INSIGHT GUIDES

PHILADELPHIA

APA PUBLICATIONS
Part of the Langenscheidt Publishing Group

INSIGHT GUIDE
PHILADELPHIA
ABOUT THIS BOOK

Editorial

Project Editor
Zoë Ross
Managing Editor
Donna Dailey
Editorial Director
Brian Bell

Distribution

UK & Ireland
GeoCenter International Ltd
The Viables Centre, Harrow Way
Basingstoke, Hants RG22 4BJ
Fax: (44) 1256-817988

United States
Langenscheidt Publishers, Inc.
46–35 54th Road, Maspeth, NY 11378
Fax: (1) 718 784-0640

Canada
Thomas Allen & Son Ltd
390 Steelcase Road East
Markham, Ontario L3R 1G2
Fax: (1) 905 475 6747

Australia
Universal Press
1 Waterloo Road
Macquarie Park, NSW 2113
Fax: (61) 2 9888 9074

New Zealand
Hema Maps New Zealand Ltd (HNZ)
Unit D, 24 Ra ORA Drive
East Tamaki, Auckland
Fax: (64) 9 273 6479

Worldwide
**Apa Publications GmbH & Co.
Verlag KG (Singapore branch)**
38 Joo Koon Road, Singapore 628990
Tel: (65) 865-1600. Fax: (65) 861-6438

Printing

Insight Print Services (Pte) Ltd
38 Joo Koon Road, Singapore 628990
Tel: (65) 865-1600. Fax: (65) 861-6438

©2001 Apa Publications GmbH & Co.
Verlag KG (Singapore branch)
All Rights Reserved
First Edition 1992
Second Edition 2001

CONTACTING THE EDITORS
We would appreciate it if readers
would alert us to errors or out-
dated information by writing to:
**Insight Guides, P.O. Box 7910,
London SE1 1WE, England.
Fax: (44) 20 7403-0290.
insight@apaguide.demon.co.uk**

This guidebook combines the
interests and enthusiasms of
two of the world's best-known
information providers: Insight
Guides, whose titles have set the
standard for visual travel guides
since 1970, and Discovery Channel,
the world's premier source of non-
fiction television programming.

Insight Guides provide both practical advice and a broad understanding of a destination's history,
culture, institutions and people,
while Discovery Channel and its
website, www.discovery.com, helps
millions of viewers
explore their world
from the comfort of
their own homes
while also encourag-
ing them to explore
it first hand.

How to use this book

Fully revised and updated, this new
edition of *Insight Guide: Philadelphia
& Surroundings* reflects the dynamic
changes in the city in recent years.
It is carefully structured both to
convey an understanding of the city
and its culture and to guide readers
through its sights and activities.
Photographs are chosen not only to
illustrate the major attractions of
this historic city, but to present a
vivid portrayal of the many faces
and moods of modern Philadelphia.
Excursions to places of interest in
the surrounding region
introduce readers to
the unique culture of
the Pennsylvania Dutch
Country as well as to
the beauty of the Penn-
sylvania countryside.

EXPLORE YOUR WORLD
DISCOVERY CHANNEL

◆ The **Features** section, indicated by a yellow bar at the top of each page, covers the history and culture of the city and surrounding area in a series of informative essays.
◆ The main **Places** section, indicated by a blue bar, is a complete guide to all the sights and areas worth visiting. Places of special interest are coordinated by number with the maps.
◆ The **Travel Tips** listings section, with an orange bar, provides a point of reference for information on travel, hotels, shops, restaurants and more. A handy index is provided on the back flap.

The contributors

Experienced teams of writers and editors, located in both Philadelphia and London, collaborated to update and expand the previous edition of *Insight Guide: Philadelphia*. The project editor was **Zoë Ross**, a London-based freelance travel guide editor, supervised by managing editor **Donna Dailey** at Insight Guides' main editorial office.

Susan Lewis, a Philadelphia-based writer, updated the city chapters and Travel Tips and wrote several new features, including The Philadelphia Story, People of Philadelphia, Culture in the City, Food and Drink, and Sports. She has been a columnist for *Philadelphia Magazine* and her work has appeared in *Reader's Digest*, *Ladies' Home Journal's Parents* magazine, and *The Philadelphia Inquirer Sunday Magazine*, among other publications.

Carol Turkington is the author of travel magazine articles and more than 30 books, including *The Complete Idiot's Guide to Cultural Etiquette*, a handbook for world travelers. A former newspaper reporter and editor, she was born and raised in the heart of Amish country and now lives in the outer suburbs of Philadelphia. She revised and wrote new features for the chapters on The Amish and Pennsylvania Dutch Country, and wrote the new chapter on the Brandywine River Valley.

Other contributors to the original *Insight Guide: Philadelphia* whose work survives in this edition include writer and editor **John Gattuso**, who has edited the *Discovery Travel Adventures* series as well as other Insight titles, along with writers **Edward A Jardim**, **Donald B Kraybill**, **Lou Harry** and **Dave Nelson**.

The book was proofread by **Lisa Cussans**, a Philadelphia native, and indexed by **Hilary Cooper**.

Map Legend

▬▬▬	State Boundary
----	County Boundary
-·-·-	National Park/Reserve
----	Ferry Route
Ⓜ	Subway/Surface Line
✈ ✈	Airport: International/Regional
🚌	Bus Station
ℹ	Tourist Information
✉	Post Office
† ⴕ	Church/Ruins
†	Monastery
☾	Mosque
✡	Synagogue
⋔	Mansion/Stately Home
∴	Archeological Site
⋂	Cave
❢	Statue/Monument
★	Place of Interest

The main places of interest in the Places section are coordinated by number with a full-color map (e.g. ❶), and a symbol at the top of every right-hand page tells you where to find the map

INSIGHT GUIDE
PHILADELPHIA

CONTENTS

Maps

Philadelphia **102**

Center City Historic
District **106**

South Street &
Queen Village **134**

Center City West **142**

Rittenhouse **166**

Parkway Museum
District **176**

Fairmount Park **185**

University City **192**

Greater Philadelphia **200**

Brandywine River Valley **224**

Pennsylvania Dutch
Country **236**

Bucks County **250**

A map of Philadephia is on
the inside front cover

A map of Philadelphia and
environs is on the inside
back cover

Introduction

Looking Closely **15**

History

Decisive Dates **18**
The Holy Experiment **21**
Birth of a Nation.................... **29**
Industrial Might **35**
A Modern Metropolis **41**

Features

The Philadelphia Story **53**
People of Philadelphia **57**
The Amish **63**
Culture in the City................. **71**
Mummermania...................... **81**
Philadelphia Food **85**
Sports **91**

Philadelphia's skyline
and the Museum of Art

Insight on ...

Philadelphia on Film 78
Architecture 148
By the Sea 230
Dutch Folk Festivals 244

Information panels

Philly Sound 47
The Mennonites 69
Pretzel Logic 89
Benjamin Franklin 110
City of Religious Liberty 118
William Penn 154
The Barnes Method 161
The Great Philly
   Cheesesteak War 203
Edgar Allan Poe 217
Valley Forge 229
Gettysburg 243

Travel Tips

Getting Acquainted .. 258
Planning the Trip 259
Practical Tips 262
Getting Around .. 266
Where to Stay 268
Where to Eat 273
Nightlife 281
Culture 283
Festivals 288
Shopping 392
Children 294
Sport 295
Further Reading 297
◆ Full Travel Tips index
   is on page 257

Places

Introduction 101
Old City 105
Society Hill and Penn's
   Landing 123
South Street and Queen
   Village 133
Washington Square West 141
City Hall to the Convention
   Center 151
Rittenhouse 165
Parkway Museum District 175

Fairmount Park 183
University City 191
South Philly 199
Urban Villages 207
North of Vine 213
Brandywine River Valley 223
Pennsylvania Dutch Country 235
Bucks County 249

LOOKING CLOSELY

No city in the United States is tied more closely than
Philadelphia to the very roots of American identity

From the very beginning, Philadelphia was a city of ideas. William Penn envisioned a City of Brotherly Love, a place where people of all faiths could worship freely under a tolerant Frame of Government. Less than 100 years later, Thomas Jefferson penned the words that severed the colonies from Britain, declaring that "all men are created equal." Eleven years later, the Founding Fathers assembled at Independence Hall to draft a new Constitution designed to "secure the Blessing of Liberty to ourselves and our Posterity," a piece of work that John Adams called the "greatest single effort of national deliberation that the world has ever seen." Benjamin Franklin, the Declaration of Independence, the Liberty Bell, the Founding Fathers – these are more than historic figures, they're players in a national mythology, the signs and symbols with which Americans still identify themselves today.

Philadelphia is also a city of firsts – site of the country's first capital, as well as the first fire company, hospital and medical school, subscription library, insurance company, stock exchange, public bank, turnpike, motion picture show, Supreme Court session, American World's Fair, daily newspaper, telephone demonstration, steam automobile and paper mill. Less earthshaking but no less beloved inventions include the Philly cheesesteak, pretzels and the Twist.

With such an inventive spirit, it's no wonder that Philadelphia was the center of young America – of finance, government, manufacturing, commerce, medicine and publishing. However, for various reasons – geography, politics and economics – by the 1900s, Philadelphia's national profile was eclipsed by its position between the financial center of New York and the national government in Washington, D.C., as well as the exodus of manufacturing and businesses to regions of cheaper labor.

Yet Philadelphia has retained its eminence in areas such as medicine and academics, and in recent years has developed a new appreciation of its historical legacy: its 18th-century homes and churches, lovely neighborhoods, spirited ethnic communities, manageable size, cultural institutions, and great shopping. The last decades have brought a dramatic new skyline, a flashy new convention center, hotels and restaurants, and a renewed sense of civic pride. Contemporary Philadelphia remains a city of ideas and (to quote its most recent slogan), "the city that loves you back."

If you've overlooked Philadelphia in the past, think again. It's the town where the nation began, a city with American soul. ❏

PRECEDING PAGES: fireworks over Independence Hall; Society Hill neighborhood; a revealing look at the Museum of Art; inside the Pennsylvania Academy of Fine Arts.
LEFT: Old City Hall.

AM

Mare glaaale.

RCVL⁹ ARCTIC⁹

Caput de ue
na reunta

Isabella

Spagnolla

OCEAN⁹ OCCIDENTALIS

Zipan
gri m=
sula

Terra incognita

Caput s.
crucis

monte fregol.

Allay m

rio demhdo
330
300 310 320 340 350 366
Z 60 Z 70 Z 80 Z 90

Clima 9
Clima 8
ptima 6
Clima 7
Clima 8 spa z
Clima 9 spa z
Z Clima 10
spa metx

30

10

90

vnus grd9 continer miliar. .6.

Decisive Dates

Pre-1600 The Lenni-Lenape tribe lives along the banks of the Delaware River.

COLONIAL TIMES: 1600–1770

Early 1600s Delaware Bay area colonized by Swedish and Dutch traders.

1681 William Penn, in repayment of a debt of £16,000, receives a charter from King Charles II for a tract of land from Chesapeake Bay to Lake Erie and the Delaware River westward.

1682 Penn arrives and negotiates peace treaties with

Native Americans. With surveyor Thomas Holmes, he lays out a city in a grid of streets between the Delaware and Schuylkill (*skoo-kul*) rivers, and names it "Philadelphia, the City of Brotherly Love." He creates a system of government called "The Holy Experiment," in which colonists are granted civil liberties and freedom to worship their individual faiths.

1683 Germantown founded.

1690 The country's first paper mill is built by William Rittenhouse along the Wissahickon Creek.

1698 Swedish settlers build Gloria Dei church.

1701 William Penn grants Charter of Privileges to Pennsylvania and leaves for England.

1719 Benjamin Franklin, aged 17, arrives from Boston and gets a job with printer Andrew Bradford.

1728 John Bartram founds the first botanical garden.

1731 Philadelphia Library, the first subscription library, founded by Benjamin Franklin.

1751 Pennsylvania Hospital, the nation's first hospital, founded by Benjamin Franklin and others.

1757 College of Philadelphia, the nation's first medical school, established. First oil streetlights used.

REVOLUTION AND INDEPENDENCE: 1700–1800

1774 First Continental Congress meet in Philadelphia at Carpenters Hall.

1775 Continental Congress elects Benjamin Franklin as first Postmaster General of the United States.

1776 The Declaration of Independence is signed at Independence Hall.

1777 Philadelphia occupied by British forces; Battle of Germantown; George Washington and his forces spend the winter at Valley Forge.

1778 British evacuate Philadelphia.

1779 University of Pennsylvania, the nation's first university, founded.

1780 Pennsylvania Bank established as the first bank authorized by Congress. Pennsylvania passes law that no child born in the commonwealth shall be a slave.

1781 British troops surrender at Battle of Yorktown.

1782 First Jewish synagogue built.

1786 First steamboat on the Delaware River.

1787 Constitution of the United States of America drafted and adopted in Philadelphia. Pennsylvania ratifies and becomes second state.

1789 First election of President of the United States.

1790 Philadelphia becomes the nation's capital for 10 years. Benjamin Franklin dies and is buried in Christ Church Burial Ground. Philadelphia Stock Exchange, the nation's first, established.

1792 Nation's first mint established in Philadelphia.

1793 Yellow fever epidemic sweeps Philadelphia, causing President Washington to move his residence and his cabinet to Germantown.

1794 First African Methodist Episcopal Church, Mother Bethel, opens on 6th Street.

1797–8 Yellow fever deaths reported to be 4,929.

ART AND INDUSTRY: 1800–1900

1801 US Navy yard established.

1805 Philadelphia Academy of Fine Arts founded, the nation's first art school and museum.

1812 Academy of Natural Sciences founded.

1814 Athenaeum founded.

1815 Fairmount Waterworks opens as a sophisticated water-pumping facility on Faire Mount.

1820s Philadelphia is the largest industrial center in the United States.

1821 College of Apothecaries opens as nation's first pharmacy school. Completion of Fairmount Dam allows more efficient distribution of water.
1824 Franklin Institute founded. Pennsylvania Railroad incorporated to construct a railroad from Philadelphia to Lancaster County.
1832 Matthias Baldwin demonstrates his steam locomotive. Railroad reaches Germantown.
1835–45 Riots affect African-American homes and Catholic churches – both St Michael's Church and St Augustine's Church are destroyed.
1849 The first skyscraper, the Jayne Building, is completed.
1855 Children's Hospital of Philadelphia founded, the first hospital for children. Pennsylvania Railroad opens a single track line from Philadelphia to Pittsburgh.
1856 Republican party holds its first national convention in Philadelphia.
1865 John Stetson founds his eponymous hat business in Philadelphia.
1867 Fairmount Park Commission established.
1874 Philadelphia Zoo opens as the nation's first.
1876 Nation's centennial celebration and first World's Fair is held in Philadelphia.
1881 First electric streetlights turned on.
1893 Reading Terminal opens, and Reading Terminal Market begins selling fresh produce and meats

STRUGGLES AND RENAISSANCE: 1900–2000

1900 City Hall opens. Philadelphia Orchestra founded.
1901 First Mummers' Parade.
1917 Benjamin Franklin Parkway, modeled after the Champs-Elysées in Paris, is completed.
1918 Influenza epidemic kills 13,000 Philadelphians.
1926 Delaware River Bridge (renamed Benjamin Franklin Bridge in 1955) opens as the world's longest suspension bridge.
1928 Philadelphia Museum of Art and Curtis Institute of Music open.
1932 PSFS building built, the first international-style skyscraper in Philadelphia.
1937 Philadelphia Orchestra appears in Disney's *Fantasia*, the first major symphony orchestra to be featured in a motion picture.
1946 First modern computer (ENIAC) developed at the University of Pennsylvania
1948 Both Republicans and Democrats hold their political conventions in Philadelphia.
1954 Schuylkill Expressway opens.

PRECEDING PAGES: an early map of America, *circa* 1507.
LEFT: Quakers sailing to America on board the *Welcome.* **RIGHT:** young Mummer in the 1930s.

1976 Bicentennial celebrations. The Please Touch Museum, the nation's first children's museum, opens.
1980 Phillies win baseball's World Series.
1985 After gun battle, police use explosives on MOVE cult that had blockaded itself at 6221 Osage Avenue. Fire kills 11 and destroys a block of rowhouses.
1987 One Liberty Place is built, the first building taller than the hat on City Hall's statue of William Penn. Bicentennial celebration of the US Constitution and the permanent lighting of the Benjamin Franklin Bridge.
1990 First Liberty Medal awarded to former president Jimmy Carter.
1991 Old City begins gallery open houses on "First Friday" of each month.

1992 Edward Rendell begins first term as mayor.
1993 Pennsylvania Convention Center opens. First Welcome America! Festival held, celebrating Philadelphia as the nation's birthplace. Avenue of the Arts is born as the city's center for performing arts.
1994 Restored Reading Terminal Train Shed opens.
1995 Ed Rendell wins second term as mayor.
1995 Independence Seaport Museum opens. Barnes collection tours the world for the first time.
1996 *Moshulu*, the world's oldest and largest four-masted iron-hulled sailing ship, is restored and moved to Philadelphia's waterfront.
1998 First Union Center Sports Complex opens on South Broad Street, with 21,000 seats.
2000 John Street elected as mayor. ❏

THE HOLY EXPERIMENT

Escaping persecution in their native Europe, religious sects such as the Quakers looked to the New World as a land of tolerance and freedom

It was a hell of a piece of real estate – and William Penn got it for a song. England's King Charles II named it Pennsylvania in honor of Penn's father, Admiral Sir William Penn, a naval commander and loyal courtier. "Penn's Woods" was an enormous tract of land, a vast empire of rich river valleys, rolling mountains and trackless forests stretching from Chesapeake Bay to Lake Erie, and spreading west of the Delaware River as far as the setting sun.

Penn was granted the charter in 1681 in repayment of a debt of £16,000 owed by Charles II to his father. An aristocrat by birth and Quaker by conversion, Penn saw the colony as a "holy experiment," an opportunity to replant and reshape English society – and turn a profit in the bargain. Quakers were having a rough go in England. More than 10,000 were thrown into jail for nonconformity. Penn himself had been locked up in the Tower of London for his espousal of radical theology. ("My prison shall be my grave before I will budge a jot," the young firebrand wrote.)

The New World seemed the Quakers' only hope and Charles II, struggling to hold onto the crown, was glad to see them go. Land-rich, cash-poor and eager to be rid of agitators, the beleaguered monarch signed Penn's charter, requiring only two beaver pelts a year and "the fifth part of all gold and silver ore found." With a stroke of the royal quill, William Penn – a 39-year-old Quaker, author of theological manifestos, colonial administrator and visionary – became the sole proprietor of a virgin territory rivaling the size of England itself.

Native dealings

Yet people had been enjoying the fruits of this land long before Penn arrived. There were the Indians, of course, a branch of the Algonquin tribe known as the Lenni-Lenape, who hunted, fished and farmed along the Delaware River

and its many tributaries. Compared to his countrymen in Virginia and New England, Penn dealt fairly with the Native Americans, requiring that they be well paid for land occupied by white settlers. Although he already held title, he insisted on buying the land for Pennsbury, his 8,000-acre (3,200-hectare) estate situ-

ated outside the city. Artists have often romanticized Penn's supposed meeting with Lenape chief Tammany at Shackamaxon Creek, though whether such a meeting occurred remains uncertain. In any case, Philadelphia was the only colonial town without a fortress or barricade, in large part because William Penn expected to live peaceably with the Lenape tribes people.

Unfortunately, fair-dealing with natives was not a Penn family trait. William Penn's son Thomas cheated the Lenape out of prime land in the so-called Walking Purchase of 1737. The Lenape agreed to sell land along the Delaware "as far as a man can go in a day and a half" – so

---

LEFT: statue honoring an early Quaker settler in Philadelphia.
RIGHT: Lenni-Lenape Native American family, 1702.

the crafty younger Penn hired trained runners to do the pacing. They covered significantly more territory than the Lenape wanted to part with.

Later, in 1763, a group of frontier vigilantes known as the Paxton Boys attacked a colony of Christianized Indians near Lancaster, killing and scalping seven and lynching 14 others who were hiding in Lancaster Jail. The Paxtons then marched to Philadelphia intending to capture the Assembly and demand more protection on the frontier. Fortunately, a delegation led by Benjamin Franklin, who

RIVER CITY

"One of the finest, and best, and pleasantest rivers in the world," the explorer Henry Hudson wrote of the Delaware River.

home near present-day Wilmington and spread north along the river to the future site of Philadelphia, where the Swedes' Gloria Dei Church, built in 1700, still stands (*see page 137*). Under the benign rule of a lusty 400-lb (180-kg) governor known (affectionately, it is presumed) as Printz the Tub, the Swedes carved out a life of rude comforts and relative prosperity. Numbering only about 2,000, the Swedish settlements were no match for the well-armed Dutch who, in 1655, informed the Swedes that they were guests in

denounced the gang as "white savages," managed to turn the marauders away – although not before promising to pay a bounty on every scalp the Paxton Boys took in their battles against "hostile" tribes.

Early Europeans

The site Penn chose for Philadelphia saw early European settlers, too. Both the Dutch and British had made several failed attempts to set down roots in the Delaware Valley ever since Henry Hudson sailed into the waterway in 1609 in search of the Northwest Passage. While the British and Dutch bickered over who owned the valley, a small colony of Swedes set up

New Holland and were expected to pay for the privilege. The Dutch, in turn, got their comeuppance about nine years later when the British took over New Amsterdam, renamed it New York, and claimed the entire Atlantic Coast from the Carolinas to New England. The Delaware Valley came under Dutch control again briefly in 1673, but a quick deal at the negotiating table put it back in British hands.

Quaker acres

Penn immediately began planning his capital city. He named it Philadelphia, the City of Brotherly Love, imagining a "greene countrie towne" of homes, gardens and orchards that, unlike the crowded cities of England, "will never be burnt and will always be wholesome." The plan he designed is essentially unchanged: a 2-mile (3¼-km) long gridiron between the Schuylkill (*skoo-kul*) and Delaware rivers, a central park (now City Hall Plaza), and four town squares equidistant from the center.

It was to be primarily a city of refuge, a great New World sanctuary where the long-persecuted masses of Europe – Quakers, Mennonites, Amish, Moravians and Pietists, among them – and all "men of universal spirit" could worship freely and live under a rational and benevolent system of government. "Ye

looked upon as a disturber of the peace and be punished accordingly."

By the time Penn arrived in 1682, house lots were being laid out by his surveyor, Thomas Holme. Tracts of 5,000 acres (2,000 hectares) were offered for sale in the countryside, with an 80-acre (30-hectare) bonus in the Liberty Lands north of the city. The land was so rich, so obviously fertile, it must have been an easy sell.

Burgeoning city

The early years were rough going for Penn's first batch of settlers, many of whom lived in caves hollowed out of the river bank. Penn had

shall be governed by laws of your own making," Penn told his colonists, "and live [as] a free, and if you will, a sober and industrious people." In his famous Frame of Government, he provided that "No person shall be molested or prejudiced for his or her conscientious persuasion or practice. Nor shall he or she at any time be compelled to frequent or maintain any religious worship contrary to his or her mind... If any person shall abuse or deride any other for his or her different persuasion or practice in matters of religion, such person shall be

ABOVE: depiction of Philadelphia's busy waterfront on the Delaware in 1730.

LAND OF MILK AND HONEY

Penn had little need to exaggerate when he wrote to a friend in England: "The soil is good, air serene and sweet from the cedar, pine and sassafras, with wild myrtle of great fragrance. I have had better venison, bigger, more tender, as fat as in England. Turkeys of the wood I had of forty and fifty pounds weight. Fish in abundance, especially shad and rock. Oysters are monstrous for bigness. In the woods are divers fruits, wild, and flowers that for color, largeness, and beauty excel..." To harried Quakers and other religious dissenters, and to poor villagers and city-dwellers across Europe, Penn's colony must have seemed a land of milk and honey.

stayed only two years during his first visit to the colony, but when he made his final visit in 1699 (this time for only 20 months), Philadelphia was already a thriving town of wharves and warehouses, merchants and craftsmen. There were three churches, fine brick homes, well over 20 taverns, and traffic of some 800 ships per year. The population stood at about 2,000, representing a polyglot mix of English, Welsh, Irish, Germans, Swedes, Finns, Dutch, African slaves, and the occasional group of Indians visiting town to trade.

The countryside was also being settled. In 1683, Daniel Pastorius founded Germantown

wharves, sprawling north and south along the Delaware. In place of a "greene countrie towne" speculators built shoulder-to-shoulder rowhouses, leaving little room for gardens and orchards. At times, brotherly love was in short supply as well. Political rivalries set Quakers against Anglicans, Quakers against Presbyterians and Quakers against Quakers. Smugglers found Philadelphia a convenient refuge from England's hated Navigation Acts, and riots of various sorts erupted with some regularity, culminating in the "Bloody Election" of 1742. Nor was Penn's town the haven of virtue and wholesomeness he envisioned. Town folk

with a group of 13 Mennonite families, and villages in Bucks and Chester counties sprang up just as quickly as land could be cleared. To the west, far-off Lancaster would become America's first inland city. Ironically, Pennsylvania's reputation for tolerance had attracted so many sects – among them Mennonites, Pietists, Presbyterians and Anglicans – that by 1700 the Quakers constituted a minority of about 40 percent, although they were still dominant in political affairs.

Yet, as with all utopias, the City of Brotherly Love fell somewhat short of the vision that inspired it. Rather than filling the street grid from river to river, the town tended to hug the

persisted in using the streets as a garbage dump. Hogs, dogs and livestock ran wild in the streets. Pickpockets and other petty criminals gave Philadelphia a reputation for lawlessness. The prospect of governing the town seemed so daunting that more than one elected official chose to pay a fine rather than serve time in city government.

Men of influence

But if Philadelphia was a little rough around the edges, there were still opportunities enough to attract a number of extraordinary individuals. Merchants such as Samuel Carpenter, Isaac Norris and Jonathan Dickenson amassed fortunes in the triangle trade between Britain, the West Indies and the colonies, bringing the city its most reliable source of income. James Logan came to Philadelphia as William Penn's secretary and made himself rich on real estate and the fur trade. A man of extraordinary intellect, he assembled one of the largest libraries in the United States, helping to make Philadelphia a center of learning and culture. Others came too – Rittenhouse, Syng, Wistar, Powel, Cadwalader, Morris – whose children and grandchildren were destined to become prominent figures in the city.

But no one would leave a greater stamp on Philadelphia than a printer from Boston who had run off as a teenager. If William Penn was the city's architect, Ben Franklin was her carpenter, hammering together ideas and institutions that would serve Philadelphia for generations. He established the United States' first hospital, first circulating library and first fire company. He expanded the colonial postal service, whipped the city's defenses into shape, helped found the College of Philadelphia (forerunner of the University of Pennsylvania) and the American Philosophical Society. He composed, edited and published the influential *Pennsylvania Gazette* and *Poor Richard's Almanack*, turning homespun aphorisms into a national creed. By the late 1750s he won a celebrated figure in Europe, where he represented colonial interests and delighted London high society.

A man of insatiable curiosity and probing intellect, Franklin numbered among his achievements as an inventor the Franklin stove, bifocals, glass armonica and the lightning rod. His experiments with electricity – ending in the famous kite-flying episode – won international acclaim and deepened Philadelphia's reputation as a citadel of knowledge *(see page 110)*.

Cultural center

Franklin's growing renown in Europe was a reflection of Philadelphia's rising status. By the mid-1700s, Penn's little Quaker village was fast becoming one of the largest cities in the British Empire. It was home to many of America's most illustrious families, a leader in commerce and trade, a center of culture on the edge of an untamed continent and the undeclared capital of America's colonies.

Penn's holy experiment evolved in unimagined ways, yielding neither the spiritual nor material riches he expected. "O Pennsylvania, what hast thou cost me!" he wrote in a letter to James Logan. "Above thirty thousand pounds more than I ever got from it, two hazardous and most fatiguing voyages, my straits and slavery here, and my son's soul almost." And yet, Penn laid the groundwork for the greatest political movement of the century, helping give birth to a nation and set the stage for a new era in the history of government. ❑

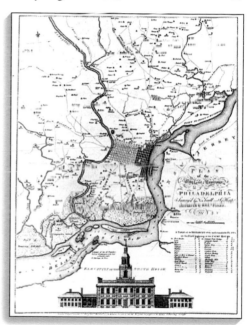

LEFT: a view of the port of Philadelphia seen from the town of Kensington.

RIGHT: William Penn's original plan for the city.

BIRTH OF A NATION

When England turned its attention to its neglected New World colony,
Americans retaliated with a bitter struggle for independence

The colonies never really panned out for Britain. There was an empire to administer, wars to fight, domestic unrest to subdue. For a while, it was a period of benign neglect for America, a time of discovery and growth. While the royals were looking the other way, America came of age.

By the early 1760s, King George III decided that it was time to put an end to all that. With the French contained in North America and the Seven Years' War winding down in Europe, he turned his attention to his increasingly restless subjects in America. And, as always, the job at hand was to squeeze as much money out of them as possible.

Intolerable acts

George III launched the effort in 1763 with a battery of laws that prohibited colonial currency and cracked down on trade between the northern colonies and the West Indies. Before the colonials could mount an effective protest, Parliament also passed the Stamp Act (1765), requiring colonists to pay taxes on legal documents, newspapers and other paper products.

To outraged Americans, the new restrictions were worse than the old Navigation Acts and smacked of the same arbitrary use of power. Newspapers decried the Stamp Act and mobs took to the streets, terrorizing tax collectors and attacking the homes of government officials. In England on a diplomatic mission, Benjamin Franklin reluctantly assented to the Stamp Act and – much to his later regret – even recommended a few friends for the post of Pennsylvania tax man. When news reached Philadelphia of Franklin's complicity, rioters went to his house and threatened his ordinarily mild-mannered wife, Deborah, who met the mob with sharp words and loaded muskets. Franklin got the message. He immediately denounced

the Stamp Act and lobbied Parliament for repeal, reminding English merchants that there were no imported goods that the colonists couldn't "do without or make themselves."

While Franklin was making his case in London, Philadelphians joined other colonists in a boycott of British goods. By March 1766,

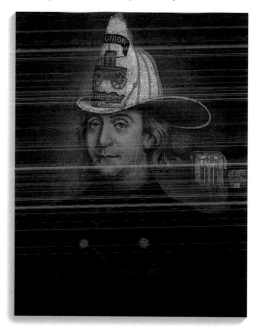

the boycott had caused so much damage to British commerce that the king relented and lifted the tax. But George III wasn't a man who took defeat lightly. In 1767 his Chancellor of the Exchequer, Charles Townshend, levied a tax on a variety of imported items, including paper, lead, glass and tea. Although the reaction in Philadelphia was less radical than in Boston or New York, the Philadelphia press denounced the Townshend Acts in scathing terms and prodded the city's merchants into a sweeping non-importation agreement. Writing anonymously, the influential lawyer John Dickinson issued his widely read *Letters from a Farmer in Pennsylvania*, attacking the legality

---

PRECEDING PAGES: the signing of the Declaration of Independence.
LEFT: a revolutionary musket. **RIGHT:** Benjamin Franklin organized the first fire company in America.

of the Townshend Acts, calling for unity among the colonies, and positing the subversive notion that taxation without representation constituted a form of tyranny.

A second colonial boycott forced the repeal of the Townshend Acts in 1770, but London wasn't ready to surrender power just yet. As a symbol of the "supremacy of Parliament," a tax on tea remained. The tea tax won no friends in Philadelphia and, when the first loads arrived in Delaware Bay, tea merchants were warned to refuse the

NATIONAL PRIDE

As the colonies united, delegate Patrick Henry declared: "The distinction between Virginians, Pennsylvanians, New Yorkers, and New Englanders is no more. I am not a Virginian, but an American."

ment against British goods. But more importantly, the First Continental Congress successfully unified the colonies in a common cause.

Independence

The situation worsened almost immediately after the delegates left Philadelphia. In Boston, a tense standoff between redcoats and patriots turned bloody. On April 19, 1775, the "shot heard round the world" was fired at Concord, Massachusetts. The die was cast; the Revolution was set in motion. "These are the

THE REPEAL
OR THE FUNERAL OF MISS AME-STAMP

shipment lest they be visited by the local "Committee for Tarring and Feathering." News of the Boston Tea Party had reached Philadelphia and, wishing to avoid a similar episode, the tea ships sped back to England.

The tea fiasco was more than the king could tolerate. Parliament's response was to impose a series of "Intolerable Acts," closing the port of Boston and dissolving the Massachusetts Assembly. Angry patriots in Philadelphia called for a colonial conference and, in September 1774, the First Continental Congress convened at Carpenters' Hall. The delegates defined their cause in a "Declaration of Rights" and drew up a broad non-importation agree-

times that try men's souls," Thomas Paine, an adopted Philadelphian, wrote in his pamphlet *The Crisis*, in support for the revolution. "The summer soldier and sunshine patriot will, in this crisis, shrink from the service of their country, but he that stands it now deserves the love and thanks of man and woman."

The Second Continental Congress convened at the Pennsylvania State House and chose George Washington as commander of "all continental forces," such as they were. On May 15, 1776, John Adams introduced a resolution urging the colonies to reorganize as states. On June 7, Richard Henry Lee called for a resolution on independence. A committee including

Thomas Jefferson, Benjamin Franklin and John Adams was appointed to draft the document, but it was Jefferson who wrote the first draft, with Franklin and Adams making only a few changes (including the deletion of Jefferson's condemnation of slavery).

It was, the delegates knew, an act of treason punishable by death. "There must be no pulling different ways: we must all hang together," John Hancock urged his fellow delegates at the signing. Ben Franklin is said to have replied: "Gentlemen, we must indeed all hang together or we shall most assuredly hang separately."

When the Declaration was read outside the State House on July 8 the bells of the city clanged in celebration, although, contrary to tradition, the Liberty Bell, hanging in the building's unsteady belltower, probably remained silent "lest... the steeple should fall down." Nor is it likely that Betsy Ross, the legendary designer of the Stars and Stripes, was asked by General Washington to supply the infant nation with its first flag, although she was a well-known seamstress *(see page 116)*.

A city abandoned

Washington's punishing defeat at New York City put an abrupt end to Philadelphia's celebration. As wounded soldiers poured into town and the dead were buried en masse in Washington Square, the redcoats marched south through New Jersey toward Philadelphia. On Christmas Day in 1776, Washington and his forces made their famous midnight crossing of the Delaware River and struck enemy camps at Trenton and then again at Princeton. When the British finally moved against Philadelphia several months later, Washington intercepted them at Brandywine Creek, but his "ragged, lousy, naked regiments" – most of them ill-equipped and with little or no training – were soundly routed.

With the sounds of battle rumbling in the distance, Philadelphia patriots prepared to evacuate. Congress fled west to Lancaster and then to York. Printing presses were carted into the countryside and the Liberty Bell was removed from the State House and hidden in a church cellar in Allentown. The streets of Philadelphia, an observer wrote, were a scene of "horses galloping, women running, children crying, delegates flying, and altogether the greatest consternation, fright and terror that can be imagined."

About three weeks later, a rebel division led by "Mad Anthony" Wayne was virtually wiped out in the Paoli Massacre, just outside the city. Several days later, the redcoats marched into Philadelphia unopposed, greeted by cheering loyalists. The Americans were forced to retreat. While the British enjoyed the comforts of Philadelphia's finest homes and taverns, Washington's freezing and hungry troops suffered at Valley Forge *(see page 229)*. Oddly,

LEFT: the Stamp Act repeal.
RIGHT: the Boston Massacre led the colonies to war.

DECLARATION OF INDEPENDENCE

Inspired by Enlightenment thought, Jefferson invoked the natural rights of all men to justify American independence. "We hold these Truths to be self-evident, that all Men are created equal, that they are endowed by their Creator with certain inalienable Rights, that among these are Life, Liberty, and the Pursuit of Happiness…" With these words, the young Virginian transformed what had been, in essence, a tax revolt into a manifesto of human rights that would influence people and governments around the world. Unanimously adopted on July 4, 1776, the Declaration of Independence severed America from the mother country in a single, decisive stroke.

General Howe and his compatriots never followed up on their victory in Philadelphia, preferring instead to indulge themselves in the pleasures of the city. The British pulled out of Philadelphia the following spring and returned to New York City, giving General Washington time to train his men properly and Congress the chance to solicit much-needed foreign aid. Benedict Arnold served for a time as the military commander of Philadelphia, only to betray the patriots at West Point.

STATE RIVALRIES

According to George Washington, after Independence, the fledgling United States were "fast verging to anarchy and confusion."

at each other's throats over boundary disputes, trade and tariffs. Economic disparity between seaports and farming towns precipitated a rebellion in Massachusetts; shots were fired between Pennsylvanians and Virginians over land; and in Europe, John Adams and Thomas Jefferson complained about inconsistent foreign policy.

Taking its cue from James Madison's Annapolis Convention, Congress called for a national conference to amend the Articles of Confederation. The delegates to the Constitu-

The bloodshed continued for another four years after the occupation, raging along the entire East Coast, before Cornwallis got bottled up by a French fleet and finally capitulated at Yorktown. The war was over and independence won, but Philadelphia, and the rest of the nation, faced an uncertain future.

"A more perfect Union"

By 1787, it was clear that the decentralized system of government established under the Articles of Confederation lacked the authority to hold the sprawling nation together. Congress had grown so ineffective that some delegates chose not to attend. The states were constantly

tional Convention, as it later came to be known, convened in May 1787 at the Pennsylvania State House, where many had signed the Declaration of Independence only 11 years earlier. Among their first official acts were the election of George Washington as president of the conference and a vow to conduct their affairs in strict secrecy. It was immediately evident that the 55 Constitutional framers would do more than amend the Articles: they would completely restructure the federal government.

The men assembled couldn't have been more qualified for the job. "An assembly of demigods," said Thomas Jefferson, whose diplomatic responsibilities held him in Paris. "If all the delegates named for this Convention at Philadelphia are present," a French diplomat remarked, "we will never have seen, even in Europe, an assembly more respectable for the talents, knowledge, disinterestedness and patriotism of those who compose it."

In addition to Washington, the most notable were James Madison, the young Virginian chiefly responsible for drafting the document; Alexander Hamilton, the radical New Yorker whose proposals included a lifetime executive and senate; the Delaware statesman John Dickinson; and Ben Franklin, who attended every session despite his old age and failing health.

elected by state and population, a four-year executive with limited veto power, and an independent "supreme" judiciary. Considering the range of opinion, the document was crafted with amazing efficiency. A final draft of the Constitution was completed in four months and adopted by the Convention only two days later. Although ratification faced opposition from various quarters, the states ultimately confirmed the Framers' work. During the signing, Franklin commented on the carving of a sun that adorned Washington's chair. "I have," he said, "often and often in the course of the session and the vicissitudes of my hopes and fears as to

Constitutional compromises

Although none of the delegates was completely satisfied with the document (three refused to sign and several resigned), Franklin voiced the prevailing opinion: "I consent to this Constitution because I expect no better, and because I am not sure that it is not the best."

In fact, it was a series of compromises that resulted in many of the Constitution's fundamental provisions: a three-branch system of checks and balances, a bicameral legislature

its issue, looked at that [sun] behind the president without being able to tell whether it was rising or setting. But now at length I have the happiness to know that it is a rising and not a setting sun."

For 10 years, Philadelphia served as the nation's capital. Robert Morris, the nation's wealthiest man, gave his Walnut Street home to President Washington as an official residence. Congress occupied the Philadelphia County Court House (now Congress Hall), and the Supreme Court convened at Old City Hall. Philadelphia, birthplace of the nation, was poised to plunge into the new century as America's most powerful city. ❏

LEFT: reenactment of the Battle of Germantown.
ABOVE LEFT: James Madison, architect of the Constitution. **ABOVE RIGHT:** George Washington.

INDUSTRIAL MIGHT

The 19th century was a time of mixed blessings in Philadelphia – an
age of meteoric industrialization tempered with bloody Civil War battles

The years following the Constitutional Convention were a golden age in Philadelphia. Although the federal government shifted its base to the District of Columbia in 1800, Philadelphia remained the wealthiest, most sophisticated and powerful city in the nation. With more than 65,000 residents, it was not only the largest urban center in America, it was the largest English-speaking city outside Great Britain. As headquarters for the Bank of the United States (1791), the Mint (1792) and the Second Bank of the United States (1816), it was the nerve center of American finance. And as one of the busiest ports on the Atlantic Coast and a leader in the trade with China, it was a major player in international commerce.

An enlightened city

Culturally, Philadelphia was still the enlightened metropolis of Franklin, Logan and other prominent men of art and science. Among the institutions established in this period were the Academy of Fine Arts (1805), the Academy of Natural Sciences (1812), the Athenaeum (1814) and the Franklin Institute (1824).

As the center of the publishing industry, it attracted major authors. Edgar Allan Poe wrote some of his best-known works while living on North 7th Street *(see page 217)*. Walt Whitman retired to a spot just across the river in Camden, New Jersey. The city also boasted some of America's most respected professionals – doctors like Benjamin Rush, Caspar Wistar and Philip Syng, and architects like Benjamin Latrobe, William Strickland and John Notman. Among artists identified with Philadelphia were Charles Willson Peale, Thomas Sully, Thomas Eakins and Gilbert Stuart.

Socially, the city was an island of comfort on the edge of a still wild continent. A "city to be happy in," Nathaniel P. Willis called it, with little of New York's chaotic ambience or

Boston's starched-collar moralism. Visitors remarked on the city's tidy brick houses, stately public buildings, and easy-going sophistication. "How… am I able to communicate a just notion of the intelligence, the refinement, the enterprise of Philadelphians," wrote Scottish author William Chambers, "their agreeable and hos-

pitable society, their pleasant evening-parties, their love of literature, their happy blending of the industrial habits of the north with social usages of the south? All this must be left to conjecture, as well as the Oriental luxury of their dwellings, and the delicate beauty of their ladies." As Gilbert Stuart was fond of saying, Philadelphia was the "Athens of America."

Iron and coal

The early 1800s were also a period of profound transformation. With the development of efficient steam engines in the late 1700s and the discovery of anthracite coal in western Pennsylvania in the early 1800s, Philadelphia

---

LEFT: after the American Civil War, steam locomotives were the height of industry.
RIGHT: John B. Stetson created his hat in the city.

was poised on the brink of the Industrial Revolution and prepared to march ahead. By the 1820s, Philadelphia was America's first and largest industrial center, turning out everything from turbines to toilets, pig iron to chandeliers. Factories, mills and foundries sprang up on the outskirts of the Old City, spouting thick black smoke over Southwark, Manayunk, Kensington and Nicetown, where the flood of new immigrants provided cheap and plentiful labor.

Although the opening of the Erie Canal diverted shipping to New York, Philadelphia became a major hub in an extensive network of turnpikes, canals and railways. Manufac-

tured goods poured from the city, and coal and other raw materials were taken in. Industrialists like William Cramp and Matthias Baldwin amassed fortunes manufacturing ships and locomotives. Haberdasher John B. Stetson made a financial killing on his cowboy hat. And countless laborers turned out products such as textiles, sugar, water pipes and cigars.

Immigrant community

But while the captains of industry were raking in family fortunes, the people who actually did the work – most of them immigrants from Ireland and Germany – were struggling to stay

RISE OF THE RAILROADS

In the 1820s, Philadelphia was competing with other East Coast ports for facilities to transport coal and produce. New York built the Erie Canal in 1825; just to the south, the Baltimore & Ohio railroad was incorporated in 1828. Philadelphia's first railroads used horse-drawn wagons to carry coal from the mines to the Lehigh River.

Of course, railroads could also be used to transport people to suburban communities such as Germantown, where wealthy Philadelphians maintained summer homes. The Philadelphia-Germantown & Norristown railroad opened in 1832, with horse-drawn cars completing the route in 45 minutes. That same year, Philadelphian

Matthias Baldwin introduced his locomotive engine, which could carry four cars of passengers the 6-mile (10-km) route in 28 minutes. Baldwin became the major supplier of US locomotive engines. After 1830, the railroads grew rapidly, with over 30,000 miles (48,000 km) of track laid in the US over the next 30 years.

The Pennsylvania Railroad was incorporated in 1846, and in 1854 opened a single track line between Philadelphia and Pittsburgh. The railroad is credited with developing the Main Line suburbs in the second half of the 19th century as the company built stations and hotels, and even dictated the minimum price of housing along the line.

alive. Starting in the 1820s, they poured into Philadelphia by the thousands, many of them poor, hungry, illiterate and desperate for work. By 1850, the population of Philadelphia County shot up to 408,000, a third of them foreign-born. Immigrants crowded into cramped apartments, ramshackle shanties and tiny "Father, Son and Holy Ghost" (or Trinity) houses with one room and one family per floor. Neighborhoods like Southwark and Moyamensing, as well as the hidden alleyways of Old City, were particularly rancid, with frequent outbreaks of cholera and yellow fever; gangs like the Moyamensing Killers and Blood Tubs roamed the streets. After

trumped-up papist conspiracy. At the height of activity in the early 1840s, a nativist gang burned down two Catholic churches and several homes in Kensington. When a pitched battle broke out a few months later between nativists and Catholics at St Philip de Neri Catholic Church in Southwark, it took the militia four days to stop the fighting, although not before 15 people had been killed and 50 wounded.

Race riots

Violence was also directed against the black community plus anyone, black or white, who was associated with the anti-slavery movement.

the cholera epidemic of 1849, the Sanitary Committee reported on the appalling conditions of Philadelphia's slums, "where extremes of filth and misery and loathsome disease met the eye; where horrid heaps of manure from hog and cow pens, putrefying garbage and refuse of every kind... gave off their noxious gases."

As if living conditions weren't bad enough, immigrants also had to face nativist agitators, who focused their bigotry on Irish-Catholics and other foreigners, whom they linked with a

LEFT: anti-Catholic rioters clash with Philadelphia police in 1844.
ABOVE: Independence Hall, 1876.

Although never widely accepted, the abolition movement had deep roots in Philadelphia, due in part to traditional Quaker condemnation of slavery. The American Anti-Slavery Society was founded in Philadelphia in 1833, and the city was a major way station in the Underground Railroad prior to the Civil War. But in the minds of nativists (and, ironically, many immigrants), abolition was associated with miscegenation, racial conflict and national disunity. Far more importantly, it threatened Philadelphia businessmen with the loss of lucrative Southern markets.

During the worst of the violence, attacks on blacks were almost a daily occurrence: churches were burned, houses looted, blacks killed in the streets. In a series of riots that broke out in 1842, a black church and an abolitionist meeting house were burned to the ground, four people were killed and more than 25 people were seriously injured. "There is probably no city in the known world," an English Quaker sadly noted, "where dislike, amounting to hatred of the coloured population, prevails more than in the city of brotherly love!"

The riots in Philadelphia reflected a broader conflict being played out throughout America.

MARTYRED END

Abraham Lincoln, cut down by an assassin's bullet, never saw his "new freedom." Citizens of Philadelphia jammed the streets to watch the president's casket inch toward Independence Hall where his body lay in state.

The Civil war spreads

As the birthplace of the nation, Philadelphia immediately joined the effort to keep the new nation whole. Philadelphians were among the first volunteers to respond to Lincoln's call for 75,000 men and its industrial might was channeled into war production. But as the war dragged on and the hope of a speedy victory seemed increasingly remote, Philadelphia's enthusiasm turned to discontent. When Robert E. Lee marched Confederate

Slavery was driving the nation apart and, by the late 1850s, the issue was approaching the flash point. In November 1860, Abraham Lincoln was elected president without a single Southern electoral vote. He visited Philadelphia en route to his inauguration, informing the crowd that "there is no need of bloodshed and war... The government will not use force unless force is used upon it." Several weeks later, Fort Sumter was bombarded by Confederate artillery. At the First Unitarian Church in Philadelphia, abolitionist minister William Henry Furness declared: "The long agony is over!" But in truth, the agony of America's bloodiest war had only just begun.

troops into Pennsylvania in the summer of 1863, Philadelphians could hardly be stirred to defend their city. Lee's army collided with Union forces (under the command of Philadelphia's own General George G. Meade) outside Gettysburg. The battle that ensued over the following three days was the bloodiest in US history *(see page 243)*. Some 7,000 Confederate soldiers were killed in a heroic but uncoordinated attempt to break Union lines. In all, the Confederates suffered more than 28,000 casualties, the Federals more than 25,000.

Four months later, Lincoln traveled to Gettysburg for the dedication of a cemetery at the battlefield. His famous address there on

November 19, 1863, majestic in cadence and brevity, reaffirmed the Chief Executive's commitment to hold the Union together: "We here highly resolve that these dead shall not have died in vain, that this nation, under God, shall have a new birth of freedom – and that government of the people, by the people, for the people, shall not perish from the earth." The war ended less than two years later.

Expansion and industry

In the post-Civil War years, Philadelphia continued to grow in leaps and bounds. Penn's "greene countrie towne" spread 7 miles (11 km) along the Delaware River, spilled across the Schuylkill River and reached out to once isolated warrens like Germantown and Manayunk. Immigrants continued to pour into the wretched precincts of Southwark and Moyamensing – by the late 1880s there were as many Italians, Poles and East European Jews as Irish and Germans. Southern blacks moved into the city as well, many occupying the slum areas between Lombard and South streets or crossing the Schuylkill into West Philadelphia. By the turn of the 20th century, Philadelphia had the largest black population of any northern city. The population, encompassing the whole of Philadelphia County, topped 1.2 million, with nearly 25 percent foreign-born. Even with the construction of thousands of new rowhouses, the housing stock remained inadequate.

Philadelphia's well-to-do were on the move, too. From the Old City, they moved west into mansions around Rittenhouse Square. In the 1880s, the wealthiest migrated again, this time to suburban estates along the Pennsylvania Railroad's exclusive Main Line. City Hall moved west, too, to a Second Empire behemoth (the largest building of its day) at Broad and Market streets. Following the trend, the University of Pennsylvania moved into new digs in West Philadelphia in 1871; Fairmount Park expanded on both sides of the Schuylkill River; the Academy of Fine Arts relocated to an ornate hall designed by Frank Furness; and several new colleges, including Drexel, Temple and Bryn Mawr, advanced the city's reputation as a place of learning.

LEFT: Philadelphians were among the first volunteers in the American Civil War.
RIGHT: a 19th-century Quaker wedding.

Throughout the postwar period, industry was king. Ironworks ringed the city. More than 33 percent of America's oil was shipped from Philadelphia, and coal continued to pour out by rail and sea. Philadelphia textile factories outproduced any in the country. Merchants like John Wanamaker, Gimbels, and Strawbridge & Clothier gave birth to retail empires. And the Pennsylvania Railroad became the largest corporation in America.

With the aftershock of war fading and the heartbeat of industry pounding in its veins, Philadelphia prepared to celebrate the nation's centennial with the biggest, most extravagant

party the country had ever seen. The Centennial Exhibition of 1876 attracted exhibitors from hundreds of countries and more than 10 million visitors. Powered by the towering 700-ton steam engine known as the Corliss Machine, the Exhibition put Philadelphia's industrial might on a world stage. It marked the final emergence of Philadelphia as a world-class city of enormous wealth and vital energy.

But for all its industrial might, Philadelphia never acquired the spitfire image of New York, its neighbor and chief competitor. Despite industrialization, Philadelphia was still the Quaker City – prosperous, progressive, learned, but still clad in gray. ❑

A MODERN METROPOLIS

Philadelphia didn't escape the big-city struggles against crime and civic disturbance, but recently it has been rediscovering its roots

The growth of industry in Philadelphia breathed new life into a very old style of government. This was the "Machine Age," and the term referred to politics as surely as it did to industry. It began in 1865 when James McManes, an Irish-born Republican ward leader, was elected trustee of the city's gas works. The first in a long line of political bosses, "King James" ran the gas works like his own personal fiefdom, doling out contracts in return for a percentage and muscling bankers, businessmen and government officials. Not that too many people really minded. In the words of one journalist, Philadelphia had become "corrupt and contented." Ballot-stuffing, vote-buying, graft and patronage were tolerated so long as the veil of gentility remained intact.

War and Prohibition

When the United States entered World War I in 1917, political bickering took a backseat to the war effort. As one of the nation's great industrial centers, Philadelphia – "workshop of the world" – was quickly transformed into the "arsenal of democracy." Almost overnight, mills and factories were retooled for wartime production. The Baldwin Locomotive Works turned out artillery shells, the Ford Motor Company made steel helmets, and the giant Hog Island shipyard, the world's largest, cranked out the better part of a navy. Patriotism ran high in Philadelphia, often to the detriment of the city's large German population. The city pulled its advertising from German-language newspapers, and classes in German were removed from the public school curriculum. Even Santa Claus was unpopular.

Two events broke the city's newfound spirit of unity. The first was a fallout in Philadelphia's ongoing political warfare. During the vicious Republican primary election of 1917, thugs hired by the Vare brothers – the city's reigning

political bosses – gave their opponent a severe beating and, in the process, killed a policeman who came to his defense. Reformers howled, thousands of ordinary citizens turned out in the streets in protest, and the hired killer was thrown into jail. Nevertheless, the Vare candidate was swept into office.

An even more devastating blow came in 1918 when the worldwide influenza epidemic swept the city. At its worst, the epidemic was claiming hundreds of lives each day. Bodies accumulated so quickly that they had to be interred in mass graves.

But it was a war of a very different kind that confronted the men returning from the battlefields of Europe: the campaign against John Barleycorn. Young men who had fought so bravely for freedom in the trenches of the Argonne – and had tasted old-world lifestyles – were soon to discover that they couldn't buy a drink in a Philadelphia saloon. Prohibition backfired in Philadelphia even more than in

LEFT: One and Two Liberty Place, gleaming skyscrapers as a symbol of modern Philadelphia.
RIGHT: Fairmount Park trolley-bus.

other cities. The illicit liquor trade turned into a gold mine for organized crime, especially for the *mafiosi* sinking roots in South Philadelphia. By some estimates, more speakeasies were doing business in the city during Prohibition than legitimate taverns had done previously. A report in *Collier's Magazine* estimated that Philadelphia's 1,185 bars, 13,000 speakeasies and 300 bordellos raked in around $40 million a year between them, and a substantial proportion of the profit was being pocketed by politicians and the police department. Gang warfare broke out in the streets as rival bootleggers battled over their turf. But in truth it

was poisoning, not murder, that took the heaviest toll. The Philadelphia coroner reported that the shocking number of between 10 to 12 deaths daily were a result of bad whiskey.

The city's response to all this mayhem was lackadaisical at best. The police, perhaps unsurprisingly given their fruitful cut of the action, seemed unwilling to intervene. An eventual shakedown in the Philadelphia police department netted some 200 cops who were on the make. Even after the mayor appointed a Marine Corps general to enforce the ban on liquor, very little seemed to change. It was clear to many observers that organized crime had infiltrated City Hall.

Speculation and decline

Even in conservative Philadelphia, it seemed, the lure of the high life was irresistible. The city may have been going to hell in a hand basket, but Philadelphians hardly seemed glum about the future. Like other Americans, they poured money into speculation, sending the price of real estate and the value of stocks through the roof. It didn't matter that the economy was standing on a mountain of credit, or that the city was being cheated of millions by the Vare machine. As long as money kept changing hands, the Pennsylvania Railroad kept chugging down the tracks, and smoke kept billowing from factory chimneys, everything seemed bullish.

But when the bottom fell out of the American stock market on Black Thursday – October 24, 1929 – the "orgy of speculation" came to a screeching halt. The Great Depression dawned slowly on Philadelphia, but no less painfully than in other cities. When the Mummers paraded down Broad Street on New Year's Day in 1930 *(see page 81)*, there were still few signs of the hardships to come. But when it hit, it sent the city reeling. Income was slashed. Unemployment skyrocketed. People were robbed of their livelihoods, their homes, their dignity. Makeshift Hoovervilles sprang up in parks and alleyways, labor strikes turned violent, and bread lines snaked along sidewalks. By 1933, 50 local banks had failed, and many of the city's most prominent industries were forced to shut down or cut back.

Thanks to obstructionists in Philadelphia's Republican administration, federal relief – in the form of President Franklin D. Roosevelt's "New Deal" – was slow to reach the city. According to the mayor, J. Hampton Moore, laziness and inefficiency were to blame for the city's economic problems. "There is no starvation in Philadelphia," he proclaimed, refusing to offer a cent in relief.

Back to war

Then, in 1941, the nation entered World War II, and the city was swept into the war effort a second time around. Once again, Philadelphia was transformed into an arsenal of democracy, churning out weapons, battleships, airplanes, uniforms, helmets and other instruments of war. Philadelphia's German and Italian communities – their newspapers, social clubs and businesses, as well as openly pro-Nazi organizations – were raided by federal agents. In order to meet labor demands, both women and African-Americans were encouraged to work in the war industries for the first time. By 1944, women accounted for 40 percent of the work force, and the number of African-American workers had doubled.

QUAKER AID

During World War II, Philadelphia's Quaker pacifists opted for service in hospitals and relief work, rather than supporting the war effort.

When Japan surrendered in 1945, Philadelphians celebrated as never before. Thousands gathered around City Hall; parties broke out in the streets; fireworks streaked across the sky.

phia's manufacturers were forced to close down, cut back or move out, leaving a glut of wartime laborers – in particular Southern blacks – without a livelihood. Many companies left altogether, relocating to the South or West United States where taxes were lower and non-union labor was plentiful. Automobiles and inexpensive housing lured thousands of predominantly white middle-class families into the suburbs. While the population of neighboring Bucks, Montgomery and Chester counties swelled, the central city's

But underlying the jubilation were disturbing questions about Philadelphia's future. The city itself was in bad shape. Neighborhoods were run-down, buildings dilapidated. Old City – home to Independence Hall, the Liberty Bell and other historic sites – was literally falling apart. With the exception of the Benjamin Franklin Parkway, Philadelphia had seen almost no new development or rehabilitation for years.

Industry was slipping, too. Without the demands of a war to sustain them, Philadel-

LEFT: hunger marchers protest, 1936.
ABOVE: Philadelphians take to the city's streets to celebrate V-J Day.

population declined. With its tax base eroding and social services on the rise, the city was in a severe financial stranglehold. By the late 1960s, the administration regularly operated on a deficit. By the late 1980s, the city was on the verge of bankruptcy.

Reform and rehabilitation

The postwar years weren't all bleak, however. Under the leadership of Richardson Dilworth and Joseph S. Clark, a coalition of activists and blue-blooded liberals pushed for reform in the city's corruption-riddled government. After exposing widespread graft, embezzlement and patronage, the reformers pushed for a new

Home Rule Charter curbing government excesses and establishing an independent mayoralty and City Council.

The newly installed Democrats embarked on an ambitious program of redevelopment. The old Chinese Wall – the elevated railway that blocked development north of Market Street – was torn down and the gleaming towers of Penn Center were erected. The dilapidated Dock Street Market was relocated to a new distribution center in South Philadelphia, clearing the way for a thorough rehabilitation of the badly run down 18th- and 19th-century homes of Society Hill. In the Old City, the federal gov-

ernment finally took action to save Independence Hall from dilapidation. In 1951, the National Park Service acquired Independence Park and quickly set to work restoring the many historic sites and buildings *(see page 105).*

The turbulent decades

As in many parts of America, the 1960s were a turbulent time in Philadelphia. A seemingly endless series of demonstrations, strikes and disturbances often paralyzed the city. Frank Rizzo, a hard-headed police inspector with a reputation for strong-arm tactics, was elected mayor in 1971, promising to restore order in

THE MOVE CONFRONTATION

In the devastating climate of crime and disorder, another event occured in which the true nightmare of the Goode administration unfolded. A radical back-to-nature group, MOVE, which had previously ignited a 1978 confrontation in which a police officer had been killed, returned to the fore, this time with even more disastrous results.

In 1978, MOVE had created an armed compound in West Philadelphia where members harassed neighbors and allowed the house to become infested with rats and cockroaches and overrun with dogs. In the 1980s, MOVE leader John Africa and his followers had relocated to another house in West Philadelphia and armed themselves

for a second confrontation. On May 13, 1985, frustrated in their attempt to talk – and then blast – the occupants out of the house, the Philadelphia police dropped a bag of explosives on the roof of the building, causing a fire that accidentally burned out of control. Eleven MOVE members, including five children, were killed, and a total of 61 nearby houses were destroyed.

After a controversial eight-month investigation, the MOVE Commission Report excoriated Mayor Goode and other key officials, but no one was legally indicted. Surprisingly, Goode defeated Frank Rizzo in the hotly contested mayoral election of 1987.

the streets and crack down on radicals. This optimistic law-and-order message was exactly what the working-class whites and upper-class conservatives wanted to hear. But Rizzo's tough talk served only to exacerbate racial, ideological and ethnic rifts.

The 1970s, however, looked set to put Philadelphia back on course. In the middle of the decade there was the Bicentennial Celebration, an event which helped focus the city's possibilities as a tourist destination and mobilize city organizations to that end. Streets were repaved, houses were renovated and closer attention was paid to the city's historic

By the time Goode took the oath of office, the contradictory trends that would characterize so many other US cities in the 1980s were already affecting Philadelphia. While so-called yuppies gentrified Queen Village, Old City, Manayunk and other borderline neighborhoods, city services were being overtaxed by an alarming rise in homelessness. While glass-and-granite towers were erected for booming corporations in Center City, drug abuse and related crime skyrocketed in the surrounding neighborhoods. A vicious struggle for power erupted among the *mafiosi* of South Philadelphia. Drug gangs and crack houses invaded

treasures. Local restaurants, businesses and retail stores joined together to promote the city, and the restaurant renaissance began.

Yet, during the early 1980s, Mayor William J. Green presided over the city for four undistinguished years of continuing social and political tensions, and a shaky financial situation. In 1984, W. Wilson Goode, Philadelphia's first African-American mayor, was voted into office on a platform of good clean government and racial healing.

FAR LEFT: MOVE follower announces a demonstration.
LEFT: Frank Rizzo with his signature tuxedo.
RIGHT: President Clinton and Mayor Ed Rendell, 1999.

the blighted neighborhoods surrounding Center City. The murder rate in the city also went through the roof at this time.

The Rendell reign

In 1991, Frank Rizzo – a bulldog to the end – made another bid to be Philadelphia's mayor, but succumbed to a heart attack in the middle of his campaign. As hundreds of mourners waited to pay their last respects outside the Cathedral of Saints Peter and Paul *(see page 176)*, it seemed that the city had reached the end of an era. Philadelphians had survived the social firestorms of the 1960s and 1970s; they had weathered the "greed is good" ethic of the

1980s. Now, as they entered the 1990s, they were primed, more than ever, for positive change, and Edward Rendell, the city's new mayor, turned out to be just the spark that Philadelphia needed.

Ed Rendell, a native New Yorker who had adopted Philadelphia as his city, being a graduate of Penn Law School and a former District Attorney, came to power with the build and bravado of a linebacker, the tireless energy of a cheerleader, and the vision of a star quarterback. What's more, he had the people skills – fueled by passion – to charm everyone, from the guy selling pretzels from a cart outside City Hall to the

corporate CEOs – whose investment in the city was so critical to its rebirth – to the government types in both the state capital, Harrisburg, and the nation's capital, Washington, D.C., who also needed to believe in him.

Rendell did not, admittedly, begin the sea of change. The seeds of positive development had already been sprinkled in the 1980s and early 1990s – organizations such as the Center City District, which focused on keeping the streets clean and safe, were firmly in place when Rendell took office. The opening of new city venues, such as Penn's Landing and Liberty Place, along with neighborhood happenings such as Old City's art open house called "First Fridays," had also already sought to enhance life for residents as well as draw commuters back to the city at weekends.

However, the Rendell Administration combined a hard line on the city budget with a strong push behind the city's strengths – in particular, identifying Philadelphia's history and culture as assets to be nurtured and expanded. In 1993 the 10-day, Welcome America! festival was instituted to celebrate the grand opening of the giant glass-and-steel Convention Center and focus attention on the city as America's birthplace.

Hotel boom

The opening of the Convention Center also helped ignite a chain reaction of innovation and development, including a hotel boom (17 openings in the city between 1998 and 2000), another restaurant renaissance, and a renewed commitment to culture and entertainment, including support for projects along the Avenue of the Arts *(see page 155)*, development and expansion of the Delaware waterfront, continued promotion of the city's historic districts, and an energetic hospitality to filmmakers *(see page 78)*. Showing true bipartisan city pride, Rendell succeeded in bringing the Republican 2000 Presidential Convention to Philadelphia, after which he went on to head the Democratic National Committee.

In 2000, at the end of his two terms, Mayor Rendell passed the keys to City Hall to former councilman John Street, who has promised to continue the upward momentum in managing the fifth-largest city in the nation. ❏

LEFT: Mayor John Street making his inaugural speech in 2000.

The Philly Sound

It was the 1950s. The big record producers hadn't yet caught on to the power of rock 'n' roll and the door was wide open for small record companies to get a tune in the charts. With good publicity, a one-hit wonder could rocket an artist to stardom. It was happening in Memphis, in Chicago and in Philadelphia. But Philly had something the other towns didn't: the TV dance show *American Bandstand*.

The show was born in 1952 when WFIL-TV realized that its lineup of British movies just didn't cut. Since the station manager had been talked into buying thousands of dollars worth of short musical films, the station went along with an idea by radio DJ Bob Horn to do a music show aimed at the kids. On the first show, Horn interviewed jazz virtuoso Dizzy Gillespie, showed clips of singer Peggy Lee, and gave birth to a TV phenomenon. But the real lifeblood of the show didn't arrive until a month later, when the station began airing promos inviting teenagers to dance in the studio.

The success of *American Bandstand* had an influence on another young disc jockey, Dick Clark. The name of his radio show, formerly called *Caravan of Stars*, was changed to *Bandstand* to cash in on the television show's success. When Horn was fired in 1956, Clark was the logical person to take over the job.

On August 5, 1957, with Clark in command, *American Bandstand* hit the national airwaves. Exposure to millions of kids brought with it a huge power to make stars. A prominent spot on the "*American Bandstand* Teenage Top 10" – a list of songs chosen on whim by Clark and his staff – could turn a nobody into an overnight sensation. Small wonder that the US Congress brought Clark up before a special subcommittee to investigate improprieties in the recording business – he was thought to own a percentage of some of the tunes he was promoting on the show.

But the kids kept right on dancing; they didn't care. The *Bandstand* format was simple. Music played, youngsters danced, performers lip-synced the lyrics of their latest record, and Dick Clark "related" to the kids with a little between-song patter. Through them, the country learned dances such as the Twist, the Duck, the Mashed Potato

---

RIGHT: disc jockey Dick Clark created a generation of teen idols and pop stars.

and the Locomotion. The kids would then rate the tunes: "I like the beat; it's easy to dance to. I give it a 95!" became a popular cliché.

The fact that *American Bandstand* was based in Philadelphia was a godsend to local crooners. Fabian, Bobby Rydell and Frankie Avalon grew up within three blocks of each other in South Philadelphia; and Chubby Checker wasn't too far away. This was the same neighborhood that had produced Mario Lanza, Eddie Fisher, Al Martino and Buddy Greco. The new idols' image was all-American. Kitted out in smart suits and conservative dresses, the *Bandstand* kids made rock 'n' roll respectable. If Elvis's gyrating pelvis disturbed

preachers and parents, Dick Clark made them feel the whole thing was just good clean fun.

But the days of the Philly Sound were soon numbered. In 1964 *American Bandstand* moved its recording location to California, emulating the nation's teenagers who had ditched the Philly Sound in favor of the Beach Boys. Since then, Philly has launched musicians including Patti LaBelle, Teddy Pendergrass, the Hooters, Tommy Conwell, recording artist and actor Will Smith and rapper The Fresh Prince, among other chart-toppers. And the Philadelphia club scene still has exciting new acts (*see page 74*). But the city hasn't really been a musical hot spot since the kids stopped doing the Hully-Gully at WFIL-TV. ❑

THE PHILADELPHIA STORY

European in design, but distinctly American in its culture, Philadelphia is as proud of its historic past as it is confident of its future

On a hot summer week in July, Philadelphia threw a rousing and successful political convention. No, we're not talking about that hot summer week, 200 and some years ago, when members of the Continental Congress arrived by horseback and stagecoach from 13 colonies to declare the birth of a new nation, the United States of America. This time it was the Republican National Convention, held the last week in July 2000, where the essentially Democratic administration and community of Philadelphia threw its arms wide open to 2,000 visitors, including delegates from 50 states and the media, who convened here to name their candidate for President of the United States. They arrived by train, bus, car and plane, checked into city and suburban hotel rooms, ate at Philadelphia restaurants, toured museums and historic attractions, listened to its music, and walked its streets, open maps in hand. At the end of the week, the convention ended and it was declared one of the best national political conventions ever.

No one was happier than the Philadelphians. It was described by some as Philadelphia's "coming out" party and the *Philadelphia Inquirer* quoted David L. Cohen, the co-chair of the host committee as saying "that the convention had achieved what some may have thought unachievable: 'To put Philadelphia on the map, once and for all... [as] one of the premier destination cities in America.'" And even before all the Republicans' bags were packed, Mayor John Street was waxing enthusiastically about "the next one."

Why all the euphoria? Why all the fuss? Technically, Mr Cohen should have talked of putting Philadelphia "back" on the map, for this quintessentially American of American cities, founded as the City of Brotherly Love, was once the center of nearly every aspect of US

culture – the national government was here, as were the national banks, the manufacturing companies, the publishing companies, the medical centers and the universities.

But Philadelphia has had its dark days as well as those filled with glory. Founded in 1681 by William Penn, an aristocratic and conservative

Quaker with radical ideas about freedom and liberty, Philadelphia has been, throughout its history, a city of contrasts and complexity. European in design yet distinctly American in its culture, Philadelphia was a living laboratory for the ideals and philosophical foundation on which America was built.

A planned city

Much of the Quaker ethic of plainness, humility and order was built into the city from the start. Unlike other cities, which grew according to their own chaotic logic, Philadelphia was laid out in advance according to Penn's simple street grid – the picture of classical order. In 1818, a Swedish

---

PRECEDING PAGES: fresh produce at the Italian Market; the annual Mummers' Parade.
LEFT: Liberty Place soars over City Hall.
RIGHT: colonial costumes at Christ Church.

traveler, Baron Axel Klinckowsrom, regarded it as "one of the loveliest cities in the world." "A beautiful city," wrote British novelist Frances Trollope in 1832, "nothing can exceed its neatness." US diplomat Charles Francis Adams thought there was "something solid and comfortable about it, something which shows permanency." "The handsomest and most populous city in the United States," said French botanist André Michaux.

Yet some back then found the orderliness unnerving. Writer Alexander Mackay, bemoan-

VOICE OF PRAISE

"I like this Philadelphia amazingly, and the people in it," reported Mark Twain, a man of many known dislikes, in 1853.

But over the years, due in varying degrees to geography, politics and the cost of labor, many of the centers shifted (education and medicine stayed). As the world became more glitzy and celebrity-driven, Quaker Philadelphia developed somewhat of an image problem coupled with an inferiority complex.

In stark contrast to its glory days as the "Athens of America," late 20th-century Philadelphia was now seemingly stuck in the shadows, sandwiched between the national government in Washington, D.C. and

ing the widespread use of brick, likened the place to "a great, flat, overbaked brick-field," and Sir Augustus Foster, an English diplomat, thought it "built too much in the shape of a chessboard to be beautiful."

But today those same visitors would probably find this classical city of brick bumped up with more exuberant styles of architecture – the Victorian extravagance of City Hall, for example, eclectic concoctions like the Pennsylvania Academy of Fine Arts, and the glass and granite skyscrapers, heirs to the pioneering modernism of the PSFS Building (see page 148). And if it's disorder you're looking for, the Italian Market is a study in chaos (see page 199).

the mega-metropolis of New York City. Philadelphia took some hard knocks from outsiders, but worse seemed to come from its own, such as native son, comedian W. C. Fields. When asked what he would like inscribed on his tombstone, Fields delivered the famous stinger, "On the whole, I'd rather be in Philadelphia."

However, the last half of the 20th century – with its exodus to the suburbs and the turbulent 1960s – was tough on all US cities. Philadelphia was not alone in fighting drugs, crime and an erosion of its tax base as residents and manufacturers fled. Philadelphia, like most cities, was in desperate need of new solutions, and the people to fight to make them happen.

An immigrant sanctuary

What saved Philadelphia were perhaps the same things that made it great 300 years ago – its ideas and its people. For all its supposed exclusivity in its clubs and society balls, few cities have opened their arms as widely to newcomers, rich or poor, and from whatever cultural or religious background.

From the beginning, William Penn envisioned Philadelphia as a city of refuge, a sanctuary for persecuted people of many faiths and nations. And to this day, the city is home to immigrant communities from around the world. In fact, immigrants and expatriates have always been among the city's most outstanding citizens and its strongest boosters. Feeling poorly treated in Boston, young Ben Franklin arrived in town with little more than a pocketful of bread and a head full of ideas. A dissolute Edgar Allan Poe rolled into town in 1838 with his 15-year-old wife and did some of his best work in a little house on North 7th Street. When *Leaves of Grass* was denounced as indecent, Walt Whitman found a new publisher in Philadelphia and a home across the river in Camden, New Jersey.

As is the case with most vibrant US cities, Philadelphia has continued to attract newcomers, including students, job seekers and visitors who have seen in this, the fifth-largest city in the United States, a livable town, where they could make a difference.

Rendell and rebirth

Ed Rendell, mayor of the city from 1992 to 2000 and dubbed "America's Mayor" by Vice-President Al Gore, has been credited with much of the success of Philadelphia's phenomenal turnaround. The beginnings had been laid in the 1970s and 1980s, as the restaurant industry blossomed, new construction changed the skyline and the Pennsylvania Convention Center was built. The Rendell Administration took the ball and ran with it, balancing the budget and nourishing the city's assets, recognizing that Philadelphia's rich historic legacy and culture could be the catalysts for its future successes. The City of Brotherly Love became in its ad campaigns "The Place that Loves You Back."

LEFT: Philadelphia's finest take a break.
RIGHT: playing the field, in the glare of modern Philadelphia skyscrapers.

By all accounts, the efforts have paid off. Nearly eight million visitors made the Philadelphia area their overnight destination both in 1997 and 1998 (more than 40 million, if you include day-trippers). Center City has about 12,700 hotel rooms and counting, over 5,000 of which were added since 1998. Restaurants continue to flourish and beget more restaurants. Shops and businesses are expanding into places like University City and Old City. Major development projects stretch from one river to the other, from an entertainment complex on Penn's Landing to a splashy new performing arts center, the Kimmel Center, on the ever-

growing Avenue of the Arts to a restoration of Fairmount Waterworks along the Schuylkill. And, most significant, a sense of pride and possibility permeates the city.

Philadelphia has grown from an 18th-century colonial town into a 21st-century metropolis with a strong sense of its past and stronger optimism about its future. A historic town within a modern city, its narrow streets and blocks of rowhouses nestle next to high-rise hotels and office buildings, whose gleaming sides of glass and steel catch the light of the afternoon sun. This reverence for the old and enthusiasm for the new exemplifies the contrasts in this city, as happy with tradition as with innovation. ❑

PEOPLE OF PHILADELPHIA

From its foundation as a colony tolerant of all faiths, Philadelphia has maintained these ideals to become one of the nation's most multicultural cities

Walk the streets of Philadelphia and – depending on the time of day – you'll see baby carriages and briefcases, street vendors and students, joggers, bikers and rowers, office workers lunching in the sunshine, groups of well-dressed business people heading towards fine restaurants and busloads of school kids on history field trips. As evening falls, you may see elegantly dressed persons headed towards a black tie gala, hear jazz riffs, blues or rock seeping from restaurants and cafés, or come across families with small children out in search of ice cream cones. Philadelphia, unlike some urban centers, is a place where people live as well as work, walk as well as ride and generally get involved in the lives of their neighborhoods. What's more, many suburbanites nestle close by, with easy commutes into the city – Philadelphians in spirit if not in the voting booth.

Neighborhoods flow seamlessly from one to another, peopled by different ethnic and cultural backgrounds so quintessentially American. Philadelphia's rich multicultural diversity is at the heart of the civic soul – as Philadelphian as the cobbled streets, Independence Hall or the Liberty Bell. William Penn's City of Brotherly Love has grown into a multicolored mosaic of over 100 neighborhoods, representing multiple cultures, cuisines and traditions.

An immigrant city

Because of its geography, Philadelphia established itself early as an immigrant port. The city was well situated, tucked between two rivers, the Delaware leading to the Atlantic Ocean and European trade, and the Schuylkill, flowing out of interior land rich with fertile farmland, coal and other natural resources.

The Lenni-Lenape Native Americans, as well as Dutch and Swedes, were already settled here when William Penn arrived with English

Quakers and German Mennonites, who were soon joined by Welsh, African-Americans and other settlers *(see page 21)*.

Whether drawn to Philadelphia because of its religious freedom and openness to the dispossessed and disenfranchised, because of its gracious rivers and rolling countryside, or simply

because the growing industrial metropolis promised jobs and new lives, people continued to arrive. While, over time, the port lost business to other coastal cities, Philadelphia still grew into one of the great immigrant cities of the 19th century. New generations of Philadelphians included Italians and other southern Europeans, Eastern Europeans, Irish, Germans, English, Scottish and Russian Jews, as well as African- and other relocating Americans. Chinese immigrants in search of their fortune settled what is now Chinatown in the late 1800s. Migrations of varying sizes continued through the 20th century – often prompted by wars or unrest in other homelands. These immigrants

LEFT: muralist painting the "University Gate" mural on Broad Street.
RIGHT: a vendor sells his wares at the Italian Market.

arrived from a wide array of countries and cultures: they crossed the Atlantic from Latvia, Lithuania, Poland, Russia, Austria and Hungary; they came from Puerto Rico, Cuba and Latin America; Asians came from China, Cambodia, Korea and Vietnam; other settlers included Indians, Filipinos, Mexicans and West Indians.

While many areas of Philadelphia are now ethnically and culturally integrated, there are also many neighborhoods still characterized by particular cultures from generations past.

ACADEMIC DRAW

Philadelphia's university, research and health care communities are among the draws for new arrivals to the city from other parts of the country and the world.

commercial purpose. Germantown was settled by Quakers and German Mennonites, most of whom were weavers *(see page 207)*. True to the founding principles of the city, the early neighborhoods of Old City and Society Hill had residents of assorted faiths – colonial delegates to the constitutional convention could find an Anglican Church across the street from a Quaker Meeting House, down the block from a Jewish congregation, across the way from a Roman Catholic Church or an African-American Congregation.

City of neighborhoods

Philadelphia is often called the "city of neighborhoods" – areas developed over its 300-year history, some old, others new, some renovated to reflect history, others more contemporary in architecture and tone. Some have residents whose families have been there for generations, others are trendy hotspots on the cutting edge.

The neighborhoods grew up with a kind of geographic logic – spreading from river to river (the Delaware to the Schuylkill) and beyond, as public transportation gave rise to the "streetcar suburbs" of West Philadelphia, Logan, Olney and Strawberry Mansion. They were bound by faiths, culture, common ideals or

As immigration increased and the city grew, other neighborhoods sprung up with larger settlements of one ethnic group or the other, such as Center City's Chinatown, the largely Italian South Philadelphia or Puerto Rican North Kensington, and the more recently settled Russian neighborhoods of the city's far Northeast. Wealth characterized other neighborhoods, such as Rittenhouse Square, which today maintains its status as one of the city's most stylish communities. Pockets of the city devoted to particular trades or commerce, such as Jewelers Row *(see page 143)* or Antique Row *(see page 146)*, also developed unique identities, many of which remain today.

Like other urban centers, Philadelphia today also has a vibrant gay community. The area between 11th and 13th and Walnut to South streets, known in the gay community as Washington West (or the "gayborhood") has a number of gay bars and cafés, as well as two gay bookstores and a gay community center *(see page 282)*. Outside Center City, Mount Airy, a largely residential community sandwiched between historic Germantown and posh Chestnut Hill, is a neighborhood that thrives on diversity and includes among its families a number of gay and lesbian couples, as well as interfaith and bi-racial couples.

University City, with its plethora of academic and research institutions, draws people from all over the world, resulting in a colorful community of people of all ages and backgrounds *(see page 191)*.

Power and prestige

For some time, the image of a powerful Philadelphia cultural élite where bloodline (Anglo-Saxon Protestant), breeding and wealth, in that order, determined political influence and social standing – eclipsed the real diversity of people that make up Philadelphia. This image was promulgated to the world by popular works of fiction such as *The Philadelphia Story*, Philip Barry's 1939 play, later made into a film starring Katharine Hepburn and Cary Grant and subsequently adapted as the 1956 musical *High Society*, starring Philadelphia native Grace Kelly *(see page 79)*. The story, although modeled on real-life socialite Hope Montgomery Scott, is hardly representative of many Philadelphians today. The characters are dashing and witty if a bit silly, frolicking on the Main Line with cocktails in hand, acid on the tongue, and society reporters yapping at their heels.

There are still some pockets of old money in Center City – the stolid townhouses on Delancey Place, for example, and exclusive social clubs – although this kind of élitism is waning. The Union League, once a bastion of white male protestants, has opened its doors to women, African-Americans and people of other faiths. "The new rich have totally overwhelmed the old rich," sociologist Professor E. Digby

Baltzell has said. While money is still important to the growth of the city, many of Philadelphia's biggest supporters are relative newcomers.

Many of Center City's old families migrated to Chestnut Hill or the Main Line, a string of suburban towns along what was the Pennsylvania Railroad's link to the western suburbs *(see page 36)*. Traveling the back roads of the Main Line into the "hunt country" of Chester and Delaware counties is reminiscent of the countryside in Europe, with long, tree-lined driveways leading up to handsome, ornate houses of various styles, many borrowing architectural cues from the old-world gentry.

But even the Main Line is loosening up, its communities reflecting much greater diversity than the stereotype admits. While high society still has its social rituals – black tie charity balls, country club memberships, private schools for the children as well as special dance and manners classes in which girls wear white gloves and boys don jackets and ties – many of these social enclaves have kept pace with the times by opening their doors a bit wider to people of other faiths and cultural backgrounds.

Just as new money has made its way into the institutional coffers, other names and faces have played critical parts in the city's development, particularly in the latter part of the 20th century.

LEFT: workmen in the Rittenhouse Square District.
RIGHT: Devon Horse Show is one of the highlights of Philadelphia's high society calendar.

The Pew Charitable Trusts, the Annenberg Foundation, the William Penn Foundation and Connelly Foundation are among those private foundations supporting projects and institutions in the area. Philadelphians from other states and countries as well as long-time residents take active roles in shaping the city's future, and the power structure today is much more consistent with the multicultural citizenry.

African-Americans

Philadelphia has had a significant African-American community throughout most of its history. A handful of African-Americans in the

late 1600s grew to 12,000 by 1820. Philadelphia was a relatively good destination for newly freed slaves and runaways from the south, both because it had a tradition of groups opposed to slavery and because it had a growing community of African churches, schools and small businesses. Quaker Mennonites had passed the nation's first anti-slavery declaration in Germantown in 1688, and Pennsylvania banned slave trade in the state in 1780, requiring that any child born to slave parents after the law must be freed at age 28. In 1787, Richard Allen, a slave who had bought his freedom five years before at the age of 23, founded Mother Bethel African Methodist Episcopal

Church, on 6th Street between Pine and Lombard streets *(see page 128).*

Through the 19th and much of the 20th century, African-Americans were largely isolated by overt bigotry, low economic status, and later, by the soft bigotry of low educational expectations and opportunities. Gradually, however, a more educated, affluent middle class has arisen, and begun to break down residential and social barriers. Black churches and their clergy have been and continue to be a strong and stabilizing force holding together the less affluent African-American communities.

Today, African-Americans comprise 40 percent of the city's population and have an active presence on corporate and nonprofit boards of directors, in educational and cultural institutions, in city government and as Philadelphia's representatives to state and national legislatures. William H. Gray III, pastor of Bright Hope Baptist Church in North Philadelphia, was a US Congressman, Chairman of the House Budget Committee and Democratic Whip. Philadelphia lawyer and Assistant District Attorney A. Leon Higginbotham, Jr became a Federal judge, served on the Federal Trade Commission, taught at Harvard and, in 1995, was awarded the Presidential Medal of Freedom. Mayor John Street is now Philadelphia's second African-American mayor.

Civic pride

Philadelphians – a mixed lot, with assorted backgrounds, diverse talents and varied goals and dreams – are a difficult population about which to generalize. Yet, if there's one thing that so many Philadelphians seem to have in common these days, it's a genuine love of the city. Volunteers conduct clean-up drives, teach children to read, help rebuild homes in depressed and downtrodden neighborhoods, and raise money for everything from schools and cultural institutions to research for cancer and Aids, among numerous other efforts. Corny as it may sound, Philadelphians are proud of their City of Brotherly Love, and the unique ideals which have guided it like a beacon through good times and bad in more than 300 years of history. ❑

LEFT: girlfriends gather after class outside the Philadelphia Free Library.
RIGHT: old-world style at the Devon Horse Show.

THE AMISH

The Pennsylvanian Amish community resolutely clings to traditional values,

following a rural way of life that has changed little since the 16th century

A long line of cars crawls along in frustration, trying to pass slow-moving Amish buggies on a busy highway in Lancaster County. It's not just a traffic jam; it's a clash between modern and traditional values. The Amish are a people apart, yet the more they try to separate themselves from the modern world, the more they attract its attention.

Responding to an invitation by William Penn, the Amish people settled the fertile countryside west of Philadelphia and, for 300 years, they have managed stubbornly to cling to many of the customs and beliefs they brought to the New World. They are the "gentle people" of pacifism and personal humility, baffling the rest of the nation's population by their tenacious hold on the past and seemingly arbitrary code of behavior. They do not use electricity; they farm with horses instead of using tractors; they shun higher education, and they do not allow the ownership of cars.

Unlike many other fundamentalist groups, however, they do not base their style of life on unquestioned Old Testament edicts. Indeed, the Amish are masters of compromise, cunningly balancing convenience against tradition and making delicate, well thought-out bargains that embrace enough of the modern world to give them prosperity while rejecting those aspects that are likely to threaten the integrity of their community and family life.

Origins

Lancaster County's 21,000 Old Order Amish are loosely linked to their other North American cousins scattered across nearly 900 congregations in 22 states and the Canadian province of Ontario. Their religious roots stretch back to the 16th-century Anabaptists who parted ways with the Protestant Reformation in 1525 in Switzerland. Although Europe was their homeland, there are no Amish there today.

LEFT: Old Order Amish continue to live a traditional, agricultural life.

RIGHT: out for a spin, Amish-style.

Adhering to the literal teachings of Jesus, the Anabaptists emphasized obedience to God's will, adult baptism, pacifism, the separation of church and state, and a disciplined church community that remained distinct from the larger world. They were dubbed rebaptizers, or Anabaptists, because they insisted on baptizing

adults who had already gone through the ritual as infants. Because adult baptism was considered both a religious heresy and a political threat, it triggered severe persecution. Thousands of Anabaptists died for their faith by drowning, burning at the stake, or decapitation.

The Amish splintered off from the Swiss Anabaptists in 1693 under the leadership of Jacob Ammann, from whom they derive their name. Hutterites, Mennonites and various Brethren groups also trace their lineage to the Anabaptists. The Amish share basic religious beliefs with other Christians, but put special emphasis on simplicity, community, obedience, humility, mutual aid, and separation from the world, a way of life galvanized by the persecution they suffered in Europe.

Discipline and control

The Amish are flourishing in North America. From a small band of some 5,000 at the turn of the 20th century, they have grown to more than 130,000. Their community has been doubling in size almost every 20 years. Large families, averaging about seven children, provide a steady stream of members, since some 80 percent or more of their children join the Amish community. In addition to having a high birth rate, the Amish have constructed a variety of

would disturb the relative equality of Amish life. The virtues of humility and simplicity also stress a smallness of ego, which promotes cooperation with the community.

Social control is another fence that cordons off the community. Obedience is considered a virtue. Children learn at an early age to obey parents, teachers and elders. At their baptism, in their late teens and early twenties, young adults promise to obey the *ordnung* – the discipline of the community passed across the generations by word of mouth. It prescribes the use of horses and traditional dress, and forbids attendance of high school and ownership of

social fences around their community to protect it from the turbulent winds of modern life.

Except for family size, the Amish emphasize small-scale values. The Lancaster community revolves around 100 church districts consisting of 25 to 35 families. Worship services, held every other Sunday, rotate from home to home because the Amish have no church buildings. Worship, work, fellowship and mutual-aid activities, such as barn raisings, revolve around the church district, affording each person a social and emotional niche. Farms and businesses are also relatively small. Large operations employing more than a dozen people are thought to lead to arrogance and wealth that

cars, televisions, electricity and computers, among many other things that are part of the everyday modern world.

The flamboyant individualism of American culture constantly threatens Amish ways. Submission to the community and concern for the corporate good takes priority over expressions of individualism, such as faddish dress, jewelry and personal photographs. The *ordnung* helps to insulate the community from the pressures of unbridled American individualism. It not only provides guidance for personal behavior but clarifies the greater importance of the community over individual whims and wishes.

The bishop of each church district interprets and enforces the rules of discipline. Respect for traditional authority held by the bishop enables the community to retain its sharp distinctions from the world. Each bishop typically is responsible for two church districts – about 50 to 60 households – enabling him to know the members quite well.

The bishops of the community gather periodically to coordinate activities and discuss troublesome issues, such as the use of computers, eating in restaurants and embryo

SETTING AN EXAMPLE

Religion is not formally taught in any sector of Amish society, including the church. Religious values are taught by example, not by formal doctrine.

Amish developed their own schools. Elders contended that eight years of education was adequate preparation for a successful life in the Amish community. After numerous legal battles in several states, the US Supreme Court in 1972 declared that Amish students could terminate their formal education at the eighth grade. Amish youth complete their education in one-room schools operated by Amish parents.

Teachers are typically single Amish women, products themselves of Amish schools, who

transplants in cattle. Individuals who violate community norms are asked to make a public confession in the church service. If they refuse, they are liable for excommunication and social avoidance, known as "shunning."

Informal education

Amish education provides another barrier around the community. Before 1950, most Amish children attended one-room schools. With the consolidation of public schools the

teach without certification or a high-school diploma. The curriculum stresses practical skills but does not include science or religion. By limiting exposure to outside ideas and non-Amish youth, Amish education erects yet another powerful wall around the community.

Other cultural fences protect Amish ways from the influence of modern life by regulating interaction with mainstream culture. Once burned by the fires of persecution, the Amish emphasize separation from the world, thus preserving the purity of Amish tradition. They believe that they are called out from the world to be a peculiar people. Although the Amish speak English, their Pennsylvania German

LEFT: Dutch Country produce is one of the thriving cottage industries in the Amish community.
ABOVE: shopping at the Central Market in Lancaster.

dialect heightens group identity and stifles interaction with outsiders. The taboo on car ownership impedes mobility. The shunning of telephones, television, radio and other types of mass media in their homes limits contamination by outside values. Avoiding membership in public organizations and political affairs also helps to draw boundaries with the larger world.

Cultural bargaining

Although the Amish have built so many fences around their community, they are also capable of reaching through them occasionally to strike bargains with the larger culture. These cultural compromises often seem like riddles or contradictions. Pragmatism permits the use and hiring of motor vehicles, for example, because that bolsters their economic well-being – but not the ownership or driving of vehicles, because such mobility would erode the integrity of the community. For the same reason, telephones are acceptable in shops or barns but not in private homes.

Amish farmers typically use tractors around their barns for heavy-duty jobs, such as powering feed grinders and hydraulic systems. In the fields, however, modern farm machinery, designed for tractors, is pulled by horses. This

RUMSPRINGA – AMISH ADOLESCENCE

Amish children are raised with love, discipline and lots of hard work. Yet even in the Amish culture, adolescence is a time of testing limits. When Amish children turn 16 or 17, they enter a period of relative freedom called *rumspringa* ("running around") when they choose a circle of friends (their "gang"). During this time, as their parents look the other way, the teens get together to socialize at Sunday night "singings" until the early hours. They decorate their buggies with fancy rigging, stash a radio under the seat – maybe even attend a movie. A few even get a driver's license and buy a car. On weekends, they get together to flirt or attend "hoedowns" with loud music and beer.

It's at the Sunday sings where courting takes place. A young man can take his girl home after a sing, and visit her at her house on Saturdays. For these visits, secrecy is key: he arrives after the family is asleep and stays until early morning, tiptoeing out the door before the family stirs. The family never discusses what the kids are up to until a few weeks before the wedding is announced.

All this is heady stuff for youngsters brought up in the traditional Amish home. Yet by the time they reach their early twenties, seven out of ten are ready to be baptized, get married and carry on the Amish traditions. *Rumspringa* ends and they become adult members of the church.

distinction protects the horse, which has evolved as the prime symbol of Amish identity in the 20th century. Twelve-volt batteries are used to stir the milk in bulk tanks, but tapping into 110-volt power lines is forbidden – largely because this would bring into Amish homes the secular values transmitted by radio and television plus a variety of modern gadgets which would undermine the simplicity of Amish life.

The complexities don't stop there. Synthetic materials that require no ironing are used to make the Amish's traditional "plain" clothes. Carriages, made in Amish shops from fiberglass and vinyl, conform to customary colors

more compromises with modern ways and accepted more technology than Amish settlements in more rural areas of the country. And even infringements of the rules are sometimes treated leniently. A young farmer is given six months to replace the rubber tires on his tractor with steel wheels. A businessman is allowed several months to complete a project before getting rid of his illicit computer.

But the forces of urbanization and industrialization have squeezed Lancaster's Amish community relentlessly. Shrinking farmland, sharply rising land prices and their own growing population have created a demo-

and styles (grey for Mennonites, black for Amish). Newer Amish homes appear remarkably contemporary with modern kitchens, bathrooms and gas appliances. But washing machines, and sometimes sewing machines and cake mixers, are powered by hydraulic pressure.

Fight for survival

The Amish of Lancaster County (see page 235) are among the most progressive Amish communities in North America. They have brokered

LEFT: Amish farming still uses horse-drawn machinery in the fields.
ABOVE: Old Order Brethren family.

graphic crisis – too many Amish and too few acres to keep them. To cope with the pressures, some families migrate to more rural areas and, whenever possible, farms are subdivided into smaller operations.

But these moves are not enough, and the Amish face the big question: would they leave their farms for factories? Once again, they compromise. Yes, they would leave the plow behind, but not for factory work, which they believe erodes the stability of family life. Cottage industries offered a way around the impasse. By starting small industries, the Amish earn a living surrounded by family and friends. Today, nearly half of Lancaster's Amish are employed in manufacturing a variety of crafts, equipment, quilts and cabinetry. Hundreds of these small shops have sprung up in the past decade, and now produce dozens of different products from doghouses to gazebos. New court rulings have allowed young Amish boys to work beside their fathers in "hazardous" trades such as carpentry, which normally would be closed to young people.

For the moment at least, the cottage industries are a happy compromise. They allow members of the community to leave their plows but stay close to ancestral roots and work in a congenial environment rich with ethnic values.

But the cottage industries also pose a danger to the future of Amish society. They place Amish entrepreneurs in frequent contact with outsiders and expose them to the thinking of the larger world. Moreover, the shops are introducing a three-tier class system – farmers, day laborers and entrepreneurs – which in the long run could ruin the equality of Amish society.

Today, these cottage industries have paved the way for an even bigger threat to the Amish way of life: the computer. Already many Old Order Amish have run afoul of their bishops, who have ruled that computers are *verboten* (forbidden). Amish small businessmen insist that they need the machines to conduct their

affairs. In fact, recent hopes for an all-Amish bank had to be abandoned when the Amish businessmen realized it would be impossible to run a bank without computers. So far, the Amish bishops have held firm – just as they ruled against credit cards ("too easy to spend money"), they see the computer and the power of the Internet as an insidious threat to the fabric of Amish life. So far, no member has been excommunicated for using a computer in business, but the rule is clear: cybernetics and Amish don't mix.

Sense of belonging

The cost of being Amish is high, but there are benefits in return – lower rates of suicide, few drug problems, and no dependency on public welfare. Amish life offers a distinct sense of meaning, belonging and identity, a rare commodity these days.

These virtues require major concessions – forgoing unbridled individualism, giving up the pursuit of pleasure and convenience. But the Amish argue that true happiness and personal satisfaction are woven into the very fabric of a stable community, and that they discover themselves as individuals only when they yield to the wisdom of tradition. As a result, some tensions between their community and the outside world are inevitable. The 1985 movie *Witness*, in which Harrison Ford played a Philadelphia cop who takes refuge in the Amish countryside, won two Academy Awards from Hollywood but received few plaudits from the Amish, who correctly foresaw a large influx of tourists arriving to indulge their wistful longing for simpler times and simpler lives. Yet, at the same time, the estimated 5 million tourists who visit Lancaster County each year spend a total equivalent to almost $30,000 for each Amish inhabitant – an invaluable boost to the prosperity of the entire community.

While many visitors may think that the Amish are a quaint and even backward people, in fact they have been successful in maintaining their simplicity of life while slowly integrating changes in the modern world. By ignoring the superficiality of American popular culture, the Amish have been able to sustain their own unique approach to life. ❑

LEFT: children follow in the footsteps of their ancestors and show respect for family values.

The Mennonites

In late summer, ripened field corn sways in the breeze like a river of molten gold. All across Lancaster County, the fields are dotted with barefoot figures in long pastel dresses. The clothes and the hair coverings set them apart as Plain people – yet they are clearly not Amish.

They are Mennonites, and they far outnumber their more conservative cousins. More worldly than Amish yet more plain than the English, the Mennonites have thrived in rural Lancaster County since the 17th century. Their tradition grew out of the Anabaptist faith of the early 1500s, when they were persecuted as anarchists and driven from Europe. Eventually, the Mennonites and the Amish split over philosophical differences, and the Mennonites moved on to Germantown in 1683 (see page 207). Eventually they spread westward to Lancaster County and beyond in search of farmland, and today number almost a million worldwide.

Like all Plain folk, the Mennonites share a reverence for humility, modesty, simplicity, honesty, and hard work. Exactly how modest members must be, however, differs from one congregation to the next. From the very beginning, Mennonites have shown a tendency to splinter into factions, usually over disagreements about what is considered worldly and thus, forbidden. There is an enormous gulf between the most liberal New Order Mennonites, who live totally in the modern world, and the Old Order Mennonites who keep completely to themselves, banning radio, TV, cars and education beyond eighth grade. However, even the most conservative Mennonites are more liberal than the Amish, and permit telephones and electricity in their plain but immaculate farmhouses.

All the Mennonite sects share a common ideal of a religious community based on the New Testament. The Bible is regarded as the sole authority on doctrine, and only adults who profess their faith are baptized. While more liberal congregations preach in English, the Old Order still use Pennsylvania German among themselves. Mennonites, among the first to endorse the separation of church and state and to condemn slavery, have traditionally obeyed civil laws. Like their Amish cousins, they refuse to bear arms or support violence, to take judicial oaths or hold public office. They are

RIGHT: a traditional Mennonite church in Pennsylvania.

linked by their belief, styles of worship, small-group Bible study and missionary work. Their retirement centers and disaster aid services are examples of their belief that word and deed must be one. Most Mennonites (except for the Old Order) believe in education and sponsor private schools and Mennonite universities. Unlike the Amish, missionary work has sent Mennonites throughout the world, establishing outposts on every continent.

The easiest way to spot the difference between Amish and Mennonite is by their appearance. While there are subtle differences between one Mennonite sect and another, in general Mennonite women wear pastel flower-print polyester dresses

(the more conservative the church, the more conservative the dress). Many Mennonite women add a cape-like triangular piece of cloth. Almost all the women wear a white net prayer covering, whose differences in shape are a mark of her congregation. The least conservative wear a tiny cap on the back of their heads with no string ties at all. Mennonite men usually wear dark pants, suspenders and a dark shirt. Small gray hats with a pinched crown are worn by even small Mennonite boys.

While Mennonites are not bound by many of the Amish restrictions – most would not object to a photograph – they move comfortably within their own culture, amidst and yet in many ways apart from the worldly influence of modern society. ❑

CULTURE IN THE CITY

No second fiddle to New York City, Philadelphia has long been a center for the arts, from its superb art museums to its world-renowned symphony orchestra

Philadelphia was declared by the painter Gilbert Stuart to be the "Athens of America" – a genteel city of democratic and cultivated sensibilities, technological advancement and abundant Greek Revival architecture. While the mantle of leadership in the arts has shifted to hectic, cosmopolitan New York City, there is still excitement in Philly's art world, with both a reverence for the Old Masters and a nurturing of new artists in nearly every form of expression.

The arts and entertainment worlds have always been a part of Philadelphia, but modern organizations have sprung up to combat the economics of a changing world. The Greater Philadelphia Cultural Alliance, originally established in 1972 to plan for the Bicentennial Celebrations, has worked since then to promote the region's 230-plus non profit arts and cultural organizations.

One difficulty has been that some of the city's finest arts groups have not had their own performance spaces and had to rent theaters on what was often a show-by-show basis. Renewed civic support in the 1990s gave new life to the arts scene. The Rendell administration oversaw the transformation of Broad Street into a fully fledged Avenue of the Arts stretching both north and south of City Hall. The Prince Music Theater on Chestnut Street became a new home for the American Music Theater Festival, which produces new musical theater works ranging from obscure revivals to experimental works. The Arts Bank, part of the University of the Arts, moved into a restored building at Broad and South streets, adding much-needed performance and rehearsal space.

The Philadelphia Clef Club for Jazz and the Performing Arts built a brand new facility on South Broad Street dedicated solely to jazz performance, history and education. The Wilma Theater moved into a splashy new theater at

Broad and Spruce streets. And right across the street, construction is underway of Kimmel Center for the Performing Arts, which will house a state-of-the-art concert hall as a new home for the Philadelphia Orchestra, and a smaller recital hall for use by several groups including the Concerto Soloists Chamber

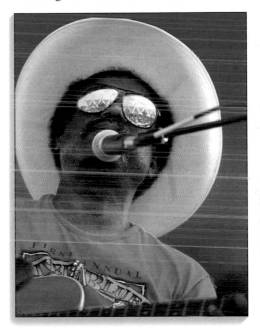

Orchestra, Philadanco and the Philadelphia Chamber Music Society. The orchestra's move will, in turn, free up the venerable Academy of Music at Broad and Locust streets as a home for the Pennsylvania Ballet and Opera Company, as well as for touring theatrical and dance productions.

Theater and festivals

Proximity to New York has been Philadelphia theater's greatest blessing and biggest curse. Early on, the town that gave birth to matinée idol Edwin Forrest, and a fair chunk of the Barrymore clan, was a launch pad for Broadway shows. But as Broadway suffered its ups and

LEFT: an open-air summer concert in Chestnut Hill's Pastorius Park.
RIGHT: Penn's Landing RiverBlues Festival.

downs over the last three decades, Philadelphia began to forge its own theatrical identity. The Theater Alliance of Greater Philadelphia evolved from the 1990 Performing Arts League. Of the estimated 120 theatrical organizations in the area, approximately 60 are members of the Alliance, which promotes general awareness of Philadelphia theater, offers discount tickets through arrangements with hotels, and administers the annual Barrymore Awards for Excellence in Theater *(see page 286).*

(see page 286).

> ### BOHEMIAN ARTS
>
> The International House and the Painted Bride Arts Center are renowned for international music, unusual dance events, performance art and offbeat films.

chamber musicals and the classics at its site in Old City *(see page 117).* Exciting work can also be found at the Philadelphia Theatre Company, a presenter of new American plays at Plays and Players Theater on Delancey Street *(see page 287).* The Wilma Theater puts on both cutting-edge drama and black comedy; and the American Music Theater Festival at The Prince Theater each year takes on the Herculean task of producing a slate of original musicals.

Smaller theaters continue to build audiences

The city has a number of subscription companies, the largest of which is the Walnut Street Theatre, offering classic and popular plays, as well as larger than life restagings of Broadway musicals. Recent offerings include *The Heiress*, *Phantom of the Opera* and *La Cage aux Folles*. You can also often find smaller, intimate theatrical productions at the Walnut's studios Three and Five. The Forrest Theatre is a touring house that brings in tried and tested Broadway shows such as *Fosse* and *Les Misérables*.

The theatrical scene has taken off, with once small theaters growing into significant players in the theatrical community. The Arden Theatre Company presents exciting literary adaptations,

along various specialist themes. The Philadelphia Shakespeare Festival puts on three of the Bard's plays each year at 2111 Sansom Street. Theater exploring the African-American experience has flourished at the Freedom Theatre on North Broad Street and the Bushfire Theater at 52nd and Locust streets, housed in a former movie palace.

Other smaller companies include The Adrienne, known for its comedies, and InterAct Theater Company and Venture Company, both known for thought-provoking drama.

A jaunt into the suburbs finds the People's Light and Theater Company in Malvern, a strong resident company that recently received national attention for its five-hour adaptation of *Sister Carrie* and its cross-cultural *kabuki*-style *Achilles*. In New Jersey, Princeton's McCarter Theater has been treated to a well-deserved artistic facelift thanks to its director, who has brought American premieres of works by playwrights such as David Rabe and Edward Albee to the theater as well as household name actors such as Ed Asner, Linda Hunt and Laura San Giacomo.

For younger crowds, the outstanding International Festival of Theater for Children brings the best in children's entertainment to five stages and their environs in West Philadelphia.

Philadelphia's music scene has experienced a good deal of action, too. Almost every other classical performance group in town plays in the considerable shadow cast by the Philadelphia Orchestra. Its singular lush sound, shaped by the eminent maestros Leopold Stokowski and Eugene Ormandy, largely accounted for its position as one of the country's great music-making ensembles of the 20th century. In 1993, Riccardo Muti passed the baton of the orchestra to German-born conductor Wolfgang Sawallisch. In addition to its regular subscription series, the orchestra performs a number of special event concerts each year, including a New

Dance and classical music

Economic troubles have tested the Philadelphia dance community to the limit. Despite its consistent excellence, the Pennsylvania Ballet was just a pirouette away from bankruptcy in 1990, before staging an eleventh-hour fund-raising coup that managed to save its life. Now it is back on its toes and is one of the city's must-sees. The highly regarded local company, Philadanco, offers an excellent modern alternative.

LEFT: the City of Brotherly Love is commemorated in art form.
ABOVE: the world-renowned Philadelphia Orchestra.

Year's Eve gala and a Hallowe'en concert where musicians (and audience members, if they choose to) show up in costume.

Until it moves into its new home at the Kimmel Center, the orchestra can be enjoyed at the Academy of Music or at its summer home at the Mann Music Center for the Performing Arts in Fairmount Park. Purists sometimes complain about the occasional honking horns and airplane roars at the Mann, but most love these concerts, especially from the vantage-point of the free seats on the lawn, where the music is often accompanied by picnic dinners, the pop of wine corks and, from the top of the hill, a terrific view of the city skyline. Jazz programs, as well as various touring dance and pop shows are also offered at the Mann.

Concerto Soloists Chamber Orchestra, featuring its musicians as solo and ensemble artists, performs the more intimate repertoire of the Baroque and Classical period, in addition to more unusual contemporary works. The group has also introduced innovative multimedia productions combining music with slide presentations of art chosen to complement the music. The ever-popular Philly Pops, led by the charismatic Peter Nero (of *Breakfast at Tiffany's* fame), continues to entertain and delight audiences with lighter fare.

Jazz, blues, rock and more

Philadelphia has a strong jazz history, nurtured by local talents such as the late great saxophonist Grover Washington, Jr. Jazz talent, both local and national, can be sampled in a number of clubs and cafés, a fairly good listing of which is in *Philadelphia Weekly (see page 262)*. The most well-known include North 3rd Street's Ortlieb's Jazzhaus and Zanzibar Blue, the Philadelphia Clef Club of the Performing Arts, and the more low-key Chris's Jazz Café on Sansom Street. Blues can be heard at Warmdaddy's at Front and Market streets, which touts itself as "the number one blues club on the East

You'll also find smaller groups for just about every taste. Orchestra 2001 offers works by 20th-century composers at various city venues. The Philadelphia Chamber Music Society performs more than 40 concerts annually, most of which are at the Pennsylvania Convention Center. Pennsylvania Pro Musica performs repertoire from Baroque, Classical, Renaissance, Medieval and modern works.

Opera buffs can check out the Opera Company of Philadelphia, which responded to financial challenges by shifting toward opera's greatest hits. This move has been popular with large numbers of newcomers, although disappointing serious-minded opera enthusiasts.

Coast." The Philadelphia Folk Song Society also offers monthly concerts.

Big name rockers play at the Electric Factory, The Mann Center, First Union Complex and Sony's E-Center across the Ben Franklin Bridge in Camden. But there's also a lot of rock, folk and other music played in more intimate settings in clubs and bars all over town. Just a few include Tin Angel on 2nd Street between Market and Chestnut in Old City, which has great acoustic (as well as electric) folk and rock, TLA (with an eclectic array of musicians and comics) and Pontiac Grille, (with louder sounds), both mainstays on South Street. Bob and Barbara's at 1501 South Street alternates funky jazz nights with other styles. Silk City at 5th Street and Spring Garden is a small club with hip new music, as are Khyber Pass and The Upstage on South 2nd and 3rd streets. North Star Bar at 27th and Poplar up behind the Art Museum has good local groups. Swingbands swing at Five Spot at 5 South Bank Street, which also offers free lessons some nights. And Bar Noir at 112 South 18th Street has a wide range of folk, jazz and other live music Sunday to Tuesday, with DJs the rest of the week.

> ### CASINO CULTURE
>
> Atlantic City, New Jersey, is a favorite hangout for Philadelphians. The casinos stage Broadway revues and lounge acts as well as big-name stars *(see page 231).*

the city), and the Jambalaya Jam, RiverBlues Festival and Singer-Songwriter Festival at the Penn's Landing outdoor arena *(see page 128).*

Visual arts

Philadelphia is filled with outdoor art treasures, due in part to a 1959 ordinance requiring all developers to allocate one percent of construction costs to the display of fine arts. The result is over 1,400 objects of public art for all to enjoy.

Your first stop on any art tour of Philadelphia should, of course, be the Philadelphia

Delaware Avenue has a lively, loud club scene, from Egypt, Maui and KatManDu to Dave & Busters, described by the *Inquirer* as "Chuck E. Cheese with a liquor license." One of the quirkier nightlife scenes is The Secret Cinema, which screens 16-millimeter film of newsreels, educational films, horror and other films at bars and locations around the city.

There are also the annual festivals, such as the Philadelphia Folk Festival, the Mellon Jazz Festival (at a variety of locations in and around

LEFT: making music on the streets of Philadelphia.
ABOVE: part of the impressive Asian Art collection at the Philadelphia Museum of Art.

Museum of Art *(see page 178),* which stands with dignity at the end of the Benjamin Franklin Parkway. If you take a walk from City Hall along the Parkway to the museum, you can also experience three works of art by three generations of the Calder family. Alexander Milne Calder sculpted the statue of William Penn that stands on top of City Hall. His son, Alexander Stirling Calder, sculpted the beautiful Swann Memorial Fountain placed in the center of Logan Circle, with the three bronze figures representing the waters of the Schuylkill, Delaware, and Wissahickon. Third generation Alexander "Sandy" Calder, abstract sculptor and inventor of mobiles, created the mobile entitled *Ghost* which hangs in the Great Stair Hall of the Museum of Art.

On a summer day, it often seems that more people are interested in running, Rocky-style, up the museum's monumental staircase than sampling the masterworks inside. This is a shame, since the museum houses a fine mix of artistic "greatest hits," including Van Gogh's *Sunflowers*, Picasso's *Three Musicians* and Du Champ's *Nude Descending a Staircase*, as well as many fascinating period rooms, Pennsylvania Dutch crafts and furnishings, and an impressive collection of Asian and Islamic art. Considerably more popular with children, however, is the museum's substantial cache of armor and armaments.

The museum becomes a festive party on Wednesday evenings, when programs are presented along special themes, with a host of extras included in your admission ticket, including gallery talks, films, tours, performances and food. And each fall, the popular Museum of Art Craft show draws more than 1,500 applicants, of which 195 are represented. Among the craft categories are basketry, ceramics, decorative fiber, wearable fiber, furniture, glass, jewelry, leather, metal, mixed media, paper and wood.

PHILADELPHIA'S MURAL ARTS PROGRAM

The Mural Arts Program began in 1984 when the Anti-Graffiti Network was established by Mayor Goode in an attempt to provide productive outlets for graffiti writers, while at the same time beautifying the neighborhood. Since then, the program has grown tremendously. Today murals are created in all parts of the city, some by professional artists, others by MAP staff artists with assistance from community volunteers. MAP also runs a number of educational programs throughout the city, giving instruction in drawing, painting and the specific techniques of mural making. The South Street area also has murals using pieces of tile, ceramic and colored cement.

The murals are not only visually striking, but many of them reflect the interests or history of the community. Some are larger-than-life paintings of well-known local heroes, such as singer Mario Lanza (Broad and Reed streets) or baseball legend Jackie Robinson (2804 North Broad Street), the laying of hands in The Peace Wall at 29th and Wharton streets and the celebration of the arts in Philadelphia Muses at 13th and Locust streets.

A great way to see the murals is to take a trolley tour given by the Mural Arts Department (see page 264), which also sells guides to the murals for those interested in exploring on their own.

The imposing size of the Museum of Art can make it easy to overlook the unassuming Rodin Museum, just a short walk down the Parkway. You'll pass *The Thinker* and a beautiful garden as you enter the largest collection of Auguste Rodin's work this side of France.

You will find a considerably more intimate setting at the Pennsylvania Academy of the Fine Arts, the first art school and museum in the country. The building itself is a work of art. It was designed by renowned Philadelphia architects Frank Furness and George Hewitt in an imaginative, if sometimes dizzying, array of styles. The museum's permanent collection offers a first-rate survey of American art, including Benjamin West's *Penn's Treaty with the Indians* and major works by Horace Pippin, Winslow Homer, Thomas Eakins and Academy founder Charles Willson Peale. The museum also mounts temporary exhibits, including work by students and faculty.

For more modern sensibilities, there is the Institute of Contemporary Art, housed in industrial-style digs on the University of Pennsylvania campus. Its definition of art includes video, performance and other alternative media. The galleries have featured works by such notables as performance artist Laurie Anderson and the controversial photographer Robert Mapplethorpe. The University Museum is also on campus, with a world-class collection of art and artifacts from traditional cultures throughout the world as well as temporary exhibits.

Back in Center City, the African-American Museum's collection includes, among other things, folk art, furnishings, and costumes. The museum also hosts concerts, dance performances and poetry readings, as well as an annual all-night jazz jam every February.

Realizing that private galleries weren't getting a whole lot of public attention, the enterprising Old City Art Association coordinated simultaneous openings for many of its member galleries. This creative buffet is now called "First Fridays," and in addition to seeing the work of local and national artists, the monthly happening has become a rare thing in Philadelphia – a great social scene. "First Fridays" have

been so successful, in fact, that University City has instituted a variation of its own called "Go West 3rd Thursdays," with a special event at a different cultural location each third Thursday. Old City also opens its doors each fall with its annual 10-day Fringe Festival, where performances and exhibits of experimental art take place in galleries, alleyways, sidewalks and unused buildings *(see page 291)*.

Noteworthy fine arts museums outside the city limits include the Wharton Escherick Museum of unique woodcuts and sculpted furnishings near Valley Forge, and the Michener Museum in Doylestown *(see page 252)*.

Cinema

The best of Philadelphia filmmakers, usually graduates of the University of the Arts or Temple University, are part of the bill at the Philadelphia Festival of World Cinema and the International Gay and Lesbian Film Festival, both of which feature the work of filmmakers from around the world.

For slightly more conventional movies, the best places are the Ritz 5 and the Ritz at the Bourse, both of which feature foreign and limited-release films. The Film Forum and the Temple University Cinematheque present a rapidly changing list of oldies for true fans who prefer celluloid to videotape. ❑

LEFT: brightly colored murals decorate the Broad Street landscape.
RIGHT: Pennsylvania Academy of Fine Arts.

CELLULOID CITY: PHILADELPHIA ON FILM

*In recent years, Philadelphia's many urban and
and suburban locations have made it a favorite
with film directors searching for realistic settings*

Once upon a time, people
who had never traveled to
Philadelphia might have had
few images of the city
beyond the Liberty Bell.
Today, thanks to Holly-
wood, an aggressive marketing effort by the local film
office and a five-county
landscape full of location
choices, Philadelphia's many vistas have been
seen on screens around the world. Under the
leadership of executive director Sharon Pinkenson
since 1992, the Greater Philadelphia Film Office
has sold the region to increasing numbers of filmmakers, which has in turn contributed to the city's
overall boom – a cumulative economic impact of
approximately $240 million in just eight years.

FILMED IN PHILADELPHIA

Philadelphia themes and locations had played on
the big screen before this, however. *Rocky* (and its
sequels) made a star of native Sylvester Stallone
and turned the steps to the Museum of Art into a
magnet for joggers and tourists alike. Other films
made here were Brian de Palma's 1980 thriller
Blow Out, with John Travolta, and the romantic
comedy *Mannequin* (1986), filmed in the palatial
Lord & Taylor Department Store. More recently,
the opening scene of Martin Scorsese's 1993 film
The Age of Innocence was filmed in the
interior of the Academy of Music. Denzel
Washington starred in the 1998 thriller
Fallen, which takes viewers from South
Philly to City Hall. Fans of the 1999 hit
The Sixth Sense may recognize the
restaurant Striped Bass as the place
where Bruce Willis shows up late for
his anniversary dinner. Blocks of the
Washington Square district became
up-scale 1880s Cincinnati in Oprah
Winfrey's *Beloved*. In 2000, Bruce
Willis and *Sixth Sense*
writer/director M. Night Shyamalan
returned to Philadelphia to film *Unbreakable*.

△ **LOCAL LANDMARKS**
Twelve Monkeys (1995) with
Bruce Willis and
Brad Pitt turned
the Eastern
State Penitentiary
into an asylum.

◁ **HIGH SOCIETY**
Main Line life was
re-created in the
romantic comedy
*The Philadelphia
Story* (1940), starring
Katharine Hepburn
and James Stewart.

▷ **BOXING BLOCKBUSTER**
Rocky won an Academy Award for best picture in 1976 and showcased South Philly's Italian neighborhood and the Blue Horizon boxing club in North Philadelphia.

△ **STAR STINGER**
When asked what he would like on his tombstone, native comedian W.C.Fields replied: "On the whole, I'd rather be in Philadelphia."

▷ **AMISH ON FILM**
Witness, a 1984 thriller starring Harrison Ford and Kelly McGillis, beautifully explored the traditional Amish life of nearby Lancaster County.

▽ **CITY LOWLIFE**
The 1983 comedy *Trading Places* starring Eddie Murphy and Dan Aykroyd light-heartedly explored the life of down-and-outs on Philadelphia's streets.

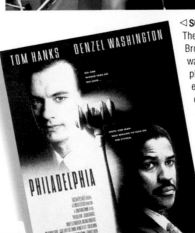

◁ **SOCIAL ISSUES**
The City of Brotherly Love was an apt place to challenge Aids discrimination in *Philadelphia* (1993), which starred Tom Hanks and Denzel Washington.

PHILADELPHIANS IN HOLLYWOOD

Philadelphians have always made their mark on the arts so it is not surprising that, as the film and television world grows ever larger, Philadelphian names have become part of the Hollywood scene.

Rocky star Sylvester Stallone is Philly's most famous son. Grace Kelly grew up in East Falls, daughter of Olympic rower and local businessman Jack Kelly, and went on to star in *High Society* and many other films before becoming a real-life princess. Comedian W.C.Fields also made it big in Hollywood but had less respect for his home town. Actor Kevin Bacon is the son of city planner Edmund Bacon and grew up in Center City. Comedian and actor Bill Cosby, one of Temple University's most famous alumni, used his life growing up in North Philadelphia as fodder for many of his comedic monologues. Also raised in the area were film director Brian de Palma, actor Will Smith *(above)*, and writer and director M. Night Shyamalan, who continues to live and make films in his native city.

MUMMERMANIA

*Only in Philadelphia do they carry on the organized silliness that is the
New Year's Mummers' Parade – a gaudy long day's journey into night*

Unlike the Mardi Gras revelers in sultry, jazz-happy New Orleans or the raucously Latin *carnavaleiros* down in Rio, there's no pre-Lenten excuse to Philadelphia's Mummers' Parade. In the City of Brotherly Love this curious residue of medieval European folklore and North American cakewalk minstrelry has somehow outlived Puritan proscription and endured various stresses and strains – the advent of women paraders, a court-ordered prohibition on the use of blackface, intrusive television cameras and the suburban migration.

Silly Philly's history

Since the dawn of the 20th century these Mummers and their descendants have been carrying on this vaguely disreputable affair, and why is anybody's guess. In their dishabille finery, they gather early on New Year's morning at Snyder Avenue in South Philadelphia and begin their trek up Broad Street, or in some recent years, along Market from Front Street. Their destination is the judges' stand at City Hall, a building whose architectural grotesquerie provides a weird counterpoint to their own procession *(see page 151)*. There, the marchers rev up their string banjos and glockenspiels, their saxophones and drums, as they arc around the square intoning the Mummers' anthem "Oh! Dem Golden Slippers," on their toes as they pursue the prize money that will make their day, at least financially, redemptive. Like their zany umbrellas and brash female impersonations, it's all a bit crazy. And, for true-blue Philadelphians, irresistible.

What is it that keeps these Mummers going? Palma Lucas of the Mummers Museum partly ascribes the phenomenon to Philadelphia's historic and geographical situation as a port of entry whose end product was "an accumulation of various traditions." Swedes, Finns, English, Scots-Irish, Germans, Italians – a mélange that

LEFT: Mummer madness, a much-loved New Year's Day tradition in Philadelphia.
RIGHT: Mummers on parade.

keeps the stew simmering. Another expert on Mummer history (and a parade judge), Professor Charles E. Welch, Jr points out that the city was a hotbed of vaudeville, burlesque and minstrel shows early in the 20th century and perhaps this also suggests some connection with New Year's Mummermania.

The phenomenon's modern version began on the first day of a new century – January 1, 1901. The city's officialdom yielded to the importunings of some municipal boosters – headed by a theatrical producer named H. Bart McHugh – and gave shape to what had been a more or less spontaneous eruption of year-end revelry.

The annual celebrations and attendant misdemeanors had largely been spawned by social clubs whose members cadged cakes from bakeries and staged balls and street fests. It had gone on throughout much of the 19th century – the first social club was the Chain Gang, founded in the 1840s in the South Philly area that is central in Mummers' tradition.

In 1806, some sober-minded Philadelphians, annoyed by the spectacle of masquerade balls that were deemed suspiciously foreign in origin, pushed a prohibition through the Pennsylvania legislature and the ban stayed until 1859. The period after the Civil War seems to have given impetus to new forms of behavior and Mummer activity increased in those years.

Actually, the roots go even deeper. The practice of shooting firearms dates as far back as the 1630s or so, when Swede and Finnish settlers began the custom – what else was there to do on the frontier? They would discharge their guns and make a hullabaloo in the days and nights just before the new year. It is from this practice that today's Mummers' organization gets its full name: the Philadelphia New Year Shooters and Mummers Association.

English settlers and Scots-Irish brought with them their traditions as well – going from house to house begging cakes and ale, performing comic plays and "fantastical" folk drama, frequently in mask. Germans and French added their seasoning to this cosmopolitan Philadelphia stew, as later, in the 20th century, did Italians with their idiosyncratic comic flair.

High-tech nonsense

What was once a spontaneous neighborhood frolic engaging the voluntary enthusiasm of ordinary folk in the late 19th century, is today a large-scale production: 25,000 participants in the four parading divisions, their investment of $30,000–$40,000 and a municipal cost of another half-million dollars or so.

It is now supervised by public officialdom and mindful of the demands of the television age – stations pay hundreds of thousands of dollars for broadcast rights. Some die-hard Mummer fans may carp at this shift in focus, but the additional revenue produces better prizes offered for the best of the parade performers. Awards are made in four categories: Comic, Fancy, String Band and Brigade, and prize money is running upward of $250,000.

A great deal of effort, as well as dollars, is spent in keeping the tradition going. There are 44 major Mummers clubs. Meetings and rehearsals take place weekly and many members drive from the suburbs. Production costs run high – some Mummers have reportedly

AMERICAN MINSTRELSY

One other major influence on the Mummers' development was American minstrelsy. The minstrel show, featuring whites in cork-daubed blackface, was a great, if largely invidious, popular form of entertainment for much of the 19th century in the United States, and it was inevitable that it would have a big impact on Mummer madness.

In 1964, however – a time of racial stress in the nation and the Civil Rights Movement – many in the black community protested the survival of what they deemed an outdated form of stereotype. Mummers at first resisted, then yielded to a judicial prohibition on blackface, and the custom was finally abandoned.

What does persist as an African-American contribution to the parade, however, is the cakewalk, a peculiar type of strutting that has become the most distinctive feature of the whole event. The cakewalk ("a strange dance developed from walking steps and figures typically involving a high prance with backward tilt") has left a solid imprint on the Mummer psyche.

The cakewalk is as much a part of the New Year parade as is the adoption and rendition of the 1879 composition by the African-American songwriter James M. Bland, "Oh! Dem Golden Slippers" as the parade's musical standard and anthem of Philadelphia.

re-mortgaged their homes to cover shortfalls.

Originally, the parade organization encompassed a Fancy Division, consisting of four clubs, and Comic Division, with eight clubs. The third division, the String Bands, came on New Year's Day in 1902 with the participation of the Trilby String Band. The newest of the divisions is the Fancy Brigades, offshoots of the Fancy Clubs. Their hallmark is lavish costumes and floats and extravagant productions.

New wrinkles and facelifts

As the parade greets the 21st century, new logistical wrinkles pop up. They are ticked off by

Recently, city negotiations have moved the parade route some years from Broad Street, which runs up the the middle of South Philly, to Market Street, which runs perpendicular to Broad in Center City. Both routes lead to City Hall, but the move makes a shorter parade route and, because it takes the parade out of South Philly, makes some people unhappy. As a result, the route has been up for discussion each year.

Other innovations have brought the joyful craziness of the Mummers to a greater audience. The "Summer Mummers" began in 1976 and march each summer – usually as part of the Independence Week celebrations – in a

observers such as Rose DeWolf of the *Philadelphia Daily News*: a shorter route and a longer time-span, shrinking crowds and a more selective preening for the TV cameras, exaggerated props and burgeoning costs. "It's almost as if it's been a victim of its own success. What used to be a nice parade that lasted six hours now can last as long as 12 hours," DeWolf says. Professional choreographers and costume designers are employed, with high-tech performances at Washington Avenue and City Hall.

LEFT: the Mummers' Parade is a spectacle of garish costumes and music.
ABOVE: 25,000 people participate in the parade.

parade that runs from the Convention Center, down Market, ending at Independence Hall. Then in 1998, the Brigades began indoor performances at the Convention Center on the evening of New Year's Day. The Mummers Museum was opened in 1979, assisted by city and state funding. The building's garish colors and Art Deco-style design match the Mummers' outlandishness, and it is a worthy stop on the tourist trail *(see page 201)*.

Whatever its trials and tribulations, adjustments and permeations, the march of the Mummers is likely to keep on cakewalking as they respond to the urge to match the nonsense of life with their own touch of absurdity. ❏

PHILADELPHIA FOOD

This is a city of great food: you can grab a pretzel from a sidewalk stand, dive into a cheesesteak, or take your pick from a wealth of restaurants

Pennsylvania Dutch food, Hershey's chocolates and wineries – not to mention orchards where you can pick your own apples, peaches and pumpkins – provide local accents to the average Philadelphian menu, but none dominate the food scene. Philadelphians have become pretty sophisticated in their palates, spoiled by an abundance of authentic markets, even in the suburbs.

Food trucks and markets

Philadelphia is famous for fast food. In 1901, Joseph Horn and Frank Hardart opened the nation's first food automat, Horn & Hardart's, where you could drop coins into a slot and get a sandwich or a piece of pie. Pretzels, the soft doughy variety (with mustard, please) have been standard street fare for nearly as long *(see page 89)*. And there is nothing like a true Philadelphia cheesesteak, a sandwich of thinly sliced beef topped with melted cheese on an Italian roll, invented in 1930 by the founders of Pat's King of Steaks *(see page 203)*.

These, along with hoagies, water ice and Tastykakes, are the fast-food favorites that native Philadelphians have grown up with, take for granted and often don't even think twice about until they leave the city and realize they don't make them elsewhere – or at least, not the same. Scrapple is also uniquely Philadelphian, but its appeal is less universal and it is difficult to describe to the uninitiated – a fried breakfast hash made from a variety of pork cuts.

But, despite this penchant for unhealthy snacks, the Philadelphia culinary scene today is much more than fast food.

Between fast food and fine dining is fine food you can get fast, and you can't get it finer or better than at one of the markets around the city. The ones most mired in history and tradition are the Italian Market on Ninth Street *(see page 199)* and the Reading Terminal Market at

the Convention Center *(see page 158)*. At first glance, the Ninth Street Market in South Philadelphia looks as if little has changed in 100 years, with crates of fresh-from-the-dock wriggling crabs, meats and fresh produce piled on wooden carts in front of fragrant cheese shops, pasta places, spice stores and the like.

The Reading Terminal Market in Center City has more of a spruced-up look but its offerings are no less authentic, with more than 80 merchants and 23 restaurants selling a wide variety of meats, seafood, vegetables and prepared foods from a host of ethnic traditions. You can shop, get some lunch, listen to musicians who are sometimes booked at the end of the market, or watch a cooking demonstration. Started in 1893, it's one of the oldest farmers' markets in America. Each summer, the market hosts, among other things, an annual Pennsylvania Dutch Festival, complete with buggy rides, farm animals, food specialties such as chicken pot pie, donuts, funnel cakes and crafts,

LEFT: a traditional American diner in South Philadelphia.
RIGHT: grilling Philly rib steaks.

including quilts, rugs and wooden toys. Pennsylvania Dutch food is a mainstay at the farmers' markets (although it might be right next to the bagels or sushi), with fresh meats and poultry, fruit pies, shoofly pies (a concoction of butter, molasses and brown sugar) and "sticky" buns.

Restaurant rebirth

Thirty years ago, you could count on one hand the number of truly exceptional restaurants that had garnered more than a local reputation. Today, Philadelphia's restau-

> ### CITY CHEESE
>
> The brand Philadelphia Cream Cheese was so named in 1880 by which time Philadelphia had earned a reputation for great food, especially dairy products.

culinary talent. This second generation of chefs – along with others inspired by the new hunger in the city for fine dining – in turn created their own successes, generating more talent, resulting in a proliferation of exceptional dining establishments.

In the Fountain Restaurant at the Four Seasons, opened in 1983, chef Jean-Marie Lacroix trained people who became chefs at other elegant eateries in and out of the city, including Bruce Lim, of Ciboulette (1988) and Francesco Martorella of Brasserie Perrier,

rants have been praised by *Esquire* magazine and voted the best in America by the readers of Condé Naste *Travelers* magazine.

The Philadelphia restaurant story is a people story. In 1970, Frenchman George Perrier opened Le Bec Fin which, with its exceptional French cuisine, has continued to win national and international recognition, and the highest accolades from critics, the hospitality industry, and patrons alike, receiving the top five-star rating from the Mobil Travel Guide for 20 years and the top five diamond rating from the American Automobile Association for over a decade. Over the ensuing 30 years, restaurants began multiplying, each success story breeding more

another of George Perrier's productions (1997). In the same period, Deux Cheminées (1979), DiLullo Centro (1985, now Toto), and Ristorante Panorama (1989) set up their dining tables, with fine china, linen and silver.

Juxtaposed to this proliferation of *haute cuisine*, others with their own unique styles and traditions – from funky to homey, to trendy to intimate – were putting down roots in various sections of Center City and beyond, including prominent women restaurateurs such as Kathleen Mulhern, who opened The Garden in 1974, Suzanna Foo, who opened her up-scale Chinese namesake in 1987, and Judy Wicks, whose White Dog Café has been combining good food with social consciousness since 1983 *(see page 193)*. Allison Barshank was the first chef at Neil Stein's trendy Striped Bass, the critically acclaimed seafood restaurant opened in 1994 in a former brokerage house with high ceilings, marble pillars, and an open kitchen.

When a local talent heats up, there's no stopping him. Neil Stein took the success of Striped Bass (which was chosen as the site for a party hosted by the President of ABC News during the 2000 Republican National Conven-

GREAT NIGHT OUT

Comments one Philadelphian: "Restaurants have so much atmosphere they qualify as entertainment. You don't need to do anything afterward."

Tangerine, a dark, sexy Moroccan mirage of a dining experience. And let's not forget his Blue Angel, an Art Nouveau French bistro, named Philadelphia's best new restaurant in *Food and Wine Magazine*'s July 2000 issue.

Throughout the renaissance, as Center City restaurants were competing for upscale dollars, Asian restaurants in Chinatown proliferated, including *dim sum* and Szechuan duck houses, as well as Vietnamese, Thai, Japanese, Malaysian, Burmese and Hong Kong-style eateries.

tion) and opened the Rouge, the first restaurant with outdoor dining on Rittenhouse Square, recreated Fishmarket and added the newest, Bleu, a French bistro and outdoor café also on Rittenhouse Square. Stephen Starr has four hot restaurants and counting in the Old City area: Continental Restaurant and Martini Bar in a former diner, ultra-chic Buddakan, heralded as one of America's best restaurants by *Travel and Leisure* magazine, serving Asian cuisine in the midst of a 10-ft (3-meter) candlelit Buddha, and

LEFT: Di Bruno Brothers cheese store is a landmark in South Philadelphia's Little Italy.
ABOVE: the ubiquitous pretzel food cart.

From bistros to haute cuisine

So, three decades after Le Bec Fin opened its doors, restaurants continue to sprout here, there and everywhere, keeping pace with the rapid rise and revival of Center City hotels, shops, cultural institutions, and neighborhoods.

Philadelphia has become a smorgasbord of dining choices. Not only do you have a choice of traditional cuisine, but there are as many different settings – from diners to fine dining rooms, bistros and cafés, with music or without, indoor and out, with views of the water, the skyline, or quaint city streets. You can head to certain neighborhoods – Old City, Rittenhouse Square, South Street, Chinatown or Manayunk, for example – where the density of eating establishments is so high they each have a "restaurant row," which usually turns out to be a block as success breeds success.

Up-scale restaurants abound in Center City from the Avenue of the Arts west, along Walnut Street and up to Logan Circle. Here you'll find Le Bec Fin, Deux Cheminées, in a house designed by Frank Furness, Opus 251 at 251 South 18th Street, and on Logan Circle, the understated Fountain Restaurant of the Four Seasons, where you'll see the

> **FOOD FESTIVAL**
>
> The Book and the Cook Festival and Fair is a 10-day festival in March that pairs up nearly 100 cookbook authors from around the world with local restaurants.

city's most sophisticated citizenry. Brasserie Perrier, Vetri, Striped Bass, Rouge 2000 and Fishmarket are here, too. Other notable seafood restaurants in this neighborhood include the Oyster House, which features a raw bar at 1516 Sansom Street; Oasis at 1709 Walnut Street, with waterfalls and an open kitchen combining seafood with Korean barbecue; and the Devon Seafood Grille on Rittenhouse Square.

Meat eaters, too, can find happiness in the numerous steakhouses that have opened up in the neighborhood, including Smith & Wollensky's on Rittenhouse Square, Ruth's Chris Steak House on Broad Street, and Morton's of Chicago on Walnut just east of Broad Street.

Italian food lovers have a wide range of dining experiences from which to choose – including the elegant La Famiglia on Front Street and Girasole, authentic Italian cuisine just a few blocks east of the Academy of Music on Locust Street, a favorite post-concert haunt for Riccardo Muti, the orchestra's former music director. There's also South Philly, where Ralph's and Dante and Luigi's vie for the title of oldest Italian restaurant in America and singers belt out arias for diners at Victor Café *(see page 199).*

Chinatown needs little explanation, except to say that it's not just Chinese. The Malaysian restaurant Penang was voted the best restaurant in Chinatown by *Philadelphia Magazine* in its annual "Best of Philly" issue for the year 2000.

Hip and happening

Old City, with its galleries, historic sights and proximity to the water, has become a hot new restaurant haven, with a slew of hip new restaurants. You can be lost among the choices, which include Rococo (1996), Fork (1997), Buddakan (1998), picked by Oprah Winfrey for the premier party for her film *Beloved*, the 1950s retro Continental Restaurant and Martini Bar (1997), Tangerine and Blue Angel, as well as the cuisines of Brazil, Afghanistan, Morocco, Mexico, Japan and India, to name a few. Whatever you pick, you're bound to come away with a list of five more choices for the next visit.

The last two decades have also seen the waterfront develop into a lively dining, drinking and dancing place. The Charthouse, part of a national chain, was one of the first restaurants to open, in 1986, the same year that the Great Plaza opened at Penn's Landing *(see page 128).* The *Moshulu* at Pier 34 is notable as an four-masted sailing ship restored as a dining attraction, its menu reflecting the ship's various ports.

You can head across the Schuylkill to University City to the restaurants of Sansom Row (White Dog Café, La Terasse, and Pod, to name a few), or head up the river to Manayunk. Main Street is wedged with restaurants like Somona, Arroyo Grill and Fish on Main, as well as a Farmers' Market *(see page 211).* ❑

LEFT: Pat's King of Steaks, creators of the Philly cheesesteak.

Pretzel Logic

A pretzel is more than a twisted biscuit, it is a storied knot of dough – as much a part of Philadelphia gastronomy as cheesesteaks, scrapple, water ice and hoagies.

Its pedigree stretches all the way back to 7th-century France. While preparing unleavened bread for Lent, a French monk twisted scraps of dough into a shape resembling arms crossed in prayer. The tasty twists were given to children as a reward for learning their prayers. Hence the Latin name *pretiola*, meaning "little gifts or prayers" or perhaps *brachiola*, "little arms."

By and by, German bakers also got the knack of the doughy delights, which they dubbed *brezel*. By the time German-speaking immigrants settled the countryside outside Philadelphia, they were more commonly known as pretzels.

While it was the Pennsylvania Dutch who brought pretzel-making to the New World (Lancaster County is still known as the "Pretzel Basket of America"), it was, in the words of one journalist, "Philadelphia who civilized it and made it into a household pet." At last count there were about 10 pretzel bakeries in the metropolitan area, turning out, by a conservative estimate, more than a million pretzels each and every day.

You can't walk far in Philadelphia without bumping into a pretzel cart on the side of the street or hearing the call of a roaming vendor -- "Pretzels, four for a dollar." "In Philadelphia, pretzels are a staple," says Edward Ermilio, owner of Northeast Soft Pretzel in Tacony. "You see people run up to a cart, grab a pretzel and then go about their business." Mind you, these are soft pretzels, the pliant, doughy variety with shiny salt-kissed skins usually smeared with mustard – completely different to the crusty, crunchy hard tack you're likely to find at the supermarket. Ermilio turns out about 20,000 pretzels a day, all hand-twisted. A first-class pretzel-bender, he says, can twist 800 pretzels an hour – that's 13 per minute. The world record is said to be an incredible 57 a minute.

But how do you tell a good pretzel from the mediocre? "What you want to look for is a golden-brown color, freshness and the proper amount of salt," says Thomas Conley, baker at the Philadelphia Pretzel Museum located at 312 Market

Street, where aficionados can hone up on the history, lore and traditions of the "Wonderful World of Pretzels." Conley's recipe turns out a puffy, bagel-like concoction that comes in a variety of shapes and sizes – nuggets, braids, hearts and rings, most hand-twisted – as well as the standard pretzel knot.

Pretzel paramours might also seek out Fisher's Pretzels at the Reading Terminal Market *(see page 159)*, where Amish girls twist foot-long strands of dough with an apparent flick of the wrist. The finished product is less salty and a bit firmer than Conley's, but always served hot from the oven and drenched in butter.

But those who think of pretzels as just another form of fast junk food, think again. Fresh pretzels are not only delicious, cheap and filling, they're also good for you – even though butter and salt can't exactly be described as health foods. They're low in calories and almost fat-free. According to popular myth, they are said to prevent motion sickness, nausea and bed-wetting in young children and, according to a doctor's report published in the *Reading Times* in 1927, they "prevent constipation," strengthen the "power of the teeth," and "increase the flow of the digestive fluids." No wonder they have such a confirmed place not only in the stomachs but the hearts of all true-blue Philadelphians. ❑

RIGHT: pretzels are a mainstay of Philadelphia life, grabbed from a pretzel cart and eaten on the go.

SPORTS

In a nation of sports lovers, Philadelphia comes high on the list of sporting cities, with seven teams playing in every major league sport

Philadelphia is a sports-loving town, with teams and events that can whip up the passion, get the blood pumping, turn ordinary citizens into zealous fans. Philadelphia has more than its share of professional sports teams, strong college and university athletics, and the stadiums and geography to host world-class competitions in everything from major league sports to tennis matches, ice skating, bicycling championships and rowing regattas. What's more, Philadelphia's got the people – from the players and fans to the thousands of recreational sports enthusiasts who fill the tennis, golf and basketball courts, playing fields and miles of trails throughout the city.

The professionals

Philadelphia is one of the few cities in the country with teams – as well as stadiums – for every major league sport. Game nights find streams of cars heading toward the three stadiums clustered in a large complex at the end of South Broad Street. The 76ers basketball and Flyers hockey teams play at the First Union Center *(see page 201)*, alongside the First Union Spectrum, where the KIXX soccer, Phantom hockey (the minor league hockey team) and the Wings lacrosse teams play.

The Eagles football and Phillies baseball teams play – for now – at Veterans Stadium. Plans are in the works to build a new football stadium in the same complex, and a new baseball park somewhere in the city – although the process of selecting just where this new park should be has become somewhat of a game itself. The Phillies team has been lobbying to build in the South Philly complex, but the city government (which is footing a big chunk of the bill) sees dollar signs and new life for other parts of the city. Then there are the coalitions of neighbors who see traffic snarls and unruly fans clogging their streets. The most recent decision

seems to be the construction of two stadiums (one for baseball, one for football) near the current stadiums as part of an improved sports complex with other development as well.

Philadelphians are passionate about their sports teams and the stars that come with them. And there's nothing like a team poised for the

national championship to rally the citizenry and light up the city with team colors and civic pride. Grown men still get all misty about about 1980, when all four major league teams went to the championships. That year, the Phillies won the world series, the 76ers made it to the NBA championship, the Flyers played in the Stanley Cup hockey finals and the Eagles went onto the 1981 Superbowl. When a team is hot, the air is thick with sports talk – at work, on street corners, at the local gas pump and grocery store. Even the statue of the quiet Quaker who founded the city, Billy Penn, perched at the very top of City Hall, has donned a cap or a shirt in support of his team.

LEFT: leading the pack at the University of Pennsylvania track.
RIGHT: the Corestates bicycle race.

Fans love the teams not only for their wins, but for the talent they bring to town, such as Phillies baseball hall of famers Mike Schmidt, Steve Carlton, Jim Bunning and Grover Cleveland Alexander, as well as Richie Ashburn, who, in his retirement became a beloved radio broadcaster for the team. When Ashburn died unexpectedly of a heart attack in 1997, thousands of fans from all over the city lined up at Memorial Hall to pay their respects to the great "Whitey Ashburn."

Basketball is a particularly beloved sport in Philadelphia, whether played on gleaming floorboards of the First Union Center or on city

1975 with star player Bobby Clarke, now team vice president and general manager. The Flyers continue to play hockey among the best in the NHL, reaching the finals five more times since the mid-'70s.

College sports and events

But the pros are only the beginning of the sports scene in Philadelphia, where intercollegiate sports events go back 200 years, and the sweat-soaked sport of boxing is practiced in small gyms scattered across the city. The Blue Horizon, at 1314 North Broad Street, is North Philadelphia's historic boxing venue open to

asphalt at neighborhood hoops all over the city, where kids (and aging kids at heart) mimic the moves of basketball greats such as Wilt Chamberlain, Julius Erving, Billy Cunningham, Hal Greer and Charles Barclay. The 76ers won the NBA (National Basketball Association) title in 1967 with the towering Chamberlain, who once scored more than 100 points in a single game. Erving was another superstar, with whom the 76ers won the championship in 1983. That year's team was immortalized by the hit single "Four-Five-Four."

The Flyers, originally tagged Broad Street bullies in the late 1960s, skated and scored their way to back-to-back Stanley Cups in 1974 and

spectators *(see page 295)*. Boxing gyms also dot the blocks of South Philly, the setting for the motion picture hit *Rocky*, written by and starring Sylvester Stallone *(see page 78)*.

The University of Pennsylvania hosts Ivy League sports at the Palestra and Franklin Fields; Temple University is home to the Apollo; and numerous other colleges and universities in the immediate region have active sports programs for men and women. College basketball's Big Five rivalry is between Philadelphia universities Temple, LaSalle, Villanova, St Joseph's and Penn. The Penn Relays at Franklin Fields date back to 1893 and number among the country's top track meets.

The Schuylkill River is home to numerous regattas, including the Dad Vail, the 2-day, largest collegiate crew race in the world, with thousands of rowers from the US and Canada competing in 100 races in 19 categories.

Philadelphia hosts a number of big sporting events that draw competitors from all over the world, such as the annual Advanta Tennis Championship, played in suburban Villanova, the historic Army-Navy game at Veterans Stadium, and the First Union USPRO cycling championship, held every June. The cycling championship runs 156 miles (250 km) along a 14½-mile (23-km) course from the Benjamin place to go is Kelly Drive, named after Grace Kelly's father, John B. Kelly, a local builder and Olympic rower. In addition to its 73 baseball diamonds, 115 tennis courts, 13 football fields, two cricket fields, six golf courses and a rugby field, Fairmount Park has miles of trails used by bikers, hikers, joggers and in-line skaters. One popular loop runs from the Museum of Art down along the east side of the river to the Falls Bridge, across the bridge and back. Another, called the Schuylkill River Trail, runs from the Museum of Art into Manayunk, through Conshohoken and all the way to Valley Forge *(see page 183)*. ❏

Franklin Parkway along Kelly Drive into Manayunk *(see page 211)*. Over a half a million spectators line the streets for this, the largest one-day cycling event in the US, drawing more than 100 entrants from over 20 countries.

A sportman's legacy

But not only professionals like to bike here, with over 100 miles (160 km) of bike lanes and trails, and over 1,800 bike racks installed over the city. If you're into participatory sports, the

LEFT: rugby players get down and dirty on one of the city's many sports fields.
ABOVE: stepping up to the plate.

DRAGON BOAT RACING

Although the "Schuylkill Navy" pretty much dominates the rowing scene, the 2,000-year-old Chinese sport of Dragon Boat racing is alive and well in Philadelphia. A brightly decorated longboat with a dragon's head at the bow and a tail at the stern, holds 20 people, who paddle 4-ft (1-meter) blades to the beat of a drum. The men's team have been national champions for years. The women's team was founded in 1997 and has members ranging from their mid-twenties to mid-seventies. While the team is competitive, it has wider aims than winning. Each member commits to practicing, attending monthly meetings and participating in some community service.

PLACES

*A detailed guide to the entire city, with principal sites
clearly cross-referenced by number to the maps*

Philadelphians think of their home as a "livable city" – not too
hectic, not too crowded, manageable. It is a town with roots,
old by American standards, but forward-looking, too – a
colonial city with a modern attitude.

Thanks to William Penn, getting around Philadelphia is a snap.
Center City, the river-to-river rectangle laid out by Penn in 1682, is
designed like a giant checkerboard. North-south streets are numbered
from the Delaware River to the Schuylkill River. East-west streets are
named, many after trees, with house numbers corresponding to the
numbered cross streets.

Within this Center City area are Philadelphia's historic colonial
neighborhoods, now known as Old City and Society Hill. Here is
where Benjamin Franklin settled, the Liberty Bell rang out in celebration, and the Framers of the Constitution forged a new nation
governed by "We, the People." Spreading west from this colonial
core are neighborhoods that settled as the city grew. As the 20th
century dawned, the mammoth City Hall was built on Center Square
at the intersection of Center City's two main streets, Broad and
Market. Today, the four districts surrounding City Hall are like four
panes in a window: the Parkway Museum and Convention Center
districts north of Market, and Rittenhouse and Washington
south of Market, straddling Broad Street. An afternoon stroll might
take you from Old City's art-gallery ghetto north of Market across
into Chinatown, through the maze of alleys in Washington Square
West to South Street, the self-proclaimed "hippest street in town."

Beyond Center City, Greater Philadelphia is a study in contrast
and color – from the ethnic enclaves of South Philly to the diverse
communities of University City and North Philadelphia. Envisioned
as a "greene countrie towne," the urban landscape is laced with open
spaces, including the 8,000-acre (3,200-hectare) Fairmount Park, the
largest municipal park in the country. Once known as the "Athens of
America," the city exhibits its love of culture at distinguished universities, galleries and learned societies as well as many museums.

And there's much more beyond the city limits. In little more than
an hour, you can be strolling along New Jersey's beaches, shooting
craps at an Atlantic City casino, eating shoofly pie in Pennsylvania
Dutch country, or soaking up Bucks County's natural beauty.

This is a livable city, indeed – a town of cobblestone alleys and
gleaming skyscrapers, of hidden courtyards and bustling streets, of
tight-knit communities and vital traditions. It is a treasure house of
history, a modern metropolis, a "city to be happy in." ❑

PRECEDING PAGES: William Penn's statue has a commanding view from City Hall
Tower; Society Hill's historic townhouses; Boathouse Row in Fairmount Park.
LEFT: Independence Hall, birthplace of the nation.

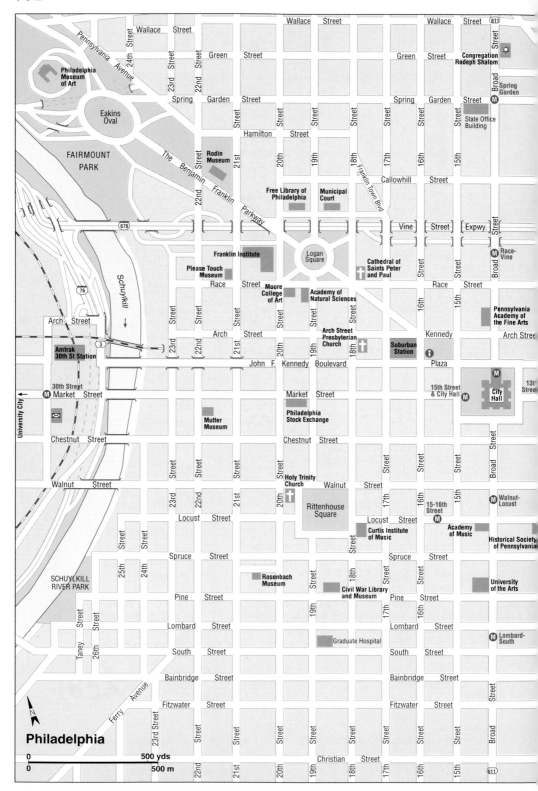

Wallace Street · 24th Street · Pennsylvania Avenue · 23rd Street · 22nd Street · Green Street · Wallace Street · 611 · Street

Philadelphia Museum of Art · Eakins Oval · Spring Garden Street · Green Street · Congregation Rodeph Shalom · Broad Street · Spring Garden

FAIRMOUNT PARK · The Benjamin Franklin Parkway · Rodin Museum · 21st · Hamilton Street · 20th · 19th · 18th · 17th · 16th · 15th · Spring Garden Street · State Office Building · Spring Garden · M

676 · 22nd · Free Library of Philadelphia · Municipal Court · Franklin Town Blvd · Callowhill Street

Schuylkill · 76 · Vine Street · Expwy. · Street · Race-Vine · M

Arch Street · Franklin Institute · Please Touch Museum · Logan Square · Cathedral of Saints Peter and Paul · Race Street · Broad

3 · Race Street · Moore College of Art · Academy of Natural Sciences · Pennsylvania Academy of the Fine Arts

Amtrak 30th St Station · 23rd Street · 22nd Street · 21st Street · Arch Street · 20th · 19th · Arch Street Presbyterian Church · 18th · Suburban Station · Kennedy · Arch Street

University City · 30th Street · Market Street · M · John F. Kennedy Boulevard · Plaza · 15th Street & City Hall · M · City Hall · M · 13th Street

Mutter Museum · Market Street · Philadelphia Stock Exchange · Market Street · Broad Street

Chestnut Street · Chestnut Street

Walnut Street · 23rd Street · 22nd Street · 21st Street · 20th Street · Holy Trinity Church · Walnut Street · 17th · 16th · 15th · Walnut-Locust · M

SCHUYLKILL RIVER PARK · Locust Street · Rittenhouse Square · Locust Street · 15-16th Street · M · Academy of Music · Historical Society of Pennsylvania

25th · 24th · Spruce Street · Curtis Institute of Music · Spruce Street

Rosenbach Museum · 18th · Civil War Library and Museum · University of the Arts

Taney · 26th · Pine Street · 19th · 17th · 16th · Pine Street · Lombard-South · M

Lombard Street · Graduate Hospital · Lombard Street

South Street · South Street

Bainbridge Street · Bainbridge Street

Ferry Avenue · Fitzwater Street · Fitzwater Street · Street

N

Philadelphia

0 _____ 500 yds
0 _____ 500 m

23rd Street · 22nd · 21st · 20th · 19th · 18th · 17th · 16th · 15th · Broad · Christian Street · 611

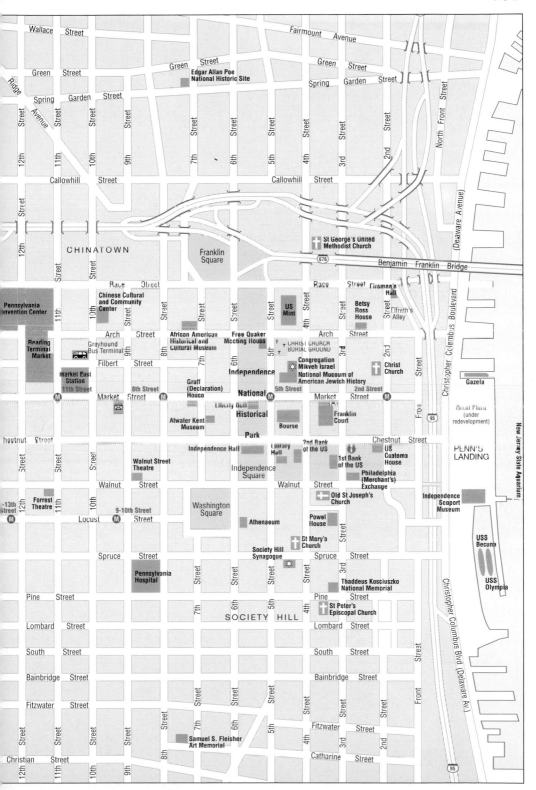

Wallace Street

Fairmount Avenue

Green Street

Green Street

Green Street

Edgar Allan Poe
National Historic Site

Spring Garden Street

Ridge

Spring Garden Street

12th Street
11th Street
10th Street
9th Street
7th Street
6th Street
5th Street
4th Street
3rd Street
2nd Street

Avenue

North Front Street

Callowhill Street

Callowhill Street

12th Street

St George's United
Methodist Church

(Delaware Avenue)

CHINATOWN

Franklin
Square

676

Benjamin Franklin Bridge

12th Street

11th Street

Race Street

Race Street

Street

Fireman's
Hall

Pennsylvania
Convention Center

Chinese Cultural
and Community
Center

10th Street

9th Street

8th Street

7th Street

6th Street

5th Street

US
Mint

4th Street

Betsy
Ross
House

3rd Street

Elfreth's
Alley

2nd Street

Christopher Columbus Boulevard

Arch Street

Arch Street

Reading
Terminal
Market

Grayhound
Bus Terminal

African American
Historical and
Cultural Museum

Free Quaker
Meeting House

CHRIST CHURCH
BURIAL GROUND

Gazela

Filbert Street

Congregation
Mikveh Israel

Christ
Church

Market East
Station
11th Street

8th Street

Graff
(Declaration)
House

Independence

National Museum of
American Jewish History

Great Plaza
(under
redevelopment)

Market Street

National

5th Street

2nd Street

Market Street

Atwater Kent
Museum

Liberty Bell

Historical

Bourse

Franklin
Court

Front

95

New Jersey State Aquarium

Chestnut Street

Chestnut Street

Street

Street

Independence Hall

Library
Hall

Park

2nd Bank
of the US

US
Customs
House

PENN'S
LANDING

Walnut Street
Theatre

Independence
Square

1st Bank
of the US

Philadelphia
(Merchant's)
Exchange

Independence
Seaport
Museum

Walnut Street

Walnut Street

Old St Joseph's
Church

13th
Street

Forrest
Theatre

11th Street

10th Street

9-10th Street

Washington
Square

Athenaeum

Powel
House

USS
Becuna

12th Street

Locust Street

St Mary's
Church

Spruce Street

Society Hill
Synagogue

Spruce Street

3rd Street

USS
Olympia

Pennsylvania
Hospital

Thaddeus Kosciuszko
National Memorial

Pine Street

7th Street

6th Street

5th Street

4th Street

Pine Street

St Peter's
Episcopal Church

Christopher Columbus Blvd (Delaware Av.)

Lombard Street

SOCIETY HILL

Lombard Street

South Street

South Street

Bainbridge Street

Bainbridge Street

Fitzwater Street

Street

Front Street

Fitzwater Street

Samuel S. Fleisher
Art Memorial

8th Street

7th Street

6th Street

5th Street

4th Street

3rd Street

2nd Street

Christian Street

12th Street

11th Street

10th Street

9th Street

Catharine Street

95

OLD CITY

Map on pages 106–7

It's been called America's "most historic square mile," largely because Philadelphia's Old City district is home to the nation's most sacred shrines and symbols of Independence

History is the obvious attraction of Old City, and simply by wandering along the narrow streets and cobblestone alleyways, you become caught up in Philadelphia's illustrious past. This is where a young journeyman printer named Benjamin Franklin set up shop, where Thomas Jefferson composed the Declaration of Independence, where the Constitution was drafted and a new kind of nation created. If you want more prompting to fully visualize history come alive, there are a number of walking tours available, including some accompanied by scholars *(see page 264)*.

But more than a journey into the past, Old City is a study in urban renewal. In the early 1950s, the National Park Service took over much of the district, cleared away the dreck and restored the area's historic sites. Rehabilitation spawned a generation of shops and galleries, architectural and design firms, theater and dance companies, restaurants and hotels.

Visitors should be aware that changes are afoot with respect to several key stopping points. In autumn 2001, the Liberty Bell will move to the new Liberty Bell Complex that will run along 6th Street from Market to Arch (on the same block of the Mall where the bell stands now). Also opening in 2001 is the new **Gateway Regional Visitor Center** on the northeast corner of 6th Street and Market on the second block of the Mall. As its name indicates, this new visitor center is intended to be a gateway to the region, and will combine the functions of the National Park Visitor Center (now at 3rd and Chestnut streets) and the city's Visitor Center (now at 16th Street and JFK Boulevard) to present a comprehensive range of visitor services for the region – in one place, you can brush up on your history, order your Phillies tickets, and plan where to have dinner that night. Plans are also underway for two more facilities to open in autumn 2002: an Independence Park Institute on the southeast corner of 6th and Arch streets, which will serve as an educational center, and the National Constitution Center, which will offer exhibits and explore the effect of the United States Constitution on people's lives.

LEFT: the famously cracked surface of the Liberty Bell.
BELOW: soldiers stand guard at Independence Hall.

Colonial core

Until the opening of the new Gateway Regional Visitor Center, the best place to start a tour of Old City is at the **Independence National Historical Park Visitor Center ❶** (3rd and Chestnut streets; tel: 215-597-8974; open daily 9am–5pm with longer summer hours), where park rangers dispense free maps and information. The center's exhibits focus on various aspects of US history, and a short film, *Independence*, directed by John Huston, runs every 30 to 45 minutes. All park buildings are staffed by knowledgeable rangers. Information about park build-

St Augustine's Catholic Church

St George's United Methodist Church

Painted Bride Art Center

Vine Street

Franklin Square

676

Ben Franklin Bridge

Race Street

Old First Reformed Church

US Mint
19

Fireman's Hall
24

Elfreth's Alley

OLD CITY

Cherry Street

Betsy Ross House
21

Elfreth Alley Museum
23

Seamen's Church Institute

95

Pier 5

Free Quaker Meeting House

CHRIST CHURCH BURIAL GROUND
18

Arch Street

Arch Street Friends Meeting House
20

Arden Theatre Company

Independence Mall

Congregation Mikveh Israel

National Museum of American Jewish History
17

Christ Church
22

Front Street

Pier 3

Spirit of Philadelphia

Gateway Regional Visitor Center (open 2001)

Gazela of Philadelphia
38

Liberty Bell

Market Street

Franklin Court

2nd Street

Christopher Columbus Boulevard (Delaware Avenue)

5th Street

Bourse

Great Plaza (under redevelopment)
39

Independence Mall

PENN'S LANDING

Chestnut Street

Independence Hall

Second Bank of the United States

First Bank of the United States

Independence National Historical Park Visitor Center

WELCOME PARK

Independence National Historical Park

Independence Square

Walnut Street

Ferry Dock
40

Rose Garden

Old St Joseph's Church
26

Independence Seaport Museum
42

Athenaeum

Willings Alley

International Sculpture Garden

Locust Street

MAGNOLIA GARDEN

Powel House
27

Dock Street

St Mary's Church
25

SOCIETY HILL

USS Becuna
43

Spruce Street
28

Columbus Memorial

Society Hill Synagogue
30

Physick House
31

USS Olympia
44

4th Street

Delancey Street

Philadelphia Vietnam Veterans Memorial
45

Thaddeus Kosciuszko National Memorial
34

3rd Street

29

2nd Street

5th Street

Pine Street

Mother Bethel African Methodist Episcopal Church
36

32

Old Pine Street Presbyterian Church

St Peter's Episcopal Church
33

Front Street

95

Presbyterian Historical Society
35

6th Street

Lombard Street

Head House Square
37

N

South Street

2nd Street

Center City Historic District

0 ————— 500 yds
0 ————— 500 m

The Moshulu

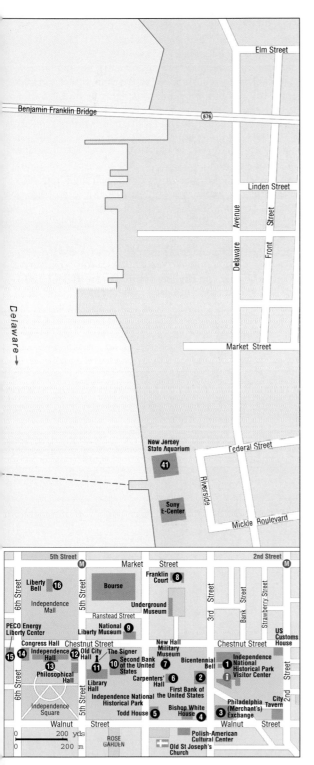

ings without individual phone numbers may be obtained by calling the Visitor Center. Also be aware that there are several park-operated buildings beyond the Old City district.

The Visitor Center is surrounded by some of the city's most distinguished and dramatic buildings. Directly across 3rd Street, the **First Bank of the United States** ❷ (Park building; 3rd Street, between Chestnut and Walnut; closed to the public) stands in "lonely grandeur." Completed in 1797, this Neo-Classical structure is a monument to the political vision of Alexander Hamilton who, as the nation's first Secretary of the Treasury, insisted that government finances be handled by a central institution. The bank's charter lapsed in 1811 and was purchased by French-born merchant, Stephen Girard, who used his resources to finance the US government during the War of 1812 *(see page 214).*

The first stock exchange

Located just to the south of the Visitor Center is the **Philadelphia (Merchant's) Exchange** ❸ (Park building; northeast corner of 3rd and Walnut streets; closed to the public), a magnificent Greek Revival structure designed by William Strickland and opened in 1834 as the nation's first stock exchange. Be sure to walk to the rear of the building for a look at the graceful curved portico. The wide cobbled way that wraps around the Exchange is Dock Street, formerly Dock Creek, where ships tied up to unload their cargo in the late 1700s.

A short walk along Walnut Street to the corner of 2nd Street brings you to the **City Tavern** (Park building; 138 South 2nd Street; tel: 215-413-1443; open lunch and dinner), a fully functioning reconstruction of the 18th-century inn where Franklin, Washington, Adams and other luminaries wrangled over the issues of the day. It is a terrific place to enjoy traditional American cuisine served by costumed staff in colonial-era surroundings. Around the corner on 2nd Street, **Welcome Park** is a plaza built in tribute to William Penn, who occupied a slate-roof house on this site during his second and final visit to the

TIP

All park-run historic buildings have free admission except the Portrait Gallery in the Second Bank and the Todd and Bishop White houses, at which a small donation is requested.

BELOW:
the Philadelphia (Merchant's) Exchange.

colony. Designed by Philadelphia architect Robert Venturi, the park is a model of Penn's original plan for the city. Next door, the Thomas Bond House is an 18th-century restoration operated by the Park Service as a bed-and-breakfast inn.

Rising like an Art Deco fortress from the corner of 2nd and Chestnut streets, the US Customs Building towers over the eastern end of Chestnut Street and Old City's unofficial restaurant row. There are numerous eateries on Chestnut between 4th and Front streets and along 2nd and 3rd streets. Choices range from sushi to spaghetti, fish to French, and high-class Italian, Middle Eastern and Afghan cuisine. The Corn Exchange Building situated at the corner of 2nd and Chestnut streets is an architectural confection of checkerboard Flemish-bond brickwork, fanciful pediments and a miniature clock tower. The **American Indian Cultural Center of the Delaware Valley** operates a small museum and craft shop (225 Chestnut Street, between 2nd and 3rd; open Monday–Friday, 9am–5pm, Saturday 11:30am–4:30pm, Sunday 1:30–4:30pm).

18th-century affluence

Return to Walnut Street and turn right toward the lovely rowhouses and gardens between 3rd and 4th streets. Here you'll find two residential houses which give a glimpse into family life in the 1790s, the **Bishop White House ❹** and **Todd House ❺** (Park buildings; 309 Walnut and 4th streets; admission by tours only, sign up at Visitors Center; entrance fee). Bishop White House was built in 1786 and occupied until 1836 by Episcopal Bishop William White, rector of Christ Church *(see page 117)*. Fully restored, the house is the very picture of 18th-century affluence, with a beautifully appointed dining room in which Washington, Jefferson, Franklin and other leading figures dined, the bishop's well-stocked

library, and – a sign of real wealth – an indoor privy. At the other end of the block is Todd House, built about 10 years earlier and, judging by the tiny rooms, modest furnishings and outdoor privy, meant for a less privileged family. John and Dolley Todd lived here for two years before John, an attorney, died in the yellow fever epidemic that swept through the city in 1793. Dolley later married "the mighty little Madison" – James Madison, that is – "master builder of the Constitution" and the nation's fourth president. She was later renowned for her graciousness as a hostess in the nation's capital and also for her heroic evacuation of the White House during the War of 1812.

From Todd House, it's a short walk through the Park Service's 18th-century garden into a lovely mall shaded by willow and dogwood trees. Straight ahead is **Carpenters' Hall ❻** (Park building; off Chestnut between 3rd and 4th streets; open Tuesday–Sunday, 10am–4pm; entrance free), a beautifully proportioned Georgian structure designed by Robert Smith in 1770–74 for the carpenters' guild. The First Continental Congress met here in September 1774 to air their grievances against George III; the building later served as a hospital during the Revolutionary War. The hall is still owned by the Carpenters' Company; the first floor is open to the public and features a display on the hall's construction.

At the front of Carpenters' Court, two smaller buildings face Chestnut Street. The **New Hall Military Museum ❼** (Park building; Chestnut between 3rd and 4th streets; open daily, 10am–4pm; entrance free), a reconstruction of New Hall built in 1791 and used by the War Department until 1792, houses Revolution era muskets, sabers, uniforms and cannonballs. It details the development of the Continental Marines, Army and Navy with dioramas, a reconstruction of a frigate gun deck, and exhibits of flintlocks and other instruments of 18th-century warfare.

Map on pages 106–7

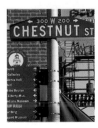

Chestnut Street is at the heart of the city's historic district.

BELOW: a carriage ride in Old City

Benjamin Franklin

He walked into town an impoverished teenager in 1723, and in just 25 years Benjamin Franklin had turned himself into a Philadelphia celebrity. By the time of his death in 1790, he had attained icon status, an international legend who had charmed the intellectual darlings of the Paris salons and helped steer the fledgling United States on their historic course.

Ben Franklin was the prototype for the Great American Success Story, a self-made man who embodied the essence of democratic meritocracy. He was a voracious improver, a child of the Enlightenment, a sort of early-American Renaissance man who, as printer, journalist, scientist and statesman, combined common sense with inspiration.

Yet, despite all the mythology, Franklin the man has always seemed a puzzle. Is the Ben Franklin who, in *Poor Richard's Almanack*, espoused such pragmatic virtues as thrift, moderation and industry the same man whose flights of imagination gave us the Franklin stove, the bifocal lens and the kite-flying experiments in electricity? A genius he may have been, but where is the grandeur, the kind of reckless élan that appealed to the romantic fancies of hero-worshipers like Thomas Carlyle and D. H. Lawrence, also two of his severest critics. He was derided as a "crafty and lecherous old hypocrite" by William Cobbett. John Keats called him "a philosophical Quaker full of mean and thrifty maxims." And both Nathaniel Hawthorne and Herman Melville regarded him as something of a mountebank, a quack dispenser of warmed-over aphorisms. He was crafty, cautious and sometimes conformist. Even his celebrated remark at the signing of the Declaration of Independence – "Gentlemen, we must now all hang together, or we shall most assuredly hang separately" – suggests a certain timorous calculation.

It is not easy to square the image of Franklin the moralist, the dour didact, with the equally evocative image of Franklin the visionary, the thinker, the "party-animal" who delighted French society, the lover of food, drink and women who were not his wife.

His dalliances in France – especially with Madame Helvetius, a rich widow to whom he vainly proposed marriage, and the younger Madame Brillon de Jouy, who liked to perch coquettishly on the lap of her "*cher Papa*" – are legendary, if never disclosed in detail. His affairs in London produced at least one child, a son who, to his father's displeasure, became an ardent Loyalist in the colonies.

A self-satisfied, middle-class man preoccupied with material pursuits? Perhaps. But Franklin left his mark all the same. And despite conservative leanings, he was a man ahead of his time.

George Washington may have been first in the hearts of his countrymen, but Benjamin Franklin was Mr America to the world at large. When he died, aged 84, his funeral drew the largest crowd – 20,000 people – ever to assemble in early Philadelphia. He was, to borrow Horace Greeley's words, "the consummate type and flowering of human nature under the skies of colonial America." ❑

LEFT: Benjamin Franklin, America's first great celebrity.

Across the walkway, in a reconstruction of a 1775 house built by Quaker Joseph Pemberton, is America's National Parks Museum Shop (Chestnut Street, between 3rd and 4th; open 9am–5pm), selling souvenirs from many national parks.

A very good house

Directly across Chestnut Street, about 20 paces down a narrow alley between 3rd and 4th streets, is **Franklin Court** ❽, site of Benjamin Franklin's last home. Franklin Court, part of the Historical Park, includes six sights of historical interest: the Courtyard Ghost structure and Underground Museum, and four houses on Market Street at the end of the Courtyard.

Franklin started work on the house in 1763 but didn't move in until 1785, when he retired from his diplomatic posts in Britain and France. All the while he sent letters home to his wife, Deborah, instructing her on everything from fireplace design to curtain hanging. "'Tis a very good house that I built so long ago to retire into," Franklin wrote. But even in retirement, Franklin had little rest. He served as President of Pennsylvania for three years and, at the ripe old age of 80, as a delegate at the Constitutional Convention. The house was torn down in 1812 by Franklin's grandchildren. Lacking plans for the structure, the National Park Service hired architect Robert Venturi to design a steel "ghost structure" representing the outline of Franklin's house and his grandson's printing office. Beneath the steel frames, viewing bays let visitors peek down into the remains of Franklin's underground kitchen and privy pit.

At the opposite end of Franklin Court, facing Market Street, a row of homes built by Franklin in the late 1780s now houses Franklin Court Museum Shop (314 Market Street; open 9am–4:30pm); a working Post Office (which uses a

Map on pages 106–7

TIP

The Polish-American Cultural Center – an exhibition space with displays featuring famous Poles, the Polish military and folk art – is among the row of handsome buildings across Walnut Street.

LEFT: inkstand used to sign the Declaration of Independence.
BELOW: statue of John Barry and Independence Hall.

"Benjamin Franklin" cancellation stamp) and postal history museum (316 Market Street; open 9am–5pm); the four-story archeological display "Fragments of Franklin Court" (318 Market Street; open 10am–4pm with longer summer hours; entrance free) in a building Franklin rented; and the Franklin Court Printing Office (320–22 Market Street; open 9am–5pm winter, 10am–6pm summer; entrance free), an 18th-century printing shop where Franklin's firebrand grandson, Benjamin Franklin Bache, once published an influential newspaper named *The Aurora*. Visitors can see the printing press in action.

The exhibits continue in Franklin Court's fascinating **Underground Museum** (entrance in Franklin Courtyard; open 9am–5pm winter, 10am–6pm summer; entrance free), which features a portrait gallery, replicas of Franklin inventions such as the glass "armonica" and library chair, a display detailing Franklin's life and work as a scientist, statesman, philosopher, printer and social organizer, an illuminated index of quotations, and an audio "drama" explaining Franklin's part in the American Revolution and the Constitutional Convention. Best of all, you can pick up a telephone at the "Franklin Exchange" and hear what George Washington, Mark Twain, D. H. Lawrence and others had to say about "the wisest American" – not all of it kindly, either.

The golden eagle has become the symbol of the United States.

Independence preserved

Walk back to Chestnut Street and turn right. Here is the **National Liberty Museum ❾** (321 Chestnut Street; tel: 215-925-2800; open Tuesday–Sunday, 10am–5pm winter, daily in summer; entrance fee), where bronze and glass sculptures and paintings celebrate the concept of freedom by honoring the diverse backgrounds of Americans. A theme museum rather than one tied to particular historical events, the exhibits tackle subjects such as violence and bigotry. There are interactive displays and an exhibition and film of Philadelphia Liberty Medal winners *(see page 46)*.

BELOW: cobbled street leading to Carpenter's Hall.

Cross Chestnut Street and turn right. Between 4th and 5th streets is the glorious facade of the **Second Bank of the United States ❿**, yet another of the park's Greek Revival jewels, designed by William Strickland in 1824. This is the house that Biddle built. Nicholas Biddle administered the Second Bank for some 20 years until President Jackson, a fervent anti-élitist, launched a fierce campaign to close it down. Today, the bank serves as **Independence Park's Portrait Gallery** (open 10am–6pm; donation requested for ages 17 and up). Many of the works are by Charles Willson Peale, one of the premier US painters of his day. Works by James Sharples, Gilbert Stuart, Thomas Sully and Peale's son, Rembrandt, are also part of the collection. The trio of ornate buildings across the street once served as banks, too. This stretch of Chestnut Street, the city's financial center in the late 19th century, was known as Bank Row.

Next to the Second Bank is a small park with a statue called *The Signer* ⓫, honoring the people who signed the Declaration of Independence. During the summer, this is a good place to find people in period costume, playing period instruments, demonstrating period games, or simply chatting with tourists.

Library Hall (Park building; 5th Street between Chestnut and Walnut; open only for scholars) stands next to the Second Bank but is set back from Chestnut Street. The original building was completed in 1789 for the Library Company of Philadelphia, destroyed in 1884 and then reconstructed in the 1950s as the library of the American Philosophical Society. The structure now houses all sorts of historical goodies, including letters and other documents written by Franklin, Jefferson and other eminent Americans.

Map on pages 106–7

Crossing 5th Street from Library Hall puts you smack in the middle of beautiful tree-lined Independence Square, known in 1776 as the State House Yard. Today, it is a lovely park in which to sit and get your bearings. The building on the corner of 5th and Chestnut streets is **Old City Hall** ⓬ (open 9am–5pm) – home of the Supreme Court from 1791 to 1800 and to city government between 1800 and 1870. Next door on 5th Street is Philosophical Hall (Park building; closed to the public), headquarters of Ben Franklin's American Philosophical Society, which has occupied the building since 1789.

Not to be missed, of course, is **Independence Hall** ⓭ (Park building; Chestnut Street between 5th and 6th; open daily 9am–5pm, longer summer hours; tours every 15–20 minutes), facing Independence Mall – the focus of the American historical experience. It was built between 1732–56 as the Pennsylvania State House and played a key role in the birth of the nation. Here the Second Continental Congress convened in 1775 to make their case against the British and, ultimately, to draft a revolutionary Declaration of Independence. Eleven years later, the Constitutional Congress met to amend the irresolute Articles of Confederation and ended up forging an entirely new government. Tours of Independence Hall start in the east wing and guide visitors into the Assembly Room, where John Hancock presided over his rebellious countrymen in 1776 and Washington served as a guiding light during the secretive proceedings of the Constitutional Convention in the summer of 1787.

BELOW: interior of Independence Hall.

Although most of the original furnishings were destroyed by the British during the Revolutionary War, a few original touches remain, including the "rising sun chair" used by Washington. The rest of the furniture dates to the late 1700s. Independence Hall also houses period restorations of the Pennsylvania Supreme Court and, on the second floor, the Governor's Chamber and the Long Room, which was used as a prison hospital for US soldiers after the Battle of Germantown, a reception hall for foreign dignitaries in the 1790s and, later, as Charles Willson Peale's museum of art and science. The **West Wing** of Independence Hall has a small "Great Essentials Exhibit" of some of the original documents critical to the founding of the United States, including the Declaration of Independence, annotated drafts of the Constitution and Articles of Confederation, and the silver inkstand used to sign them.

Now closed to the public, the bell tower was designed by William Strickland and erected in 1828, about 37 years after the unsteady original was torn down. The bell hanging in the steeple is not the Liberty Bell but a substitute – the John Wilbanks bell – installed in 1828 and still rung on national holidays.

The Lights of Liberty show features the voices of Charlton Heston, Ossie Davis, and Frank Langella, among others, playing historical figures, with Ralph Archbold portraying Benjamin Franklin. Whoopi Goldberg narrates a special children's version.

Finally, standing off Independence Hall's west shoulder, **Congress Hall** (6th and Chestnut streets; open 9am–5pm, longer summer hours) housed the United States legislature between 1790 and 1800. Here, the Bill of Rights was adopted, and the second president was inaugurated, demonstrating that peaceful transition of power under the new country's system of government worked. Inside, the Senate and House chambers are replete with fine studded leather, mahogany furnishings and other 18th-century fineries.

Let freedom ring

Across 6th Street on the southwest corner of 6th and Chestnut is the PECO **Energy Liberty Center** (tel: 1-877-GO-2-1776; open daily April–October at 10am, tours Tuesday–Saturday at dusk, every 10–15 minutes), where you can purchase tickets for the Lights of Liberty Show. This sound and light show takes visitors on an hour's nighttime walking tour through National Historic Park, telling the story of the struggle for American independence from 1765–76. Visitors hear through individual audio headsets and view visuals projected onto the walls of historic structures at five stops.

The **Liberty Bell** (Independence Mall, Market Street between 5th and 6th; open 9am–5pm, longer summer hours), in anticipation of large crowds for the country's Bicentennial in 1976, was moved from Independence Hall to a glass-and-steel pavilion in the plaza directly across Chestnut Street. In 2001, it is scheduled to be moved to a new Liberty Bell Complex on a different part of the same block. This is probably the most famous bell in the world, which is somewhat ironic given its checkered history. First of all, there is that giant crack marring its face. Consider, too, that the colonial Philadelphians who lived nearby

BELOW: the Liberty Bell is a popular tourist attraction.

THE LIBERTY BELL

The circumstances surrounding the very making of the bell represent a kind of comedy of errors. Originally intended for the State House tower, the Liberty Bell was first cast in London by the venerable Whitechapel Bell Foundry and sent by ship to Philadelphia in 1752. Before it could be installed, someone decided to put it to the test and, perhaps ineptly, gave it a ring that promptly produced its famous crack. The bell was recast by two Philadelphia craftsmen, John Stow and John Pass. To their chagrin, bell number two sounded a rather unmelodious bong, and Pass and Stow recast it once again – in the process immortalizing themselves with the inscription "Pass and Stow" on the bell's waist.

The bell tolled several times in honor of the momentous events attending the American Revolution; for the joyous news of Cornwallis's surrender at Yorktown in 1781 and the signing of the Treaty of Paris two years later; for the sad news of George Washington's death in 1799 and again for Lafayette's in 1834. The bell cracked again in 1835 while being rung for the death of Chief Justice John Marshall. It tolled once more, to commemorate Washington's birthday in 1846, and since then it has stayed mute except for a handful of occasions on which it has been gently tapped.

were wont to grumble about its insistent ring at inopportune moments. And later, in the 19th century, plans to scrap it as an antiquated heap of metal were considered on more than one occasion.

To the east of the Liberty Bell Pavilion is the **Bourse**, a block-long Victorian beauty built in 1893–95 as a commodities exchange and now a shopping mall. Illuminated by a domed skylight, the three-tiered arcade makes a convenient place to pick up a gift, grab a bite to eat or simply cool off on a hot day.

Independence Mall continues north, where construction of the new Gateway Regional Visitors Center, Independence Park Institute and the National Constitution Center is planned for the block between Arch and Race *(see page 105).* Franklin Square, between 6th and 7th streets north of Race, is the least used of William Penn's original five town plazas. It is now strangled by the entrance to the Benjamin Franklin Bridge, which arches more than 8,000 ft (2,500 meters) across the Delaware River. Isamu Noguchi's jolting stainless-steel sculpture, *Bolt of Lightning*, a memorial to Benjamin Franklin, towers over the foot of the bridge, offering a rather peculiar welcome to motorists as they enter the city.

Gallery ghetto

Northwest of Independence Mall, Old City is quite clearly a neighborhood in transition, with handsome colonial buildings standing shoulder to shoulder with sooty, 19th-century warehouses, many of them transformed into artists' lofts, galleries and up-scale condominiums. On the edge of Independence Mall, tucked into a quiet brick walkway between 4th and 5th streets, is the **National Museum of American Jewish History** ⓱ (35 North 5th Street; tel: 215-923-3811; open Monday–Thursday 10am–5pm, Friday 10am–3pm, Sunday noon–5pm; entrance

Map on pages 106–7

Old City is packed with places to eat – everything from haute cuisine *to* Pennsylvania Dutch pies.

BELOW: the Lights of Liberty show.

Independence Day celebrations have a special resonance in Old City.

BELOW:
Betsy Ross House.

fee). Most of the gallery is given over to an exhibit exploring the growth and diversity of the American Jewish experience from the establishment of the first Jewish community in New Amsterdam (later New York City) in 1654 to the present. A side gallery is devoted to changing exhibits, including a yearly special on ceremonial art, "Contemporary Artifacts." Sharing the building is the historic **Congregation Mikveh Israel**, founded in 1740, whose early members included Haym Salomon, a financier of the Revolutionary War and Nathan Levy, whose ship, the *Myrtilla*, carried the Liberty Bell to America.

Churches and Meeting Houses

The **Free Quaker Meeting House** (Park building; southwest corner of 5th and Arch streets; closed to the public) and Christ Church Burial Ground face each other a little farther north on 5th Street. The meeting house was built in 1783 for the "Fighting Quakers," a splinter group that broke from the pacifist Society of Friends in support of the American Revolution. **Christ Church Burial Ground** ⓲ (southeast corner of 5th and Arch streets) is the final resting place of Benjamin and Deborah Franklin and several signatories to the Declaration of Independence. The gates are often locked, but you can look at Franklin's grave from the corner, and the Park Service sometimes conducts tours (tel: 215-597-8974).

For an even better view of the cemetery, stroll to the **US Mint** ⓳ (151 North Independence Mall East; tel: 215-408-0114; open September–April Monday–Friday, May–June Monday–Saturday, July–August daily; entrance free). You can take a free self-guided tour of Uncle Sam's money factory, have a quick lesson in numismatics and watch as thousands of coins are cranked out every weekday. The windows in the visitors' gallery give a bird's-eye view of the burial ground, Independence Mall and the Liberty Bell Pavilion.

From the Mint, it's a short block on Race Street to the Old Reformed Church (southeast corner 4th and Race streets; tel: 215-922-4566), built in 1837, taken over by a paint factory after 1882, reclaimed by its congregation 80 years later, and beautifully restored. A block north, the Benjamin Franklin Bridge intrudes on a pair of historic churches – St George's United Methodist Church (4th Street between Race and Vine; tel: 215-925-7788), the oldest Methodist church in the US, and St Augustine's Catholic Church (4th Street between Race and Vine; tel: 215-627-1838), established in 1796, burned down by anti-Catholic rioters in 1844, and rebuilt a few years later by architect Napoleon LeBrun.

A two-block walk back to Arch Street brings you to the **Arch Street Friends Meeting House** ⓴ (Arch Street, between 3rd and 4th; tel: 215-627-2667; guided tours Monday–Saturday 10am–4pm; donation), built in 1804 on land granted to the Quakers by William Penn. Dioramas inside features scenes from Penn's life. Continuing down Arch Street – past the firehouse, the giant bust of Benjamin Franklin (it's made of thousands of pennies), and the lovely homes hidden away in Loxley Court – is the **Betsy Ross House** ㉑ (239 Arch Street; tel: 215-627-5343; open Tuesday–Sunday 10am–5pm winter, summer daily; donation). Though some dispute that Betsy Ross lived here and that she sewed the first flag, she and her husband John are still thought to have lived and run their upholstery business here from 1773–86. Whatever the truth, the restored rooms give a fascinating glimpse into a seamstress's busy (and cramped) life in this tiny 1740 house.

Next to the Betsy Ross House is the **Seamen's Church Institute** (249 Arch Street; tel: 215-922-2562; open Monday–Friday 9am–4:30pm; entrance free). Founded in 1843, the church first operated on a boat known as "The Floating Church of the Redeemer," ministering to seamen arriving in Philadelphia's port. While its ministry continues today, the Seamen's Church Institute also houses a small museum with ship models and a history of the maritime industry.

It's a short walk from here to **Christ Church ㉒** (2nd Street between Market and Arch; tel: 215-922-1695; guided tours Monday–Saturday 9am–5pm, Sunday 1–5pm, closed public holidays and Monday–Tuesday January–February; donations welcome). With its soaring white steeple, elegant arched windows and magnificent interior, Christ Church is one of Philadelphia's most handsome colonial buildings and was the city's most prominent structure well into the 1800s. Washington, Franklin and Betsy Ross worshiped here.

Historic streets

Walking north on 2nd Street takes you past the **Arden Theatre Company**, and a few of the new art galleries that have multiplied in recent years. Many are housed in airy old factories, some with cast-iron facades dating back to the 1890s. The Old City Art Association (tel: 215-625-9200) has started a tradition called "First Fridays" – on the first Friday evening of each month galleries host "open houses," drawing crowds to the district's historic streets. The Fringe Festival happens for about 10 days in September, when galleries, eateries, and unused buildings become the sites of artistic perfor-

Map on pages 106–7

BELOW: 18th-century Elfreth's Alley.

mances and exhibitions (tel. 215-413-9006 for information). You'll find clusters of galleries on 2nd Street between Market and Race, and on 3rd and Cherry streets between Market and Vine. Many specialize in contemporary or ethnic works and furniture from the 1950–60s. To the north, the **Painted Bride Art Center** (230 Vine Street; tel: 215-925-9235) presents art exhibitions and programs in dance and music.

Elfreth's Alley, a hidden enclave of early 18th-century houses, said to be the nation's oldest continuously inhabited street, is two blocks north between 2nd and Front streets. The alley began as a pathway for carts to and from the waterfront. The first houses were built in 1713 by Jeremiah Elfreth, a blacksmith who rented homes to seafarers and craftsmen. Today, all but one of the homes are privately owned. No. 126 is the **Elfreth's Alley Museum ㉓** (tel: 215-574-0560 or 877-353-7384; open February–December Tuesday–Saturday 10am–4pm, Sunday 1–4pm, January Saturday 10am–4pm, Sunday noon–4pm; entrance fee).

A few steps away, **Fireman's Hall ㉔** (147–9 North 2nd Street; tel: 215-923-1438, open Tuesday–Saturday 9am–4pm; entrance free) is packed with old fire engines, helmets, water cannons and other equipment documenting the history of firefighting from 1731, a few years before Benjamin Franklin founded the Union Fire Company, the nation's first, back in 1736. ❏

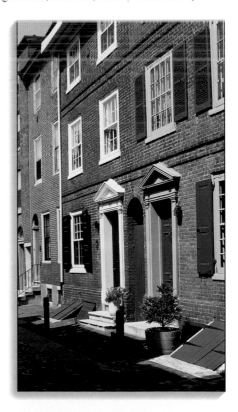

The City of Religious Liberty

William Penn called Philadelphia his "Holy Experiment" with good reason. State-sponsored religion was viewed as necessary to maintain a society with consistent moral values, so Philadelphia's system of government, which guaranteed its citizens the freedom to worship in different ways, was considered irresponsible and dangerously contrary to English law, to which its citizens were still subject.

However, religious tolerance was part of Penn's Quaker philosophy, which he had learned as a teenager in England and for which he had been imprisoned several times. Quakers believed that each human being has an "inner light" of God within him. Churches, ordained clergy and liturgical rite were unnecessary; Quakers opted for simple meeting houses where individuals could communicate with God if they felt so moved.

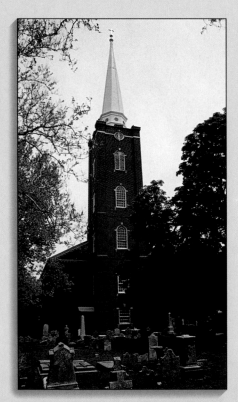

Given the opportunity to start his own community in 1681, Penn challenged the notion that adherence to one set of beliefs was necessary for civil order. He believed that true civic liberty was impossible without religious freedom. His 1701 Charter of Liberties began expressing this fundamental concept: "FIRST, Because no People can be truly happy tho' under the greatest enjoyment of civil Liberties, if abridged of the Freedom of their Consciences as to their Religious Profession and Worship... I do hereby grant and declare, That no Persons inhabiting in this Province or Territories who shall confess and acknowledge One Almighty God..."

Word of such unusual freedom spread and this small town attracted settlers from all over Europe who sought refuge from religious persecution in their homelands. People worshiped in private homes, in barns, in stores, and in one case in a brewery, while they gathered funds to erect houses of worship. Churches began to spring up and people from different denominations, countries and faiths worshiped next door to one another.

Gloria Dei Church, built by Swedish settlers in 1677, was joined by the first Quaker meeting house on Front Street in 1682. In 1695, the Greater Quaker meeting house and Christ Church, the city's first Anglican church, were constructed half a block from each other. The First Baptist Church was founded in 1698, as was the First Presbyterian Church, with whom joint services were held for a while. The Old First Reformed Church was organized in 1727 and the First Moravian Church in 1741. St Michael's and Old Zion Lutheran churches opened in 1743 and 1766, respectively. Despite protests from some quarters, the city council did not interfere in the celebration of Roman Catholic mass, prohibited by law in England. Jesuit priest Father Joseph Greaton, a resident of Philadelphia since the 1720s, built St Joseph's Chapel near 4th and Walnut streets in 1733.

Members of the city's first Jewish congregation, Mikveh Israel, began meeting in private homes in 1737 and became formalized in 1740 when Nathan Levy, American-

LEFT: St Peter's Church, built in 1761.
RIGHT: Old Pine Street Church; the Statue of Religious Liberty.

born son of a merchant from New York, turned over the deed to a burial ground on Spruce Street above 8th. The congregation then constructed a synagogue on Cherry Street above 3rd, dedicated in 1782.

In 1761, the Anglican community added St Peter's at 3rd and Pine and St Paul's on 3rd near Walnut. When St Joseph's became too small, a new Catholic church, St Mary's, was built down the street. The cathedral is also credited with beginning the Catholic parish school system when it opened St Mary's Academy in the 1770s. Predominantly German Holy Trinity Church at 6th and Spruce, and Irish Catholic St Augustine's at 4th and Vine opened in 1789 and 1796. The Second Presbyterian Church opened in 1743 at 3rd and Arch streets, and the Third Presbyterian Church, known as Old Pine, became a separate congregation in 1768.

The next year marked the founding at 4th and Vine of St George's Methodist Church, which would, in 1794, give root to three African-American churches, Mother Bethel Methodist Church, St Thomas's Episcopal Church and Mother Zoar United Methodist Church. Universalist Baptists Church, organized in 1790, and Rodeph Shalom, an Ashkenazic synagogue, were constructed in 1796. By the late 1700s, Philadelphia had 30 different congregations, most within blocks of Independence Hall. The Whitefield Meeting House had also been constructed in 1740 at 4th and Arch to accommodate speakers and religious groups which did not have places of their own.

The congregations did not merely coexist, but assisted each other in times of need. Early congregations such as the Baptists and Presbyterians shared facilities, as did the African-Americans. Christ Church contributed to Mikveh Israel in 1782 when the Jewish congregation faced financial difficulties.

Of these 30 congregations, 19 exist today, 12 of which still worship at their original locations. They continue to work together through Old Philadelphia Congregations, formed in 1975. Clergy from each faith meet monthly and have sponsored projects to promote understanding and fellowship. ❑

SOCIETY HILL AND PENN'S LANDING

Map on pages 106–7

Philadelphia's loveliest neighborhood, Society Hill, has the biggest concentration of 18th-century homes in the country; down on the waterfront the city's maritime history is preserved at Penn's Landing

Named for the Free Society of Traders, to whom William Penn granted land between Walnut and Pine streets, this chiefly residential neighborhood emerged in the late 1700s, shared by both working-class and wealthy families in a lively milieu of craftsmen, merchants, shopkeepers and seamen. The finest churches were within earshot of the rowdiest taverns, the most prestigious homes within smelling distance of the open-air market.

When well-heeled families started moving into more fashionable homes around Rittenhouse Square *(see page 165)*, the old neighborhood began a long decline that turned much of it into a slum. Had it not been for the efforts of preservationists in the 1950s, many of the historic homes would have fallen to the wrecking ball. The many years of rebuilding and renovating, painting and primping, have paid off grandly.

Today, Society Hill contains some of the most charming streets, lovely homes and priciest real estate in the city. It's a walker's paradise, with cobbled alleyways and hidden courtyards, brick sidewalks and tree-shaded lanes, and historic houses, large and small, that have been lovingly and accurately restored.

PRECEDING PAGES: setting sail from Penn's Landing. **LEFT:** a man of Independent means. **BELOW:** the US Customs building.

Grand houses, old churches

You can slip into Society Hill through the iron gate of the **Rose Garden**, on the 400 block of Walnut Street behind the Second Bank of the United States. The brick walkway leads to the type of quiet courtyard that makes strolling through Society Hill such a delight. Uncovered here is a section of original cobblestone. As the marker alongside explains, while William Penn laid out the streets in 1681, the City did not assume responsibility for paving until 1762. Follow the path across Locust Street into the smaller Magnolia Garden, planted in modern times in deference to George Washington's fondness for magnolias. Here, in early spring, magnolia and azalea blossoms surround the flagstone walk with splashes of red, white and sherbet-pink. It's a wonderful place to read the Sunday paper and sip coffee, or to take a few restful moments before pressing on.

The **Philadelphia Contributionship for the Insurance of Houses from Loss by Fire**, the oldest fire insurance company in the country, founded by Ben Franklin, is headquartered around the corner at 212 4th Street. Franklin and his pals started the "hand-in-hand" company in 1752. Its firemark – four hands locked in a fireman's carry – still hangs on buildings throughout Society Hill and Old City. Franklin's company refused to insure houses with trees nearby, so a competitor, the

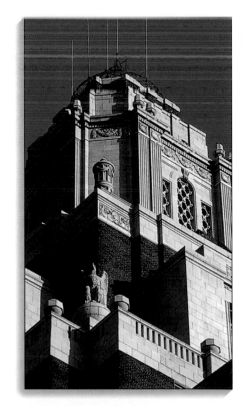

Mutual Assurance Company for Insuring Houses from Loss by Fire, the second oldest insurance company in America, filled the gap. The Green Tree Company was once at Locust and 4th streets in buildings occupied by the Shippen, Wistar and Cadwalader families, the cream of Philadelphia society. It was frequented by John Adams, George Washington and a host of the city's most distinguished guests. Now the Episcopal Diocese of Pennsylvania, organized in 1784, uses the house as its Church House (tel: 215-627-6434; open 9am–4:45pm).

Next door to the Church House is **St Mary's Church** ❷❺ (4th Street between Locust and Spruce; tel: 215-923-7930; open Monday–Saturday 9am–4:45pm; entrance free). Founded in 1763 when St Joseph's around the corner became too small for the congregation, St Mary's is the city's oldest Catholic church. Take a look inside for the two-tiered stained-glass windows. A brick walkway on the north side of the church leads to the cemetery, where Revolutionary naval commander John Barry is buried along with a number of prominent Philadelphians.

Across the street from St Mary's Church, narrow St James' Place leads into **Bingham Court**, a generous plaza surrounded by modern townhouses designed by the noted architect I.M. Pei. The north entrance leads across Willings Alley to the inner courtyard of **Old St Joseph's Church** ❷❻ (Willings Alley, between Walnut and Locust, 4th and 3rd streets; entrance free). Founded in 1733, St Joseph's is Philadelphia's oldest Catholic parish. As an inscription at the door explains, this was the only place in the British empire where Catholic Mass was permitted by law – a tribute to William Penn's policy of tolerance. Although enjoying legal status, Catholics were looked on with suspicion if not outright contempt. According to tradition, Ben Franklin advised the Catholic fathers to confine their church behind an iron gate for protection.

BELOW: Head House Square, Society Hill's shopping district.

How the other half lived

Return to Bingham Court and follow St James' Place across to 3rd Street. To the right, just past two handsome houses adorned with ornate wrought-iron balconies, is **Powel House** ㉗ (244 South 3rd Street; tel: 215-627-0364; tours Thursday–Saturday noon–5pm, Sunday 1–5pm, and by appointment; entrance fee), one of the grandest colonial homes in Philadelphia, built in 1765, and a classic example of Georgian style. As mayor of Philadelphia and one of the wealthiest men in town, Samuel Powel entertained Washington, John Adams, the Marquis de Lafayette and other friends in the lavish reception room, dining room and ballroom. And the Powels knew how to party. John Adams – always the starched-collar Bostonian – described a Powel fête as "a most sinful feast… [with]… everything that could delight the eye or allure the taste; curds and creams, jellies, sweetmeats of various sorts, twenty sorts of tarts, fools, trifles, floating islands, whipped sillibub, &c., &c." Nearly demolished in the 1930s, Powel House has been restored in painstaking detail from the splendid crystal chandelier, Chippendale chairs (George Washington liked them so much he ordered 20 for Mount Vernon) and Nanking china (a gift from the Washingtons), to the rack upon which Samuel hung his wig before going to bed. Before leaving, be sure to stroll through the 18th-century garden in the rear courtyard.

Remnants of 18th-century life line the streets of Society Hill.

Take a few steps south on 3rd Street for a look at the beautiful old brownstones once owned by Michel Bouvier, great-great-grandfather of Jacqueline Kennedy Onassis, then retrace your steps to Old St Paul's Episcopal Church, built in 1761, redesigned by William Strickland in 1830, and now used as offices for the Episcopal Community Services. St James' Place continues past a row of modern townhouses to I.M. Pei's Society Hill Towers, a trio of apartment buildings conspicuously out of sync with the neighborhood's colonial style. The Society of Free Traders once kept an office on this knoll overlooking Dock Creek, where ships arriving from Britain and the West Indies unloaded their freight. Years later, the area was occupied by the sprawl of Dock Street Market, since relocated to a modern facility in South Philadelphia.

BELOW: George Washington, "father of the country."

Heading downhill on 2nd Street brings you back to the 18th century in a hurry. The first brick building on your right is Abercrombie House (270 South 2nd Street), a handsome Georgian home built for a Scottish sea captain in 1759. Across the street, the modest brick building that seems to lean to one side is **A Man Full of Trouble Tavern**. Constructed in 1759 and, sadly, now closed, this endearing little building was typical of the taverns that once huddled around the waterfront where a sea-dog could find dinner, a few tankards of grog and a place to stay the night.

Delightful detour

Before continuing to Head House Square (see page 128), you can stroll down **Spruce Street** ㉘ into the residential heart of Society Hill, where lovely 18th- and 19th-century homes have been brought back to life with interesting contemporary touches. Some of the larger houses, like the Davis-Lenox House (No. 217) and the Wharton House (No. 336), were occupied by the well-to-do. But many homes are fairly

A Halloween hay bale makes a sunny seat in Society Hill.

modest, with two or three stories and relatively tight interior space. Peek down the alleyways at Philip and American streets (between 2nd and 3rd streets). On the next block, St Joseph's Walkway returns to Bingham Court, passing a pocket of houses on the left named Bell's Court. These homes have only one room on each story – Philadelphians call them Father, Son and Holy Ghost, or Trinity houses – and are typical of working-class dwellings in the early 1800s.

On the opposite side of Spruce Street, St Peter's Way crosses to a lovely playground between Cypress and Delancey streets. **Delancey Street** ㉙, one of the most charming and secluded in the city, is lined with 18th-century homes such as the Alexander Barclay House and Trump House, tiny private courtyards (Drinker's Court) and imaginative modern conversions.

Throughout the neighborhoods, you may notice touches of 18th-century living. The metal brackets outside some second-story windows hold "busybody mirrors", which let upper-floor occupants see who is at the front door. It is said that Ben Franklin invented the mirror so he could see his wife coming down the street while he "entertained" young ladies in the upstairs parlor.

Church tour

Farther along Spruce Street, between 4th and 5th, is the impressive white mass of the **Society Hill Synagogue** ㉚ (426 Spruce Street; tel: 215-922-6590; open Monday–Friday 10am–3pm; entrance free). Originally a Baptist church from 1829, the building has an 1851 façade designed in the Greek Revival style by Thomas U. Walter, architect of the Capitol's dome in Washington, D.C.

Cypress Street leads out of Lawrence Court to 4th Street and the **Physick House** ㉛ (321 South 4th Street; tel: 215-925-7866; hourly tours Thursday–Saturday noon–4pm, Sunday 1–4pm, shorter winter hours; entrance fee). Built in 1786 by Henry Hill, this magnificent freestanding mansion – one of the finest Federal-style homes in the country – is fully restored. Furnishings date from 1815–37, when the house was occupied by Philip Syng Physick, "father of American surgery." Among the doctor's many innovations are surgical devices displayed upstairs, including a ghastly looking gall bladder remover that was used without the benefit of anaesthesia.

BELOW:
Penn's landing stretches along the Delaware River.

South of Spruce Street, Society Hill is graced with a number of historic churches. The **Old Pine Street Presbyterian Church** ㉜ (4th and Pine streets; tel: 215-925-8051; open Monday–Friday 9am–5pm; entrance free) has stood, in one form or another, since 1768. Originally, the church looked like its Georgian-style neighbor, St Peter's, but it was badly damaged during the Revolutionary War. A renovation in the 1800s turned it into a Greek Revival temple, with Corinthian columns and a second-story entrance. John Adams worshiped here and, during the British occupation, redcoats used the church as a hospital. Several Revolutionary War veterans are buried in the cemetery, including 100 Hessians – German mercenaries hired by the British to put down the Yanks.

A block away, **St Peter's Episcopal Church** ㉝ (3rd and Pine streets; tel: 215-925-5968, open for tours, Monday–Friday 9am–3pm, Saturday 10am–noon, Sunday 1–3pm; entrance free) retains the simple dignity of its original Georgian design. Built between 1758–63 by Robert Smith, master builder of both Carpenters' Hall and Christ Church, this "chapel of ease" was established for well-to-do parishioners who were tired of slogging through the mud to Christ Church. Apart from the six-story steeple, which was added in 1852 by William Strickland, St Peter's looks much as it did more than 200 years ago. The high-backed box pews are original (Washington sat in No. 41), and the church's unusual layout, with the chancel in the east end and the pulpit in the west, remains intact. Outside, a brick path wanders past the graves of painter Charles Willson Peale, naval hero Stephen Decatur, financier Nicholas Biddle, and a delegation of Indian chiefs who died in the yellow fever epidemic of 1793.

Across the street, the **Thaddeus Kosciuszko National Memorial** ❸ commemorates the Polish patriot who aided the American cause in the Revolution. After an illustrious career as a military engineer in America, Kosciuszko led a failed revolt against the Czarist occupation of Poland. Wounded, imprisoned and later exiled by the Russians, he returned to Philadelphia and boarded at this house between 1797–98, where he received distinguished visitors, among them Vice-President Thomas Jefferson. The exhibit, which includes a slide program and a recreation of Kosciuszko's bedroom, details the career of the man who, in Jefferson's words, was "as pure a son of Liberty as I have ever known."

Around the corner on Lombard Street, there are three church buildings of note. The **Presbyterian Historical Society** ❸ (425 Lombard Street; tel: 215-627-1852), the national archives and research center for the Presbyterian Church, is a balanced Federal structure set in a walled garden. In the garden, are statues by Alexander Stirling Calder of important figures in the history of the

Map on pages 106–7

TIP

Visitors to the Old Pine Street Presbyterian Church should make a point of catching Jazz Vespers, a musical treat offered every third Sunday of the month.

BELOW:
the USS *Olympia* and USS *Becuna* at Penn's Landing.

Presbyterian Church. About a block west, Congregation Bnai Abraham (527 Lombard Street; tel: 215-374-9280; open for services) is an imposing building with an arched arcade and stained-glass rosette over the entrance.

Around the corner, **Mother Bethel African Methodist Episcopal Church** ㊱ (6th Street, between Pine and Lombard streets; tel: 215-925-0616; open Tuesday–Friday 10am–4pm, Saturday by appointment; entrance free) is believed to be the oldest property continuously owned by African-Americans in the country. The church was founded in 1787 by Richard Allen, a former slave and preacher who broke with Old St George's Methodist Church when he and other black parishioners were relegated to the upstairs gallery. The new congregation's first church was an old blacksmith shop that Allen had hauled to the site on a horse-drawn wagon. Allen and his followers won the city's respect for their selfless efforts during the yellow fever epidemic of 1793. Later, as the center of Philadelphia's largest black neighborhood, Mother Bethel hosted abolitionists like Frederick Douglass and runaway slaves along the Underground Railroad *(see page 37)*. Allen's tomb is in the basement.

Retail therapy

From Mother Bethel, it's a short walk down Pine or Lombard streets to **Head House Square** ㊲, Society Hill's only shopping area. In colonial times, the brick shed in the center of 2nd Street sheltered the town's "New Market," started in 1745. (The first market was on the east end of High Street, now called Market Street, in Old City.) The little brick house at the end – Head House – was added in 1804 and used as a meeting place for volunteer firemen. A fire bell once hung in the cupola. Today, Head House Square has smart shops and restaurants. On summer weekends, the market shed is given over to a lively crafts fair.

BELOW: Saturday market at Head House Square.

New Market complex – a terraced, glass-walled shopping area just off Head House Square – has gone through various incarnations, and is now a cabaret and theater space. The bank across 2nd Street from the Head House – strikingly out of place with its arched windows, ornate cornices and cast-iron pilasters – was modeled after the Loggio Consiglio in Padua, Italy, although it is now greatly altered.

On the waterfront

In Benjamin Franklin's day, Philadelphia's waterfront was a bustling hive of sailing ships, warehouses, taverns, sail makers and counting houses. But, like New York, Baltimore and Boston, Philadelphia tore down the rotting piers and seedy whiskey joints that once choked its waterfront and turned it into a riverside park dubbed **Penn's Landing** (121 North Columbus Boulevard, between Market and South streets; tel: 215-629-3200). Pedestrian walkways connect the riverfront to Center City at Market, Chestnut, Walnut and South streets. Just north of Market Street, if it is in port, you can see the *Gazela* ㊳, which is Philadelphia's participant in the Tall Ships festivals. Built in 1883, the *Gazela* is a 177-ft (54-meter) long square- rigged ship.

Between Market and Walnut is the **Great Plaza** ㊴, site of a massive Family Entertainment Center designed to include a 20-screen Cineplex, an IMAX theater, the Please Touch Museum (relocated from the Parkway Museum District), year-round ice-skating, theme restaurants and shopping. The Great Plaza, filled with markers detailing river geology, population growth, and other information about Philadelphia, is also the site of an open-air amphitheater where pop groups perform free concerts almost every weekend during the summer and where the Philadelphia RiverBlues Festival, Jambalaya Jam and other special events are held each year *(see page 74)*.

Map on pages 106–7

The **Ferry Dock** ⓸ is where you can catch the RiverLink ferry (Walnut Street; tel: 215-925-LINK; open April–December) across the river. On the New Jersey side of the Delaware sits the **New Jersey State Aquarium** ⓸ (Mickle Boulevard, Camden; tel: 856-365-3300; open April–September 9:30am–5:30pm, shorter winter hours; entrance fee), the Camden Children's Garden, and the Sony E-Center, a year-round facility with a 25,000 capacity amphitheater. The Aquarium boasts one of the world's largest fishtanks, with more than 1,500 fish, and has exhibits of seals, penguins, sharks and many exotic species.

Historic masted ships are docked at Penn's Landing.

At the southern end of the Great Plaza is the angular concrete structure of the **Independence Seaport Museum** ⓸ (211 South Columbus Boulevard; tel: 215-925-5439; open daily 10am–5pm; entrance fee). The collection focuses on the history of the port, with displays on 19th-century shipbuilding and navigation and a fascinating array of nautical gizmos, model ships, scrimshaw and other artifacts associated with the life of early American mariners. South of the museum, an international sculpture garden leads toward the marina, where visitors can watch traditional wood boat-building at the museum's Workshop on the Water. The USS *Becuna* ⓸, a guppy-class World War II submarine that served in 1944 as submarine flagship under General Douglas McArthur and later in the Korean and Vietnam wars, and the USS *Olympia* ⓸, a 19th-century cruiser pressed into service during the Spanish-American War, are berthed a few steps away and open to the public (tel: 215-925-1898; open 10am–4:30pm; entrance fee). Nearby, the **Philadelphia Vietnam Veterans Memorial** ⓸ (Delaware Avenue and Spruce Street) is modeled after the now-famous "Wall" in Washington, D.C.

BELOW: a view of Penn's Landing from New Jersey.

Waterfront attractions

The Delaware River waterfront has, in recent years, become a hotspot for nightclubs and restaurants too numerous to mention, as well as a departing place for boat tours *(see page 264)*. A few places north of Penn's Landing include Dave and Buster's (325 North Columbus Boulevard, Pier 19 North; tel: 215-413-1951) a casual restaurant/arcade with billiards, Iwerks Theater and golf simulators, and Holiday Boat Tours (Columbus Boulevard at Callowhill Street; tel: 215-629-8687; narrated tour daily at 1pm, 4pm and 7pm).

At the southern end of Penn's Landing docks are the *Spirit of Philadelphia* (South Columbus Boulevard at Lombard Circle, office Pier 3 at Penn's Landing; tel: 215-923-1419) with dining and entertainment, and the *Moshulu* (Pier 34 and Columbus Boulevard, near South Street; tel: 215-923-2500), the latter of which claims to be "the world's oldest and largest four-masted restaurant sailing ship." ❑

SOUTH STREET AND QUEEN VILLAGE

Map on page 134

South Street is Philadelphia's haven of hip boutiques and ethnic restaurants, with an emphasis on fashion that is in contrast to neighboring Queen Village, the city's oldest area

When Philadelphians talk about **South Street** ❶ they aren't referring to its entire river-to-river stretch, which forms the unofficial southern border of Center City. They're talking about the strip from Front Street to about 7th Street, where on weekends the pedestrians move faster than the bumper-to-bumper "cruisers." Memorialized by the 1963 rock 'n' roll hit "South Street" by the Orlons, it's this area which is called the "hippest street in town." Here is where the action is – where an eclectic assortment of people comfortably mingle among the eccentric and conventional assortment of boutiques, shops, restaurants, bars and cafés. Here you will find the graying hippies, punks, androgynes, hip-hoppers, gays, college kids, teenagers, singles, young marrieds and, during the day, parents with strollers in tow.

PRECEDING PAGES: party time on South Street. **LEFT:** street life. **BELOW:** flower power.

Pushcarts to punks

Toward the end of the 19th century, this was the commercial center of the city's largest Eastern European Jewish neighborhood. Pushcarts and storefronts lined the street. These days, you can still get a hint of the old neighborhood around 4th Street, the two-block stretch south of Bainbridge  that is dubbed **Fabric Row** ❷ and which is lined with old-fashioned fabric shops, tailors and dressmakers. The so-called South Street renaissance got rolling in the 1950s, when Philadelphia planned a crosstown expressway that was slated to wipe out everything along the street from the Delaware to the Schuylkill rivers. Residents complained, but had little luck fighting City Hall.

Reluctantly, many of them packed up and moved onto greener pastures. But like many civic projects in Philadelphia, the expressway debate dragged on for years, never quite resolving one way or the other. Meanwhile, artists discovered this low-rent district and started moving in, ignoring the possibility that the bulldozers might be rumbling toward their doorstep at any moment.

But thanks to a vocal rainbow coalition made up of African-Americans, Irish and hippies, the bulldozers never came. By this time, too, many of the artists, artisans and alternate-lifestylers were buying their own studios and buildings, which is one of the reasons why South Street has retained so much of its artsy, edgy attitude and hasn't sprouted a fast-food joint on every corner. (Although there is a McDonald's on 6th and South, it is cleverly disguised by two-story exterior walls painted with a colorful jungle mural, which helps it blend right in with the neighborhood.)

Traditional Italian pizza is a South Street favorite.

There are chain stores now, such as Tower Records, The Gap, Pearl Art (art supplies), but they have helped add stability to the revolving door of businesses that often seem to close before they open. But South Street gets its high-octane mystique from the quirky, funky shops and restaurants interspersed throughout the neighborhood, the colorful signs and storefronts, and the diversity of people on the street. What "makes" South Street what it is is the fact that it is genuinely exciting to walk through, especially on Friday and Saturday nights when all the crowds hit the sidewalk. It is South Street because the merchants and workers who live here make it as much a community as a marketplace. It is South Street because even the chain stores and the yuppies who discovered the area in the 1980s seem to have adapted to the atmosphere of the neighborhood rather than forcing the neighborhood to conform to their up-scale liking.

Exploring South Street

Begin a tour of the area at Front Street, where the South Street pedestrian bridge to Penn's Landing provides a scenic view of the Delaware River and a modern sculpture of people strolling mimics the activity of humans below. The block from Head House Square at 2nd and South streets *(see page 128)* is a transition block from open-air river views to the quaint congestion of South Street, with an assortment of restaurants offering everything from traditional American diner fare to Irish, Cajun, and Italian cuisine. The real heart of South Street runs from 2nd to 6th streets. Here weekend visitors often find themselves pressed elbow to elbow outside the many cafés, galleries and the funky little shops.

From snacking to dining, South Street offers something for every taste bud – from cheesesteaks and hamburgers to ice cream and water ice to fiery Indian,

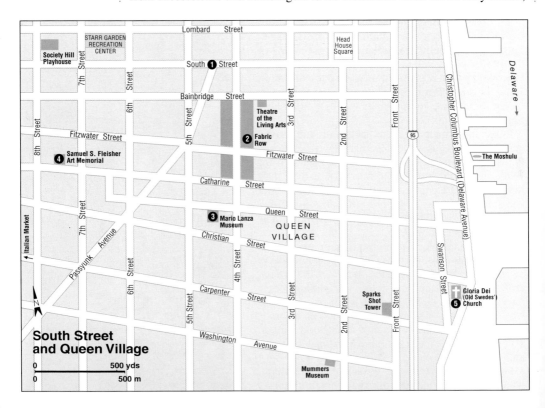

Mexican and Chinese foods to Italian cuisine and many more too numerous to mention. A few highlights include the **Knave of Hearts**, a romantic little nook and a pioneer in the 1960s revival of South Street. **Bridget Foy's** at 2nd Street, and **Jon's** at 3rd Street, both offer outdoor tables for gazing and grazing, and a prime view of the South Street carnival.

At night, you are likely to hear music blasting from local rock clubs, where graying local legends who never made the big time keep wailing away with apologies to no one (and none is expected). **Jim's Steaks** boasts the best cheesesteaks on South Street. **Johnny Rockets**, on the corner of 5th Street, is a great place to take kids of any age for hamburgers, sodas or shakes. It's a retro 1950s-style diner with miniature jukeboxes at every table, where you can perch on a stool at the counter or slide into one of the red vinyl booths.

Around the center of the strip between 3rd and 4th streets is the **Theater of the Living Arts**, a South Street landmark that has survived a number of incarnations. During the hippie heyday, it was a theater operated, for an infamous season, by André Gregory of *My Dinner with André* fame. It later became a revival house showing foreign and domestic movies. After a failed attempt to turn it back into a playhouse, it's now one of the city's prime venues for touring bands that can't quite fill the city's larger concert halls.

South Street offers a curious and quirky assortment of shops – from old-fashioned shoe stores to trendy boutiques, to a few erotic shops and everything in between. Highlights include **Xog**, one of the best and longest-lived of the "fashion with an-attitude" boutiques, **American Pie**, a hodgepodge of crafts, jewelry, chimes and other handcrafted goods; and **The Works Gallery**, both featuring exquisitely crafted furnishings, pottery, sculpture and other *objets*

Map on page 134

BELOW: South Street is alive with musical beats.

d'art. The place with king-sized plastic ants crawling over the storefront is **Zipperhead**, another South Street original where fashionable punks and would-be punks come to check out the latest in the studs-and-leather look.

South Street has its own collection of literary and music retail establishments. **Tower Books** is one of the larger bookstores in the city, with thousands of titles and a knowledgeable staff. At the corner of 5th Street, the **Book Trader** offers a wide range of used books and terrific posters, an annex in the rear with used records (remember them?) and occasional book readings and musical performances. There is also **Garland of Letters**, a New Age bookstore with enough crystals to choke Shirley MacLaine; the subject matter tends toward spirituality, astrology, philosophy and methods of healing that do not require a physician *(see page 293)*.

Toward the western end, you'll find **Tower Records** and the Tower Records Classical Annex. Together, the stores offer the most comprehensive selection of tapes and CDs in the city.

Queen Village

South Street is the main thoroughfare of an area that, since the 1960s, has been known as Queen Village. Before that it was Southwark, and before that Wiccaco. Whatever the name, it's the oldest settled part of the city. As early as 1640, more than 40 years before William Penn arrived with his Quaker immigrants, Swedish settlers erected log cabins in this area as well as a crude blockhouse that served as the area's first church.

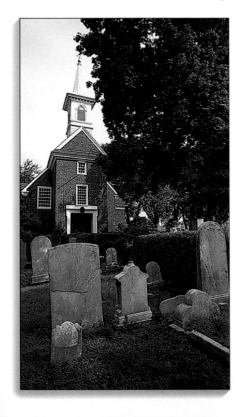

BELOW:
Gloria Dei (Old Swedes') Church.

Stretching from Lombard Street to Washington Avenue and from Front to 5th streets, the neighborhood claims some of Philadelphia's oldest houses and churches. Like South Street, the area has been greatly affected by highway construction plans. But here, the highway, I-95, was actually built, clearing away much of what had become a slum while leaving historic buildings relatively intact.

Though much of Queen Village is residential, South Street's eclectic ambience extends several blocks south of the main strip, depending upon which street you pick. Tattoo and body piercing parlors abound right off South Street on 4th, where you can also find the Famous 4th Street Deli – operated by the same family for three generations. In contrast, the trendy Martini Café and the Beau Monde Creperie can be found on 6th Street. Assorted used book and music shops are scattered here and there.

Look for the murals here and elsewhere in Philadelphia. Murals of cut glass have found homes on a number of walls of residences and shops in Queen Village.

On 4th and Queen streets stands Settlement Music School, where the late tenor Mario Lanza used to study, and which houses the **Mario Lanza Museum ❸**, a collection of Lanza paraphernalia (416 Queen Street, 3rd Floor; tel: 215-468-3623; open Monday–Saturday, 10am–3pm, closed Saturday–Sunday July–August; entrance free). The school itself sponsors a series of concerts, teaches 3,000 students, and has always been a major force in nurturing the city's up-and-coming musical talent.

Map on page 134

Also serving as both classroom and museum is the **Samuel S. Fleisher Art Memorial** ❹ (719 Catharine Street; tel: 215-922-3456; open Monday–Friday 11am–5pm and, while school is in session, Monday–Thursday 6:30–9:30pm, Saturday 10am–3pm, closed August), one of those places that even locals know little about. The free art school features five exhibitions a year of emerging local talent, supplemented by a collection of Russian icons and 14th- to 16th-century European paintings housed in the Italian-style Fleisher Sanctuary.

In the far southeast corner of Queen Village stands **Gloria Dei (Old Swedes')** **Church** ❺ (Christian Street between Columbus Boulevard and I-95; tel: 215-389-1513; open daily 9am–5pm). Now a national historic site, this is Pennsylvania's oldest church, dating back to 1698–1700. The courtyard encompasses a cemetery, the 18th-century Guild House, Parish Hall, caretaker's house and rectory. The church itself features carvings brought from Gothenburg in 1642, models of the *Fogel Grip* and *Kalmar Nyckel*, two ships that carried early Swedish settlers to "New Sweden," hanging from the ceiling *(see page 228)*, and a pair of wooden angels that were part of another Swedish ship.

While you're in the neighborhood, if you look up, you may notice **Sparks Shot Tower** at Front and Carpenter streets. The 142-ft (43-meter) tower is all that remains of an early 19th-century ammunition plant built by plumber Thomas Sparks and his partner John Bishop. They developed an innovative method for making shotgun pellets by dropping molten lead through a series of screens into barrels of cold water, where it hardened into balls. Bishop, a Quaker pacifist, suffered a crisis of confidence and sold his half of the business when, during the War of 1812, he became sickened by the factory's product being used to shoot down people instead of game. ❑

Sparks Shot Tower looms over the neighborhood.

BELOW: funky shops and bars of South Street.

WASHINGTON SQUARE WEST

Map on page 142

This 36-block area is a lively mix of Bohemians, businesses, historic sites, antiques shops, three medical centers, cozy restaurants and a variety of shopkeepers and residential areas

Washington Square West isn't as quaint as Society Hill *(see page 123)*, but it's certainly no slouch in the character department. More daring in spirit than its genteel neighbor, and a bit rougher around the edges, here you will find a labyrinth of alleyways lined with houses that take you right back in time. Add to this fine architecture and a dash of jazz, and you'll see why this is one of Philadelphia's most varied and colorful neighborhoods.

A placid patch of green shaded by sky-high walnut and sycamore trees, **Washington Square ❶** anchors the neighborhood at the eastern border. One of William Penn's original town plazas, the square served as a potter's field during the American Revolution. The 5,000 British and American soldiers who were laid to rest here are memorialized by the **Tomb of the Unknown Soldier,** where an inscription reads: "Liberty is a light for which many men have died in darkness." Later, during the tragic yellow fever epidemic of 1793, hundreds of victims were interred in the square in unmarked graves.

By the middle of the 1800s, Washington Square had become a high class residential neighborhood. A few of the fine homes still stand on Washington Square West and Walnut Street, although most are now occupied by businesses.

PRECEDING PAGES: Pennsylvania Hospital. **LEFT:** Athenaeum reading room. **BELOW:** Antique Row bicycle store.

Printing center

Some years later, the square became the center of Philadelphia's prestigious publishing industry. The massive **Curtis Center ❷**, once the headquarters of the *Ladies' Home Journal* and *Saturday Evening Post*, still dominates the northeast corner of the square and is the home of original tenants, publishers W.B. Saunders (6th and Walnut streets; tel: 215-238-6450; open Monday–Friday 9am–5pm, Saturday 8am–5pm; entrance free). Inside the lobby you can see the **The Dream Garden**, an impressive 15x50-ft (4x14-meter), 260-color glass mosaic mural created in 1916 by Louis C. Tiffany Studios on the basis of a painting by Maxfield Parrish. Lea and Febiger, the oldest publisher in the US, was once located in the palazzo on Washington Square South, now home to the **Locks Gallery** (600 Washington Square South; tel: 215-629-1000) and its collection of contemporary art.

The grand Renaissance-style palace on 6th Street is the **Athenaeum ❸** (219 South 6th Street; tel: 215-925-2688; gallery open Monday–Friday 9am–5pm; entrance free; tours and research by appointment), a private library built in 1845 and one of the country's foremost repositories of Victorian design. Filled with antique art and furnishings, the building looks much as it did 100 years ago, when bibliophiles came here to read, study and chat with other members. A changing exhibit is displayed on the first floor.

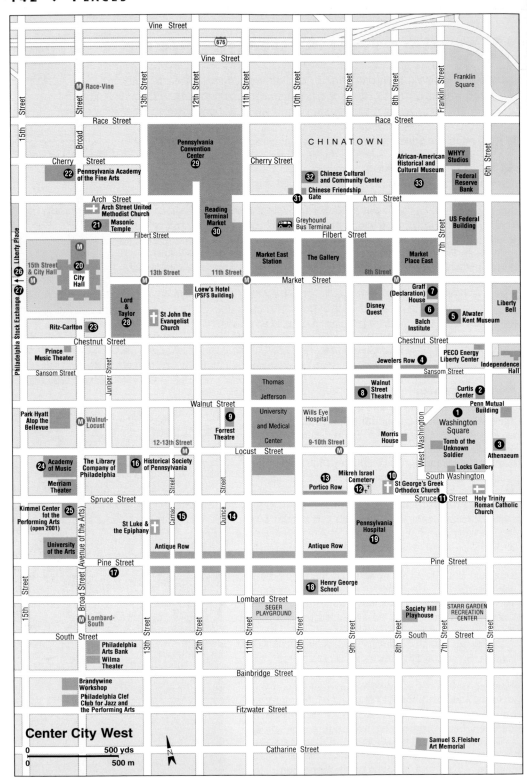

Vine Street

676

Vine Street

Race-Vine

Race Street

Race Street

CHINATOWN

Franklin Square

Cherry Street

Pennsylvania Convention Center
29

Cherry Street

African-American Historical and Cultural Museum
33

WHYY Studios

22 Pennsylvania Academy of the Fine Arts

Chinese Cultural and Community Center
32

Federal Reserve Bank

Arch Street

Arch Street

US Federal Building

Arch Street United Methodist Church

Chinese Friendship Gate
31

21 Masonic Temple

Reading Terminal Market
30

Filbert Street

Filbert Street

Greyhound Bus Terminal

Loew's Hotel (PSFS Building)

Market East Station

The Gallery

Market Place East

15th Street & City Hall

13th Street

11th Street

Market Street

26

City Hall
20

Disney Quest

Graff (Declaration) House 7

Liberty Bell

27

Lord & Taylor
28

St John the Evangelist Church

6

Balch Institute

Atwater Kent Museum 5

Ritz-Carlton 23

Chestnut Street

Chestnut Street

Prince Music Theater

Sansom Street

Jewelers Row 4

PECO Energy Liberty Center

Sansom Street

Independence Hall

Thomas Jefferson

Walnut Street Theatre 8

Curtis Center 2

Park Hyatt Atop the Bellevue

Walnut Street

Walnut-Locust

University and Medical Center

Wills Eye Hospital

Penn Mutual Building

Washington Square 1

9 Forrest Theatre

Morris House

Tomb of the Unknown Soldier

3

12-13th Street

Locust Street

9-10th Street

West Washington

Athenaeum

24 Academy of Music

The Library Company of Philadelphia

16 Historical Society of Pennsylvania

Locks Gallery

Mikreh Israel Cemetery

South Washington

Merriam Theater

13 Portico Row

10

12

St George's Greek Orthodox Church

Spruce Street

Spruce Street

11

Holy Trinity Roman Catholic Church

Kimmel Center fot the Performing Arts (open 2001) 25

St Luke & the Epiphany

15

14

Pennsylvania Hospital
19

University of the Arts

Antique Row

Antique Row

Pine Street

Pine Street

17

18 Henry George School

Lombard Street

Lombard-South

SEGER PLAYGROUND

Society Hill Playhouse

STARR GARDEN RECREATION CENTER

South Street

South Street

Philadelphia Arts Bank Wilma Theater

Bainbridge Street

Brandywine Workshop

Philadelphia Clef Club for Jazz and the Performing Arts

Fitzwater Street

Center City West

Samuel S. Fleisher Art Memorial

0   500 yds

0   500 m

N

Catharine Street

Map
on page
142

The Colonial-style reconstruction next door to the Athenaeum was the residence of the late Mayor Richardson Dilworth, a Democratic reformer described by a colleague as "D'Artagnan in long pants and a double-breasted suit." The **Penn Mutual Building**, located at Walnut and 6th streets, is a rambling, Classically oriented composition with a towering glass-and-concrete addition. (Note the original Egyptian Revival façade of the old Pennsylvania Insurance Company still standing on Walnut Street.) The Italianate bank directly across the square was built for the Philadelphia Savings Fund Society in 1869.

North of the Square

With jewelry stores of every type, **Jewelers Row ❹**, between 7th and 9th streets north of Walnut, has been Philadelphia's diamond district since 1851.

The austere-looking **Atwater Kent Museum ❺** (15 South 7th Street; tel: 215-922-3031; open Tuesday–Saturday 10am–4pm; entrance fee Tuesday–Friday) interprets the history of Philadelphia from its Quaker roots to the present with exhibits of household objects and other materials used by local citizens through the years. A children's wing displays toys, dolls and games. Fans of Norman Rockwell will be attracted by the museum's varied collection of *Saturday Evening Post* covers and posters by the celebrated artist who captured so much of the homely nature of American life.

A few steps away, the **Balch Institute ❻** (18 South 7th Street; tel: 215-925-8090; open Monday–Saturday 10am–4pm; entrance fee) is a glorious celebration of America's ethnic diversity, with a library, archives, museum and education center, focused on immigration, ethnic life and multiculturalism in the US Changing exhibits usually focus on a particular theme or ethnic group; past shows have covered ethnic arts, Immigrants in the media, ethnic communities in Philadelphia, and refugee communities in the US The Institute also conducts tours of the city's historic ethnic sites.

Next door to the Balch, the **Graff (Declaration) House ❼** (7th and Market streets; open 10am–4pm; entrance free) is a reconstruction of the house in which Thomas Jefferson wrote the Declaration of Independence *(see page 31)*. When Jefferson rented the upstairs parlor in 1776, the house, built and owned by bricklayer Joseph Graff, was located on the quiet outskirts of town. A short film is shown on the first floor; Jefferson's rooms are recreated on the second.

Footlights and fanfare

A quick walk west on Walnut Street brings you to two theaters. The **Walnut Street Theatre ❽** (825 Walnut Street and 9th Street; tel: 215-574-3550) is the oldest continuously used theater in the US Before Broadway stole the show, thespians such as Edwin Forrest, Edwin Booth, Sarah Bernhardt and Ethel Barrymore regularly walked the boards at this venerable hall, now fully modernized. These days the Walnut Street Company keeps busy with a series of dramas, musicals and Shakespeare on its main stage and smaller, contemporary or experimental work in its studio. Before moving on, be sure to catch the *Starman in the Ancient Garden* statue across the street.

TIP

Although individual jewelers' shops on Jewelers Row may vary, generally they are open weekdays and Saturdays 9:30am–5:30pm, Wednesdays until 8:30pm, Sundays 11am–5pm.

BELOW: *Starman in the Ancient Garden* sculpture

Jazz musicians are a frequent sight on the streets around Washington Square.

BELOW:
George Washington watches over the Tomb of the Unknown Soldier.

Farther along Walnut, the **Forrest Theatre** ❾ (1114 Walnut Street; tel: 215-923-1515) packs in the crowds with big-time touring Broadway shows such as *Phantom of the Opera* and *Les Misérables*. The Forrest is named after stage idol Edwin Forrest, a Philadelphian whose passionate style and fiery disposition made him a national sensation. It's difficult to imagine just how popular Forrest was in his day. When he was panned by London critics, for example, his fans in Philadelphia retaliated by pelting a rival British actor, William Macready, with rotten eggs and tomatoes. When Macready later appeared in New York City, Forrest partisans stormed the theater, sparking a riot that killed 22 people in the blackest moment in American stage history.

Return to 8th Street and walk south for a look at some of the neighborhood's architectural landmarks. The townhouse at No. 225 South 8th Street is **Morris House**, built in 1786 when this area was still on the outskirts of town. The large fanlight over the door, heavy cornices, and black-and-red brickwork – known as Flemish bond – are hallmarks of the late-Georgian style. The **Musical Fund Hall**, just around the corner on Locust Street, was designed by Philadelphia architect William Strickland in the 1820s. In its brief career as the city's main concert hall, it sponsored engagements by Charles Dickens, William Makepeace Thackeray, singer Jenny Lind, and many other artists. In 1856, it hosted the first Republican National Convention, only two years after the formation of the party. The nominee, John C. Fremont, lost to James Buchanan in the general election. The building has since been converted into condominiums.

A block south, at 8th and Spruce streets, **St George's Greek Orthodox Church** ❿ (open for worship) is housed in a Greek Revival structure originally designed for an Episcopal congregation by the Philadelphia architect John

FREEDOM IS A LIGHT FOR WHICH MANY MEN HAVE DIED IN DARKNESS

IN UNMARKED GRAVES WITHIN THIS SQUARE LIE THOUSANDS OF UNKNOWN SOLDIERS OF WASHINGTON'S ARMY WHO DIED OF WOUNDS AND SICKNESS DURING THE REVOLUTIONARY WAR

THE INDEPENDENCE AND LIBERTY YOU POSSESS ARE THE WORK OF JOINT COUNCILS AND JOINT EFFORTS OF COMMON DANGERS, SUFFERINGS AND SUCCESS.
WASHINGTON'S FAREWELL ADDRESS · SEPT. 17, 1796

Haviland, who is entombed beneath the church. The interior is a heady Byzantine transformation of the original conservative Episcopal style, replete with gold-foil iconography, ornate woodwork and glowing stained glass.

Spruce Street and alleyways

Walking east on **Spruce Street** ⓫ will take you past two blocks of beautifully restored 19th-century houses. At least they look like houses. In fact, between 7th and 8th streets they are façades only, with a modern office building behind.

Holy Trinity Roman Catholic Church, erected by German immigrants in 1789, stands at 6th and Spruce streets. The church's small cemetery contains the graves of Acadian (French-Canadian) refugees who were kicked out of Nova Scotia by the English in 1755 and sheltered in Philadelphia.

To the west on Spruce Street, between 8th and 9th streets, is tiny **Mikveh Israel Cemetery** ⓬ (tel: 215-922-5446 for visiting information), consecrated in 1740 and one of America's oldest Jewish cemeteries. The congregation now has its synagogue at 44 North 4th Street on Independence Mall East, sharing a building with the National Museum of American Jewish History *(see page 115)*. Haym Salomon, an exiled Polish Jew who helped finance the American Revolution, is buried here, as is Nathan Levy, whose ship, the *Myrtilla*, transported the Liberty Bell from England. The cemetery's most celebrated occupant is Rebecca Gratz, a friend of Washington Irving and model for the character of Rebecca in Sir Walter Scott's popular novel *Ivanhoe*.

The handsome brick houses on the 900 block of Spruce Street – each with a marble portico at the entrance – are known as **Portico Row** ⓭ and were designed by the distinguished Philadelphia architect Thomas U. Walter.

You can begin to explore the neighborhood's cozy alleys farther along Spruce Street, past the weathered brownstones between 10th and 13th streets. Many of these alleys are tree-lined, with brick sidewalks, and "streets" no wider than a large cart. First try **Quince Street** ⓮, where the University of Pennsylvania's **Mask & Wig Club** (No. 310) – a bizarre yellow chateau – is tucked away amid tiny brick homes and ivy-covered cul-de-sacs. To the north of Spruce Street, Quince leads into the labyrinth of Sartain, Manning, Irving and Jessup streets. To the south, it cuts across Pine Street to a corridor of trim homes at Waverly Street and another at Addison Walk. The maze of alleyways entered at **Camac Street** ⓯ (between 12th and 13th) is even more complex, with side alleys branching off every few steps. According to the *WPA Guide to Philadelphia*, published in 1937, this sheltered byway was "the scene of brawls by day and crimes by night… lined with brothels and taverns [and] rotted in a mire of debauchery."

Camac Street was also known for the many clubs, including the **Philadelphia Sketch Club** (235 Camac Street; tel: 215-545-9298), which once boasted artists N.C. Wyeth and Thomas Eakins among its members, and which presents shows in its gallery from time to time. The **Charlotte Cushman Club**, founded in 1907 as a residence for visiting actresses, is located in a snug townhouse at No. 239. The club is best known

Map on page 142

TIP

The Inn Philadelphia, a restaurant with garden and piano bar, is tucked away at 251 South Camac Street (tel: 215-732-2339) and is a cozy place to spend an evening.

BELOW: Antique Row on Pine Street.

for its prestigious Charlotte Cushman Award; among its recipients have been Richard Burton and Helen Hayes. An appointment is needed for a tour of the building, but theater-lovers will certainly be tickled by the offbeat memorabilia. The **Plastic Club** (247 Camac Street; tel: 215-732-7492 or 610-664-1997 for tours; workshops 10am–2pm; entrance fee) was founded in 1897 as a club for women artists, and still conducts workshops open to the public.

You can follow Panama Street to 13th Street, where the 1839-built **Church of St Luke and the Epiphany** (Pine and Spruce streets; tel: 215-732-1918; open by appointment) stands in Greek Revival splendor.

A short walk north brings you to the **Library Company of Philadelphia** (1314 Locust Street; tel: 215-546-3181; reading room and gallery open Monday–Friday 9am–4:45pm) and the **Historical Society of Pennsylvania**  (Locust Street between 12th and 13th streets; tel: 215-732-6200; open Tuesday, Thursday, Saturday 10am–4:45pm, Wednesday 2–8:45pm; entrance fee), which have complementary collections. The Library Company, now a working research library, was founded in 1731 by Benjamin Franklin and was the first circulating library in America. Documenting US history through the printed word from the colonial period to about 1880, it also has a print department and collections on African-American and women's history. The Historical Society features one of the best exhibits on local history, as well as changing exhibits

Wealth and health

You can wrap up this tour by walking two blocks south to **Pine Street** ⓲, known as **Antique Row**. There are a couple of dozen antiques shops between 13th and 8th streets, not to mention a number of shops specializing in jewelry, folk art and vintage clothing. Serious collectors will find first-rate selections and expert advice at **Albert Maranga Antiques** (1100 Pine Street), **Schaffer Antiques** (1032 Pine Street), **M. Finkel and Daughter** (936 Pine Street) and **Reese's** (928–930 Pine Street), among others. **Indigo** carries a colorful collection of folk art from the Americas, Africa and Asia; **Maide Franklin** features a fine collection of jewelry. **Giovanni's Room** (325 South 12th Street) is a bookstore specializing in gay, lesbian and feminist material.

This area, between 11th and 13th and Walnut to South streets, has a number of gay bars and cafés, a couple of other gay bookstores, and a gay community center. For more complete listings, pick up a copy of the *Philadelphia Gay News* at any of the Center City newsstands *(see page 262)*.

If all this shopping makes you hungry, try one of several eateries (including a pizzeria and café) that cater to the neighborhood's Bohemian crowd. And you can't go wrong with the mountainous apple pie smothered in two huge scoops of French-vanilla ice cream at **Not Just Ice Cream** on Locust Street.

A detour south on 10th Street brings you to the **Henry George School** ⓲ (413 South 10th Street; tel: 215-922-4278; museum open by appointment), birthplace of the visionary economist whose *Progress and Poverty* was a bestseller in the 1880s. George believed that a "single tax" on land would narrow the gap

BELOW: antiques stores do brisk business in Philadelphia.

between rich and poor. At the height of his single-tax movement, he nearly became mayor of New York City, running as the candidate of the United Labor Party. He died in 1897, just four days before the election. Although few people remember George these days, there are still faithful Georgists who feel that the self-educated economist's ideas are as valid now as 100 years ago. The school houses a modest museum of memorabilia and offers seminars.

Backtrack on 10th Street just north of Pine for a quick look at Clinton Street, one of the neighborhood's prettiest and most exclusive. The walled complex of buildings at Clinton and 9th streets is **Pennsylvania Hospital ⑲** (entrance at 8th and Spruce streets; tel: 215-829-3971; Welcome Center open Monday–Friday, 8:30am–5pm, guided tours of 10 or more by appointment with 2–4 weeks notice; entrance free). The oldest hospital in the country, it was founded in 1751 by Benjamin Franklin. You can get a good look at the original buildings by walking along the iron fence on Pine Street and then entering through the 8th Street gate. The east wing was completed in 1775; the west wing and central pavilion – a masterpiece of Federal architecture – were finished about 30 years later. The statue of William Penn was given to the hospital by Penn's grandson John, who found the piece in a London junkyard and had it shipped to Philadelphia. It's said that at the stroke of midnight on New Year's Eve, the statue steps off its pedestal for a stroll around the grounds. A tour of the hospital takes you through the historic medical library and surgical amphitheater where distinguished physicians such as Benjamin Rush, Philip Syng Physick and Caspar Wistar made breakthroughs in the healing arts. The hospital's treasures include a collection of surgical instruments, a chair used by Penn, several Sully portraits, and Benjamin West's painting *Christ Healing the Sick in the Temple*. ❑

William Penn stands before his landmark, the Pennsylvania Hospital.

BELOW: Philadelphia is a medical mecca.

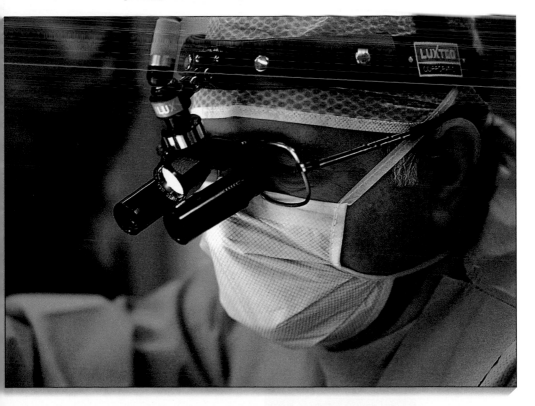

ARCHITECTURE: HISTORY UNDER CONSTRUCTION

Philadelphia's architecture spans the history of the US, from Federal and Georgian, to Victorian, to modern-day gleaming glass skyscrapers

As you walk westward from the Delaware River through the city, many buildings help track Philadelphia's historical and architectural development.

Old City and Society Hill were settled first and have fine examples of Georgian architecture, such as Christ Church (1727–44) at 2nd and Market and Independence Hall (1729) along Chestnut between 5th and 6th. Both are brick, with symmetrical design and classical details. Society Hill's narrow residential streets retain original colonial homes.

The 1800s saw the use of the Greek Revival style in the Second Bank of the United States (1818–24) on Chestnut Street, and the Merchant's Exchange (1832) at 143 South 3rd Street, both by William Strickland. The mid-1800s gave rise to more ornate styles: the Cathedral of Sts Peter and Paul (1846–64) on Logan Square, by Napoleon LeBrun and John Notman, has a grand Italian Renaissance interior. An outstanding example of Victorian architecture by Frank Furness is the Academy of Fine Arts (1872–76) on Broad Street.

The 20th century has spanned a range of styles, from the Neo-Classical Girard Trust Building (1905–8), now the Ritz Carlton Hotel, to skyscrapers including the International-style PSFS Building (1930–31) (now Loews Philadelphia Hotel). More recently, Two Liberty Place (1990) and the Bell Atlantic Tower (1991) have joined the skyline.

▷ **GLASS SPIRES**
One Liberty Place (1987), at 960 ft (293 meters), was the first building to top William Penn's City Hall hat.

△ **CITY LANDMARK**
Second Empire-style City Hall is the largest municipal building in the US, topped by a 27-ton cast iron statue of William Penn, long the tallest point in the city.

▷ **ART AND ARCHITECTURE**
The imposing Classical style of the Philadelphia Museum of Art, with its grand Corinthian columns at the entrance, resembles a modern-day Greek Temple.

△ COLONIAL GEM
Elfreth's Alley is generally considered to be the oldest continuously inhabited street in the country.

▽ GRAND AVENUE
An aerial view of Benjamin Franklin Parkway illustrates its impressive swathe across the city's landscape.

▽ HOME SWEET HOME
Built in 1798, Strawberry Mansion in Fairmount Park is one of the finest surviving Federal-style residences.

▽ OLD MEETS NEW
The train shed of Reading Terminal Market is the only surviving single span arched train shed in the US.

A GRACIOUS THOROUGHFARE

In 1917, the Benjamin Franklin Parkway made a bold mark on the city, and is an outstanding example of the Beaux Arts design popular among early 20th-century architects and planners. The Parkway, both gracious and functional, created a broad green diagonal connecting City Hall to the new art museum being built atop Faire Mount, the site of the city's new waterworks.

Designed by Jacques Greber and Paul Phillipe Cret, the Parkway was modeled after the Champs Elysées in Paris. It begins at Logan Circle, the site of one of Penn's original town squares, with the delightful Swann Fountain (*above*) in the center. The wide tree-lined avenue ends below the museum at Eakins Oval, named after the Philadelphia painter Thomas Eakins.

The Philadelphia Museum of Art (built 1916–28) sits at the top of an expansive staircase flanked by more fountains. Influential in its design was Julian Abele, chief designer for Horace Trumbauer and the first African-American graduate of the University of Pennsylvania's school of architecture. The view back down the Parkway to Center City from the top of the steps is magnificent.

CITY HALL TO THE CONVENTION CENTER

Map on page 142

The vast monolith of City Hall looms over Center City, surrounded by Philadelphia's main business, arts and shopping districts, and the exhibition venue of the Convention Center

T hey started working on it back in 1871, it took no less than 30 years to complete, and about halfway through the project somebody tagged it "the biggest and ugliest building in America." City Hall, at once monstrous and magnificent, sits squarely on the bull's-eye of downtown Philadelphia like an urban version of some inscrutable Egyptian pyramid, evoking ambivalent awe. Walt Whitman sized it up as "a magnificent pile… weird, silent, beautiful," and the American Institute of Architecture later pronounced it "the greatest single effort of late 19th-century architecture."

Love it or hate it, you'll find it hard to ignore this endearing hangover from the gaudy age of architectural excess. It stands right in the heart of Center City, at the intersection of the two major thoroughfares of Broad and Market streets, former site of William Penn's 8-acre (3-hectare) Center Square. To the west is Philadelphia's business district, bristling with a fresh wave of glass-and-granite skyscrapers. To the east is a cavernous new Convention Center and the city's largest shopping area. And to the north and south along Broad, the newly named Avenue of the Arts, are the homes of world-class cultural institutions, including the oldest opera house and art school-museum in the United States.

Heart of the city

Designed by John McArthur and Thomas U. Walter, and adorned with hundreds of sculptures by Alexander Milne Calder, Philadelphia's **City Hall** ❷⓿ (Broad and Market streets, tour office in East Portal, room 121; tel: 215-686 1776/2840; tower open Monday–Friday 9:30am–4:15pm for six people at a time, sign up in room 121, 90-minute tours, including tower, 12:30pm; entrance free) is the largest municipal building in the country. Its style is classified as Second Empire – reflecting, perhaps, a sense of optimism that bespeaks the American romance with Victorian architecture in the latter part of the 19th century. Its massive granite walls are 22 ft (6 meters) thick at the base, and its central tower, the world's tallest masonry structure without steel reinforcement, rises 510 ft (145 meters) above street level. Calder's famous 27-ton statue of William Penn adds another 37 ft (10.5 meters).

Until the 1980s, a gentlemen's agreement prevented the construction of any building whose height would exceed the top of William Penn's hat, but with the construction of developer William S. Rouse's Liberty One in 1987 *(see page 157)*, quickly followed by others, Philadelphia's skyline has grown over recent years to reflect its place as a contemporary city alive with change.

LEFT: grand interior of City Hall.
BELOW: Christmas on Broad Street.

The observation deck atop City Hall Tower is just below William Penn's toes, and though it is no longer the highest point in the city, the panorama is still wonderful, giving a great sense how Penn's city plan has evolved. To reach the observation deck, take the elevator from the northwest corner (15th Street and JFK Boulevard) to the seventh floor and then follow the red lines. A second elevator takes you the rest of the way. But be prepared to wait. During peak season and weekends, it can take an hour or more before you get lifted into the heavens. If you'd like a closer look at some of City Hall's splendid public rooms, take the free 90-minute tour. It includes, among other sights, Conservation Hall, the City Council Chambers, the Supreme Court, and the Mayor's Reception Room.

The imposing medieval-style building to the north of City Hall is **Masonic Temple ㉑** (1 North Broad Street; tel: 215-988-1916/7; tours Monday–Friday 10am, 11am, 1pm, 2pm and 3pm, Saturday 10am and 11pm except July–August; entrance free). This is the headquarters of the Grand Lodge of Free and Accepted Masons of Pennsylvania and one of the most spectacular Masonic structures in the world. Designed in 1868 by 27-year-old James Windrim, the building is a monumental patchwork of architectural styles.

A free tour guides visitors through seven lavishly decorated lodge halls, each reflecting a major architectural style – Oriental, Gothic, Ionic, Egyptian, Norman, Renaissance and Corinthian. The scale of the place is dazzling, the workmanship masterful, and the Masons' predilection for arcane symbols is evident throughout the building. The tour ends at the Masonic Museum, which features all sorts of paraphernalia, much of it originally owned by historical figures such as the Marquis de Lafayette, Andrew Jackson, Ben Franklin and George Washington.

A City Hall statue is sihouetted against the Masonic Temple.

BELOW: modern sculptures enliven the concrete plazas of Center City.

Walk north on Broad Street past the Gothic spires of the Arch Street Methodist Church, erected in 1865, to the **Pennsylvania Academy of the Fine Arts** ㉒ (118 North Broad Street; tel: 215-972-7600; open Monday–Saturday 10am–5pm, Sunday 11am–5pm; entrance fee except Sunday 3–5pm), the oldest art school and museum in the country. Frank Furness' Victorian tour de force is as much a work of art as the paintings it contains. Highly eclectic and idiosyncratic, this building is a fine example of the stylistic mix-and-match that became Furness' hallmark. The interior is a riotous counterpoint of deep-blue ceilings, red-veined marble floors, Moorish arcades, gilt accents and purplish walls with a gold floral pattern. You might expect the building to overpower the art, but it doesn't – the Pennsylvania Academy is fortunate to own one of the strongest collections of early American art in the country.

Exhibitions change regularly, but you're more than likely to find works by Charles Willson Peale, Benjamin West, Gilbert Stuart, Washington Allston, Mary Cassatt, Winslow Homer, Andrew Wyeth and the Academy's most celebrated student and teacher, Thomas Eakins, who was dismissed from the faculty for his insistence on using female nude models in a class that included women. The Academy also shows contemporary work, much of it by students or faculty members, particularly in the first-floor Morris Gallery. Call ahead for details on gallery talks, receptions and daily tours.

Map
on page
142

South on Broad

Retrace your steps to City Hall, looping around 15th Street for a look at downtown's best-known (if not best-loved) public sculptures, including Joseph Brown's *Benjamin Franklin, Craftsman*, Jacques Lipchitz's *Government of the*

BELOW:
Pennsylvania
Academy of
the Fine Arts.

William Penn

Like some benevolent *padrone*, William Penn has perched serenely atop City Hall since 1894, overseeing the real estate he acquired in 1681 from Charles II in satisfaction of a debt the king owed Penn's father. But if this statue – 37 ft (11 meters) tall and 547 ft (165 meters) above ground – strikes the visitor as precarious, it is an apt impression: Penn's grip on Philadelphia was never too firm. Who owned what, how the place was to be governed, theological hair-splitting that pitted Quaker against Anglican and Quaker against Quaker – it was at times an unbrotherly stew that mired the affairs of the Founder, who didn't spend all that much time here anyway.

Turmoil was nothing new to Penn. He lived through civil strife and regicide, fire and plague. Born in 1644 in London, he was sufficiently nonconformist (after embracing Quakerism, he was expelled from Oxford) for Admiral Penn to dispatch his upstart son on a Continental tour. But Quakerism stuck with Penn, providing the touchstone for his utopian designs on Pennsylvania.

A religious liberal, Penn preached and pamphleteered and got into familial and civil hot water. Confined to the Tower of London for a spell, he churned out more tracts in prison. In 1672, he married Gulielma Maria Springett, who was pregnant eight times in their first 13 years of marriage. She died in Penn's arms in 1694. Two years later he married another Quaker, 24-year-old Hannah Callowhill, begetting seven children by her.

Penn first visited his colony in 1682, just after his 38th birthday. He had promoted it so well that a couple of thousand settlers were already on hand to greet him. Penn named Philadelphia and shaped its block pattern along orderly grid lines, did land deals with the Indians and went back to England in 1684. He returned for his second, and final, visit 15 years later.

Although remembered for his tolerant leanings, Penn had his complexities. The free-holding aspirations of his settlers clashed with his own seigneurial impulse. Although he insisted on fair-dealing with Indians, he regarded them as little more than noble savages. While Quakers were among the earliest to denounce slavery, Penn himself was a slaveholder. Yet Penn's "holy experiment" laid the foundation for America's first melting pot, predating by nearly a century Jefferson's declaration that "all men are created equal."

From the very beginning, however, Penn was vexed by changing political and economic fortunes. Mired in debt, he considered selling the colony back to the British crown in 1712 for less than its original value, but the deal was dropped when he suffered a stroke. It would take another 64 years and a revolution to bring an end to the Penn arrangement.

The statue atop City Hall, crafted by Scottish-born Alexander Milne Calder, adorns a French Renaissance-style building presided over by a succession of Americans tending the affairs of a polyglot community. The city is the legacy of a man who took his final leave of it in 1701. In all, Penn had spent less than four years in Pennsylvania. ❑

LEFT: the young William Penn, already a fervent Quaker and campaigner.

People, Claes Oldenburg's colossal *Clothespin*, and Robert Engman's pretzel-like *Triune*. Much of the artwork here is a product of Philadelphia's one percent rule, which earmarks this percentage of municipal costs for public art.

Heading south on Broad Street, you'll pass the domed and gleaming white Neo-Classical **Ritz-Carlton ㉓** (10 Avenue of the Arts; tel: 1-800-241-3333), formerly the Girard Trust Company and later Mellon bank. Built between 1905 and 1908 it is a loose adaptation of the Roman Parthenon, designed by Stanford White and Frank Furness. Take a look into the luxurious lobby, where giant columns loom like redwood trees, and the central rotunda looks down (through a glittering chandelier) on the ballroom below. Ask at the desk about the availability of tours. The **Land Title Building**, an early skyscraper built in 1897, is on the next corner. And the Union League (1865) – a private club organized by well-to-do patriots during the Civil War – is housed in a Second Empire brownstone mansion with a sweeping double staircase at the corner of Sansom Street.

A block away, the venerable old Bellevue-Stratford Hotel has been reborn as the **Park Hyatt Atop the Bellevue**. After a multimillion-dollar face-lift, the street level has been converted into high-class retail space where a handful of up-scale stores like Polo Ralph Lauren and Tiffany & Co. do business in marble and mahogany digs. A more moderately priced food court on the lower level is a good place for a quick lunch, where you can get everything from hoagies and pizza to Mexican food, salads, Chinese and sushi.

The hotel also accommodates several fine restaurants including The Palm, a fancy steakhouse known for gargantuan slabs of beef and a high-profile clientele, Ciboulette and, on the top floor, Founders, sky-high and ultra-elegant with thrilling views of Center City. The popular jazz club and restaurant, **Zanzibar Blue** (200 South Broad Street; tel: 215 732-5200), sets its stage on the lower level, accessible from Broad Street.

Avenue of the Arts

Jazz is just one of the musical forms you'll hear on Broad Street, recently tagged the "Avenue of the Arts." The proliferation of theaters and other performance venues, particularly south of City Hall, has been intense. One of the most interesting is the Prince Music Theater, specializing in new and innovative music and drama, just west of the avenue on Chestnut (1412 Chestnut Street; tel:215-972-1000).

Opened in 1857, the **Academy of Music ㉔** (232–46 Broad Street; tel: 215-893-1999 box office/ 215-893-1935 for tours) is the oldest music hall in the US still in use. Designed by Napoleon Le Brun and Gustave Runge, and renowned for its fine acoustics, the Academy has welcomed a host of illustrious speakers and musicians, among them Abraham Lincoln, Tchaikovsky, and conductors of the Philadelphia Orchestra, among them Leopold Stokowski, Eugene Ormandy, Riccardo Muti and Wolfgang Sawallisch. As well as its musical achievements, the Academy, with its Neo-Baroque interior modeled after La Scala in Milan, is one of the best-loved buildings in the city, fondly referred to as the "Grand Old Lady of Broad Street."

Map on page 142

Hop aboard the Phlash bus to reach the main attractions.

BELOW: lobby of the Ritz Carlton Hotel.

The Pennsylvania Ballet Company is world-renowned.

However, the Philadelphia Orchestra has for some time sought a new space with acoustics more tailored to a symphony orchestra concert (as opposed to opera) hall. After years of public ambivalence typical of many new projects in the city, construction is now in progress for a new concert venue at the junction of Spruce and Broad streets. The **Kimmel Center for the Performing Arts** ㉕ will be one of the major new players on the Avenue of the Arts. Designed by architect Rafael Viñoly, acoustics designer Russell Johnson and theater designer Richard Pilbrow, the Kimmel Center will consist of a 2,500-seat Concert Hall for the Philadelphia Orchestra, as well as a 650-seat Recital Theater, which will be used by the American Theater Arts for Youth, the Philadelphia Chamber Music Society, Concerto Soloists Chamber Orchestra of Philadelphia, and Philadanco. The Academy of Music, on the other hand, will be maintained as home to the Pennsylvania Ballet and the Opera Company of Philadelphia *(see page 285)*, and will host Broadway and other visiting productions.

The performance theme continues across Broad Street. The **Wilma Theater** (265 South Broad Street; tel: 215-893-9456) has moved into a splashy new hall. The new halls are joining the Arts Bank (southeast corner of Broad and South streets), which offers theater and rehearsal space in a renovated bank. There is also the **Merriam Theater**, which features Broadway shows, concerts, opera, and pop music and the **Pennsylvania Ballet** (1101 South Broad Street; tel: 215-551-7000) and the **Opera Company of Philadelphia** (510 Walnut Street; tel: 215-928-2100), the **Philadelphia Clef Club for Jazz and the Performing Arts** (736–8 South Broad Street; tel: 215-893-9912), the **Brandywine Workshop** (730 South Broad Street; tel: 1-800-546-2825) and the **University of the Arts** (320 South Broad Street; tel: 1-800-616-ARTS), which is

BELOW:
Philadelphia's
Academy of Music.

housed in one of John Haviland's stark Greek Revival structures at Pine and Broad streets. The school shows work by students and guest artists in the main hall and at the Rosenwald-Wolf and Mednick galleries across the street. (For more details on performances and tickets for events, *see page 283*.)

Map on page 142

Corporate muscle

Big changes have been made in the business district west of City Hall, too. A fresh crop of office towers on Market Street is pumping new vigor into an area that hasn't seen much action since the early 1960s, when the **Penn Center** complex rose from the ruins of the old Chinese Wall. The twin towers of I.M. Pei's Commerce Square at 20th and Market streets, site of the snazzy Cutter's Grand Café, and the granite-and-glass towers of both the Mellon Bank Center and 1919 Market Street are among the most conspicuous additions to the skyline. But the real head-turner in this area is **Liberty Place** ㉖ (17th and Market streets), a pair of glass-plated towers (Liberty One and Liberty Two) reminiscent of New York City's Chrysler Building.

The two-level shopping arcade at Two Liberty Place (entrance at 16th and Chestnut streets) is a glossy addition to the neighborhood, with lots of polished marble tiles, shiny brass trims and a sunlit central rotunda, as well as an upstairs food court with a vast array of choices for a quick lunch. The shops and eateries are predictably trendy, although Sfuzzi, a swanky Italian restaurant and bar, and the Rand McNally travel bookstore are worth a special look.

You can watch the wheels of capitalism turn two blocks away at the **Philadelphia Stock Exchange** ㉗ (1900 Market Street; tel: 215-496-5000; open Monday–Friday 8am–5pm; entrance free) which, dating from 1790, is

LEFT:
Market Place East.
BELOW:
views of City Hall
from Broad Street.

the oldest stock exchange in the US The trading floor is built around an eight-story atrium where visitors can follow the action through plate-glass windows while lounging in a small "forest" complete with waterfalls, fountains and thousands of plants.

Market Street was once called High Street, but the eastern end was the site of the city's first market and in common parlance it was referred to as "market street" for so long, the name was officially changed.

Market East

To the east of City Hall, Market Street used to be dominated by discount shops and department stores, reflecting, perhaps, its early history as the locus of city shopping. As development moved westward towards the center of the city, large departments stores developed.

The granddaddy of all department stores was the former John Wanamaker, now **Lord & Taylor** (13th and Market streets), a Philadelphia institution since the 1870s, when department store pioneer John Wanamaker (the first merchant to introduce the use of price tags) moved his first dry-goods shop into the old Pennsylvania Railroad depot. Alas, Wanamaker's was sold in 1995 to become Lord & Taylor. The current building was completed in 1911 and features a magnificent five-story Grand Court where Wanamaker's old mascot, a giant bronze eagle, keeps an eye on shoppers waiting in line at the gourmet counter. The airy Grand Court is the site of spectacular Christmas light shows and a great place to stroll during the daily organ concerts, performed on a 30,000-pipe organ – said to be the largest in the world. The fate of the organ under new ownership remains uncertain, however.

St John the Evangelist Church (13th Street, between Market and Chestnut streets; tel: 215-563-4145; open Monday–Friday 9am–5pm) is located around the corner on 13th Street. Built in 1832, it was the second Roman Catholic cathedral in Philadelphia.

BELOW:
Christmas lights
at Lord & Taylor.

With the arrival of the Pennsylvania Convention Center, east Market Street has continued to change dramatically, particularly around City Hall, where there is now a Marriot Hotel, a Loew's Hotel located in the old PSFS Building, and a Hard Rock Café on the corner of 12th and Market streets, adjacent to the Market Street entrance to the Convention Center. The **PSFS Building** at 12th and Market streets, built between 1930 and 1932 and long known for its giant neon sign, was the first American skyscraper to be built in the International style, the forerunner of the glass-skinned monoliths that sprang up in the country the 1950s and 1960s.

Convention Center district

The **Pennsylvania Convention Center** (Visitor Services at the Convention Center, tel: 215-418-4735 for information about free tours available by appointment only), a 1.3 million-sq ft (1.2-million sq meter) facility hosting major exhibition shows and events, runs along Arch Street from 11th to 13th streets, with its main entrance at 12th and Arch streets. There is also a grand entrance on Market Street, where the head house for the Reading Terminal Railroad used to be. Inside the center an escalator leads up into the cavernous Grand Hall, which was formerly the railroad's train shed.

The new facility passes over **Reading Terminal Market** ③ (12th and Arch streets; tel: 215-922-2317; open Monday–Saturday 8am–6pm), a boisterous food bazaar that has existed in one form or another for more than 100 years. Today, vendors offer a bewildering array of everything from sushi to scrapple, *bok choi* to baklava. In addition to fresh produce, meats and seafood, you'll find a slew of Philadelphia specialties: chocolate-chip cookies from the Famous 4th Street Deli, Rick's Philly Steaks, related to the original Pat's King of Steaks *(see page 203)*, Bassetts' irresistible ice cream and the Termini Brothers' scrumptious Italian pastries – not to mention hearty meats, sweets and baked goods brought to Philadelphia by members of the Pennsylvania Dutch community *(see page 85)*.

And that's only the beginning. In the mood for seafood? Try Pearl's Oyster Bar. Fancy a blue-corn enchilada? Have a bite at the 12th Street Cantina. How about an ice-cold brew at the Beer Garden? Rib sticking Southern cuisine at the Down Home Diner? Scrapple and eggs at the Dutch Eating Place? And be sure to save enough room for one of Fisher's famous pretzels.

Having satiated yourself, shopping is next on the agenda at **The Gallery** (entrance on 9th and Market streets; tel: 215-625-4962; open Monday–Saturday 10am–7pm, Wednesday and Friday until 8pm, Sunday noon–5pm), a four-block mall stretching from 12th to 8th streets with three major department stores and some 200 shops and restaurants set in an airy, skylit atrium. Between 8th and 7th streets, the old Little Brothers Department Store – a beautiful white cast iron structure – has been transformed into **Market Place East**, a mixed-use complex of shops, restaurants and offices. You'll find even more shopping opportunities a block away on Chestnut Street.

Map on page 142

The Convention Center district is a great place to eat.

BELOW: outside and inside the popular Reading Terminal Market.

Map
on page
142

Authentic Chinese cuisine can be found all over Chinatown.

BELOW: a mural marks the site of the African-American Museum.

Ethnic influence

If you're still hungry, drift over to **Chinatown**, where about 45 restaurants are packed between 9th and 11th streets on one side, and Vine and Arch streets on the other. Nearly all are Chinese, of course, but there are also excellent Vietnamese and Thai places, and most are reasonably priced. Gift shops and grocery stores carry a bonanza of exotic Asian goodies. You can stock up on fortune cookies at the Chinese Cookie Factory, Chinese pastries at Diamond Bakery (232 North 10th Street), or Chinese noodles at the East Asia Noodle Company (212 North 11th Street) and New Tung Hop (133 North 11th Street).

While you're in the neighborhood, be sure to see the 40-ft (11-meter) **Chinese Friendship Gate** ③ at 10th and Arch streets, built by craftsmen in 1984 as a sign of friendship between Philadelphia and Tianjin. The **Chinese Cultural and Community Center** ㉜ (125 North 10th Street) is modeled after a Mandarin palace and is the annual site of a traditional 10-course banquet in celebration of the Chinese New Year *(see page 288)*.

Just east of Chinatown is the first major museum devoted exclusively to African-American culture, the **African-American Historical and Cultural Museum** ㉝ (701 Arch Street; tel: 215-574-0380; open Tuesday–Saturday 10am–5pm, Sunday noon–5pm; entrance fee). Exhibits explore the African-American experience and influence in American life, including the arts, architecture, sports, politics, religion, technology and medicine. Previous shows have chronicled the history of the slave trade, migration of African-American families to various Philadelphia neighborhoods, and the role of Philadelphia's community in the Civil Rights movement. Every February, the museum hosts "Jazz 'til Sunrise," an all-night jazz jam featuring noted jazz artists. ❏

The Barnes Method

When they talk about "The Method" in Philadelphia, chances are they're not talking about Stanislavsky or Strasberg but about Dr Albert Barnes. He was an eccentric art collector whose Method has made Philadelphia the center of a heated debate in the art world. At issue is whether a private collector has the right to keep a world-class art collection out of the public eye and whether the edicts of a late collector should dictate how people view masterpieces.

Barnes made his millions by inventing Argyrol, an antiseptic. He channeled his fortune into a collection of French Impressionists that, at the time, was looked down upon by critics. He made his bid for respectability in 1923, showing his collection at the Pennsylvania Academy of the Fine Arts. The reviews were not good. Outraged, Barnes acquired a 12-acre estate in Merion, built a gallery to house his collection, and set up the Barnes Foundation, a non-profit, tax-exempt educational organization.

The collection consisted of some 800 paintings – including 180 Renoirs, 60 Matisses, 59 Cézannes, 19 Picassos and assorted Seurats, Modiglianis, Rousseaus, El Grecos and Titians. Firmly against the use of historical explanation and the comments of both critics and the artists themselves, Barnes concluded that art should be analyzed scientifically. To that end, the paintings in his collection were hung in deliberate patterns stressing context, surrounded by antiques. He also removed the works' dates and titles. And only students of his Method saw them, at least until 1961, when a lawsuit challenged the right of the Barnes Foundation to be tax-exempt as long as the works were not available to the public.

After that, the Barnes Foundation was more accessible, but still under the strict edicts of Barnes's will. No photographs were allowed, paintings were not to be loaned out, rehung or reproduced. Critics weren't welcome.

The rules eased a bit when attorney Richard Glanton, a trustee of Lincoln University, was named president of the Barnes Foundation in 1990. Barnes had offered his collection to the University of Pennsylvania if it would teach the Barnes Method, but it was Lincoln which agreed to it.

Glanton and his successor, Kimberly Camp, have made many changes at the Foundation, arousing objections from both loyal students of Barnes and local neighbors, who resist the idea of an international tourist attraction down the block. In 1992, to finance renovation of the gallery, much of the collection was sent on a worldwide tour. New leadership has (with court approval) increased visitor attendance from 500 to 1,200 per week, and opening times from two to three days a week. Also, tensions have eased as more people discover the art and eccentricity, and the 11-acre arboretum that is the Barnes (300 North Latche's Lane, Merion; tel: 610-667-0290; open by reservation September–June Friday–Sunday, July–August Wednesday–Friday; entrance fee). ❑

RIGHT: two eccentrics together – Dr Albert Barnes and Salvador Dalí.

RITTENHOUSE

Map on page 166

From the vast mansions of Philadelphia's 19th-century rich, to the Bohemian shopping streets filled with boutiques and bookstores, Rittenhouse is reminiscent of New York's Greenwich Village

Rittenhouse is the *grande dame* of Philadelphia – a few years past her prime, perhaps, but still handsome, haughty and resolutely upper-crust. This was the Philadelphia of old families and old money, an enclave of Victorian splendor in a sea of "Quaker gray," a place where one finds, in novelist Henry James's polished description, a "bestitching of the drab with pink and green and silver."

Rittenhouse Square

At the heart of the neighborhood is **Rittenhouse Square ❶**, named in honor of colonial clockmaker-astronomer David Rittenhouse who, like his predecessor Benjamin Franklin, was president of the American Philosophical Society and a major figure in both science and government. Rittenhouse Square hit its stride in the late 1800s when the wealthy families that once occupied the narrow streets of the colonial city moved into more spacious and stylish homes west of Broad Street. It was a period of explosive growth in Philadelphia. Energized by the meteoric rise of an industrial élite, a new breed of architects like John Notman, Wilson Eyre and Frank Furness were compelled toward ever more exuberant and eclectic designs that were more in keeping with the city's new status as an industrial giant.

While many of the old-line well-to-do families have moved away to Chestnut Hill or the suburban comforts of the Main Line, a few remain to keep the home fires burning, and new residents with means continue to settle in the area. For although a number of the grand Victorian mansions that once surrounded Rittenhouse Square have been replaced by contemporary apartment buildings, this is still one of the most prestigious addresses in the city, and has community groups active to keep it that way. Rittenhouse Square, with its 6 acres (2.5 hectares) of green intersected by shaded benches and curving walkways, is both a geographical and social crossroad that brings together a cross-section of neighborhood residents.

Young professionals can be seen power-walking in the morning and power-lunching in the afternoon; fur-clad dowagers walk their dogs; homeless people hang out in the shade; mothers watch their kids play on the bronze goat and dip their feet in the reflecting pool. People on their lunchbreaks picnic on the benches, and some of the surrounding restaurants have been reported to deliver sandwiches to patrons ordering from here by cellphone. During the May Flower Market, the square is a rainbow-colored sea of petals and pollen. In spring, the Clothesline Exhibit transforms it into an enormous open-air gallery where artists pin up their work in the hope of catching a collector's eye.

PRECEDING PAGES: aerial view of Rittenhouse Square. **LEFT:** music-maker. **BELOW:** St Mark's Church detail.

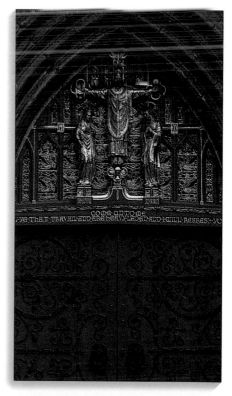

Strolling the square

As you walk the perimeter of the square, you can see traces of the old glory days coexisting gracefully with the new. At 18th and Walnut streets, the **Van Rensselaer Mansion ❷**, one of the country's great Beaux Arts mansions, is currently occupied by the up-scale Anthropologie (tel: 1-800-309-2500), selling clothing and household items with exotic designs from other cultures. Although much of the interior has been gutted, the ornate mantels, domed stained-glass skylight and the unusual ceiling paintings of Venice are still intact.

Fresh flowers brighten up the neighborhood.

Next to the Van Rensselaer Mansion, the **Presbyterian Ministers' Fund**, the oldest life insurance company in the country, is housed in the dignified Alison Building, the ground floor of which is a rambling Barnes & Noble store, where you can browse, sip cappuccino and listen to readings by noted authors.

On the northwest corner of the square, John Notman's Romanesque **Church of the Holy Trinity** (Walnut Street between 19th and 20th streets; tel: 215-567-1267; open by appointment), once the city's most fashionable congregation, is overshadowed by the modern sawtooth profile of the **Rittenhouse Hotel** (210 West Rittenhouse Square; tel: 215-546-9000), where afternoon tea is a tradition at the cozy Cassatt Lounge, which has its own outdoor garden. Smith & Wollensky Steak House beckons at street level and views of Rittenhouse Square can be found in Treetops (tel: 215-790-2533), specializing in American and Continental cuisine.

A row of Victorian townhouses still occupies the southwest corner of the square adjacent to the **Ethical Society**, a "humanist religious fellowship" dating from 1920 that offers "Sunday platforms" on a wide range of topics and issues. At the southeast corner, the once posh **Barclay Hotel** stands next to the **Curtis**

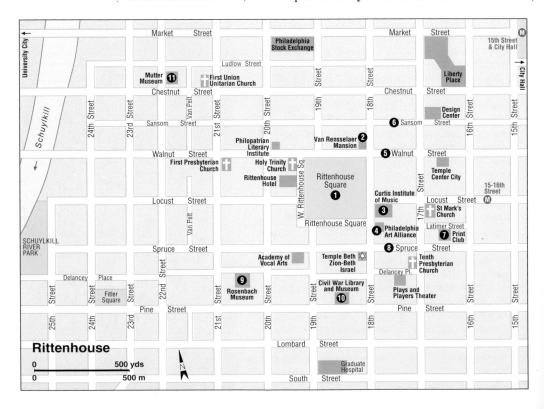

Map
on page
166

Institute of Music ❸ (18th and Locust streets; tel: 215-893-7902), a world-renowned conservatory established in 1924 by Mary Louise Curtis Bok Zimbalist, daughter of publishing magnate Cyrus Curtis. Among Curtis's well-known alumni are Leonard Bernstein, Gian-Carlo Menotti and Samuel Barber. Performances, including free student concerts, are held at the concert hall.

On the other side of the Barclay is the **Philadelphia Art Alliance ❹** (251 South 18th Street; tel: 215-545-4302; open Tuesday–Sunday 11am–5pm; entrance free), housed in the grand old Wetherill Mansion. Exhibits change about every eight weeks and range over the spectrum of fine arts – painting, sculpture, crafts, photography, drawing – by well-known artists and unknowns. Call ahead for a schedule of free readings, recitals, performances and lectures.

Continuing north along 18th Street, you'll find fashionable and comfortable restaurants on the square, **Rouge 98** (210 South 18th Street; tel: 215-732-6622) and **Devon Seafood Restaurant** (225 South 18th Street; tel: 215-546-5940), both of which in good weather open onto the sidewalk with *al fresco* dining.

Neighborhood feel

As in other parts of Philadelphia, every street has a distinctive character. **Walnut Street ❺** along the northern border and running east of the square, is the heart of what is called Rittenhouse Row, which includes a bevy of smart shops, including Rodier, Lagos, Burberry and Jacques Ferber. If you're a book-lover, you can choose between Borders and Barnes & Noble on Walnut or visit a local landmark, the family-run **Joseph Fox Bookshop** (1724 Sansom Street; tel: 215-563-4184). Narrow **Sansom Street ❻**, north of and parallel to Walnut, with its edgy attitude, bookstores, theaters and restaurants, is like a slice of New York's Greenwich Village.

The neighborhood also offers prime gallery-hopping. There are a number of galleries in the Rittenhouse Square area, including those specializing in Impressionist work, 19th- and early 20th-century paintings, and French decorative arts *(see page 283)*.

Between the stores, the galleries, the professional office spaces, and nearby cultural institutions, there are a lot of people out at lunch and dinner. Luckily, there's a restaurant for just about every taste and budget in this neighborhood, although along Walnut Street there's a concentration of places for more elegant dining. There's no matching **Le Bec Fin** (1523 Walnut Street; tel: 215-567-1000), one of the country's finest French restaurants, or **Susanna Foo** (1512 Walnut Street; tel: 215-545-2666), cited by critics for consistently imaginative Chinese cuisine. There are many more dining options in the area to choose from, but none of them are for budget travelers *(see page 273)*.

A short jaunt south on 17th Street past the opulent **Warwick Hotel** brings you to Locust Street, where **St Mark's Church** (Locust between 16th and 17th streets; tel: 215-735-1416; open for worship, group tours by appointment), a Gothic Revival masterpiece designed by John Notman, has stood since 1851. The handsome buildings across the street are the handiwork of several prominent architects, including Notman and Wilson Eyre.

TIP

Striped Bass (1500 Walnut Street; tel: 215-732-4444) has garnered great reviews for its food and its dining room is striking. Fans of the film *The Sixth Sense* may recognize it as the place where Bruce Willis showed up late for his anniversary dinner

BELOW: Rittenhouse Square in bloom.

In 1995, local merchants formed a consortium called "Rittenhouse Row," to strengthen the perception of the swank area as one with the finest restaurants and shops, art galleries and cultural venues in the city.

Continue south on 17th Street and detour into narrow Latimer Street, where you'll find changing exhibits of prints and photographs at the **Print Club ❼** (1614 Latimer Street; tel: 215-735-6090; open Tuesday–Saturday; entrance free), founded in 1915. Check the gift shop for one-of-a-kind prints, stationery and handmade books. Latimer Street is occupied by a number of other clubs, including the Pennsylvania Society of the Colonial Dames of America, and is a great place to peek into some of the lush gardens behind mansion walls.

South of the square

To the south of Rittenhouse Square, the neighborhood is largely residential, with an occasional florist, antiques shop or doctor's office at street level. **Spruce Street ❽** is the most interesting architecturally, with a fine row of brownstones between 20th and 21st streets, and homes by Frank Furness (2132–34 Spruce Street and 235 South 21st Street), Wilson Eyre (315–17 South 22nd Street) and George Hewitt (2100 Spruce Street). The Tenth Presbyterian Church (17th and Spruce streets; tel: 215-735-7688; open by appointment), a combination of styles and materials, is a paragon of Victorian eclecticism, with a prominent bell-tower. The mansion behind the church was once owned by Harry K. Thaw, who, in a scandalous episode, shot his wife's lover, the New York architect Stanford White. It seems that White flaunted the affair by using Mrs Thaw as the model for his nude sculpture *Diana*, which once stood atop New York's old Madison Square Garden and is now housed at the Philadelphia Museum of Art.

A block away, at 18th and Spruce streets, **Temple Beth Zion-Beth Israel** (tel:215-735-5148; open Monday–Thursday 9am–5pm, Friday 9am–3pm, Sunday by appointment), is an imposing structure built of a lustrous local stone.

BELOW: gracious living in the square.

The 2000 and 1800 blocks of **Delancey Place** – the quietest and most exclusive street in the neighborhood, if not the entire city – have long been associated with Philadelphia's oldest families. The genteel atmosphere makes a perfect setting for the **Rosenbach Museum** ❾ (2010 Delancey Place; tel: 215-732-1600; open mid-September–July Tuesday–Sunday 11am–4pm, arrive by 2:45pm for tour; entrance fee), a collection of some 30,000 rare books, 275,000 manuscripts, and a houseful of art and antiques gathered by brothers Philip and A.S.W. Rosenbach, considered the foremost rare-book expert of his day. Tours are led by knowledgeable guides and are tailored to visitors' interests – if there is something special you would like to see, call a few days in advance and the curators will try to have it on display. Exhibits change frequently, but highlights are likely to include original drawings by Honoré Daumier and William Blake; 15th-century illuminated manuscripts of *The Canterbury Tales*; a page or two of James Joyce's handwritten draft of *Ulysses*; the *Bay Psalm Book* (the first book printed in America); the only known first edition of *Poor Richard's Almanack*; rare editions of Melville, Defoe and Carroll; drafts of poetry by Ezra Pound, Wallace Stevens and Marianne Moore; and letters by Franklin, Washington, Jefferson, Roosevelt and hundreds of others.

Also on Delancey you'll find the premises of **Plays and Players** (1714 Delancey Street), the city's oldest community theater group and an intimate venue for an evening of drama.

Another of Philadelphia's little-known jewels resides about two blocks away at 1805 Pine Street. It's the **Civil War Library and Museum** ❿ (tel: 215-735-8196; open Tuesday–Saturday 11am–4:30pm; entrance fee) of the Military Order of the Loyal Legion of the United States, a three-story repository of Civil

Map on page 166

Rare books are on display at the Rosenbach Museum.

BELOW: unusual architectural details abound in the square.

Map on page 166

War artifacts, documents and paraphernalia, and a 12,000-volume library. Over the years, the Loyal Legion has accumulated hundreds of firearms, swords, broadsides, photographs and paintings as well as such curiosities as Ulysses S. Grant's death mask, a lock of Abraham Lincoln's hair, and the stuffed head of Major General George G. Meade's trusty war horse, Old Baldy, wounded five times in battle and now the museum's mascot.

To the west, Pine Street runs past townhouses and stores to a tidy pocket park called Fitler Square. **Schuylkill River Park**, a pleasant little patch of trees and benches with playground and a dog run, is just two blocks beyond. If you're in the area, you can wander through some of the neighborhood's quiet alleyways. Panama Street, between 18th and 19th streets, is a tree-lined hideaway of ivy-covered homes (check out the Tudor conversion at No. 1920); tiny Addison, Smedley and Croskey streets are worth exploring, too.

Heading north

Head north on 22nd Street, turn right on Spruce Street and then left on Van Pelt, which is lined with renovated carriage houses. Follow Van Pelt across Locust Street and pass through the archway into **English Village**, an enclave of Tudor-style homes built around a flagstone plaza. Return to 22nd Street and continue north to the First Union Unitarian Church (Chestnut between 21st and 22nd streets; open Monday–Friday 8am–6pm, Sunday 10am–1pm; entrance free), the only Center City church designed by Frank Furness.

A half-block away, at 22nd and Ludlow streets, is yet another of Philadelphia's little-known, and somewhat grisly, treasures: the **Mutter Museum** ⓫ (19 South 22nd Street; tel: 215-563-3737, ext. 242; open Monday–Saturday 10am–4pm, Sunday noon–4pm; entrance fee). Founded in 1858 as a medical teaching aid, the museum – housed at the College of Physicians of Philadelphia – is a collection of medical instruments, artifacts and specimens.

BELOW: spooky specimens at the Mutter Museum.
RIGHT: artists find inspiration in the square.

There are fairly innocuous exhibits on technology – an early heart-lung machine, obstetrical instruments, and a doctor's office from the early 1900s, among other things. But in the pathology section, it's time to leave if you're the squeamish type. There are graphic displays of just about every eye and skin disease one would care to imagine, a plaster cast made at the autopsy of Chang and Eng, the original Siamese twins, a mummified "Soap Lady" from the early 1800s, an ovarian cyst the size of a bowling ball, a human horn (that's right, a horn), the skeleton of the so-called Kentucky giant, and a variety of organs, limbs and decapitated heads pickled in formaldehyde, including the brain of murderer John Wilson and the liver shared by Chang and Eng.

And if you think that's weird, how about hundreds of foreign objects (buttons, pins, bones and bullets) that Dr Chevalier Jackson pulled from his patients' throats with a special device invented for the task, vesicles removed from Chief Justice John Marshall's bladder by renowned Philadelphia doctor Philip Syng Physick, a chunk of John Wilkes Booth's thorax, and a tumor removed from President Grover Cleveland's jaw. This is not a museum for the faint of heart. ❏

PARKWAY MUSEUM DISTRICT

Map on page 176

Philadelphia's museum district is a long stretch between Center City and the green expanses of Fairmount Park; here you can learn all about art and science along a single street

Philadelphia has a number of museums located along **Benjamin Franklin Parkway ❶**, a grand European-style boulevard that runs from City Hall *(see page 151)* to the Philadelphia Museum of Art, urging travelers toward the bucolic space of Fairmount Park *(see page 183)*. This is Philadelphia's Champs Elysées, a swath through Penn's orderly street grid adorned with fountains, flags, flowerbeds and more than 25 outdoor sculptures.

Designed in 1917 by French-born architects Jacques Greber and Paul Philippe Cret – exponents of the City Beautiful movement of the early 1900s – the Parkway was conceived as a sign of civic maturity, a declaration that the Quaker City had shed her mundane persona and was poised to take on the trappings of a great urban center *(see page 149)*.

The Parkway starts at **John F. Kennedy Plaza ❷**, a favorite spot for people lunching outdoors. The plaza, adjacent to City Hall, is the site of Robert Indiana's word-sculpture *Philadelphia LOVE,* said to be "the most plagiarized piece of artwork in the country." The mushroom-shaped building at the corner of 16th Street is the **Philadelphia Visitors Center**, where maps and brochures are available and tourists can purchase tickets for a variety of events. Across the street from the Visitors' Center is Suburban Station, a busy commuter station built in 1929.

PRECEDING PAGES: the Philadelphia Museum of Art. **LEFT:** Popeye floats down the parkway. **BELOW:** *The Thinker* at the Rodin Museum.

Logan Square

From JFK Plaza, it's a 10-minute walk to **Logan Square ❸**, one of William Penn's original town plazas, now girdled by a busy traffic circle. Originally the site of a cemetery and gallows, old Northwest Square was renamed in 1825 in honor of James Logan, who had come to Pennsylvania as William Penn's secretary. Logan was not only a first-rate businessman – he made a fortune in the fur trade and in real estate – but a man of uncommon learning. His personal library was one of the most extensive in the colonies and is now maintained by the Library Company of Philadelphia *(see page 146)*. The parkway plan transformed the square into a circle to facilitate traffic around the area.

At the center of Logan Square is **Swann Memorial Fountain**, an evocative rendering of three reclining nudes (representing Philadelphia's three rivers – the Delaware, Schuylkill and Wissahickon) executed by Alexander Stirling Calder. His father, Alexander Milne Calder, sculpted the statue of William Penn perched at the top of City Hall. In turn, Stirling Calder's son, Alexander Calder, continues the tradition. His mobile *Ghost* hangs in the Museum of Art, and local wits have said this makes the Calder family the Father, Son and Holy Ghost of the Parkway.

On the east side of the square is the **Cathedral of Saints Peter and Paul** ❹ (tel: 215-561-1313; open daily 8am–3pm, small group tours by appointment; entrance free), a venerable Italian Renaissance structure designed by Napoleon Le Brun and John Notman. Begun in 1846 when Logan Square was still on the outskirts of town, the cathedral is one of the only major buildings on the square that predates the parkway.

The twin Neo-Classical structures on the north side of the square are the **Free Library of Philadelphia** ❺ (19th and Vine streets; tel: 215-686-5322; open Monday–Wednesday 9am–9pm, Thursday–Friday 9am–6pm, Saturday 9am–5pm, Sunday, except summer and holidays, 1–5pm; entrance free) and **Municipal Court**, built between 1917 and 1927 and modeled after matching palaces on the Place de la Concorde in Paris. Bibliophiles should check for special exhibits at the library's Rare Book Department, as well as an excellent collection of Dickens memorabilia at the William Elkins Library and the world's largest library of orchestral music.

It's easy to find your way around central Philadelphia.

Exploring science

Walk clockwise around the square to the **Franklin Institute** ❻ (20th and Parkway; tel: 215-448-1200; open Monday–Thursday 9:30am–5pm, Friday–Saturday 9:30am–9pm, Sunday 9:30am–6pm; entrance fee), one of the premier science museums in the country. With acres of exhibition space and hundreds of interactive displays, the institute is a playground for the mind. Everywhere you turn, there's something to touch, explore, discover or play with. The Science Center is the core of the museum, covering ecology, aviation, astronomy, physics, mathematics and just about everything else of interest to budding Einsteins.

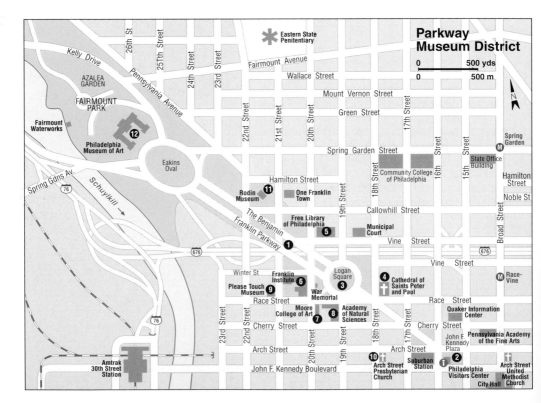

Map on page 176

Walk through a giant heart, climb into a jet fighter, take a bicycle ride on a one-inch cable three storys above the ground, "freeze" your shadow, have a look at "liquid air," and see how a four-story Foucault's pendulum demonstrates the Earth's rotation. At the Mandell Futures Center, visitors can explore the trends and technologies that will shape the 21st century.

Don't miss the Tuttleman IMAX Theater, which shows spectacular IMAX films on a four-story domed screen with 56 speakers. And if you've got the time, go stargazing at the state-of-the-art Fels Planetarium. The Franklin Institute is also home to the **Benjamin Franklin National Memorial** (entrance free) which, in addition to a fascinating collection of Frankliniana, features an enormous marble statue of the institute's namesake and inspiration.

Around the square, the **Moore College of Art ❼** (20th and Parkway; tel: 215-568-4515; open Monday–Friday 10am–5pm all year, Saturday Sunday noon–4pm winter only; entrance free), an art college for women, shows changing exhibits of contemporary art, sculpture, photography and architecture.

The **Academy of Natural Sciences ❽** (19th and Parkway; tel: 215-299-1000; open Monday–Friday 10am–4:30pm, Saturday–Sunday 10am–5pm; entrance fee) is easy to find, with a pair of bronze dinosaurs near the entrance. Founded in 1812, the Academy is the nation's oldest science research museum of natural history. Permanent exhibits include Dinosaur Hall and a butterfly habitat, featuring African, Costa Rican and Malaysian butterflies. There is also a Live Animal Center where visitors can watch through large observation windows the care of a diverse collection of wild animals that have been injured or orphaned, and a hands-on children's nature center called Outside/In, where kids can explore local habitats, examine fossils and handle live animals.

If you're traveling with young children, also be sure to put the **Please Touch Museum ❾** (210 North 21st Street; tel: 215 963 0667; open daily 9am–4:30pm; entrance fee) on your list, the first museum in the country dedicated to children aged seven years and younger. Located behind the Franklin Institute near the corner of 21st and Race streets, this former warehouse has been transformed into a three-story romper room where kids can let their imagination run wild. Children can make fairytales come to life, crawl inside a giant Space Geode, see themselves on television, get behind the wheel of a bus, and much more. The Education Store carries all sorts of nifty items for busy hands and inquisitive minds and is a great place to shop for the kids back home.

Religious architecture

While you're in the neighborhood, make a short detour to **St Clement's Episcopal Church** (Cherry and 20th streets; tel: 215-563-1876; open Monday–Friday 7am–6pm, Saturday 7am–noon, Sunday 7am–2pm, 4–5pm), a picturesque brownstone structure designed by John Notman in 1855. A "high" Episcopal church, St Clement's has a great musical program at high mass every Sunday.

Four blocks away, the **Arch Street Presbyterian Church ❿** (southeast corner of 18th and Arch streets; tel: 215-563-3763; open Tuesday–Thursday by

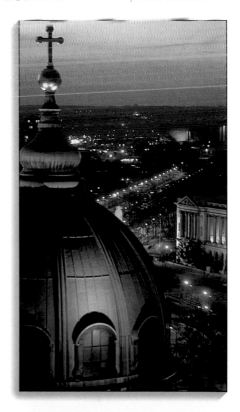

BELOW: the Cathedral of Saints Peter and Paul.

appointment) is also worth a look. Built in 1855, the church is a harmonious blend of styles brought together with massive Corinthian columns, copper dome and cheerful orange trim. The interior is a study in Classical proportion.

Across the street, the splendid Bell Atlantic Tower steps skyward in a cascading series of setbacks. Its two smart neighbors – One and Two Logan Square – are worth a look, too. Parched travelers may want to stop for a while at the Dock Street Brewery and Restaurant at Two Logan Square for a home-town brew *(see page 274)*.

Art treasures

Back on the parkway, just past Logan Square, the twin pylons of the Civil War Soldiers and Sailors Memorial stand sentinel on either side of the boulevard, acting as a gateway to the Philadelphia Museum of Art.

A block farther, the **Rodin Museum** ⓫ (22nd and Parkway; tel: 215-763-8100; open Tuesday–Sunday 10am–5pm; donation) is an island of tranquility set behind an elegant portal, a replica of the gateway Rodin constructed for his own home in France. Given to the city by movie-house mogul Jules Mastbaum, who commissioned Paul Cret and Jacques Greber to design the building, the museum houses the largest collection of Rodin's work found outside France, including *The Thinker*, *The Gates of Hell* and *The Burghers of Calais*.

The Rodin Museum is administered by the larger **Philadelphia Museum of Art** ⓬ (26th and Parkway; tel: 215-763-8100; open Tuesday–Sunday 10am–5pm, Wednesday 10am–8:45pm; entrance fee), which stands like a modern-day acropolis atop Faire Mount, its monumental staircase inviting visitors into the cavernous lobby. These are the same stairs on which Sylvester

BELOW: the Museum of Art is a masterpiece of neo-classical architecture.

Stallone made his triumphant trot in the wildly popular film *Rocky (see page 78)*. The museum has an extensive collection of European art, as well as an Asian wing and American and 20th-century collections.

A collection of European paintings from the 14th to 19th centuries contains highlights such as Van der Wyden's *Crucifixion with Virgin and St John* and Van Eyck's *Saint Francis Receiving the Stigmata*. There is also a fine medieval collection, which features a 12th-century French abbey, through to Peter Paul Rubens' *Prometheus Bound*, Poussin's *The Birth of Venus*, Renoir's *The Bathers* and Van Gogh's *Sunflowers*, not to mention works by Rousseau, Monet, Gauguin, Manet and other latter-day Masters.

Elsewhere in the museum, an entire wing dedicated to 20th-century art traces the influence of innovators like Picasso, Klee, Brancusi and Duchamp on the postwar work of Warhol, Oldenburg, Johns, Stella and others. A renowned American collection features the work of Pennsylvania Dutch and Shaker craftsmen, period rooms, and well-known Philadelphia painters such as Charles Willson Peale, Thomas Eakins and Mary Cassatt.

A 16th-century Hindu temple and Japanese teahouse are but a few of the treasures in the Asian wing. A fascinating gallery of arms and armor details the extraordinary talents of Renaissance metalworkers, and an excellent photography exhibit features the work of Alfred Stieglitz.

This renowned museum can be overwhelming and it's impossible to see everything in a single visit, so be selective. A good way to start is to join one of the free hourly gallery tours or a "spotlight" tour of a particular work or artist. Check the schedule for films and lectures. And visit the museum shop for the city's best collection of art books.　　　　　　　　　　　　　　　　□

Map on page 176

Stately statues grace the courtyard of the Museum of Art.

BELOW: Swann Memorial Fountain at Logan Square.

FAIRMOUNT PARK

Map on page 185

*William Penn's original hope for the city of Philadelphia as a
"greene countrie towne" finds its strength in the expanse
of Fairmount Park, the largest city park in the United States*

The backyard of the Philadelphia Museum of Art *(see page 178)* is the **Azalea Garden** ❶, a 4-acre (2-hectare) bouquet of azaleas, rhododendrons and magnolias that opens onto the vast expanse of **Fairmount Park** (tel: 215-685-0000). The Fairmount Park System, the largest part of which is Fairmount Park itself, spreads over 8,900 acres (3,560 hectares) and is the largest municipal park in the country, with 100 miles (160 km) of hiking trails and bridle paths, 3 million trees, hundreds of statues, 105 tennis courts, 73 baseball fields, six pools, six golf courses, amphitheaters, a zoo and more than 20 historic homes. (The entire system includes parkland throughout the city, including Pennypack Park in the northeast, Cobbs Creek in West Philadelphia, the original squares in Center City and numerous pocket parks.)

Fairmount Park spreads over 4,400 acres (1,760 hectares) on both sides of the Schuylkill River, stretching up into the northern reaches of the Wissahickon Valley *(see page 207)*. The park is so large, it's necessary to drive or take the Fairmount Park trolley-bus, which departs from the JFK Plaza visitors center every 20 minutes most days of the week. The trolley-bus stops regularly along the 17-mile (27-km) loop around the park.

At the water's edge

If you're walking from the Museum of Art, you can wander down to the **Fairmount Waterworks** ❷, a glorious old pumping station that looks like a cluster of Greek temples perched on the river's edge.

When the efficiency of the city's first water pumping facility on Center Square (now the site of City Hall), operational from 1801–15, proved less than ideal, the operation was moved to beautiful Neo-Classical structures on the higher ground of Faire Mount, where distribution of water could be assisted by gravity. With the completion of the Fairmount Dam in 1821, the operation of the Philadelphia Waterworks was regarded as a technological marvel. It became, for a time, the second most visited tourist site (after Niagara Falls) in North America and operated until 1909. However, soon there was no room to add sand filtration beds to purify the river water which had become heavily polluted by up-stream industry and the city's growing population.

The Waterworks were then used as an aquarium from 1911 to 1962 and a public swimming pool from 1962 to 1973. In the 1970s, the site was declared a National Historic Landmark and fundraising efforts for restoration as a historic site began. The project is now in its final phase, scheduled for completion in 2001, with restoration of the old Engine House, the two Mill Houses, the Caretaker's House and Gazebo.

PRECEDING PAGES:
Boathouse Row.
LEFT: rowers on the
Schuylkill River.
BELOW: recreation
on Kelly Drive.

A classic view over the green fields of Fairmount Park.

Also on site will be an Interpretive Center with interactive exhibits, a restaurant and landscaped gardens. On a nice day, you're liable to see cyclists and in-line skaters taking a break, and people stopping for a snack at **Lloyd Hall** ❸ (1 Boathouse Row; tel: 215-684-3936; open Monday–Friday 10am–10pm, Saturday–Sunday 9am–5pm), a Fairmount Park recreational facility with a gymnasium, café, outside patio, and a place to rent bicycles. This is the beginning of the **Schuylkill River Trail**, a level bike path that runs more or less continuously from the Museum of Art to Valley Forge *(see page 229)*. The trail uses the Fairmount Park trail along Kelly Drive, moves onto Main Street in Manayunk *(see page 211)*, and then onto the unpaved Manayunk Canal Towpath for a short distance, before continuing on through Conshohocken, Bridgeport and onto Valley Forge. If you're feeling energetic, this is a great way to get a sense of the variety Philadelphia has to offer.

Boathouse Row has been home to boathouses since the early 1800s. The existing boathouses were constructed after the 1868 Fairmount Park Commission was granted authority to review and approve plans for boathouse construction. Now a historic landmark, Boathouse Row is home to sculling clubs and a host of local high school and university crew teams.

Historic houses

Fairmount Park is dotted with historic houses, some of which are open for viewing, but they can be difficult to locate along the winding roads that run through the park. The Museum of Art conducts tours of seven houses that are fully renovated: Laurel Hill, Lemon Hill, Sweetbriar, Strawberry Mansion, Woodford, Mount Pleasant and Cedar Grove; the last two are administered by the museum and staffed by park guides (Park House Guides Office, west foyer Museum of Art; tel: 215-684-7926; open Tuesday–Friday 9am–5pm). The Philadelphia Trolleyworks company (tel: 215-925-TOUR) also runs a trolley-bus tour through the park with stops at the houses *(see page 264)*.

BELOW: Fairmount Park in bloom.

If you plan to continue your explorations on foot, you can carry on along the river or take Lemon Hill Drive to **Lemon Hill** ❹ (Poplar Drive, East Fairmount Park; tel: 215-232-4337; open Tuesday–Saturday 10am–4pm; entrance fee), the only historic home within walking distance of the Museum of Art. The property was originally owned by Revolutionary financier Robert Morris until he ran foul of his creditors and landed in debtor's prison. Henry Pratt bought the estate at a sheriff's sale and built the present house in 1800. Named after Pratt's hothouse lemon trees, the property is a graceful example of Federal design with large, lacy fanlights, unusual oval parlors overlooking the river, and a fine collection of period furnishings.

From Lemon Hill, it's a short drive along the river (turn at the Grant Monument) to **Mount Pleasant** ❺ (Mount Pleasant Drive, East Fairmount Park; tel: 215-235-7469; open Tuesday–Sunday 10am–5pm; entrance fee), a majestic Georgian mansion constructed in 1761 by a Scottish sea captain, John Macpherson, who made his fortune as a "privateer" –

a pirate in service of the monarch – a line of work that cost him an arm. Macpherson occupied his later years as a farmer, publisher and inventor of a "vermin-proof bed." In 1779, Benedict Arnold bought the house for his bride, Peggy Shippen, but was convicted of treason before either could move in. Described by John Adams as "the most elegant seat in Pennsylvania," Mount Pleasant remains a masterpiece of Georgian style, with beautifully restored woodwork, Chippendale furniture, portraits by Benjamin West and Charles Willson Peale, and a lush rear garden.

You'll pass more modest **Rockland** (1810) and **Ormiston** (1798) along the road to **Laurel Hill ❻** (East Edgely Drive, East Fairmount Park; tel: 215-235-1776; call for opening times; entrance fee), a pretty summer estate built in 1760. Farther along the loop, **Woodford ❼** (33rd and Dauphin streets, East Fairmount Park; tel: 215-229-6115; call for opening times; entrance fee) is a stately Georgian manor house built in 1756 by William Coleman, a member of Franklin's Junto, and later occupied by David Franks, who turned the house into a center of Tory activity during the British occupation. Home of the Naomi Wood collection of American antiques, Woodford is brimming with 18th century furnishings, including scores of household items such as foot warmers, wind harps, wick trimmers and antique books.

Nearby, **Strawberry Mansion ❽** (near 33rd and Dauphin streets, East Fairmount Park; tel: 215-228-8364; call for opening times) was built in two stages: the central section in 1798 and the matching wings in the 1820s. The largest house in the park, it got its name in the 1840s when strawberries and cream were served to visitors. Today, the house is fully restored with a variety of period furnishings.

Map on page 185

It's a 5-minute walk beyond the boathouses to the Samuel Memorial, a terraced sculpture garden featuring the work of several artists, including Jacques Lipchitz and Waldemar Raemisch.

BELOW: grand mansions of Fairmount Park.

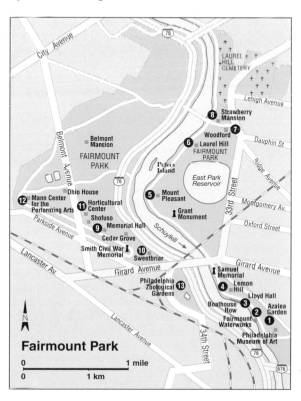

Fairmount Park

Map on page 185

Closer to the Schuylkill River on the west side, Boelson Cottage, built in the 1680s, is the oldest structure in Fairmount Park and possibly the oldest surviving house in Pennsylvania.

BELOW AND RIGHT: animals and birds from all over the world can be seen at Philadelphia Zoo.

The west side

The huge green dome you see looming over the trees belongs to **Memorial Hall ❾** (Belmont Avenue and South Concourse Drive, West Fairmount Park; tel: 215-685-0000; open Monday–Friday), a monumental exhibition hall built as a museum in 1875 for the Centennial Fair and one of only two buildings that remain from the celebration. The other is **Ohio House**, a modest Victorian structure made out of Ohio stone at States Drive and Belmont Avenue. Both buildings are now used for office space, but visitors can get information at Memorial Hall and are welcome to view its breathtaking central hall.

Exiting from the rear of Memorial Hall, it's a short way on North Concourse Drive through the twin spires of the **Smith Civil War Memorial** to two very different historic homes. **Cedar Grove** (Lansdowne Drive, West Fairmount Park; tel: 215-235-7469; open Tuesday–Sunday 10am–5pm; entrance fee), a farmhouse built in 1745 and moved stone by stone from its original Northern Liberties site, is a fine example of Quaker simplicity. A short walk away, **Sweetbriar ❿** (Lansdowne Drive, West Fairmount Park; tel: 215-222-1333; open Wednesday–Sunday 10am–4pm; entrance fee) is the Neo-Classical home of merchant Samuel Breck, built in 1797 as a sanctuary from the yellow fever epidemic sweeping the city.

Also not far from Memorial Hall is the **Horticultural Center ⓫** (Horticultural Drive, West Fairmount Park; tel: 215-685-0096; Visitor Center open daily 9am–3pm, grounds daily 7am–6pm; entrance free), which includes a greenhouse complex and a 22-acre (9-hectare) arboretum. Nearby is **Shofuso** (Lansdowne Drive, West Fairmount Park; tel: 215-878-5097; open May–October, Tuesday–Sunday; entrance fee), known as the Japanese House. Originally built for display in 1954–55 at New York's Museum of Modern Art, it was moved to Philadelphia when the exhibit ended. Shofuso is a replica of a 16th-century Japanese home behind a walled garden. Guides will be happy to show you around, and tea ceremonies are occasionally conducted.

West of Belmont Avenue is the **Mann Center for the Performing Arts ⓬** (George's Hill; box office tel: 215-878-7707; season June–September), an outdoor amphitheater where you can hear the Philadelphia Orchestra, as well as touring rock, jazz and pop shows. There are outdoor restaurants at the top of the hill and the view of the city skyline is wonderful.

The last stop on the tour is yet another Philadelphia first. Founded in 1859, opened in 1874, the **Philadelphia Zoological Gardens ⓭** (3400 West Girard Avenue; tel: 215-243-1100; open daily; entrance fee) is the oldest zoo in the US The 42-acre (17-hectare) site is home to nearly 2,000 animals from around the world, many in recreated habitats. Highlights include the 5-acre (2-hectare) African Plains, a 2½-acre (1-hectare) Primate Reserve, a Reptile and Amphibian House, Jungle Bird Walk, Bear Country, a Children's Zoo, and the "Treehouse," an 1876 building transformed into six different environments. Exhibits featuring rare or exotic species are brought in each season. To get an overview of the park, try the elevated Monorail Safari, which gives a bird's-eye view along the 1-mile (0.5-km) track. ❑

UNIVERSITY CITY

*Philadelphia has long been an academic center in the US
and many of its colleges are clustered around University City,
an area that benefits from the lively student atmosphere*

Map
on page
192

The saga of the University of Pennsylvania begins in 1740 with the campaign for a Charity School at 4th and Arch streets "for the instruction of Poor Children Gratis… and also for a House of Publick worship." Unfortunately, the school never did get solidly off the ground, financially speaking, and a few years later the ubiquitous Benjamin Franklin stepped in to spearhead a drive to transform the benevolent school into a less secular, more public oriented institution. The academy that was founded evolved into the College of Philadelphia and then into the nation's first university in 1779; it shifted its place of operations in 1802 to 9th Street, between Chestnut and Market.

This second home sufficed for seven decades, until a new provost took over and denounced the location as a "vile neighborhood, growing viler every day." Fashionable Philadelphians had already begun abandoning Center City and heading west. And so did the university. "Penn" shifted its campus across the Schuylkill River to the west bank, some 15 blocks from the paternal glance of William Penn atop City Hall. Construction of a bridge in 1805 had created easier access from the east, but it was the university's relocation that quickened the developmental pace. And in 1892, the founding of what became Drexel University nearby designated the area as University City.

Today, aside from its academic attractions, University City is home to several medical centers, museums, a variety of restaurants, and historic residential communities. Bridges connect University City to Center City on five streets: JFK Boulevard (both ways), Market (westbound), Chestnut (eastbound), Walnut (eastbound), and South (both ways).

Getting around University City

A walk through the neighborhood, following a roughly circular route, discloses much of the area's character – the cloistered campuses, ivy-covered halls, exuberant collegiate atmosphere, grand Victorian architecture, and ethnic diversity – like a little college town against the backdrop of a modern city. The boundaries of the neighborhood run roughly from the Schuylkill River to 45th Street and from Baltimore Avenue to Market Street. As in Center City, the streets are laid out in a grid, making orientation easy.

The **30th Street Station** ❶ (30th Street and JFK Boulevard), which can be reached by any SEPTA (Southeastern Pennsylvania Transportation Authority) subway-surface trolley or Market Street subway train, acts like a sort of reception hall for University City. Occupying nearly a full city block, the station, of Greek design and faced with Alabama limestone, was opened in 1933 by the once mighty but now vanished Pennsylvania Railroad *(see page 36)*. Today, the

PRECEDING PAGES:
Benjamin Franklin
presides over the
Penn campus.
LEFT:
graduation day.
BELOW: enjoying
college sports.

newly renovated station (complete with a food court and stores) has been handed over to Amtrak and is that line's second busiest depot.

Drexel University (main tel: 215-895-2000) is near the station, with many of its buildings clustered between Market and Chestnut, 31st and 33rd streets. Although much of the campus is newly but unimaginatively constructed, there are some older buildings of note. The Paul Peck Alumni Center at 32nd and Market streets is a Frank Furness building that opened in 1876 for the first World's Fair (and may in the future be open to the public). The most important of Drexel's original buildings remains in use – the Main Building at 32nd and Chestnut streets, now a National Historic Landmark. The structure, built in a classic Renaissance style with terracotta decorative touches and a truly heroic interior court, is a stunning example of late 19th-century design.

History and art

University City draws students from all over the world.

The University of Pennsylvania is the dominant presence in University City and is the largest employer in Philadelphia. The university's athletic facilities are along the Schuylkill River between Walnut and South streets. They include the Class of 1923 Ice Rink (3130 Walnut Street; tel: 215-898-1923; open September–March, Monday–Friday; entrance fee), tennis and squash courts, the **Palestra**, the university's indoor basketball and track arena, and **Franklin Field**, the site of Ivy League football, the Penn Relays and other sports.

Of particular interest in this area is the **University of Pennsylvania Museum of Archeology and Anthropology ❷** (3320 South Street; tel: 215-898-4001; open Tuesday–Saturday 10am–4:40pm, Sunday 1–5pm; entrance fee), known in common parlance simply as the University Museum. The museum, which

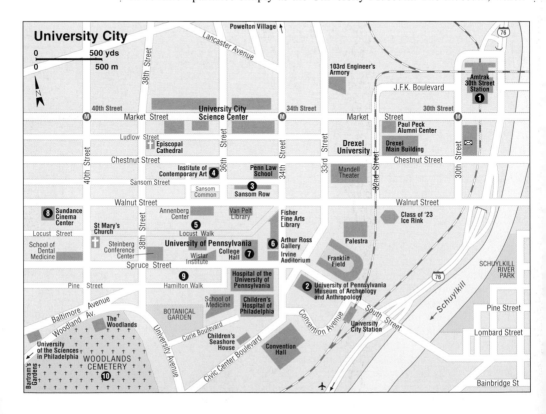

Map
on page
192

conducts research in 18 different countries, boasts one of the most distinguished archeological collections in the world, with 32 exhibition galleries and special emphasis on the arts and cultures of the classical Old World civilizations as well as the native people of Polynesia, Africa and the Americas. The museum building itself is significant – a huge, though incomplete 19th-century building that was designed in an almost dizzying variety of architectural styles.

South of the museum is the Penn Tower hotel and its pedestrian bridge to the hospital complex, which includes the University of Pennsylvania's main hospital and the Children's Hospital of Philadelphia. Beyond the bridge on the southeast side of the street sits Convention Hall which has been used as a sound stage for a number of films, including *The Sixth Sense* in 1999 *(see page 78)*.

Walk back north on 34th Street (passing on the northwest corner of 34th and Spruce streets the Irvine Auditorium, a ziggurat-like 1929 building designed by Horace Trumbauer) to Sansom Street just west of 34th Street, known as **Sansom Row** ❸. The south side is a lovely block of rowhouses built around the time of the Civil War. No. 3420 was for a time the home of the famous 19th-century spiritualist and founder of the Theosophical Society, Madame Helena P. Blavatsky. The building, divided into small eclectic dining rooms, now houses the **White Dog Café** (tel: 215-386-9224), named in honor of the anonymous white dog Madame Blavatsky successfully draped over her infected leg as a cure. It is one of the most stylish restaurants in University City, and among the most characteristic of the neighborhood's colorful milieu. More than an eating place, White Dog hosts lectures and discussion groups, throws parties to celebrate local causes, and produces a tri-annual newsletter on its activities. It also has music in its piano parlor at weekends.

TIP

During the school year, the Nesbitt Design Art Gallery at 33rd and Market streets shows student work in various media. Call 215-895-2548 for days and times.

BELOW:
Locust Walk runs through the heart of the Penn campus.

At the west end of Sansom Row, at 36th Street, is Sansom Common, a shopping and dining area surrounded by the Institute of Contemporary Art and the University of Pennsylvania Bookstore at 36th and Walnut streets. The **Institute of Contemporary Art** ❹ (118 South 36th Street; tel: 215-898-7108; open Wednesday–Friday noon–8pm, Saturday–Sunday 11am–5pm; entrance fee) features cutting-edge photography, performance and plastic arts. The Penn Bookstore is run by Barnes & Noble, with a large inventory beyond text books.

Penn campus

The Penn campus begins in earnest at 34th and Walnut streets. A stroll down **Locust Walk** ❺, an eastward pedestrian extension of Locust Street running from 34th to 40th streets, offers a splendid way to examine the university's central campus. Architecturally, it is a patchwork of many styles, as if the school's trustees had decreed that each building had to represent an entirely different school of design. The result is like sorting through an architectural grab bag, whose contents, if pleasing individually, are unsettling en masse.

Some of the most intriguing university buildings are clustered at the east end of Locust Walk. Notable among them is the old University Library, built in 1888–90, and now the **Fine Arts Library** (34th and Walnut streets). The building, perhaps the masterwork of local architect Frank Furness (whose buildings dot University City), is so richly ornamented that it seems like a fairytale castle constructed of a warm reddish stone. Named a National Historic Landmark in 1985, part of the library is devoted to the **Arthur Ross Gallery** ❻ (220 South 34th Street; tel: 215-898-1479; open Tuesday–Friday 10am–5pm, Saturday–Sunday noon–5pm; entrance free), which features changing exhibits from the university's art collection.

College Hall ❼, an exemplary model of the Victorian Gothic style, lies across the court from the Van Pelt Library. It was built in 1871–72 to house the university upon its move from 9th and Chestnut streets, and reflects the influence of John Ruskin, the eminent English art historian and critic, who long championed the decorative use of contrasting colored stone and other materials.

Locust Walk runs west, alternately a shaded enclave between ivy-covered stone, an open bridge over busy 38th Street, and a walk through the high rise dormitory complex, before ending at 40th Street, which has the Dental School to the left and a line of retail stores to the right. Around the corner at 40th and Walnut streets is the new **Sundance Cinema Center** ❽, a project by Robert Redford's Sundance operation, which features films on seven screens (with advance reservations), a restaurant, tapas bar, espresso bar and a media research library.

Locust Walk between 36th and 38th streets is paralleled two blocks south by **Hamilton Walk** ❾. Another of the many leafy walkways that cut through the Penn campus, Hamilton Walk is bordered by the former Men's Dormitories, which run along Spruce Street. A sprawling structure adorned with gables, gargoyles and unusual stone figures, the building is a beautiful evocation of a medieval English university.

The somewhat odd-looking sculpture directly in front of the Fine Arts Library – only one of many art pieces on campus – is Claes Oldenburg's Split Button.

BELOW: at one of life's crossroads.

Across the walk are the starkly vertical lines of the Alfred Newton Richards Medical Research Laboratories, designed in 1959 by local architect Louis Kahn. Hidden away just south of the Richards building is a **Botanical Garden**, an unexpected pleasure in this otherwise urban academic environment and a great place for footsore tourists to break for lunch. From the end of Hamilton Walk, it's a short jaunt to **Delancey Place**, a handsome enclave of rowhouses.

Map on page 192

Beyond the campus

South and west of Penn the neighborhood becomes mostly residential. Many streets are lined with architecturally interesting houses in various states of repair. Across Woodland Avenue is **Woodlands Cemetery** ⓿, burial ground for many of Philadelphia's distinguished families. Farther down Woodland Avenue at 43rd Street and Kingsessing Avenue is the **University of the Sciences in Philadelphia**, the first college of pharmacy in the western hemisphere.

Powelton Village, tucked into the northeast corner of University City several blocks directly north of the Drexel campus, is characterized by large Italianate and Victorian homes as well as several blocks of charming rowhouses.

South of University City on a patch of green hugging the Schuylkill River lies **Historic Bartram's Gardens** (54th Street and Lindbergh Boulevard; tel: 215-729-5281; garden open daily 10am–5pm, house and museum store open March–December Tuesday–Sunday, tours at 12:10, 2:10 and 3:10pm; entrance fee). John Bartram, friend to Benjamin Franklin and one-time botanist to King George III, began this 44-acre (18-hectare) oasis in 1728. Visitors can tour the house, barn and cider press, wander through the gardens, walk along the river trail, and learn about excavations dating as far back as the 15th century. ⌑

BELOW:
Furness Library
on Penn campus.

CENTER OF LEARNING

Higher education in Philadelphia dates back to 1749, when Benjamin Franklin founded a preparatory school, which would become, in 1755, the College of Pennsylvania. In 1779, a medical school was added, qualifying it as the nation's first university, the University of Pennsylvania, where nine signers of the Declaration of Independence would either teach, study, or serve as trustees.

Penn, as it is also known, was only the beginning. Drexel University, founded in 1891, is right next door, and Temple University in North Philadelphia, founded in 1884, educates more than 31,000 students in 14 schools and colleges. The Philadelphia area has the largest concentration of higher educational institutions in the country, with 88 colleges and universities, 27 of which are in the city limits, covering a broad spectrum of learning. They include: five medical schools; 24 teaching hospitals; the renowned Curtis Institute of Music, established in 1924; the Pennsylvania Academy of Fine Arts; the University of the Arts, devoted exclusively to the visual and performing arts; and schools of Quaker beginnings – Bryn Mawr, Haverford and Swarthmore. Just 45 miles (72 km) from the city is Lincoln University, the first institution of higher learning to provide education to men of African descent.

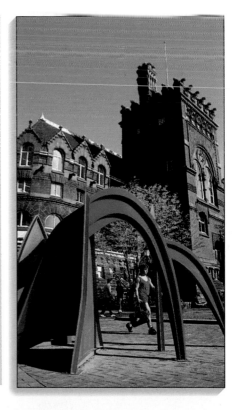

nia's FINEST

lian

SAGE

EAKS CHOPS FILETS
for your
FREEZER

SOUTH PHILLY

*Philadelphia's most multicultural area has a long immigrant
history dating back to the Swedes in the 17th century. Today this
ethnic diversity is most evident in the area's markets and restaurants*

Map
on page
200

It's almost midnight at the Melrose Diner *(see page 274)*. And, as usual, the place is packed and buzzing with life. A bunch of teenage boys makes a ruckus in a corner booth, trying to attract the attention of the girls with the teased-up hair at the counter. Waitresses whiz by like they're on roller skates, doing a juggling act with meat loaf and apple pie. A group of night-shift guys swab gravy off their plates, toss down a second cup of coffee, then drag themselves to work. A few blocks away, a couple of shirtless kids slap a handball against a wall. Their buddies hang out on the corner, staking out the turf. Over at Victor Café *(see page 278)*, opera-singing waiters serve up heaped bowls of fettuccine, and then belt out an impromptu version of *Il Pagliacco*. And at 9th Street and Passyunk Avenue, the late-night crowd lines up for the neighborhood's famous cheesesteaks at Pat's and Geno's.

While all this is going on, somewhere in South Philly, in one of the thousands of anonymous rowhouses that crowd the streets, an old woman tucks her grandchildren into bed with stories of the Old Country. She tells them about her long voyage across the ocean, and the day she first stepped foot on American soil. It's an American story. A story of immigration. And in so many ways, the essential story of South Philadelphia.

Little Italy

On balance, Nietzsche said, the most admirable of all Europe's people are the Italians, the most perfect humanists. Their American cousins have exhibited this genius for humanism in enclaves like South Philadelphia since around 1880, when the migratory urge began the depopulation of Italy's Mezzogiorno. These ragged *paesani* were poor in possessions but rich in culture, determination and family spirit.

Lots of others – Irish, Germans, Jews from Eastern Europe, blacks from Dixieland – came to South Philly too, and in recent years there has been an influx of new faces from Asia – Vietnamese, Cambodians and Chinese sinking roots into the rowhouse terrain, building new lives in a strange land. But it is the Italians who have left the most indelible mark here.

South Philly is a tight-knit community. Kids play stickball in the streets, old folks perch on stoops and gossip, church bells chime all day, and the smells of countless delis, bakeries, pastry shops and pizzerias permeate the air.

At the heart of the neighborhood, in all of its bustling, ramshackle glory, is the **Italian Market ❶**, six blocks of butchers, bakers and pasta-makers strung along 9th Street between Christian and Washington. There's a slew of discount stalls, too, hawking everything from bootleg videos to cut-rate shoes. And yes,

PRECEDING PAGES:
prime cuts.
LEFT: Rocky
keeps an eye on
Veterans Stadium.
BELOW:
the Italian Market.

Many Italian food shops are South Philly institutions.

this is the market Sylvester Stallone jogged through in the original film *Rocky*. (At Rocky's Gym, located a block from the market at 8th and Carpenter streets, aspiring pugilists prove Oscar Wilde's observation that life imitates art.)

Touring this Little Italy in the early 1920s, Christopher Morley wrote that the market "breathes the Italian genius for good food." And so it does, although these days you're also likely to find Chinese, Vietnamese and black hucksters. The merchandise is much the same as it was 70 years ago. There are piles of fruit and vegetables, wriggling crabs, miles of fresh linguine, and everything from 6-ft (1.5-meter) salamis to suckling pigs hanging in storefront windows.

Starting at the northern end of the market, a quick tour might include a taste of crusty, brick-oven bread at **Sarcone's Bakery**, homemade pasta at **Superior Ravioli**, a sackful of herbs, teas and coffee beans at **Spice Corner**, a wedge of provolone at **Di Bruno Brothers' House of Cheese** or a bowl of moist mozzarella at **Claudio's Italian Market Cheese**, a look at the latest culinary gadgets at **Fante's**, and then a pound or two of fresh linguine at **Talluto's**.

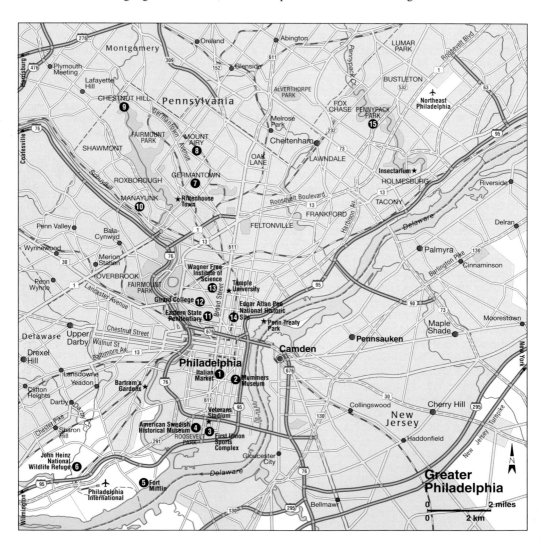

Greater Philadelphia

At the end of the market, reward yourself with one of **Geno's** or **Pat's** "world-famous" cheesesteaks *(see page 203)*. Or there are several other restaurants in walking distance of the market, including **Ralph's** (760 South 9th Street; tel: 215-627-6011), dating from 1900 and run by four generations of the same family; **The Saloon** (750 South 7th Street; tel: 215-627-1811), a boisterous steak and pasta place; **Dante's and Luigi's** (762 South 10th Street; tel: 215-922-9501; closed Monday), inexpensive but with the mystique of a Mafia hit a few years back; as well as several Vietnamese places around 8th and Christian streets. Farther south you'll find **Termini Bros.** (1523 South 8th Street; tel: 1-800-882-7650), a bakery and pastry shop that has been family-run since 1920. The shopping continues at a less hectic pace farther south along Passyunk Avenue, where a mix of clothing stores, restaurants, ice cream parlors and barbershops tend to do a brisk neighborhood business.

High kicks

Passyunk Avenue swerves through the street grid and intersects Broad Street, which, as any true-blue South Philadelphian can tell you, is the path of the Mummers' New Year's Day Parade *(see page 81)*. Today, the area's many Mummers organizations number hundreds of members, and the Mummers' Parade – one of the largest in the country – stretches for more than 2½ miles (4 km) north along Broad Street to City Hall.

If you can't wait until New Year's Day to see the Mummers do the high step, you can get a taste of the Mummer experience at the **Mummers Museum** ❷ (100 South 2nd Street; tel: 215-336-3050; open Tuesday–Saturday 9:30am–5pm, Sunday noon–5pm; entrance fee). Housed in an unusual (and oft-maligned) building that is supposed to represent the strutters' flamboyant outfits, the museum chronicles the tradition and history of Philadelphia Mummery with exhibits of elaborate, feathered costumes, video and audio displays. The famous Mummers string bands offer weekly concerts at the museum between April and September and at special events throughout the city.

At the south end of Broad Street, three large arenas draw fans from all over the region for major league baseball, football, basketball and hockey, as well as spectators for concerts, ice shows, the circus and various championship events. **Veterans Stadium** (Broad Street and Pattison Avenue) is home to the Phillies baseball and the Eagles football teams *(see page 295)*. Just south of Pattison Avenue, the **First Union Sports Complex** ❸ (events tel: 215-336-3600; box office open Monday–Friday 9am–6pm, Saturday–Sunday of event 10am–4:30pm) is home to the Flyers ice hockey and the 76ers basketball teams, the Philadelphia Wings Lacrosse team, as well as Comcast SportsNet, a 24-hour sports cable network, Philadelphia's National Professional Soccer League team (KIXX) and the Philadelphia Phantoms. Tours of **First Union Center** including the Comcast SportsNet, the press box and locker rooms, are available for groups of 15 or more with advance reservations. Individuals may call for information and be added on to tours if there is room (tel: 215-389-9543; entrance fee).

TIP

Most shops in the Italian Market are open Monday to Saturday, but the best time to visit is Saturday morning, when chefs, amateur and professional, stock up for a week, and the vendors, eager to sell produce before the weekend, offer the best deals

BELOW: costumes at the Mummers Museum.

Map on page 200

The earliest immigrants

Of course, Italians weren't the first immigrants to settle in these parts. Way back in the 1640s, four decades before William Penn ever stepped foot on American soil, a hardy bunch of Swedish pioneers hacked out farms and built log cabins in the place where rowhouses and family grocery stores now stand.

You can learn more about the brief but fascinating history of New Sweden, as well as achievements of later Swedish-Americans, at the **American Swedish Historical Museum** ❹ (1900 Pattison Avenue; tel: 215-389-1776; open Tuesday–Friday 10am–4pm, Saturday–Sunday noon–4pm; entrance fee). Set on the edge of Roosevelt Park in a building modeled after Sweden's 17th-century Eriksberg Castle, the museum features a collection of artifacts and art works displayed in galleries designed in a variety of Swedish architectural styles. The museum also sponsors annual festivals such as Valborgsmassoafton in April, a crayfish party in August, and Lucia Fest, with candlelit procession, in December. All feature folk dancing, traditional Swedish food and holiday music.

History buffs may want to travel even farther south to old **Fort Mifflin** ❺ (Island and Fort Mifflin roads, near the airport off I-95; tel: 215-685-4192/492-1881; open April–November Wednesday–Sunday 10am–4pm; entrance fee), site of the gallant but failed defense of Philadelphia during the American Revolution. Construction of the fort was started by the British in 1772 on what was then known as Mud Island, but it was abandoned to the Americans after the Declaration of Independence. In 1777, the rebel force at Fort Mifflin was instrumental in preventing the British fleet from reaching Philadelphia and resupplying the redcoats occupying the city. Hundreds of Americans died during two weeks of constant bombardment, and the redcoats finally broke through. But the delay was sufficient to protect General Washington's army at Valley Forge *(see page 229)*. The fort was rebuilt in 1795, and used as a prison for as many as 300 Confederate soldiers during the Civil War. Now a National Historic Landmark, many of the buildings inside the thick stone walls have been restored, and guided tours, usually led by costumed soldiers, include the firing of a 19th-century cannon.

BELOW:
unfurling the flag
at Fort Mifflin.

The **John Heinz National Wildlife Refuge** ❻ at Tinicum (Visitor Center at 86th and Lindbergh avenues; tel: 215-365-3118; open daily; entrance free) is a short drive from Fort Mifflin. Thanks to the efforts of local conservationists, 1,200 protected acres (480 hectares) have been set aside along the woods, tidal marshes and mud flats of Darby Creek. Tinicum was first settled in 1643 by Johann Printz, who put his village on what was then an island at the mouth of Darby Creek. Even then, draining and landfilling the marshes was considered an effective way of reclaiming alluvial soil for planting. Much of the area, including **Philadelphia International Airport**, stands on landfill. Today, Tinicum is among the last unspoiled areas in the environmentally rich wetlands around the metropolitan area. The reserve serves as a nesting ground for more than 70 species of bird as well as a stopover for migratory birds. The 3-mile (5-km) loop trail and boardwalk lead hikers across the lagoon and into the woods and thickets. ❑

The Great Philly Cheesesteak War

They have been locking horns for more than 30 years: Pat's King of Steaks (1237 East Passyunk Avenue; tel: 215-468-1546) and Geno's (1219 9th Street; tel: 215-389-0659), South Philly's cheesesteak champs, facing off like opposing chess pieces across the intersection. There are other – some heretics even say better – cheesesteak stands in Philadelphia (Jim's Steaks at 4th and South streets is often mentioned as a contender), but the rivalry between Pat's and Geno's has catapulted them to legendary status. Publicly, the owners downplay the issue. "There's a subtle rivalry between the two of us," says Frank Olivieri, Jr, grand-nephew of Pat, the founder. "Sure, we're always looking out the window to see what the other guy is doing, but it's mostly media hype. We're friends on the battlefield and we're friends off the battlefield." Geno's owner agrees: "Competition is healthy," Joe Vento says. But the rivalry is "not what people think. We're friends."

Still, like longtime sparring partners, the two can't help but throw a few jabs. Olivieri says his cheesesteaks are the people's choice. The secret, he says, is the well-seasoned, nearly 70-year-old grill. He claims that Pat's outsells Geno's 12–1. Vento challenges this and says that Geno's is a larger operation. "You put 10 people over [at Pat's], it looks packed. You put 30 people at my place, and it's nothing. We can push 'em out faster and keep the lines down." He's also proud of his cleanliness. "I don't buy that greasy spoons make better steaks."

About the only thing the two agree on is who started selling steak sandwiches first. "Pat's did it first," concedes Vento, who opened his stand in 1966 – although who first added cheese is still debatable. It all began in 1930. Pat's founders, brothers Pasquale and Harry Olivieri, then working as hot-dog vendors, slipped grilled chopped beef into a hot-dog roll for a hungry taxi driver. The cabbie liked the new-fangled sandwich so much he came back for more, and pretty soon Pasquale and Harry knew that they had a hot item on their hands. Years later, after the brothers opened shop at their Passyunk Avenue stand, one of the cooks got bored eating plain steak on a bun, so he melted some cheese on top. The rest was history.

Since then, the cheesesteak has proved a remarkably adaptable concoction. Imaginative chefs substitute pork or chicken, mozzarella or provolone, pile on mushrooms, hot sauce, tomatoes, peppers, eggplant and mounds of fried onions. A few have even developed a vegetarian variety.

But in South Philly, the only choice you have to make is Pat's or Geno's. And loyalty is a serious matter. "Geno's is the best," customers chime, hoisting hefty sandwiches toward their mouths. "Tastes better, friendly people. No contest. They're not chintzy with the onions either." "Pat's is number one," customers on the opposite side of the street say. "The first, the original, the best." ❑

RIGHT: don't leave town without sinking your teeth into one of Philly's famous cheesesteaks.

URBAN VILLAGES

Philadelphia is often described as a city of neighborhoods, each with its own identity, and you couldn't ask for a better example than the "urban villages" clustered in the city's northwest corner

Map on page 200

E stablished at different times and under very different circumstances, Philadelphia's urban villages, Germantown, Chestnut Hill, Mount Airy and Manayunk, have little more in common than their general location. Once separate towns with discrete borders, the area was annexed by Philadelphia in the 1830s. Germantown is the oldest, founded just two years after Philadelphia. While the community has struggled through hard times, it is rich with historic sites. Chestnut Hill began as a real estate development for well-to-do Philadelphians and remains an enclave of beautiful homes and ritzy shops. Manayunk started as a mill town but has, since the 1980s, undergone sweeping gentrification along its trendy, boutique-lined Main Street.

Three neighborhoods, three very different personalities. Taken together or separately, they make a terrific day trip "outside" the city. Although public transportation is available from Center City, driving may be more convenient, especially if you plan on visiting more than one neighborhood.

PRECEDING PAGES: portrait of Manayunk. **LEFT:** Manayunk's trendy Main Street. **BELOW:** Battle of Germantown reenacted at Cliveden.

Germantown

Lying about 6 miles (10 km) northwest of Philadelphia, **Germantown ❼** was founded in 1683 by Quaker and Mennonite immigrants who were invited by William Penn to join his "holy experiment" in the New World *(see page 21).* Led by Pietist scholar Francis Daniel Pastorius, the original 13 families – mostly Dutch or German-speaking Swiss – laid out the village on a gentle rise along Wissahickon Creek. The little town grew quickly, gaining an early reputation in weaving, printing and publishing. When the British captured Philadelphia in 1777, Lord Howe stationed the bulk of his army in Germantown. George Washington launched a daring four-pronged attack against the redcoats from here, but fog and poor timing scuttled the plan, and despite fierce combat along Germantown Avenue, Washington was forced to retreat to Valley Forge *(see page 229).* In 1793, Philadelphians fled to Germantown to escape another invader – the yellow fever epidemic carried by mosquitoes from swampland in the lower elevations of the city. Later, many returned, building summer retreats in the surrounding countryside.

Germantown grew in waves as technology made it more accessible to the city. In the 1870s, when the railroad line from Center City to Chestnut Hill reduced the trip to Germantown to a mere half-hour commute, prosperous Philadelphians could afford to live there year round and mansions sprung up near every train stop. Around the turn of the 20th century, rowhouses appeared as housing for factory workers in the industrial boom.

BELOW: Stenton Mansion, James Logan's country retreat.

Today, Germantown is a treasure of 18th- and 19th-century architecture, most of it on a 3-mile (5-km) stretch of **Germantown Avenue** between Windrim and Phil-Ellena streets, originally an old Indian trail where early European settlers drew lots for land. Although sections of the old village are run down, there are still tranquil tree-lined sidestreets such as Walnut Lane and Tulpehocken streets, where colonial and Victorian homes are lovingly maintained.

Exploring Germantown

William Penn's brilliant secretary, James Logan, was among the first to build a Germantown retreat, and it is the farthest east of the group. **Stenton Mansion** (4601 North 18th Street; tel: 215-329-7312; open Thursday and Saturday 1–4pm, Tuesday–Wednesday by appointment; entrance fee), a magnificent Georgian house built in 1728, was Logan's refuge from his professional obligations – a place where he could entertain Indian friends, indulge his interest in science, and delve into his 2,000-volume library, one of the largest in the colonies. Only five of the original 500 acres (200 hectares) remain in this partially blighted neighborhood, but the barn, greenhouse and much of the Logan family's furnishings are intact. Washington camped here before confronting the British at the Battle of Brandywine, and the British commander Lord Howe chose it as his headquarters before the Battle of Germantown.

The **Germantown Historical Society** on Market Square is a good place to start. Market Square, once the village center and site of the firehouse, stocks and market shed, is now occupied by an imposing Civil War monument. An 1888 Presbyterian church stands on the site of what was the Church of German Reformed Congregation of Germantown, dating from 1733, and the Federal-style Fromberger House, which dates from the late 1790s, now houses the **Historical Society Visitors Center and Museum** (5501 Germantown Avenue; tel: 215-844-0514; open Tuesday–Friday 9am–5pm, museum open Tuesday, Thursday 9am–5pm, Sunday 1–5pm; entrance fee for museum and library). The museum offers an overview of local history and a large collection of 18th- and 19th-century tools, toys, household goods and textiles. The library contains archives and books relating to Germantown history.

Down the street toward Philadelphia, **Grumblethorpe** (5267 Germantown Avenue; tel: 215-843-4820; open April–December Tuesday, Thursday, Sunday 1–4pm; entrance fee) is a solid stone house built as a country home for wine importer John Wister in 1744 and employing a style of Georgian architecture unique to the Germantown area.

Across the street from the Historical Society, the **Deshler-Morris House** (5442 Germantown Avenue; tel: 215-596-1748; open April–December Wednesday–Sunday 1–4pm; entrance fee) sheltered President Washington during the yellow fever epidemic. Cabinet meetings were held here, prompting the nickname the "Germantown White House." Washington liked the place so much he returned the following summer with wife Martha and her two grandchildren. Maintained by the National Park Service, the house has been restored with period furnishings and a garden.

Continue north to **Wyck** (6026 Germantown Avenue; tel: 215-848-1690; open April–mid-December Tuesday, Thursday, Saturday, 1–4pm and year-round by appointment; entrance fee), a modest Quaker home built in 1700 with original furnishings and a fascinating 200-year-old garden.

About a half-block north, the **Mennonite Information Center** (6133 Germantown Avenue; tel: 215-843-0943; meeting-house open by appointment; entrance fee) is located next to a meeting-house built in 1770 on the site of the sect's first American house of worship. Mennonites and Quakers, many of them weavers from Crefeld, Germany, were Germantown's first settlers in 1683 *(see page 58)*. The meeting-house has a front meeting room and a back room where visitors can see the table on which, on February 18 1688, the first written protest against slavery in the New World was signed.

Concern about slavery continued, and during the Civil War Germantown residents participated in the Underground Railroad by hiding runaway slaves. **Johnson House**, several blocks north (6306 Germantown Avenue; tel: 215-438-1768; open Thursday, Friday, 10am–4pm, Saturday 1–4pm; entrance fee), built in 1768, saw heavy fighting during the Battle of Germantown and was a safe house in the Underground Railroad. Across the street, the **Concord Schoolhouse** (6309 Germantown Avenue; tel: 215-843-0943; open by appointment; entrance fee), constructed in 1775, contains original desks, chairs, books and the old school bell. The Upper Germantown Burying Ground is adjacent, with headstones dating to the colonial and Revolutionary War period.

A block away, **Cliveden** (6401 Germantown Avenue; tel: 215-848-1777; open Thursday–Sunday noon–4pm; entrance fee), Germantown's most lavish 18th-century mansion, occupies a 6-acre (2.5-hectare) park. Built in 1763 by Benjamin Chew – a lawyer, Loyalist, and the last Chief Justice of the colonial period – the house was used as a fortress by the British during the Battle of Germantown. Cliveden's 2-ft thick (0.5-meter) walls still bear pockmarks left by American musket balls and grapeshot. The house is beautifully maintained and, thanks to the reams of documentation saved by the Chew family, is a thoroughly accurate renovation. During the assault on Cliveden, Washington placed his artillery on a knoll across the street, where the lovely Federal-style Upsala has stood since 1798.

Mount Airy and Chestnut Hill

Although the neighborhoods no longer have definitive boundaries, **Mount Airy** ❽ extends roughly from Upsal Street north to Cresheim Valley Drive. Mount Airy is the largely residential neighborhood between Germantown and Chestnut Hill and has become known as one of the most integrated communities in the region, with numerous inter-faith, inter-racial and gay couples living among traditional nuclear families. Two churches here are historically significant. The Church of the Brethren (6611 Germantown Avenue), erected in 1770, is the first of the Dunkard sect, a branch of the Mennonites named for their distinctive practice of baptism. Nearby, St Michael's Lutheran Church (6671 Germantown Avenue), founded in 1717, is the oldest Lutheran congregation

Map on page 200

BELOW: historic Mount Airy church is made of local stone.

TIP

If you're in
Germantown on
Tuesday, Friday or
Saturday, be sure to
stop at the Farmers'
Market on West
Haines Street for
scrapple (processed
pork), cinnamon buns
and other
Pennsylvania Dutch
delights.

BELOW: Ebenezer
Maxwell Mansion
in Mount Airy.

in the country. The existing structure is the third on the site, although the Lutherans' schoolhouse, built in 1740, still stands.

Turning south off Germantown Avenue (back near the Mennonite Information Center) onto Tulpehocken Street, you will find large Victorian homes, built in the mid- to late-1800s with prosperity from the railroad line *(see page 36)*. The **Ebenezer Maxwell Mansion** (200 West Tulpehocken Street; tel: 215-438-1861; open Friday–Sunday 1–4pm; entrance fee) is an elaborate Victorian home built in 1859 and furnished with a clutter of Philadelphia-made furniture and late-Victorian decor.

If you continue north on Germantown Avenue, you'll come to **Chestnut Hill ❾**, the city's most exclusive residential district. Chestnut Hill was a remote area of farmland and forest until Henry Houston, a director of the Pennsylvania Railroad and the area's largest landholder, arranged a commuter line. Houston constructed a grand country inn (now Chestnut Hill Academy) and church (St Martin's in the Field), both on West Willow Grove Avenue, as well as scores of fashionable homes intended to lure well-heeled Philadelphians to the suburbs. Houston's son-in-law, Dr George Woodward, continued the work well into the 1900s. Woodward drew inspiration from English and French country homes in an effort to develop comfortable housing for both affluent and working families. Among the best examples of the Houston/Woodward style are French Village at Elbow and Gates lanes; the Benezet Street and Winston Road houses; Houston's private castle, Drum Moir, at West Willow Grove Avenue; and the court houses around Pastorius Park. The **Chestnut Hill Historical Society** (8708 Germantown Avenue; tel: 215-247-0417; open Monday–Friday 9am–5pm) is a good source of information, offering rotating exhibits of local interest, an archive of documents, and architecture guides for local tours.

Woodmere Art Museum (9201 Germantown Avenue; tel: 215-247-0476; open Tuesday–Saturday 10am–5pm, Sunday 1–5pm; any donation requested), housed in Charles Knox Smith's magnificent Victorian mansion, features changing exhibits from the permanent collection of 19th-century art as well as work by contemporary Delaware Valley artists. The museum also conducts art classes and sponsors a concert and lecture series.

Farther north, at the very edge of Chestnut Hill, the University of Pennsylvania maintains the serene **Morris Arboretum** (100 Northwestern Avenue; tel: 215-247-5777; open daily 10am–4pm, extended summer hours). Developed by John and Lydia Morris (heirs to the Morris Iron Works fortune) in the late 1800s on their former summer estate, the 92-acre (37-hectare) arboretum maintains nearly 2,000 kinds of plants, and includes a fragrant rose garden, Japanese gardens, a swan pond, as well as outdoor sculptures and an exhibit about medicinal plants that explores the relationship between plants and people.

While you're in Chestnut Hill, it's worth visiting **Rittenhouse Town** (206 Lincoln Drive, enter from Wissahickon Avenue; tel: 215-438-5711; open April–October Saturday–Sunday noon–4pm; entrance fee), founded in 1690 by a group of Mennonites *(see page 69)*. William Rittenhouse was a papermaker and the first Mennonite minister in the US Located here was America's first paper mill and it was also the birthplace of David Rittenhouse, scientist and first director of the United States Mint *(see page 116)*.

Map on page 200

Manayunk

It was once a big jump from blue-blooded Chestnut Hill to blue-collar **Manayunk ⑩**, but not anymore. Since up-scale stores and eateries have opened on Main Street, this compact working-class burg has been drawing fresh crowds of city and suburban folk alike. Built on a steep hillside rising from the Schuylkill River, Manayunk was once one of Philadelphia's most productive industrial neighborhoods. With the swift current of the Schuylkill River to power its factories and the mule-drawn barges of the Schuylkill Canal to transport materials, Main Street's 14 mills turned out blankets, upholstery, cloth and other textiles by the ton.

The old Manayunk Canal towpath is now a popular recreation spot.

Although the textile industry was decimated by the Great Depression, nevertheless a few manufacturers survived and many of the old mills have now been converted into fancy condominiums or office buildings The sons and daughters of the original Polish, Irish and Italian immigrants are still here, very often occupying the same modest rowhouses as their parents. At the top of the hill you can still see the much grander mansions that were occupied by the wealthy mill-owners in their 19th-century heyday.

The big attraction in Manayunk is **Main Street**, a strip of trendy shops and galleries tucked into a parade of colorful storefronts. The bars, restaurants and outdoor cafés garner terrific reviews, too *(see page 279)*. Manayunk is a Lenape Indian word meaning "the place we go to drink," and with gastronomes packing local eateries, the name is as fitting today as it was 300 years ago.

BELOW: cycling along the Manayunk Towpath.

At the weekend in good weather, you're apt to see bicyclists taking water ice or ice cream breaks along the Manayunk Towpath, a gravel path that runs alongside the Manayunk Canal and is used as part of the Schuylkill River trail, a bikepath that extends from the Philadelphia Museum of Art *(see page 178)* to Valley Forge National Historic Park *(see page 229)*. If you're inspired to head in either direction by bike yourself, Metropolis Bicycles at 4159 Main Street has bikes for rent.

If you need even more incentive to break out of Center City, keep other events in mind: Manayunk has its share of street festivals, too. In mid-May, Canal Day celebrates the birth of the Manayunk Canal in 1823, which helped contribute to Philadelphia's leading position in 19th-century industry. Usually quiet back streets are thronged with spectators who come to watch cyclists conquer the grueling "Manayunk Wall" during the annual First Union US Pro Cycling Championship in June. Also in June is the Annual Manayunk Arts Festival, a juried outdoor art festival that is part of the city's Welcome America! Festival *(see page 290)*. These summertime events provide great opportunities to see Manayunk at its best and to meet the old and new "Yunkers" who have transformed a graying mill town into a thriving contemporary urban village. ❏

NORTH OF VINE

Although not the most frequented area of the city by tourists,
largely due to some run-down enclaves, there are sights
of interest in the north – a reminder of the area's glory days

Map
on page
200

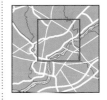

The area of Philadelphia north of Vine Street is a vast urban sprawl that covers everything north of Center City and east of Germantown Avenue *(see page 207).* North Philadelphia is a rather indistinct, amorphous expanse that takes in a wide range of ethnic enclaves, sprawling suburban housing, faded industrial centers, inner-city blight and a wooded city park. It wasn't always this way. In the mid-1800s, parts of North Philadelphia were considered very fashionable. North Broad Street in particular was a magnet for the burgeoning class of industrialists seeking large lots of land for sumptuous new homes. Unfortunately, however, many of these neighborhoods have long since fallen on hard times.

But nestled just north of Center City are the neighborhoods of Fairmount, Spring Garden and Northern Liberties, much of which were settled in the 19th century and which have undergone successful gentrification in recent years. Here you'll find a mixture of large townhouses and smaller rowhouses, high-rise apartment complexes and small businesses, in addition to several prominent historic landmarks as well.

LEFT: a meditative
moment.
BELOW: Eastern
State Penitentiary.

Correction and education

Just a few blocks from the Museum of Art *(see page 178)* is the **Eastern State Penitentiary** ⓫ (22nd and Fairmount streets; tel: 215-236-3300; open May, September, October Saturday–Sunday, June–August Wednesday–Sunday 10am–5pm; entrance fee except Sunday 10–11:30am; no children under seven), closed as a prison facility in 1972 and reopened recently as a historic landmark. Designed by John Haviland and constructed between 1823 and 1836, this building was an innovative experiment in prison design, reflecting the Quaker philosophy that criminals could be reformed by isolating them in solitary confinement, allowing reflection and prayer. Tours require hardhats (which are supplied) and include a look at cells, the work area and the guard central tower, as well as exhibits of inmate-made weapons, mug shots and photographs and stories of famous inmates such as the gangster Al Capone. There are also several art exhibits exploring themes of prison existence.

Several blocks north of the Penitentiary is **Girard College** ⓬ (Girard and Corinthian streets; tel: 215-787-2680; open Thursday 10am–2pm and by appointment other days; entrance free), an oasis of green grass and white marble behind iron gates. The compound of Classically inspired structures centers around Founder's Hall, a building of breathtaking scale designed by 29-year-old Thomas U. Walter in 1833 and regarded as one of the finest examples of

Greek Revival architecture in the US Founder's Hall houses the Girard Collection, which preserves the furnishings, housewares, artworks and other belongings of Stephen Girard, the college's founder and an important financier of the early American government.

Girard was born in Bordeaux, France, to a family of merchant mariners. At the age of 14, he signed on as a cabin boy aboard a merchant vessel and remained at sea for several years. He was only 23 when he became captain on a ship that traded in the West Indies, and he then took part in the American coastal trade, building up his own business at the same time that he represented a New York mercantile company.

Britain's blockade of American ports during the stormy political period before the Revolution led Girard to settle in Philadelphia, where he launched a successful business career. He built a fleet of merchantmen that was to provide him with a great fortune. In 1812, he acquired the building that had been the Bank of the United States, along with its assets, and transformed it into the Bank of Stephen Girard. Girard and the German-born John Jacob Astor – both destined to become the richest men in America – spearheaded a drive to sell government bonds to finance the War of 1812 against Britain.

At the age of 75, Girard began carefully planning the administration of his estate, including large bequests to both Philadelphia and Pennsylvania, and setting aside $6 million of his fortune for the establishment of a school for white male orphans.

The school, Girard College, was opened in 1848, 17 years after its founder's death. Legal battles challenging the terms of Girard's will had been fought before the school was opened, and another protracted legal conflict ensued in the

BELOW: the Greek Revival beauty of US Founders Hall.

mid-20th century over the stipulation that admission was restricted to white males. Finally, in 1968, non-whites were admitted following a ruling by the US Supreme Court. Today, students are white and of color, boys and girls, and children of single parents who require financial assistance.

Map on page 200

A major anchor of the north Broad Street community is **Temple University** (1801 North Broad Street; tel: 215-204-7000), founded in 1884, with more than 28,000 students in 16 schools and colleges, including professional schools in law, dentistry and medicine.

Three blocks west of the Temple campus is the little-known **Wagner Free Institute of Science** ⓭ (17th and Montgomery streets; tel: 215-763-6529; open Tuesday–Friday 9am–4pm; children under 18 must be accompanied by an adult; donations welcome), built in 1860. Its founder was William Wagner, a wealthy merchant with a penchant for stones, bones and stuffed animals and a desire to share the discoveries made on his expeditions. He hired John McArthur, Jr, architect of City Hall, to design the impressive Greek Revival building to house his collection and provide space for his scientific lectures. Today, the museum remains almost exactly the same as it was more than a century ago and continues to provide free educational lectures and programs on scientific subjects, including geology, anthropology, archeology and paleontology.

Literary landmark

To the east of Broad Street, just north of Old City, is a neighborhood known as the Northern Liberties, part of the "Liberty Lands" that William Penn parceled out as bonuses to people who bought building lots in the city proper. Gentrification has crept up from Center City, but the area is still peppered with

BELOW: learning lessons at Girard College.

Map on page 200

factories, warehouses and vacant lots. Most visitors come to the area to pay homage to a literary genius at the **Edgar Allan Poe National Historic Site ⓮** (530–32 Spring Garden Street; tel: 215-597-8780; open June–October daily, November–May Wednesday–Sunday 9am–5pm; entrance free).

The site encompasses two structures, one occupied by Poe between 1842 and 1844 and the neighboring house, which now contains a modest display on this famous author's life and work and where rangers show you around a bit before letting you explore on your own. The Poe house itself is bare and unfinished from the upstairs bedrooms to the spooky dark basement. Even the walls are stripped down to the plaster. Poe moved often when in Philadelphia, and sold most or all of his furniture when he eventually left town. This was the last house in which Poe lived in Philadelphia. However the house is undergoing extensive renovation due to be completed by 2001.

To the north of Poe's house, the area gets dicey for travelers. Philadelphia, like many large northern cities, lost a large chunk of its manufacturing pre-eminence in the mid-20th century, as many industries moved south or overseas in search of cheaper labor and raw materials, leaving large patches of blighted, abandoned homes and factories. However, the spirit of entrepreneurship lives on, and smaller manufacturing and service businesses have dotted the area. Even in the blighted areas, oases of small modern housing are springing up to replace abandoned, deteriorated homes.

A bright spot here is **Taller Puertorriqueño** (2721 North 5th Street; tel: 215-426-3311; open Tuesday 2–6pm, Wednesday–Saturday 10am–1pm, 2–6pm), a cultural center and community workshop located in the Hispanic neighborhood's colorful business district. A brilliant three-story mural is painted on the side of the building. A gallery shows an occasional traveling exhibit and work by local artists. Ask about up-coming lectures, workshops and seminars.

The great northeast

The scene is somewhat different to the east of 5th Street in the old manufacturing centers such as Frankford, Richmond, Fishtown and Tacony along the Delaware River. In the earliest days of European settlement these were small agrarian villages separated from main Philadelphia by farms and pastures. But by the late 1600s, small mills and workshops were springing up along Pennypack Creek, providing the area with flour, lumber, textiles and iron tools.

The steam engine freed factories from swift-running streams and, at the onset of the Industrial Revolution, this northeastern area flourished, cranking out iron, steel, textiles and other manufactured goods, and attracting thousands of immigrant laborers.

Thanks to the Fairmount Park Commission, there is a patch of green in these post-industrial neighborhoods; the 1,300-acre (520-hectare) **Pennypack Park ⓯** runs 8 miles (11 km) along Pennypack Creek, with miles of hiking and biking trails, picnic areas, peaceful woods, a 150-acre (60-hectare) bird sanctuary and, near Verree Road and Bloomfield Avenue, an environmental center with many interesting exhibits on the wildlife and ecology of this inner-city wilderness. ❏

BELOW: the hallowed halls of Girard College.

Edgar Allan Poe

Edgar Allan Poe was born in Boston in 1809, the son of two touring actors, David Poe and Elizabeth Hopkins. Not that he ever knew his parents; at the age of two he was orphaned and moved to Richmond, Virginia to live with a wealthy merchant, John Allan, from whom he gained his middle name. In 1827 Poe enlisted in the army, but his military career held little sway over his desire to write and he arranged his own dismissal by disobeying orders.

Poe then moved to Baltimore to live with his aunt, Maria Clemm, and her young daughter Virginia, during which time he began publishing short works of fiction and poetry. Returning to Richmond, he became editor of the *Southern Literary Messenger*, in which he published his own critical reviews of contemporary authors, including a young Charles Dickens. However, the magazine's owner was less fond of the hard-hitting attacks on popularist authors than the readers and, in January 1837, Poe "resigned" his post.

The same year Poe moved to Philadelphia to undertake editorial work for *Burton's Gentleman's Magazine*, by which time his reputation in literary circles as a writer was secure. A year earlier he had married his 13-year-old cousin Virginia, the inspiration for his immortal poem *Annabel Lee*, and they lived here with her mother and their beloved cat, Catterina.

It was in the house on North 7th Street that this sensitive man of letters composed some of his famous stories, among them *The Fall of the House of Usher*, *The Murders in the Rue Morgue* and *The Gold Bug*. And it was here in Philadelphia that he enjoyed success as a literary critic of the first order and found the greatest domestic contentment.

Poe lived at several different addresses during his Philadelphia years, but this house is the only one that has survived. It was a happy menage: "Eddy" (as Poe was called by the family), his beloved "Sissy" with her gentle bearing, pale complexion and raven hair, and her mother whom he called "Muddy." Unfortunately, in 1842 Virginia suffered her first attack of consumption, the family moved to New York two years later, and the poet lost his "beautiful Annabel Lee" there on January 30, 1847. She was only 24.

The poet wrote these haunting lines in her memory:

It was many and many a year ago,
In a kingdom by the sea,
That a maiden there lived whom
* you may know*
By the name of Annabel Lee;
And this maiden she lived with
* no other thought*
Than to love and be loved by me.

The blow was devastating and it wasn't long before the disconsolate widower was gone as well. Poe was found lying on a Baltimore street corner on October 3, 1849, and four days later he died in a Maryland state hospital.

As a lasting credit, Poe transformed the short story into an art form, perfected the thriller genre, and gave the world some of the finest literary criticism of his time.   ❏

RIGHT: Edgar Allan Poe, one of America's finest 19th-century writers.

BRANDYWINE RIVER VALLEY

Map on page 224

An easy 20-minute drive southeast of Philadelphia leads to a valley of old homesteads, hamlets and quiet country roads, with a strong history of 19th-century American industry

s you head out of Philadelphia on Route 1, you'll come to the valley of the Brandywine River, which twists through 20 miles (40 km) of rolling hills and estates. The river itself is really no more than a creek where two east and west branches meet at Chadds Ford, eventually joining the Delaware River at Wilmington. In the shadow of this babbling brook, scions of the Wyeth and the du Pont families settled down to pursue their dreams, leaving behind a legacy of industrial innovation, seasoned with equal parts scandal and success.

Originally the territory of the Lenni-Lenape tribe, the Brandywine Valley was subsequently colonized by the Dutch, the Swedes, the English – and finally by the du Ponts and Wyeths. It was the river power that first attracted E.I. du Pont and his two sons, who saw a need for high-quality gunpowder in the New World and set about creating a company that would be the foundation of the worldwide industrial powerhouse that bears the family name.

PRECEDING PAGES: fall foliage in Bucks County; young faces of the Pennsylvania Dutch Country. **LEFT:** spectacular shades of fall. **BELOW:** John Chads House.

Chadds Ford

Much later, the valley nurtured another family's dream of quite a different sort. Decades ago, the haunting play of light and shadow on the Brandywine hills first attracted illustrator N.C. Wyeth to settle here, followed by his son Andrew and grandson Jamie. You can find the greatest collection in the world of Wyeth paintings in **Chadds Ford ❶**, at the Brandywine River Museum (Rt 1, Chadds Ford; tel: 610-388-2700; open daily 9:30am–4:30pm except Christmas; entrance fee). The museum, housed in a renovated Civil War-era gristmill, also displays the largest US collection of English Pre-Raphaelite paintings, as well as collecting and preserving American art with an emphasis on the art history of the Brandywine Valley, American landscape and still life. Its circular, brick-floored core with dramatic walls of glass showcase spectacular views of the Brandywine River and the rural landscape that inspired many of the artists represented in the museum.

The museum and grounds are owned and managed by the Brandywine Conservancy, an environmental organization founded in 1967 to protect the area from massive industrial development. In keeping with the conservancy's spirit of preservation, the museum grounds are planted with native wildflower gardens and a 1-mile (2-km) riverwalk which you can follow to the 18th-century bluestone **John Chads House ❷** (Rt 100; tel: 610-388-7376; open May–September Saturday–Sunday noon–5pm, October–April by appointment; entrance fee). The house was built in 1725 for the innkeeper and ferry operator who gave his name to Chadds Ford (the extra "d" was a Victorian flourish.) It was built on the banks of the creek by

The Chadds Ford Museum has a striking layout.

John Wyeth, Jr, its simplicity reflecting Chads' Quaker heritage. The original oak floors and paneling are fine examples of early 18th-century Pennsylvania architecture, ensuring its place on the National Register of Historic Places.

Right across the street is the **Chadds Ford Winery ❸** (632 Baltimore Pike, Chadds Ford; tel: 610-388-6221; open May–December daily noon–6 pm; free tour, entrance fee for wine tasting). This small premium winery, located in a renovated 17th-century colonial barn, first began production in 1982. Today the winery produces 30,000 cases of wine, making it the largest in Pennsylvania and in the top 10 on the East Coast. You can take the winemaking tour and wine tasting, browse the gift shop, or picnic on the outdoor deck and grounds.

While you're in Chadds Ford, don't miss **Brandywine Battlefield Park ❹** (tel: 610-459-3342; open Tuesday–Saturday 9am–5pm, Sunday noon–5pm). The park is the site of the Battle of Brandywine, which took place during the Revolutionary War *(see page 31)*. Still standing are the quarters of the Marquis de Lafayette and the spot where General Washington set up his headquarters before retreating for the tragic winter at Valley Forge. A permanent interpretive exhibit and an audio-visual presentation tell the story of the battle and its relation to the Philadelphia Campaign of 1777, while changing exhibits cover other topics of interest to the American Revolution.

From here it's just a few minutes' drive to **Kennett Square ❺**, a quiet town originally home to the Lenni-Lenape tribe. Named after a village in England, the town was incorporated in 1855 and was known for strong anti-slavery sentiments. Kennett Square was a hotbed of abolitionism – Harriet Tubman lived and worked here and Quakers helped slaves to freedom along the Underground Railroad *(see page 37)*.

BELOW: Flower Garden Walk at Longwood Gardens.

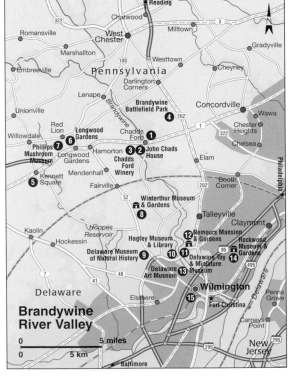

Map
on page
224

Flowers and mushrooms

About 3 miles (5 km) northeast of Kennett Square you'll find **Longwood Gardens ❻** (Rt 1; tel: 610-388-6741; visitor center and outdoor gardens open daily, conservatory open April–October daily, open-air theater performances June–August; entrance fee). Once the country estate of industrialist Pierre S. du Pont, who rescued it from the sawmill's blade just in time, Longwood is famous for its superb gardens and elaborate fountains, lakes, woodlands, wildflowers, rose garden and greenhouses with exotic tropical displays.

Pennsylvania produces more mushrooms than any other state, and Kennett Square alone provides about 25 percent of the entire US mushroom crop.

Entering the gardens is a bit like falling down a rabbit hole into Wonderland; you enter through a low building built right into the side of a hill and emerge on the other side into the park – a great leafy world filled with bird song and wind chimes. There's no such thing as an "off season" here, where even in the dead of winter you can visit the heated conservatories for miniature walk-through eco-climates of deserts and rainforests. The greenhouses and the conservatory are particularly colorful from November through to April, but masses of flowering plants adorn the conservatory year round. The conservatory is also home to year-round classes, special events, and the very popular Children's Garden Maze. May is the month of maximum blooms, when 50,000 bulbs burst into flower. More than 11,000 types of plants are the main summer outdoor attractions, and spectacular half-hour illuminated displays at the main fountain garden take place June through August on every Tuesday, Thursday and Saturday evening after dark.

The property was first sold by William Penn to Quaker farmers Samuel and Joshua Peirce, who planted a small arboretum here in 1700 known as Peirce's Park. Over the years it changed hands several times, until Pierre du Pont bought the property in 1906. Like many du Ponts, Pierre was a gardening fanatic whose eclectic tastes included a love of theater. As a result, Longwood Gardens offers not just flowers and trees but fireworks, colorful fountain displays set to music, organ and vocal concerts, kids' workshops and other special events throughout the year. December is a very special time, with holiday music shows and fountain-light outdoor shows.

If all that exploring makes you peckish, stop for a bite to eat at the cafeteria or the formal Terrace Restaurant, both located a short walk from the conservatory. During warm weather you can eat outside.

On your way out of Longwood, check out the **Brandywine Valley Tourist Information Center** (Rt 1, Kennett Square; tel: 1-800-228-9933) to get a good idea of what's happening in the area. Just a few steps down the street is the **Phillips Mushroom Museum ❼** (909 East Baltimore Pike, Kennett Square; tel: 610-388-6082; open daily 10am–6 pm). If you like mushrooms, there's no better place to visit. You can sample different types of mushrooms and enjoy a promotional movie on the joys of cultivating the fungus. Don't miss the gift shop offering everything from wild mushroom caviar and mushroom fettuccine to mushroom-decorated ties, lamps, key chains, mobiles and birthday cards. Of course, the shop also sells mushrooms – plain, exotic, fresh, marinated, dried and canned.

BELOW: waterlilies in the conservatory of Longwood Gardens.

Du Pont treasures

To continue your tour of the Brandywine Valley, hop on Route 52 south, stopping just 30 miles (50 km) south of Philadelphia and 6 miles (10 km) north of Wilmington at the **Winterthur Museum and Gardens** ❽ (Rt 52; tel: 302-888-4600; open Monday–Saturday 9am–5pm, Sunday noon–5pm; reserve in advance by phone for 1- and 2-hour decorative arts tours).

Exotic and native plants bloom at Winterthur Gardens.

Winterthur houses the nation's largest collection of early American decorative arts, set in a mansion on 1,000 acres (400 hectares) of landscaped meadows and woods. It was home to Henry Francis du Pont, a superb landscaper and the most prodigious collector of decorative arts made or used in the US from 1640 to 1860. Du Pont inherited the original 18th-century country house in 1927 and proceeded to transform it into a 175-room home filled with US furniture, art and accessories, such as entire portions of a Philadelphia mayor's house, a Pennsylvania Dutch farm, a 19th-century Delaware inn and the family room of a 17th-century Massachusetts dwelling. A free-standing staircase and several rooms were originally part of the Montmorenci estate in North Carolina.

Each room has its own treasures – an old general store, a Chinese parlor built to showcase wallpaper hand-painted in 1770 in a continuous panorama of Chinese village life. There are about 5,000 pieces of Chinese porcelain, in addition to chandeliers, paintings, maps, statues, tapestries, silverware and more – du Pont's collection of *objets d'art* is the largest in the world. Interactive displays in the galleries explore the history and development of Early American decorative arts.

BELOW: Chadds Ford Winery offers tours and tastings of local wines.

The spectacular gardens, which peak in early May, include rare rhododendron and azaleas and a 60-acre (25-hectare) garden of native and exotic plants complemented by landscaped ponds, meadows and woodlands.

Still driving south on Route 52, you'll come to the **Delaware Museum of Natural History** ❾ (4840 Kennett Pike, Wilmington; tel: 302-658-9111; open Monday–Saturday 9:30am–4:30pm, Sunday noon–4:30pm, closed public holidays; entrance fee) The museum, which contains a variety of natural history exhibits in natural settings, includes an extensive shell collection, mounted African animals and extinct birds. A discovery room features hands-on exhibits and activities, and films are shown on a regular basis. The museum was founded by John du Pont, direct descendent of Henry du Pont.

A few miles south on the Brandywine River is the **Hagley Museum and Library** ❿ (Rt 141; tel: 302-658-2400; open March–December daily, January–March Saturday–Sunday). Built on the original site of the 1802 du Pont mills, Hagley was the du Ponts' first US home. It was here that the 19th-century workers lived; today it is an outdoor museum spreading over 240 acres (100 hectares) along the Brandywine. A National Historic Landmark, this nonprofit institution is dedicated to America's economic and technological heritage. Exhibits and demonstrations depict the evolution of the US economy and include a wooden waterwheel, turbine-powered roll mills, an operating steam engine and a restored 1870s machine shop. Working models in the Millwright Shop demonstrate the production of black powder. The Henry Clay Mill is an old stone cotton-spinning shop featuring dioramas, models and narrated displays tracing economic development along the Brandywine from the 17th century to the present day. A restored workers' community on nearby Blacksmith Hill features a one-room schoolhouse and a worker's house.

Overlooking the Brandywine is **Eleutherian Mills,** the Georgian-style mansion built in 1803 by company founder Eleuthere Irenee du Pont, a French nobleman and son of Louis XVI's finance minister The mansion and its furnishings reflect the tastes of the five generations of du Ponts who lived there. The barn contains 19th-century farm tools, weather vanes, vehicles, a Conestoga wagon and antique cars. Nearby are the first office of the du Pont Company, Lammot du Pont's workshop and the formal French garden.

If your kids aren't wild about manufacturing displays, they may enjoy a stop instead at the **Delaware Toy and Miniature Museum** ⓫ (Rt 141; tel: 302-427-8697; guided tours by reservation Tuesday–Saturday 10am–4pm, Sunday noon–4pm, closed public holidays; entrance fee) just past the entrance to the Hagley. It offers a collection of more than 100 antique and contemporary dollhouses, as well as dolls, toy trains, boats and planes from the 18th century to the present day. Special displays include a Victorian Christmas parlor with a traditional Christmas scene and miniatures in ivory, silver and porcelain.

Haven't had enough of the du Pont grandeur? Then continue on Route 141 to the **Nemours Mansion and Gardens** ⓬ (Rockland Road; tel: 302-651-6912; open May–November Tuesday–Sunday, tours 9am, 11am, 1pm, 3pm; under 16s not permitted). The 102-room Louis XVI-style estate of Alfred I. du Pont displays antiques, Oriental rugs and paintings and tapestries dating from the 15th century. Nemours is set on 300 acres (120 hectares) of woodlands and

Map
on page
224

TIP

Catch a show at Wilmington's Grand Opera House (818 North Market Street; tel: 302-658-7879), a restored theater once home to Buffalo Bill Cody and John Philip Sousa.

BELOW: Winterthur Museum near Wilmington.

Map on page 224

The tall ship Kalmar Nyckel *brought the first settlers to the Delaware Valley.*

manicured gardens with examples of the family's extravagant life, including vintage automobiles and a bowling alley. You can take a bus tour through the gardens, one of the finest examples of French-style horticulture in the US.

Leaving Nemours, take Route 100 south to the **Delaware Art Museum ⓭** (2301 Kentinere Parkway, Wilmington; tel: 302-571-9590; open daily; entrance fee except Wednesday pm and Saturday am), which contains one of the most important collections of English Pre-Raphaelite art in the country, in addition to paintings by US artists Thomas Eakins, Winslow Homer, Maxfield Parrish and the Wyeths. The museum also focuses on Delaware history from the first settlement to modern times. A children's gallery offers hands-on activities.

If you're interested in more decorative arts, you're just a short distance from an 1851 manor house, the **Rockwood Museum and Gardens ⓮** (610 Shipley Road, Wilmington; tel: 302-761-4340; open Tuesday–Saturday 11am–4pm; entrance fee). Guides conduct tours of the rural Gothic house and you can explore the gardens, including unusual varieties such as a weeping beech planted around 1856. A cast iron and glass conservatory is filled with tropical plants.

Wilmington

From Rockwood, it's just a short drive to **Wilmington ⓯**, first christened New Sweden and then renamed Willingtown by its Quaker founders to honor local merchant Thomas Willing in 1731. To get an idea of all the tourist activities, check out the Greater Wilmington Convention and Visitors Bureau (100 West 10th Street; tel: 302-652-4088 or 1-800-422-1181).

BELOW:
Nemours Mansion.

Just a few blocks away is the Delaware History Center, which dominates the 500 block of Market Street Mall in downtown Wilmington. The **Delaware History Museum** (504 Market Street; tel: 302-655-7161/656-0637; open Tuesday–Friday noon–4pm, Saturday 10am–4pm, closed public holidays; entrance fee) is located in a renovated Art Deco Woolworth store and features three galleries of interactive exhibits on Delaware history, including costumes, toys and art. The Old Town Hall, built in 1798–1800, served as a center of political and social activities in Wilmington's mercantile-milling economy. Today it's owned by the Historical Society of Delaware and is used for exhibitions. Willingtown Square consists of six historic houses relocated into an urban park in 1976.

To get a feel for Wilmington before the du Ponts made it their home, head out to the waterfront to visit the *Kalmar Nyckel* **Shipyard and Museum** (823 East 7th Street, Wilmington; tel: 302-429-7447; open Monday–Saturday 10am–4pm, Sunday noon–4pm, closed public holidays; entrance fee). The *Kalmar Nyckel* was the ship that brought the first European settlers to the Delaware Valley in 1638. There are tours of the shipbuilding facilities led by costumed guides, plus a replica of the tall ship.

You can continue your tour of the city's Swedish roots at **Fort Christina** (7th Street; tel: 302-652-5629; entrance free) next to the shipyard. Here you can still see the rocks where the first settlers landed, some of the original log homes, and read historical plaques on walls surrounding the park. ❑

Valley Forge

There were no battles fought at Valley Forge, but more Continental soldiers died here than in any single engagement during the American Revolution. The enemies at this grueling six-month encampment were hunger, cold, fatigue and disease. Driven back from their defense of Philadelphia, repelled at Brandywine and at Germantown by the better equipped and organized British army, George Washington's beleaguered troops pulled back to Valley Forge, where they built log huts and, without proper clothes, shoes or blankets, sustained themselves on "firecake," a bland mixture of flour and water. Hundreds came down with dysentery, pneumonia and typhus. Of the 12,000 who retreated to Valley Forge in December 1777, 2,000 never returned.

Only loyalty to Washington and American independence held the camp together. Yet, despite heavy losses, desertions and rumors of mutiny, the ragtag Continental Army was transformed at Valley Forge into a capable, cohesive fighting force, due in part to the efforts of Prussian officer Baron Friedrich von Steuben, who arrived from France with a letter of introduction from Benjamin Franklin.

A skilled officer, von Steuben helped transform the soldiers into an integrated army. He drilled them relentlessly, reorganizing troop structure, teaching musket volleys and shoring up discipline. In June they intercepted the British army in New Jersey on its way out of Philadelphia, staving off a British counterattack at the Battle of Monmouth. The war dragged on for another five years, but the triumph over circumstance at Valley Forge propelled the Continental Army to victory.

Today, the site of Washington's fateful encampment is preserved at Valley Forge National Historical Park (Rt 23 and North Gulph Road; tel: 610-783-1077; open daily 9am–5pm; entrance fee for historic buildings), 18 miles (28 km) northwest of Philadelphia. The Visitors Center has exhibits, a gift shop, an 18-minute film and free maps of the park. A number of original 18th-century

buildings, including Washington's HQ, still stand on the 3,000-acre (1,200-ha) site, as do reconstructed huts. Look at the Washington Memorial Chapel, with carillon recitals after Sunday services and concerts scheduled throughout the summer. Near the chapel is the World of Scouting Museum (tel: 610-783-5311; open Saturday–Sunday 11am–4pm; entrance fee), which chronicles the scouting movement from its founding.

Near the park is the unusual and quirky Wharton Escherick Museum (Horseshoe Trail Road; tel: 610-644-5822; open March–December Saturday 10am–5pm, Sunday 1–5pm, Monday–Friday groups only 10am–4pm, reservations required; entrance fee), home and studio of artist Wharton Escherick (1887–1970). Escherick, called the "Dean of American Craftsmen," began his artistic life as a painter, but became best known for his sculptural furnishings. The museum was created in 1971 to preserve his uniquely designed studio, which houses a collection of over 200 works, including paintings, ceramics, sculpture and furnishings. ❑

RIGHT: a costumed interpreter recalls historic events at Valley Forge.

BY THE SEA: PHILLY'S GREAT GETAWAY

Since 1801, when the New Jersey coast was first pushed as a tourist attraction, it has been a Philly favorite, only 90 minutes' drive from Center City

The colorful beach towns along the coast from the tip of Cape May to the shoals of Long Beach Island appeal to a variety of tastes and interests. From the Victorian houses of Cape May to the revelries of Wildwood, the glitz of Atlantic City to the family ambience of Ocean City, the Jersey Shore just can't be beat.

BEACH COMMUNITIES

Cape May's beach is small and, due to erosion, getting smaller every year, but there is a board-walk and a pedestrianized walkway of quaint shops. Once a family community, Wildwood began luring a younger crowd in the 1970s, earn-ing the nickname "Childwood." It is still a rite of passage for high school graduates, and two weeks in June known as "Senior Weeks" can get hectic, but it has the best boardwalk in New Jersey.

Stone Harbor, Avalon and Sea Isle City have a lower profile than their neighbors; Stone Harbor is noted for its bird sanctuary. Next door to Mar-gate is Ventnor, where the Atlantic City board-walk begins. This is bicycle-riding territory, with elegant oceanfront homes.

Farther north is Long Beach Island, 18 miles (29 km) long with a series of little towns along the main boulevard. It attracts a mix of teenagers, families and well-off holidaymakers. At the northern tip is historic Barnegat Lighthouse, which offers magnificent views.

> ▷ PINK ELEPHANT
> At Margate you'll find a 90-ton, six-story-high elephant named Lucy. Built as a real-estate promotion in 1881, now she's a National Historic Landmark.

△ SUNSET SAILING
Both Sea Isle City and Avalon attract tourist and local sailing enthusiasts to the bay side of the island with popular fishing and party boats.

△ SOLITUDE SEEKERS
Just across the bridge from Atlantic City, Brigantine, a quiet residential island, has uncrowded beaches. At the northern tip there's a small nature preserve.

◁ OCEAN CITY
The best of the beach towns, with a boardwalk and family activities. No alcohol is allowed.

▷ EXOTIC ESCAPE
The Trump Taj Mahal forms a palatial backdrop to Atlantic City's boardwalk. It contains nine restaurants, a casino and 1,250 hotel rooms.

PLACE YOUR BETS: ATLANTIC CITY

With the approval of gambling in 1976, this decaying resort was granted a new lease of life. The first casino, Resorts International, opened in 1978.

Atlantic City attracts more than 33 million visitors a year. The games are essentially the same wherever you go – blackjack, baccarat, roulette, and the ubiquitous slot machines. You can stroll from one gaming hall to another or catch a ride on one of the boardwalk's famous wicker rolling chairs. Tropicana has the indoor Tivoli Pier, a 2-acre amusement park complete with Ferris wheel; the immense Trump Taj Mahal *(above)* is like an electrified pasha's palace; the Showboat plays Dixieland jazz in the lobby. These are only a few. If the street names sound familiar, they are the same as used in the board game Monopoly, invented here in 1930.

In the second week in September, the Miss America Pageant takes over the town. Say what you will about this long-running beauty contest – a sore point for feminists – it is one of the most popular diversions in the country.

◁ **THRILL SEEKERS**
The boardwalk at Wildwood has all the latest rides and water slides at two amusement piers – Mariner's Landing and Morey's Pier. Day passes are available.

▽ **CAPE MAY**
At the tip of the peninsula is this laid-back resort of gingerbread homes and bed-and-breakfasts. Tours of the historic district are offered during the summer.

△ **KIDS' HAVEN**
Numerous New Jersey beach resorts offer amusement parks catering to children and families.

PENNSYLVANIA DUTCH COUNTRY

Map on pages 236-7

Home to the traditional farmsteads of the Amish and Mennonite communities, Lancaster County is a constant tourist draw, as well as being the location of the historic battle of Gettysburg

Philadelphia

Only two hours from Philadelphia, the bucolic countryside of Lancaster County makes a worthwhile trip for a day or a weekend. Religious dissenters who settled this land in the early 1700s were an independent group, and they've managed to hang onto their beliefs, traditions and language despite the constant encroachment of mainstream culture.

Yet there's a right way and a wrong way to explore Lancaster County. If you hop on Route 30 at Philadelphia, you'll find it's a painful process, bogged down by bumper-to-bumper traffic as neon billboards scream their come-ons for "genuine Amish" attractions and "traditional" smorgasbords. Lancaster County is a minefield of both tourist attractions and tourist traps, and sometimes the difference can be subtle. The confusion is compounded by the fact that the local tourism industry capitalizes, sometimes shamelessly, on the Amish way of life *(see page 63)*. Sadly, too many visitors never stray from Route 30, and their only experience of the Amish culture is the tacky tourism industry version of *faux* farms and giant *papier-mâché* Pennsylvania Dutchmen grinning goofily from above the roadsides.

PRECEDING PAGES:
Pennsylvania's
heartland.
LEFT: Lancaster
County lad.
BELOW: Kutztown's
folk festival.

Fortunately, there's a better way, if you're willing to head off along meandering side roads that snake throughout the county. Buy a good map and you'll see countless small roads running at right angles to the major tourist arteries of routes 222, 23, 340, 30 and 741. Take any of these tiny tracks north or south, and within minutes you'll find yourself in the middle of a modern-day Brigadoon, where the only sounds are the muted lowing of the cattle, the creaking of a buggy, and the whisper of the wind across patchwork acres of summer wheat. If you've had the foresight to bring bikes, get them out now. Otherwise, park your car and take a hike along a country road and discover the measured rhythm of the real Lancaster County.

The road to Lancaster

There are many ways to get to Lancaster itself. One of the best is to take the Pennsylvania Turnpike and jump off at **Morgantown ❶** (exit 22). In the village of Morgantown, turn right onto Route 23 and head west toward **Churchtown ❷**, a sleepy little village of stone mansions, cozy cottages and antiques stores. This is a good place to set up headquarters – try the historic Inn at Twin Lindens *(see page 271)*, which boasts one of the most romantic places to stay in the entire eastern seaboard. Famous for elegant breakfasts and fabulous dinners, you'll need to book far ahead to guarantee a room. It's worth it.

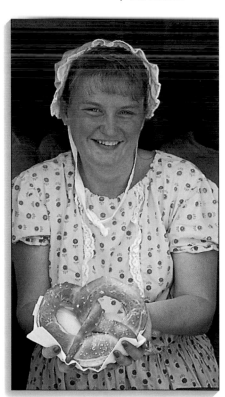

Lancaster County offers idyllic images of rural life at almost every turn.

Right outside Churchtown is the Amish-owned **Smucker's Harness Shop** (2014 Main Street), known throughout the world for fine handmade harnesses and sleigh bells. Smucker's outfits the Budweiser Clydesdales and made the late John Denver's wedding saddle. Take a look in the back, where you'll see Amish saddlers quietly stitching on antique sewing machines as Amish tots frolic on the floor under your feet. Even if you don't know anything about horses, a stop at Smucker's can give you a sense of how the "real Amish" live and work.

A short detour east will bring you to **Hopewell Furnace National Historic Site ❸** near Pottstown, where an entire iron-manufacturing village has been restored to its early 19th-century appearance (tel: 610-582-8773; open daily; entrance fee). In summer costumed guides demonstrate the skills necessary to keep the community running and the furnace at full blast. The site is surrounded by **French Creek State Park ❹**, with lakes, campsites and hiking trails.

A taste of things Amish

As you continue west, be sure to stop at the roadside stands to stock up on luscious fruits and vegetables, homemade bread and pies, and home-canned relishes, jams and jellies. Some stands offer quilts and other gift items, and all are operated by Amish or Mennonites. If you're feeling peckish, consider a stop at **Shady Maple Smorgasbord** (1324 Main Street, East Earl) – more of an experience than a restaurant. This huge barn of a place may look as if it's designed for tourists, but it's a favorite hangout for the locals, too, who come to enjoy the fabulous array of authentic home-cooked Pennsylvania Dutch food, prepared and served by Mennonites. If you come for early breakfast, you'll see the trestle tables filled with Amish families, who know a good breakfast bargain

BELOW: following the traditional Amish way of life.

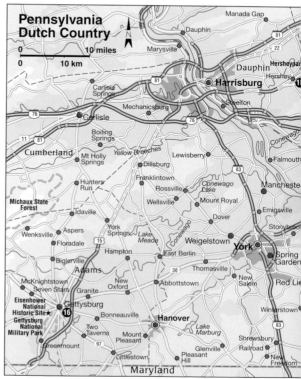

Map on pages 236–7

when they see it. This is also a favorite stop for local Amish builders and contractors on their way to work. Downstairs you'll find gift shops filled with good quality, low priced Amish-made wooden toys and furniture.

Continue west on Route 23 toward Blue Ball, where you can pick up Route 322 and head toward **Ephrata ❺**, home of the Ephrata Cloister (632 West Main Street; tel: 717-733-6600; open Monday–Saturday 9am–5pm, Sunday noon–5pm; entrance fee), where in 1732 more than 300 celibate German followers of Pietist Conrad Beissel built a community of log-and-stone buildings. Known for printing, basketmaking and milling, the cloister founded a school in the 1740s and nursed 500 wounded soldiers during the Battle of Brandywine, but faded into unimportance by the 1800s (there isn't much of a future in celibacy.)

Also at Ephrata, you'll find the **Artworks at Doneckers** (100 North State Street; tel: 717-738-9503; open Monday–Tuesday, Thursday Friday 11:45am–5pm, Saturday 10am–5pm; entrance free), selling the work of 50 artists and artisans who work together in a former shoe factory. The Doneckers complex also features a top French restaurant (333 North State Street), The Inns at Doneckers (40 restored rooms in four different locations) and a sophisticated fashion-and-housewares store (409 North State Street).

Antiques roadshow

At this point, if you're an antiques buff, you may want to head north on Route 272 for a visit to the market and auction house of the **Green Dragon** (North State Street; tel: 717-738-1117; open Friday 9am–10pm; entrance free). At seven large market buildings and many other smaller stores, the Green Dragon merchants offer everything from lace to milk cans. As the locals say, "If you can't buy it at

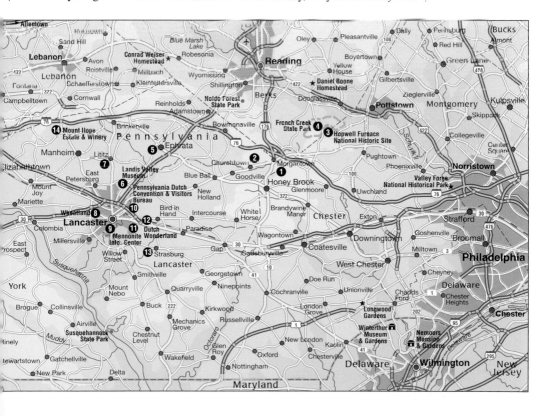

the Green Dragon, it chust ain't fer sale!" Then move east on Route 272 to **Adamstown**, where on most weekends you'll find more than 30,000 dealers of 18th- and 19th-century collectibles and antiques. Three times a year they really put on a show, attracting another 4,800 dealers from around the country. Midway between Ephrata and Adamstown you may want to stop for a bite as Zinn's Diner (Route 272), a heavily advertised eatery/gift shop/recreation park that serves decent local food. There may be a line of tourists, but locals love to come here, too.

Crops flourish in Lancaster County.

Heading back on Route 272 south again toward Lancaster, don't miss the **Landis Valley Museum ❻** (2451 Kissel Hill Road; tel: 717-569-0401; open Tuesday–Saturday 9am–5pm, Sunday noon–5pm; entrance fee), a reconstructed 19th-century village of shops, workshops and houses where guides recreate the crafts, skills and day-to-day chores of the 1800s. The 1999 movie *Beloved* was filmed on location here. The museum also offers a variety of workshops and events throughout the year, including Harvest Days (fall), Herb Faire (summer), and Days of Belsnickel (winter). If your children are getting bored, across the road from the museum is the **Hands On House**, two floors of please-touch fun and educational activities guaranteed to keep youngsters totally captivated.

From there, travel west on Route 772 to **Lititz ❼**, a peaceful 18th-century Moravian village with a tree-shaded town square lined with stores and anchored by the restored Victorian General Sutter Inn (14 East Main Street). When the wind is right, you can smell the chocolate from the Wilbur Chocolates Factory. There's no factory tour, but you can visit the **Wilbur Chocolates Candy Americana Museum** (48 North Broad Street; tel: 717-626-3249; open Monday–Saturday 10am–5pm; entrance free) to see a demonstration candy kitchen, antique signs, and confectioners tools. Nothing goes better with chocolate than pretzels,

BELOW:
Amish farmers
harvesting wheat.

so stop at the other end of the street at the **Sturgis Pretzel House** (219 East Main Street), the first commercial pretzel bakery in the US. Then take your booty to the Lititz Springs Park (Main Street) for a picnic beside the stream.

Just outside downtown Lancaster, you can discover 250 years of local history at the **Lancaster County Historical Society** (230 North President Avenue; tel: 717-392-4633; open Tuesday, Thursday 9:30am–9:30pm; Wednesday, Friday–Saturday 9:30am– 4:30pm; entrance free). Nearby is **Wheatland** ❽ (1120 Marietta Avenue), the home of James Buchanan, the only Pennsylvania native to become President of the United States. The 19th-century estate is a showcase of Victorian furnishings and some of Buchanan's personal possessions.

Lancaster City

Convenient parking in downtown **Lancaster** ❾ puts you within walking distance of Central Market (Penn Square), the nation's oldest publicly owned farmers' market and a great place to buy from Amish and Mennonites standholders. Every Tuesday, Friday and Saturday you'll find not just the freshest, cheapest fruits, vegetables, meat and fish around, but piles of Amish quilted goods, Plain aprons and hats and Amish dolls. Three gourmet food stands offer tasty lunch takeaways, but you'll also find Pennsylvania Dutch specialties: Lebanon bologna, red beet eggs, potato chips, moon pies, whoopie pies, shoo fly pies, and fresh horseradish. If you'd rather take a lunch break at a restaurant, try Carr's, right across the alley, or stop in at the popular J-M's Bistro (300 West James Street), an affordable yet fabulous eatery just a few blocks away.

Surrounding Central Market on all four sides you'll find a Dickensian cobblestone alley of tiny art shops, antiques dealers, and jewelers – and the

Map on pages 236–7

TIP

Most of the streets in downtown Lancaster are one-way, and are laid out in straight intersecting lines.

BELOW: Amish quilts.

Traditional designs decorate the Dutch Country's visitors center.

Heritage Center of Lancaster County (13 West King Street; tel: 717-299-6440; open May–November, Tuesday–Saturday 10am–4pm; entrance free), a decorative arts museum featuring furniture, rifles, silverware and Pennsylvania Dutch quilts. If you're a theater buff, walk one block south and check out the recently restored **Fulton Opera House** (12 North Prince Street), which has been offering local and touring talent on its Victorian stage since 1852.

For a view of the rest of the downtown area, join one of the costumed guides of **Lancaster Walking Tours** (100 South Queen Street; tel: 717-392-1776; open April–October, Monday–Saturday 10am and 1:30pm, Sunday 1:30pm; entrance fee), who lead visitors around the houses, churches and markets.

Plain folk culture

If you feel you really must visit an "Amish" attraction, head out of King Street (Rt 462/Business Rt 30/Lincoln Highway East). Stop first at the **Pennsylvania Dutch Convention and Visitors Bureau** ❿ (501 Greenfield Road; tel: 717-299-8901 or 1-800-PA DUTCH for automatic information; open Monday–Thursday 8am–6pm, Friday 8am–7pm, Sunday 8am–5pm) or the **Mennonite Information Center** ⓫ (2209 Mill Stream Road just off Rt 30; tel: 717-299-0954; open Monday–Saturday 8am–5pm). At the tourist bureau, you can rent an audio-tape tour, which gives you an in-car guide to the area's major attractions. The Mennonite Center offers a tour guide service – for a minimum of two hours a guide will join you in your car for a tour of the countryside. Guides who speak French, Spanish and German can be requested with prior notice.

Continue on Route 30 another few miles east of town to the **Amish Homestead** (2034 Rt 30 East; tel: 717-768-3600; open daily 11am–4pm; entrance fee), among the best of the many "authentic" Amish attractions. This 71-acre (30-hectare) farm is operated and inhabited, in part, by an Amish family. Guides explain the beliefs and practices of the Plain people during a tour of the 1744 farmhouse and farm buildings. Skip the wax museums and anything that features cardboard cut-outs of Amish life. Your kids may also talk you into stopping at **Dutch Wonderland** ⓬ (2249 Rt 30 East; tel: 717-291-1888; phone for opening hours; entrance fee) – it's no Disneyworld, but a low-tech amusement park for the younger set.

East of Lancaster are the small towns of **Bird-in-Hand**, **Paradise** and **Intercourse**. You'll hear plenty of jokes about the origin of the name of Intercourse but there's no accepted explanation. Some think it's a corrupted version of "entercourse," referring to the entrance to an old racecourse outside town. Others believe the village grew up at the intercourse of two roads, the Old King's Highway from Philadelphia to Pittsburgh (now the Old Philadelphia Pike) and the road from Wilmington to Erie. The place is inundated with tourists sporting "Intercourse is for Lovers" T-shirts, which strikes a discordant note since this part of the county features some of the area's most beautiful scenery. For a more informative view of the area, try the People's Place on Main Street in Intercourse, where an interesting 25-minute film explores Amish history and customs.

BELOW: quilters at work at the Kutztown festival.

Map on pages 236–7

About 10 miles (16 km) south on Route 896 is **Strasburg** ⓭, where you can learn about the development of America's railroads at the **Railroad Museum of Pennsylvania** (Rt 741 East; tel: 717-687-8628; open May–October daily; entrance fee), and then hop aboard the Strasburg Railroad's historic steam locomotive for a 45-minute round-trip to Lancaster. The town has a number of other attractions, from an "Amish village" to buggy rides and miniature golf. While you're in the area, you might consider one of the religious shows at the **Sight and Sound Millennium Theater** on Route 896 in Strasburg (tel: 717-687-7800 for times; entrance fee). Presented on one of the world's largest stages, these dramatic productions (featuring scores of actors, live animals and special effects) are close to Broadway standards. Be aware in advance that the shows present a fundamental Christian orientation.

West of Strasburg on Route 272 in the village of Willow Street (yes, it's a town!) you'll find the **Hans Herr House** (1849 Hans Herr Drive; tel. 717-464-4438; open April–December Monday–Saturday 9am–4pm; entrance fee), the oldest meeting-house used by Swiss Mennonite immigrants. Built in 1719 and restored in 1970, the house is also the oldest dwelling in the county. Staff offer tours that provide a good introduction to early Mennonite history *(see page 69)*. The first Saturday in August is Herr House Heritage Day, where you can find demonstrations of gardening, soap-making, and other events of rural life.

For shoppers more interested in designer clothes, Route 30 is also home to two huge outlet malls just a few blocks apart. Tanger Outlet and Rockvale Square sell everything from brand-name clothing to power tools. Buses from New York City, Maryland and Delaware tote hordes of shoppers to these outlets, proving Lancaster is a place with more than just Dutch Country offerings

BELOW:
transportation remains simple in Amish country.

Map
on pages
236–7

America's favorite chocolate is even celebrated on lampposts.

BELOW: Hershey Kisses on the factory line.

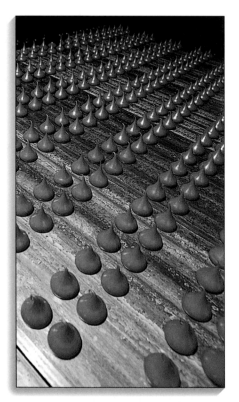

One of the best ways to get up close to the Amish is by traveling to one of the many local fairs, which they like to attend as well as the tourists. Remember that here, as is the case in all dealings with the Amish, photography is not appreciated – having their photo taken is a violation of their religious beliefs against graven images. The most popular of the fairs are the **Pennsylvania Dutch Folk Festival** (Schuylkill County Fairgrounds, Summit Station) and the **Kutztown Pennsylvania German Folk Festival** (Kutztown Fairgrounds), both in early July *(see page 244)*. The fact that Kutztown and Summit Station aren't in Lancaster County is just a technicality – these two fairs are still the best ways to experience Amish culture without feeling as though you are trespassing. You'll be able to observe horse-shoeing, glass-blowing, sheep-shearing, ox-roasting and other country fair activities.

Summer weekends also bring the **Pennsylvania Renaissance Faire**. Here, a troupe of costumed performers turn the grounds of the **Mount Hope Estate and Winery** ⑭ (off the Pennsylvania Turnpike at exit 20) into a 16th-century English country fair complete with jousting, Shakespearean performances (significantly abridged) and dancing. In winter, the estate reopens for an Edgar Allan Poe Hallowe'en *(see page 217)* and a Charles Dickens Christmas Past.

Chocolate haven

A bit farther to the west is **Hershey** ⑮ and **Hersheypark** (100 West Hersheypark Drive; tel: 1-800-HERSHEY; open May–Labor Day daily; entrance fee), home of the world-famous chocolate company, where the air exudes chocolate and Hershey kisses decorate the lampposts. Hersheypark has some serious fun for rollercoaster aficionados – new in 2000 was the Lightning Racer, the only wooden racing coaster in the world, with a double track and two staggered lifts. Riders fly on a wild ride of 15 drops at speeds beyond 50 mph (80 km/h). There are 60 other rides – seven other coasters (more than any other park in Pennsylvania), six water rides, and more than 20 rides designed for the very young. You can catch a variety of entertainment from dance revues to dolphin shows. Included in the admission is a stroll through the 11-acre (4.5-hectare) ZooAmerica, featuring 200 animals native to North America.

If all this wears you out, try a stroll through the lush 23-acre (10-hectare) Hershey Gardens (Hotel Road), or take a ride through **Hershey's Chocolate World** (800 Park Boulevard; tel: 717-534-4900; open daily; entrance free). More action occurs over at the Hershey Park Arena, Stadium and Star Pavilion, one of the most versatile entertainment complexes in the east. The 30,000-capacity outdoor stadium hosts top sports teams, including Hershey Wildcats soccer. Smaller concerts and events take place at the Star Pavilion. The 7,225-seat Arena has been the home to the Hershey Bears Hockey Club since 1938, in addition to hosting ice shows, circuses and other events. A new $75 million, 12,500-seat arena was built in 2001.

Continuing southwest, you will reach the historic town of **Gettysburg** ⑯, site of the famous Civil War battle *(see opposite page)*. ❑

Gettysburg

History buffs shouldn't miss a side trip to Gettysburg National Military Park, just two hours west of Lancaster, where in the summer of 1863 Confederate and Union forces fought the bloodiest battle in US history *(see page 38)*. When Confederate General Robert E. Lee and his 75,000 men collided with the 97,000 northern army of General George C. Meade, the three-day fight that followed marked the turning point in the American Civil War. More men died that July than in any other battle on American soil.

The climax came when Major General George E. Pickett led 12,000 Confederate troops in a desperate charge across an open field. Blasted by artillery and rifle fire, Pickett's men could not break the Union line. When the dust cleared 50 minutes later, 10,000 men and more than 5,000 horses lay dead.

Four months later, Abraham Lincoln delivered his famous Gettysburg Address at the adjacent cemetery where 3,500 Civil War soldiers are buried.

The Gettysburg battlefield is located in and around the historic town of Gettysburg, with more than 100 historic buildings radiating from the town center at Lincoln Square. One block north of the square the Gettysburg Convention and Visitors Bureau (35 Carlisle Street) offers various tour options, including walking, driving, bus, carriage, horseback and candlelit ghost excursions. If you drive yourself, consider hiring a licensed battlefield guide to accompany you at the National Park Service (97 Taneytown Road), next door to the Gettysburg National Cemetery.

Continue your tour with the Wills House (1 Lincoln Square), the spot where Lincoln worked on his address and slept the night before he delivered it. Eight blocks west along Chambersburg Street, Lee's Headquarters and Museum is where General Lee struggled with his ill-fated battle plans. Next, stop by the restored Civil War era home of the only woman killed in the battle, Jennie Wade, who was struck by stray bullets in her kitchen while baking bread for Union soldiers

(758 Baltimore Street). The original wooden doors still carry the scars of hundreds of bullets. At the National Civil War Wax Museum (297 Steinwehr Avenue) an audio-visual presentation has more than 200 lifesize figures in 30 scenes, a reenactment of the battle and an animated Lincoln giving his address.

Before venturing out onto the battlefield itself, stop by the National Military Park Visitor Center (tel: 717-334-1124; open daily) to look at artifacts and a 3-D sound and light show of the battle. Once you've got a bit of background, you're ready to tackle the battlefield itself. The 6,000-acre (2,400-ha) park is the largest battlefield shrine in the US, with over 1,000 monuments and 20 museums. It looks very much like it did 130 years ago, with its farms, gray stone walls, and rolling pastureland. Take along a map, a guide, or a taped tour to help you navigate.

Presidential buffs also won't want to miss the Eisenhower National Historic Site (19 Taneytown Road), the only private home ever owned by former US President Dwight D. Eisenhower and his wife Mamie. ❑

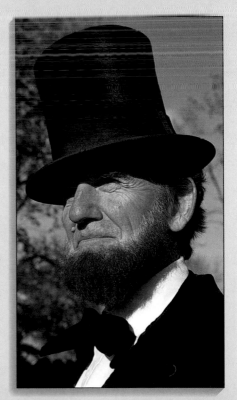

RIGHT: a costumed actor portrays Abraham Lincoln at Gettysburg's Memorial Day parade.

PENNSYLVANIA DUTCH FOLK FESTIVALS

The twin Pennsylvania Dutch folk festivals in southeast Pennsylvania are renowned in an area already crammed with fairs from summer to fall

The Pennsylvania Dutch Folk Festival and the Kutztown Pennsylvania German Folk Festival are rated among the best festivals in the entire country. Both honor authentic, hardworking Pennsylvania Dutch life *(see page 235)* with plenty of good entertainment.

For more than 50 years, there was just one Pennsylvania Dutch folk festival – the "Kutztown Pennsylvania Dutch Folk Festival" at Kutztown University. But in 1995 the festival was sold and moved to the Schuylkill County Fair Grounds in Summit Station, and renamed the "Pennsylvania Dutch Folk Festival." The university then created its own "Kutztown Pennsylvania German Folk Festival" at the original site. Both fairs occur at about the same time in early July each year.

Both festivals offer similar experiences in a typical fair setting, ranging from master glassblowers to quilters and weavers. You can attend an Amish wedding and explore a one-room schoolhouse. Traditional food is also plentiful: chicken dinners, pot pie, funnel cakes, Dutch fries, German sausage sandwiches, buffets, corn on the cob, waffles, shoo fly pie, soft pretzels – not to mention all the other typical fair foods.

Kids can find plenty to do: there are puppet shows, folk tales and songs, magicians, ventriloquists and children's musicians, marble games and petting zoos, as well as giant wooden toys to crawl through, a 19th-century horse-drawn merry-go-round, and pony rides.

Just about every 19th-century craft is represented, with sheepshearing, wool-dyeing, fiddling, blacksmithing, weaving, woodcarving, metalworking, papercutting, pottery, chair caning, soapmaking, quilting, breadbaking, ox-roasting, broommaking, beekeeping, and old-fashioned popcorn-making.

△ **FESTIVAL FARE**
With an invitation to *"Komm rei, huck dich un essa"* ("come in, sit down, and eat"), there's plenty of food on offer.

◁ **COMMUNITY SPIRIT**
Many traditional crafts are enjoyed as group activities by young and old, such as this gathering of quilters.

⊳ HAY DAYS

Hay stacks to play around in and sweet treats such as candy apples are a favorite among local Amish children during the two main Dutch Country festivals.

△ BUGGY BLISS

The horse-drawn buggy is a novelty ride for visitors at country festivals, but it is the main form of transportation for the Amish, who don't drive motorized vehicles.

⊳ DUTCH DESIGN

Many crafts, such as the hand-painting of tools and vessels in bright, primary colors, have been handed down the generations and are now popular souvenirs.

▽ PENNSYLVANIA QUILTS

A row of quilts made to traditional Pennsylvania Dutch designs are left out to dry before being sold to locals and tourists at fairs around the region.

HEEMET FESCHT – HOME FESTIVAL

The tongue twisting Pennsylvania German name Heemet Fescht simply means "Home Festival," and to residents of Kutztown that's exactly what it is – a celebration of 19th-century home life. Held on a 40-acre (16-ha) working farm at Kutztown University, this annual festival in September is a nostalgic look back in time. Visitors can wander through a historic garden, learn what life was like in a one-room schoolhouse, check out working farm demonstrations or take a horse-drawn wagon ride. Crafters are on hand to explain everything from seat-weaving and woodcarving to fraktur (decorated writing) and flintknapping (making stone tools). No home festival would be complete without some good Pennsylvania German home cooking, and the Heemet Fescht serves it all, from chicken corn soup to red beet eggs. The festival also offers lectures on cultural heritage and local lore, classes in the 130-year-old schoolhouse, a church service in the old dialect of Pennsylvania German, and a collection of nearly 10,000 Pennsylvania German artifacts.

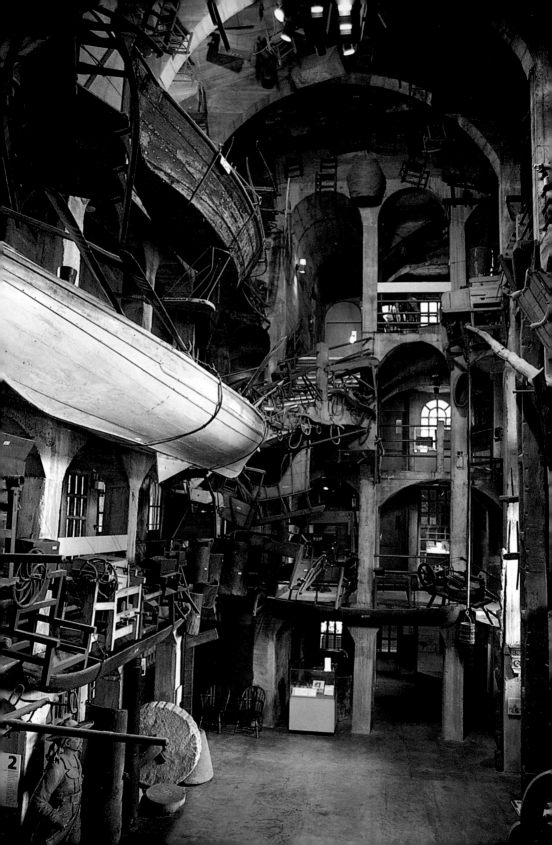

BUCKS COUNTY

An hour north and a world away from Center City, Bucks County is graced with some of the most beautiful landscapes in the Delaware Valley: a sanctuary of woods, farms, creeks and wildlife

Map on page 250

Philadelphia

No sooner did William Penn design the layout of Philadelphia than he ran off to the suburbs, choosing to make his home in the woods of Bucks County. And stressed-out city dwellers have been following on his trail ever since. "The country life is to be preferred for there we see the works of God," Penn wrote. And 300 years later, travelers seeking a peaceful getaway are still finding the place heavenly.

River mansions

William and Hannah Penn set up house at **Pennsbury Manor** ❶ (400 Pennsbury Memorial Road, off Rt 13 south of Morrisville; tel: 215-946-0400; open Tuesday–Saturday 9am–5pm, Sunday noon–5pm; entrance fee), an 8,000-acre (3,200-hectare) estate situated on a bend in the Delaware River about 26 miles (40 km) north of the city. Penn spent from 1682–84 and 1699–1701 at the plantation before returning to England in 1701. "Let not poor Pennsbury be forgotten, or neglected," he wrote his servants, "keep the housen, the farme & the Gardens, till we come." But Penn never returned, and the property fell to ruin.

That might have been the end of Pennsbury had it not been for a group of historians, architects and preservationists who quite literally brought the estate back to life. Meticulously reconstructed from archeological studies and Penn's own detailed instructions, the property is now a working recreation of a colonial estate, fully furnished with one of the state's best collections of 17th-century antiques. The grounds are available for self-guided viewing. During guided tours (call for times), costumed guides show visitors around the mansion, smokehouse, stable, kitchen, carpenter's shop, brew house and other outbuildings. There is a packed schedule of special events, including workshops for children, garden tours, a 17th-century country fair, Christmas festivities and plenty of demonstrations of open-hearth cooking, beer-making, woodworking and other crafts.

Near Pennsbury Manor is the colonial town of Historic **Fallsington** ❷ (4 Yardley Avenue, off Rt 1; tel: 215-295-6567; hourly tours May–October Monday–Saturday 10am–4pm, Sunday 1–4pm; entrance fee for guided tours), where Penn came to worship while residing in the country. It preserves several 18th-century buildings around a charming village square, including three Quaker meeting-houses and a log cabin. Walking tour maps are available at the Historic Fallsington Information Center, and guided tours of the buildings are available.

Two other historic homes in the area are also worth a visit. The **Margaret R. Grundy Memorial Library and Museum** ❸ (610 Radcliffe Street, Bristol;

PRECEDING PAGES: early morning fog over the Delaware. **LEFT:** Mercer Museum's central court. **BELOW:** fall foliage in Tinicum Park.

tel: 215-788-9432, library tel: 215-988-7891; open September–June Monday–Friday 1–4pm, Saturday 1–3pm, July–August closed Saturday; entrance free) is an elegant Victorian home, with a fine collection of period furnishings, that overlooks the Delaware River. Tours of the house and library, which is a modern structure built largely underground, are available by appointment.

Andalusia ❹ (1237 State Road, Andalusia; tel: 215-245-5479; tours by appointment only; entrance fee), one of the country's finest Greek Revival homes, is also on the Delaware River. Originally a simple country house, it was redesigned by financier Nicholas Biddle, who hired Thomas U. Walter to handle the renovation. The 220-acre (90-hectare) estate is still owned by the Biddle family, who preserve the house and its magnificent furnishings.

If you're traveling with children under the age of 13, you may want to set aside a day for nearby **Sesame Place** ❺ (100 Sesame Road, Langhorne, off Rt 1; tel: 215-752-7070; open daily mid-May–Labor Day, September–mid-October, Saturday–Sunday, hours vary; entrance fee), a *Sesame Street* theme park, with a range of rides, water slides, shows and other attractions such as Vapor Trail, Runaway Rapids, Slimey's Chutes, Mumford's Water Maze and the indoor Games Gallery designed to engage young minds and bodies.

Artists and writers

Doylestown ❻, the Bucks County seat, is directly north of Center City. An important stagecoach station in the 1700s, today it is a Main Street town of gingerbread houses, interesting shops and first-rate inns and restaurants.

Most tourists, however, come to Doylestown to see the **Mercer Mile**, three fantastic structures built between 1908 and 1916 by Henry Chapman Mercer, a

Henry Mercer built Fonthill in the style of a Tudor castle.

LEFT: the salon in Mercer's home, Fonthill.

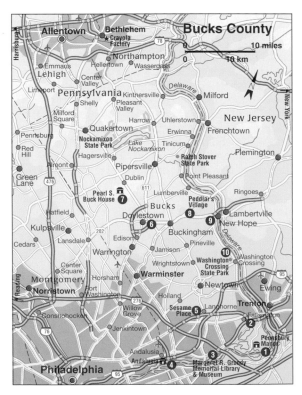

brilliant, if somewhat eccentric, archeologist, artist and historian. After years of studying ancient cultures in the US and abroad, Mercer turned his attention to the tools and handicrafts of the Delaware Valley, searching the countryside for tools, utensils and other artifacts made obsolete by the Industrial Revolution. He called the collection "Tools of the Nation Maker," and with more than 40,000 objects, it remains the largest of its kind in the world.

Mercer was also something of an artist. While researching local crafts, he became fascinated with a nearly forgotten style of Pennsylvania German pottery. He adapted the style to tile-making and eventually developed a commercial clay shop to produce tiles and other ceramics of his own design. By 1905, Mercer's Moravian tiles had become a major exponent of America's Arts and Crafts movement, and his work was being commissioned for such varied buildings as Grauman's Chinese Theater in Hollywood, the Harvard Lampoon building, the National Press Club in Washington, D.C., the Pennsylvania Capitol in Harrisburg, and high-class hotels all over the world.

The first building Mercer designed was **Fonthill** (East Court Street and Rt 313/Swamp Road; tel: 215-348-9461; open Monday–Saturday 10am–5pm, Sunday noon–5pm; entrance fee), a Tudor-style castle completed in 1910 and constructed entirely of reinforced concrete, a material that was just beginning to be used by professional architects. He built the castle from the inside out without benefit of detailed blueprints, improvising techniques as he went along, even pouring concrete over a farmhouse and incorporating it into the structure. The rooms are irregular, the windows unmatched and stairways sometimes go nowhere, but the overall effect of the vaulted salons, maze-like floor plan and the thousands of brilliantly colored tiles is quite astonishing. It's probably safe

Map on page 250

BELOW: the Moravian Pottery and Tile Works.

to say that you have never seen anything like it. Guided tours of Fonthill are offered several times a day; make reservations several hours in advance.

Mercer started the neighboring **Moravian Pottery and Tile Works** (130 Swamp Road; tel: 215-345-6722; open Monday–Saturday 10am–4:45pm; entrance fee) even before Fonthill was completed. Modeled after several Californian missions, this second concrete fantasy served as a tile factory well into the 1950s. The Bucks County Parks Department reopened the Tile Works as a working museum in the 1970s and it continues to turn out tiles using Mercer's original designs and techniques, although on a much smaller scale. Tours of the Tile Works leave every half hour.

Mercer followed the Tile Works with yet another medieval-style castle designed to house his massive collection of pre-industrial tools and farm implements. The **Mercer Museum** (84 South Pine Street, Doylestown; tel: 215-345-0210; open Monday–Saturday 10am–5pm, Tuesday until 9pm, Sunday noon–5pm; entrance fee) is crammed with everything from old stagecoaches to sausage-makers. Much of the collection is dramatically suspended by wires in the four-story central court. An iconoclast in almost everything he did, Mercer felt that the unusual display allowed visitors to see ordinary objects from a new perspective. Whatever his reasoning, the effect is likely to make your jaw drop.

The **James A. Michener Museum** (138 Pine Street, Doylestown; tel: 215-340-9800; call for opening times; entrance fee), named in honor of Doylestown's well-known author, is directly across the street from the Mercer Museum. The museum is located on the grounds of the former Bucks County Jail. Prison walls surround part of the site, and the warden's house now serves as gallery space for the museum's collection of 20th-century American art. The center's shows feature selections from the permanent collection in addition to work by regional artists.

You can also visit the homestead of another renowned Bucks County writer, Pearl S. Buck, author of *The Good Earth* and winner of both the Pulitzer and Nobel prizes. The **Pearl S. Buck House** ➐ (520 Dublin Road, Perkasie; tel: 215-249-0100; tours March–December, Tuesday–Saturday 11am, 1pm, 2pm, Sunday 1pm, 2pm; entrance fee) is part of a 60-acre (25-hectare) spread known as Green Hills Farm. The early 19th-century farmhouse is also now headquarters of the Pearl S. Buck Foundation, an international children's-aid agency.

In and around New Hope

A 10-minute drive southeast of Doylestown on Route 202 brings you to **Peddlar's Village** ➑, a complex of about 80 boutiques and restaurants specializing in antiques, folk art, fashions and handcrafted gifts. The shops are built around a landscaped "village green" with a pond, waterwheel, gingerbread-style gazebo and award-winning gardens. Bargain hunters should try Penn's Flea Market across Route 202 for that once-in-a-lifetime discovery, although serious antiques hunters may do better at more out-of-the-way dealers and flea markets.

BELOW:
a peaceful ride
on a country lane.

It's a 5-mile (8-km) drive on Route 202 south to the village of **New Hope ⑨**, a former ferry crossing on the Delaware River that now caters to the hordes of tourists who flock here every weekend. As a result, traffic can be horrendous, so be sure to give yourself plenty of time. A small mill town in the 1700s, New Hope boomed with the opening of the Delaware Canal in 1832. Although the railroad came along and put the waterway out of business in the early 1900s, by then New Hope was attracting a newer, different sort of crowd. The arrival of William Lathrop, Daniel Graber, Edward Redfield and other influential painters led to the growth of a lively artists' colony. And today, artists and collectors are still flocking to New Hope for the galleries and special exhibitions.

The **Delaware Canal**, named a National Heritage Corridor, is also still in operation, although the mule-drawn barges of the **New Hope Canal Boat Company** (149 South Main Street, New Hope; tel: 215-862-0758; entrance fee) now carry tourists rather than coal and lumber. The **Locktender's House**, where you pick up the barge, has been preserved and has a small free museum (tel: 215-862-2021 for information).

More than 200 historic buildings in New Hope are listed on the National Register of Historic Places. At South Main and Ferry streets, for example, the **Logan Inn** surrounds the shell of the original Ferry Tavern, which opened for business in the 1720s and is now the departure site for Bucks County Carriages, offering carriage rides through town (tel: 215-862-5883). Nearby, old Town Hall, now the **New Hope Tourist Information Center** (Main and Mechanic streets; tel: 215-862-5880; open daily), and **Vansant House** date to the latter half of the 18th century. Built in 1784, the **Parry Mansion** (New Hope Historical

Map
on page
250

*Country flea markets
are fun for buyers
and sellers alike.*

BELOW: mule-drawn
barge on the
Delaware Canal.

While in New Hope you can catch a ride on the New Hope & Ivyland Railroad (West Bridge and Stockton streets; tel: 215-862-2332; entrance fee) which runs a Baldwin steam locomotive on a 9-mile (14-km), 50-minute round-trip between New Hope and Lahaska.

BELOW:
historic Logan Inn in New Hope.

Society, 45 South Main Street; tel: 215-862-5652; open May–December, Friday–Sunday 1–5pm, group tours by appointment; entrance fee) now serves as a museum of decorative arts, displaying rooms in five different period styles, dating from 1775 to 1900.

New Hope is also home to the **Bucks County Playhouse**, which has been offering summer stock for more than 50 years from a renovated gristmill. And don't forget New Hope's sister city across the bridge in New Jersey. **Lambertville**, New Hope's less commercial alter-ego, is filled with homey restaurants, quirky shops and a more low-key attitude – in short, a perfect place to take shelter from New Hope's crowded sidewalks.

History buffs should make a point of visiting **Washington Crossing State Park** ❿ (1112 River Road, Washington Crossing; tel: 215-493-4076; open Tuesday–Saturday 9am–5pm, Sunday noon–5pm; entrance fee), where George Washington launched his daring Christmas attack on the British and Hessian camp at Trenton, an event that is reenacted every Christmas Day. The park is divided into two units. About 2 miles (3 km) south of New Hope is the **Thompson-Neely House**, where the general and his officers met to plan the attack. A short drive away, the 110-ft (30-meter) **Bowman's Tower** (open Tuesday–Sunday 9am–4:30pm), built in 1930 to commemorate a Revolutionary War lookout point, affords a spectacular view of the valley. An 80-acre (30-hectare) Wildflower Preserve (tel: 215-862-2924; open daily 9am–5pm; entrance free) surrounds the tower; a naturalist is usually on hand to answer questions and suggest tours along the many trails. About 5 miles (8 km) south, the second unit includes the **Washington Crossing Memorial Building** where a replica of Emanuel Leutze's famous painting, *Washington Crossing the Delaware*, hangs.

Rolling rivers and covered bridges

But the real flavor of Bucks County lies along the back roads and untrammeled spaces of its many farms and natural preserves. From New Hope, River Road winds along the Delaware River to the three charming towns of **Lumberville**, **Erwinna** and **Uhlerstown**. Along the way, at **Point Pleasant**, you can rent canoes and inner tubes for a float down the river. You'll find the area's loveliest parks in these northern reaches of the county, too, including the fascinating boulder field of **Ringing Rocks County Park**; the peace and isolation of **Bull's Island State Park**; the 1,450-acre (580-hectare) **Lake Nockamixon**, which is the largest body of water in the county; Tohickon Valley County Park and **Ralph Stover State Park** in the stunning Tohickon Valley; Peace Valley just north of Doylestown; and the 19th-century Erwin Stover House and **Tinicum County Park** overlooking the Delaware River in Erwinna.

Northern Bucks is also home to most of the county's 12 covered bridges, most built in the 1870s. Contact the Bucks County Conference and Visitors Bureau (152 Swamp Road, Doylestown; tel: 215-345-4554) for a guide.

A wine-tasting tour is a good way to see the countryside. Bucks County has several wineries that welcome visitors, including: **Buckingham Valley Vineyards** (1521 Rt 413, Buckingham; tel: 215-794-7188; open Tuesday–Sunday; entrance free), **New Hope Winery, Inc.** (6123 Lower York Road, Rt 202, New Hope; tel: 215-794-2331) and **Sand Castle Winery** (755 River Road, Erwinna; tel: 610-294-9181; open daily). **Chaddsford Winery** also has tastings at its retail shop (Rts 202 and 263, Peddlar's Village; tel: 215-794-9655; open daily). And, of course, Bucks County is famous for its cozy inns and classy restaurants, many in historic buildings *(see pages 271 and 280).* ❏

Map on page 250

Tubing the Delaware River is a favorite summer pastime.

BELOW: folk art on sale in New Hope.

INSIGHT GUIDES
TRAVEL TIPS

New Insight Maps

Maps in Insight Guides are tailored to complement the text. But when you're on the road you sometimes need the big picture that only a large-scale map can provide. This new range of durable Insight Fleximaps has been designed to meet just that need.

Detailed, clear cartography
makes the comprehensive route and city maps easy to follow, highlights all the major tourist sites and provides valuable motoring information plus a full index.

Informative and easy to use
with additional text and photographs covering a destination's top 10 essential sites, plus useful addresses, facts about the destination and handy tips on getting around.

Laminated finish
allows you to mark your route on the map using a non-permanent marker pen, and wipe it off. It makes the maps more durable and easier to fold than traditional maps.

The first titles
cover many popular destinations. They include Algarve, Amsterdam, Bangkok, California, Cyprus, Dominican Republic, Florence, Hong Kong, Ireland, London, Mallorca, Paris, Prague, Rome, San Francisco, Sydney, Thailand, Tuscany, USA Southwest, Venice, and Vienna.

👁 INSIGHT GUIDES
The world's largest collection of visual travel guides

CONTENTS

Getting Acquainted

The Place 258
Climate 258
Culture & Customs 258

Planning the Trip

What to Bring 259
Entry Regulations 259
Health 259
Money Matters......................259
Getting There 260
Special Facilities 261

Practical Tips

Business Hours 262
Media 262
Postal Services 262
Public Holidays 262
Telecommunications 263
Tourist Offices......................263
Embassies & Consulates 263
Tour Companies 264
Security & Crime..................264
Medical Services 265
Religious Services.................265
Tipping 266

Getting Around

On Arrival 266
Public Transportation.............266
Taxis 267
Ferries 267
By Car..................................267

Where to Stay

Choosing a Hotel...................268
Hotel Listings 268
Bed-and-Breakfasts..............272
Youth Hostels 272
Campsites............................272

Where to Eat

What to Eat 273
Liquor Laws 273
Restaurant Listings 273

Nightlife

Nightclubs, Comedy & Music.281
Jazz & Blues 282
Gay & Lesbian Venues...........282

Culture

Art Galleries 283
Cinema 284
Music....................................285
Dance Companies.................286
Theater 286

Festivals

Annual Events 288

Shopping

Shopping Areas.....................292
What to Buy 293

Children

Aquariums & Zoos.................294
Farms & Orchards 294
Museums...............................294
Theme Parks.........................295

Sports

Spectator 295
Participant 295

Further Reading

History & Culture...................297
Food 298

Getting Acquainted

The Place

State: Pennsylvania (PA).
Capital: Harrisburg.
Largest city: Philadelphia.
Situation: 39 53° N, 75 15° W, on the same approximate latitude as Madrid and Athens. Located in southeastern Pennsylvania, Philadelphia is bordered by the Delaware River, which leads to the Atlantic Ocean, and bisected by the Schuylkill River, which leads from the Delaware inland.
Population: 5.8 million in the Philadelphia metropolitan area, approximately 1.6 million of whom live in Philadelphia proper. Of these 1.6 million, 39 percent are African-American, 5.6 percent Hispanic, 2.7 percent Asian, and 0.2 percent Native American. (African-Americans comprise 20 percent, Hispanics 4 percent, and Asians 16 percent of the larger Philadelphia region.)
Area: 135 sq. miles (350 sq. km) – Philadelphia County. The Philadelphia five-county area includes the counties of Philadelphia, Bucks, Montgomery, Chester, and Delaware. Camden County, New Jersey is right across the Delaware River.
Time Zone: Eastern Time Zone or GMT minus 5 hours.
Currency: US dollars ($US), divided into 100 cents (¢).
Weights and measures: imperial.
Electricity: Standard is 110 volts; if you plan to use European-made electrical appliances, lower the voltage with a transformer and bring a plug adaptor.
International dialing code: (1).
Local dialing codes: Telephone numbers preceded by 1-800 are toll free in the US The prefix for all other numbers in the city of Philadelphia and in some northern suburbs is 215 unless otherwise noted. Most of the western suburbs use the prefix 610. Use a prefix for all calls; dial 1 first for calls using a different area code.

Climate

Philadelphia's weather runs the gamut: hot and sticky in summer, biting cold in winter, pleasant but occasionally rainy in spring, cool and crisp in fall. Summer brings sudden rainstorms, winter has a few dustings of snow, although it doesn't usually last. Keep in mind that Philadelphia weather is unpredictable. Unseasonal cold or warm spells are not uncommon, Indian summers sometimes extend balmy weather well into October, and snow can fall as late as March.

Monthly Range:

January	26–40°F (-3.3–4.4°C)
February	26–41°F (-3.3–5°C)
March	33–50°F (0.5–10°C)
April	43–62°F (6–16.7°C)
May	53–73°F (11.7–22.8°C)
June	63–81°F (17.2–27.2°C)
July	68–95°F (20–35°C)
August	66–93°F (19–34°C)
September	60–80°F (15.6–26.7°C)
October	49–66°F (9.5–19°C)
November	39–54°F (4–12°C)
December	29–43°F (-1.7–6°C)

Culture and Customs

Just 90 miles (150 km) south of New York City, Philadelphia has adopted some of the same raw energy and frenetic pace – tempered somewhat by its Quaker sensibilities and traditions. While its population is a mosaic of native Philadelphians, transplanted Americans from other regions, and foreign immigrants, it maintains a distinct identity. Like William Penn, the city's Quaker founder, it has its share of incongruities. Generally speaking, Philadelphia's Quaker tradition respects wealth but eschews ostentation, values

Fascinating Facts

Did you know that Philadelphia is a city of firsts? As well as being the United States' first capital, throughout its proud history it has given birth to America's first:
● hospital
● fire company
● insurance company
● subscription library
● zoo
● medical school
● motion picture show
● turnpike
● computer
● daily newspaper
● stock exchange
● public bank
● world's fair
● bifocal glasses
● steam automobile

self-reliance but is generous to people in need, welcomes outcasts but is clannish, values learning and culture but can be provincial in taste and outlook, reveres the past but can also be progressive.

With rare exceptions, English is spoken everywhere in Philadelphia. Like all immigrant cities, there are ethnic pockets where other languages are spoken – Chinese in Chinatown, Vietnamese, Cambodian and Italian in a few South Philadelphia locations, Spanish in the Latino community of North Philadelphia – but even in these few areas English is spoken in nearly all stores and restaurants. If you travel to Pennsylvania Dutch Country or meet Amish people in Philadelphia you may notice that they speak a Pennsylvania German dialect, but they speak English to outsiders.

Planning the Trip

What to Bring

Philadelphia has four distinct seasons. Summer is hot and humid, with an occasional cloudburst. Winter is bone-chilling and unpredictable. Heavy snow is unusual but not unheard of. The best plan for spring and fall is to dress in layers, so that you can put clothes on or take them off as the weather dictates.

Although fancy restaurants and high-class hotels expect visitors to dress appropriately (some require jackets and ties for men,) Philadelphians are, by and large, an informal lot. Most casual shops and restaurants don't mind if you wear neat shorts, a light shirt and tennis shoes during the summer, although it is always prudent to call ahead to check. In the hip parts of town, especially on South Street, just about anything goes.

Most visitors prefer to walk around Center City rather than drive or take a bus, so be sure to wear comfortable shoes or sneakers.

Entry Regulations

VISAS AND PASSPORTS

A passport, a visitor's visa and evidence of intent to leave the US after your visit are required for entry into the US by most foreign nationals. Visitors from the United Kingdom and several other countries (including but not limited to Japan, Germany, Italy, France, Switzerland, Sweden, Ireland and The Netherlands) staying less than 90 days may not need a visa if they meet certain requirements. All other foreign nationals must obtain a visa from the US consulate or embassy in their own country. An international vaccination certificate may also be required depending on your country of origin.

Exceptions to this rule are Canadians entering from the Western Hemisphere, Mexicans with border passes and British residents of Bermuda and Canada. Normally, these people do not need a visa or passport, although it's always best to confirm visa requirements before leaving your home country.

Once admitted to the US, you may visit Canada or Mexico for up to 30 days and re-enter the US without a new visa. If you happen to lose your visa or passport, arrange to get a new one at your country's nearest consulate or embassy.

CUSTOMS

All people entering the US must go through customs. Be prepared to have your luggage inspected and follow these guidelines:
1. There is no limit to the amount of cash you can bring into the US. If the amount exceeds $10,000, however, you must declare this and file a special report;
2. Any objects brought for personal use may enter duty-free;
3. Adults may enter with a maximum of 200 cigarettes or 50 cigars or 2 kilograms of tobacco and/or 1 liter of alcohol duty-free;
4. Gifts valued at less than $400 can enter duty-free;
5. Agricultural products, meat and animals are subject to complex restrictions: to avoid delays, leave these items at home unless absolutely necessary;
6. Illicit drugs and drug paraphernalia are strictly prohibited. If you must bring narcotic or habit-forming medicines for health reasons, be sure that all products are properly identified, carry only the quantity you will need while traveling, and have either a prescription or a letter from your doctor.

To obtain information, contact: **US Customs**, 1301 Constitution Avenue NW, Washington, D.C. 20229. Tel: 202-927-6724; in Philadelphia: 2nd and Chestnut streets. Tel: 215-597-4605.

EXTENSIONS OF STAY

Visas are usually granted for six months. If you wish to remain in the country longer than six months, you must apply for an extension of stay at the **Immigration and Naturalization Service**, 2401 East Street, Washington, D.C. 20520. Tel: 202-514-4330; in Philadelphia: 1600 Callowhill Street. Tel: 215-656-7144.

Health

The bad news is that health care in the US is extremely expensive. If you don't already have insurance that is accepted in the US, ask your travel agent about a travel plan that, at the very least, covers emergency medical care. The good news is that Philadelphia boasts some of the country's most prestigious hospitals and medical schools. If you become ill while traveling, Philadelphia is, all things considered, a good place to be.

Bear in mind that many private practitioners expect payment upon delivery of services. If you are unable to pay at the time of your visit, or you don't have insurance, you may be turned away.

Money Matters

CASH & TRAVELERS' CHECKS

US money is based on the decimal system. The basic unit, a dollar ($1), is equal to 100 cents. There are four basic coins, each worth less than a dollar. A penny is worth 1 cent (1¢); a nickel worth 5 cents (5¢); a dime worth 10 cents (10¢); and a quarter 25 cents (25¢). In addition there are several denominations of paper money. They are: $1, $5, $10, $20, $50, $100 and rarely, $2 bills. Each bill is the same color, size and shape, so make sure you check the dollar amount on the face of the bill. It's advisable to arrive with at least $100 in cash (in small bills) to pay for ground transportation and any other incidentals.

It's always a good idea to carry internationally recognized travelers' checks rather than cash. Travelers' checks are usually accepted by retailers in lieu of cash, or may be exchanged for limited amounts of cash at many banks. Bring your passport with you to the bank.

Money may be sent or received by wire at any Western Union Office (tel: 1-800-325-6000) or American Express MoneyGram office (tel: 1-800-543-4080). The following addresses may also be useful:
Western Union
1618 North Broad Street.
Tel: 215-232-2299.
American Express
16th Street and JFK Boulevard.
Tel: 215-587-2300.
615 Chestnut Street.
Tel: 215-592-9211.

Credit cards
Major credit cards are very useful (American Express, Visa, Master-Card, Diners Club, Carte Blanche, Discover, etc.) and will be necessary if you want to rent a car

Exchange Bureaux

In addition to select hotels and the airport, foreign currency may be exchanged at the following Center City locations:
American Express Travel Service
16th Street and JFK Boulevard.
Tel: 215-587-2300.
First Union
1500 Market Street.
Tel: 215-786-5980.
123 South Broad Street.
Tel: 215-985-8237.
Mellon PSFS Bank
1234 Market Street.
Tel: 215-561-1290.
Thomas Cook Currency Services
1800 JFK Boulevard.
Tel: 215-563-7348.

(see page 267). They are widely accepted at shops, restaurants, hotels and gas stations, although not all cards are accepted by every vendor. To be safe, try to carry at least two kinds (American Express and Visa, for example.)

Some credit cards may also be used to withdraw cash from automatic teller machines (ATMs) located throughout Center City and the outlying areas. Check with your bank or credit-card company for the systems your cards will operate.

Getting There

BY AIR

Philadelphia International Airport (general information: tel: 215-937-6937) serves both domestic and international destinations. It is in South Philadelphia, about 25 minutes by car from Center City. The airport has a general number for gate times on all flights (1-800-PHL-GATE), as well as a helpful website (www.phl.org) with maps of terminals and the first feed of the runways on the web.

An information desk is located at each of the terminals, A, B, C, D, E, and as of spring 2001, F. There are currency exchanges at Terminals A,B, D and E. A retail mall is located between Terminals B and C, and smaller food courts, in-line stores and carts sell throughout the airport. A new international terminal is scheduled to be completed by spring 2002. Baggage claim is located on the lower level, as are buses, taxis and rental car firms and hotel shuttles.

Other airports
Atlantic City International Airport services most major East Coast cities. Carriers include Northwest Airlink, United Express, US Air and TW Express. It's about a 90-minute drive from Atlantic City to Philadelphia (see page 230).

Newark International Airport in north New Jersey and **Baltimore/ Washington International Airport** in Maryland are two hours by car from Philadelphia.

Airline tickets
Several airlines operate ticket offices in Center City:
American Airlines
1500 Market Street.
Tel: 1-800-433-7300.
Delta Airlines
1617 JFK Boulevard.
Tel: 1-800-221-1212.
Korean Air
2 Penn Center Plaza.
Tel: 215-665-9080.
Olympic Airways
1515 Market Street.
Tel: 215-977-8601.
US Air
123 South Broad Street.
Tel: 1-800-428-4322.

BY BUS

Greyhound Bus Lines, America's largest bus company, has connections to cities and small towns throughout the country. The company routinely offers discounts such as a $99 go-anywhere fare (subject to certain restrictions.) Call the Greyhound office nearest you for information regarding special rates and package tours.
Greyhound Bus Lines
1001 Filbert Street.
Tel: 215-931-4027(main number) or 215-931-4035 (ticket information).

Greyhound also has a number of suburban stations just outside Philadelphia, including:
Bristol
2634 Durham Road.
Tel: 215-785-3044.
King of Prussia
234 East DeKalb Pike.
Tel: 610-768-7047.
Willow Grove
800 Fitzwatertown Road.
Tel: 215-659-3443.

BY CAR

Several highways lead to the city of Philadelphia. From New York City, the New Jersey Turnpike (exit 4) leaves you about 20 minutes outside of Philadelphia near Camden, New Jersey. From Washington, D.C. or Baltimore, I-95

Airlines

Major carriers that service Philadelphia International Airport include:

Air Aruba
Tel: 1-800-88ARUBA.

Air Canada
Tel: 1-800-776-3000.
www.aircanada.com

Air France
Tel: 1-800-237-2747.

Air Jamaica
Tel: 1-800-523-5585.

Air Tran
Tel: 1-800-825-8538.
www.airtran.com

America West
Tel: 1-800-235-9292.
www.americawest.com

American Airlines
Tel: 1-800-433-7300.
www.amrcorp.com

American Eagle
Tel: 1-800-433-7300.
www.amrcorp.com

ATA-American Trans Air
Tel: 1-800-293-FLY-ATA.
www.ata.com

British Airways
Tel: 1-800-247-9297.
www.british-airways.com

Continental Airlines, Continental, Continental Express
Tel: 1-800-525-0280.
www.flycontinental.com

Delta Airlines, Delta Connections
Tel: 1-800-221-1212.
www.delta-air.com

Lufthansa
Tel: 1-800-645-3880.

Midway
Tel: 1-800-446-4392.
www.midwayair.com

Midwest Express
Tel: 1-800-452-2022.
www.midwestexpress.com

National Airlines
Tel: 1-800-825-2880.
www.nationalairlines.com

Northwest Airlines
Tel: 1-888-EASTWIND.
www.nwa.proair.com

TWA, TransWorld Connection
Tel: 1-800-221-2000.
www.twa.com

TransStates Airlines
Tel: 1-800-221-2000.
www.transstates.com

United Airlines, United Express
Tel: 1-800-241-6522.
www.ual.com

US Air, US Airways Express
Tel: 1-800-428-4322.
www.usairways.com

(also known as the Delaware Expressway) follows the Delaware River directly through the center of the city.

From the west, the Pennsylvania Turnpike intersects I-76 (the Schuylkill Expressway); and from Atlantic City, the Atlantic City Expressway leads to the Walt Whitman Bridge and the Benjamin Franklin Bridge.

Bridges crossing the Delaware River connecting Philadelphia to New Jersey include: the Walt Whitman Bridge, Benjamin Franklin Bridge, Betsy Ross Bridge and Tacony-Palmyra Bridge.

BY RAIL

Amtrak offers services from Philadelphia's majestic 30th Street Station (originally built for the Pennsylvania Railroad) to hundreds of destinations across the country. Tel: 1-800-872-7245 for schedules, fares and other information.

Trains to New York City and Washington, D.C., run hourly (if not more often). Travel time to New York is approximately one to two hours. Travel time to Washington, D.C. is about two hours.

Special Facilities

TRAVELERS' AID

If you're stranded in the city, you may request assistance from any of these offices:

Greyhound Bus Terminal
9th and Filbert streets.
Tel: 215-238-0999.
open: Monday 10am–3pm, Tuesday 10am–4pm, Wednesday–Thursday 9am–4pm, Friday 10am–1pm.

Social Services Building
311 South Juniper Street.
Tel: 215-523-7580.
open: Monday–Friday 8:45am–4:45pm.

DISABLED AND ELDERLY TRAVELERS

For information on **SEPTA**'s services for elderly and disabled riders, tel: 215-580-7365 or 215-580-7853 (TDD). SEPTA operates Paratransit, a door-to-door van service for those who are unable to ride the bus or train. Riders must register with SEPTA in advance and make reservations. Tel: 215-580-7000 or 215-80-7712.

Moss Travel Information Service at the Moss Rehabilitation Hospital, (1200 West Tabor Road; tel: 215-456-9600 or 215-456-9602; open Monday–Friday 9am–5pm) provides disabled travelers with information on accessibility and other issues both in the United States and abroad.

Amtrak Access provides information on Amtrak's rail services for those with disabilities. Check out their website (www.amtrak.com) under Services and Locations, or write to them at 60 Massachusetts Avenue, N.E., Washington D.C. 20002.

Useful addresses
Mayor's Commission on the Disabled
Tel: 215-686-2798.
Philadelphia Corporation for Aging Seniors Helpline
Tel: 215-765-9040.

Practical Tips

Standard business hours are 9am–5pm. Many banks open a little earlier, usually 8–8:30am, and nearly all close by 3pm. A few have Saturday morning hours.

Major department stores are open 10am–7pm Monday to Saturday, until 8pm on Wednesday, and noon–5pm on Sunday. A few large supermarkets are open 24 hours. Most shops in downtown Philadelphia close by 5 or 6pm, but those in the larger malls such as Liberty Place and The Gallery may stay open later. Also, many shops are open later on Wednesdays.

Media

NEWSPAPERS AND MAGAZINES

Philadelphia has two major daily newspapers, both owned by the same firm. *The Philadelphia Inquirer* is considered to be the thinking person's paper, with award-winning journalists and in-depth coverage. Look for the Friday Weekend section for entertainment information. *The Daily News*, which calls itself the "People Paper," is published in a tabloid format, with good overviews of the news, a large sports section and popular special sections. Both papers list upcoming events.

There are a number of weekly newspapers, most available at corner boxes, delicatessens, laundromats and bookstores throughout Center City, with listings or advertisements for local nightclubs, galleries, restaurants, museums and shops. *The City Paper* and *The Philadelphia Weekly* are the two most popular.

Other newspapers are geared to particular groups, including *The Philadelphia Tribune*, an African-American newspaper, *Philadelphia Gay News*, and *Parents Express* and *MetroKids*, two free weeklies devoted to issues about children.

Philadelphia Magazine is a glossy magazine, published monthly, and contains feature articles covering culture, social life, politics and people in the Delaware Valley. The restaurant reviews are great for tips on the latest developments on the Philly food scene. *Datebook*, the rundown of upcoming events, is also very helpful.

Many bookstores in Center City carry a wide range of magazines. These include Tower Books, Borders Book Shop, Brentanos, and Waldenbooks. A selection of major daily newspapers are available at newsstands throughout Center City.

International magazines and journals can be purchased at **Afterwords** (218 South 12th Street).

TELEVISION & RADIO

Philadelphia is served by more than 10 television stations. With cable service, the number can go over 50. There are the three original commercial networks: ABC, NBC and CBS, as well as the WB channel and Fox Broadcasting. The Public Broadcasting System (PBS) is viewer supported and commercial-free.

There are more than 50 radio stations on the FM and AM dial in the Philadelphia area. Major news headlines, weather and traffic reports can be found at KYW, 1060 on the AM dial. Some of the major stations include: WIP (610 AM) sports; WRTI (90.1 AM) jazz and classical music; WHYY (90.0 AM) national public radio; WYIS (690 AM) Spanish language; WWDB (860 AM) 1980s hits; WYSP (94.1 AM) rock; WHAT (1340 AM) African-American

Postal Services

Standard postal hours are 8:30am–5pm Monday to Friday, 9am–noon Saturday. A few post

All government offices, banks and post offices are closed on public holidays, many of which are observed on the closest Monday, creating several three-day weekends. Public transportation does not run as often on these days. For a list of annual events, see page 288.

● January 1: New Year's Day
● January (3rd Monday): Martin Luther King Jr Day
● February: President's Day
● March/April: Easter Sunday
● May: Memorial Day
● July 4: Independence Day
● September: Labor Day
● October: Columbus Day
● November: Veterans' Day; Thanksgiving Day
● December 25: Christmas Day

offices have extended hours, including the Main Post Office (2970 Market Street; tel: 215-895-8000; open daily 24 hours) and the William Penn Annex (9th and Chestnut streets; tel: 215-592-9610; open Monday–Friday 8:30am–6pm, Saturday 8am–4pm). There are also three self-service postal centers: the Main Post Office, Roosevelt Mall (Welsh Road and Roosevelt Boulevard; open 8:30am–5pm) and Philadelphia Airport Concourse C *(see page 260)*, which is open 24 hours, but is only a drop-off post.

Stamps are also sold at vending machines at some convenience stores, gas stations, hotels and transportation terminals.

Other post offices in Center City include:

B. Free Franklin Station
316 Market Street.
Tel: 215-592-1289.
Continental Station
615 Chestnut Street.
Tel: 215-627-1171.
Fairmount Station
900 North 19th Street.
Tel: 215-232-4600.
John Wanamaker Station
1234 Market Street.
Tel: 215-557-9944.

Middle City
2037 Chestnut Street.
Tel: 215-567-3772.
Penn Center Station
Subway Concourse, 2 Penn Center.
Tel: 215-496-9679.

Courier services
For overnight or expedited delivery of letters and packages, contact **Federal Express** (tel: 1-800-238-5355), **DHL** (tel: 1-800-345-2727) or **United Parcel Service** (tel: 1-800-272-4877) for the office or drop box nearest you.

There are Federal Express offices in Center City at: 121 South Broad Street; 615 Chestnut Street; 11th and Market streets; 1617 JFK Boulevard; 1500 Market Street; 1900 Market Street; 2 Penn Center; 820 Spring Garden Street. United Parcel Service is at 15 East. Oregon Avenue, tel: 215-895-8984.

Telecommunications

Payphones can be found throughout the city: at restaurants, bars, hotels, gas stations, public buildings and many street corners. To operate, drop in at least 35¢ and dial your number. If you need to deposit more change, a recorded voice will tell you the amount. The prefix, or area code, in the Philadelphia area is 215. The prefix for areas immediately west and north of this calling region is 610. The prefix for the Lancaster area is 717. The prefix for Cherry Hill and the surrounding areas of New Jersey is 856. The rest of southern New Jersey is 609. You must dial the prefix for all calls, and must dial 1 before the prefix in all areas outside of the area code that you are dialing from.

If you need assistance, dial 0 and wait for the operator to answer. For directory information, dial the area code and 555-1212 or 411. Take advantage of toll-free 1-800 numbers whenever possible. Long-distance rates tend to be lower on weekends and after 5pm.

To dial other countries, first dial the international access code 011, then the country code: Australia

(61); France (33); Germany (49); Italy (39); Japan (81); Mexico (52); Spain (34); United Kingdom (44). If using a US phone credit card such as **Sprint** or **At&T**, dial the company's access number, then 01, then the country code.
Sprint
Tel: 10333.
AT&T
Tel: 10288.

Telegrams & faxes
Western Union (tel: 1-800-325-6000) can arrange telegram, telex and facsimile transmissions. **MCI International** (tel: 215-496-3200) handles business telexes and faxes. Check the phone directory or call for the nearest office.

Fax machines are available at most hotels but prices are higher. Printers, copy shops, stationers, office supply shops and convenience stores may also have them.

Tourist Offices

Greater Philadelphia Tourism Marketing Corporation
123 South Broad Street.
Tel: 215-599-0776 or 888-GOPHILA
www.gophila.com
Free trip planning guide, information

Embassies and Consulates

Austria
123 South Broad Street.
Tel: 215-772-7630.
Finland
112 Christian Street.
Tel: 215-465-5565.
France
1 Liberty Place.
Tel: 215-851-1474.
Germany
1617 JFK Boulevard.
Tel: 215-665-3263.
Israel
230 South 15th Street.
Tel: 215-546-5556.
Italy
6th and Chestnut streets.
Tel: 215-592-7329.
Japan
1735 Market Street.
Tel: 215-963-5565.

about hotels, current events, and ways to put together an itinerary.
Philadelphia Visitors Center
16th Street and JFK Boulevard.
Tel: 215-636-1666.
Philadelphia Convention and Visitors Bureau
1515 Market Street.
Tel: 215-636-3300.
www.pcvb.org
Information for large groups.
Independence National Historical Park Visitor Center
3rd and Chestnut streets.
Tel: 215-597-8974/1785.
www.nps.gov/inde
Brandywine Conference and Visitors Bureau
200 East State Street, Suite 100, Media, PA 19063.
Tel: 610-565-3679.
www.brandywinecvb.org
Bucks County Conference and Visitors Bureau
152 Swamp Road, Doylestown, PA 18901-9999.
Tel: 1-800-836-BUCKS or 215-345-4552.
Pennsylvania Dutch Convention and Visitors Bureau
501 Greenfield Road, Lancaster, PA 17601.
Tel: 717-299-8901.
www.padutchcountry.com

Mexico
Bourse Building.
Tel: 215-922-4262.
The Netherlands
45 Brennan Drive, Bryn Mawr.
Tel: 610-520-9591.
Norway
112 Christian Street.
Tel: 215-462-2502.
Panama
124 Chestnut Street.
Tel: 215-574-2994.
Spain
3410 Warden Drive.
Tel: 215-848-6180.
Sweden
8 Penn Center, Suite 2001.
Tel: 215-496-7200.
Switzerland
Public Ledger Building.
Tel: 215-922-2215.

Valley Forge Convention and Visitors Bureau
600 West Germantown Pike, Plymouth Meeting, PA 19462.
www.valleyforge.org
Atlantic City Convention and Visitors Bureau
2314 Pacific Avenue, Atlantic City, NJ 08401.
Tel: 1–888-AV-VISIT.
www.atlanticcitynj.com
Chamber of Commerce of Greater Cape May
PO Box 556, Cape May, NJ 08204.
Tel: 609-884-5508.
www.beachcomber.com/Capemay

Tour Companies

It is worth noting that some tours are seasonal, and may close or offer more limited options in the colder months.

African-American Historical Tours
1510 Cecil B. Moore Avenue, Suite 301.
Tel: 215-768-8157.
www.gatours.com
Educational, cultural and historical tours of African-American sites.
American Jewish Committee Historic Tours
Tel: 215-665-2300.
A two-hour walking tour of historic sites connected to Jewish history.
American Trolley Tours
Tel: 215-333-2119.
Tours of historic Philadelphia. Pick-up from hotels and visitors centers.
Black History Strolls and Tours
Tel: 215-242-1214.
Walking and bus tours of historic district with emphasis on African-American history and culture.
Centipede Tours
Depart from Welcome Park, 2nd and Chestnut streets.
Tel: 215-735-3123.
Candlelight walks of historic district led by costumed guides. Available in many languages. May to October.
Chef's Tour of the Italian Market
Tel: 215-772-0739.
Behind the scenes tour by Absolutely Philadelphia includes history, recipes, and sampling of various Italian delicacies. Some tour packages include lunch.

Foundation for Architecture
1727 Chestnut Street, 2nd floor.
Tel: 569-215-3187.
Call the foundation for a schedule of over 20 walking tours focusing on the city's architectural history.
Friends of Independence National Historical Park
313 Walnut Street.
Tel: 215-597-7919.
One-hour evening tours of Independence Park; summer only.
International Visitors Council
1515 Arch Street.
Tel: 215-683-0999.
A non-profit corporation offering multilingual bus and walking tours of Philadelphia's historic district and Amish country for groups.
Italian Market Tour
Tel: 215-334-6008.
Celeste Morello, author of *The Philadelphia Italian Market Cookbook*, leads a unique tour through the market.
Joseph Poon's Wokking Tour of Chinatown
1002 Arch Street.
Tel: 215-928-9333.
Tour of Chinatown's attractions, including food by chef Joseph Poon.
Lights of Liberty
6th and Chestnut streets.
Tel: 215-LIBERTY.
Sound and light show.
Murals of Philadelphia Tour
Tel: 215-568-5245.
Philadelphia Ghost Tour
5th and Chestnut streets.
Tel: 215-413-1997.
A walking tour through the historic neighborhoods of Old City and Society Hill that fills the visitor in on local spooky tales. May–November.
Philadelphia Hospitality Tours
Tel: 215-790-9901.
Non-profit organization offers customized group tours and behind the scenes access to Philadelphia treasures.
Philadelphia Trolley Works
Tel: 215-925-TOUR.
Narrated tour with on-off privileges at 20 stops through the city.
Poor Richard's Walking Tours
Tel: 215-206-1682.
www.phillywalks.com
Much praised tours of different parts of the city given by PhD

students in history from the University of Pennsylvania.
Quaker Tours
5th and Arch streets (Free Meeting-house).
Tel: 610-566-2037.
Walking tour through Old City, focusing on the Quaker influences.
The Tippler's Tour by Historic Philadelphia, Inc.
Begins at 244 South 3rd Street.
Tel: 215-629-5801.
Pub crawl visits 18th-century watering holes in Philadelphia, 5:30pm Friday through December.
Underground Railroad Trail to Freedom Tours
Tel: 215-636-3316.
Provides lists of tour operators for Underground Railroad tours in Philadelphia and Lancaster County. Brochure available at Philadelphia Visitors Center *(see page 263)*.
Brandywine Tours
Tel: 610-358-5445.
Tours of Brandywine River Valley.
Executive Events
4647 Point Pleasant Pike, Doylestown, PA 18901.
Tel: 215-766-2211.
Group and individual guided tours specializing in Bucks County.
Historic Lancaster Walking Tour
100 South Queen Street, Lancaster, PA 17603.
Tel: 717-392-1776.
Walking tours of downtown Lancaster led by costumed guides.
Lancaster Bicycle Touring
41 Greenfield Road, Lancaster, PA 17602.
Tel: 717-396-0456.
Guided bicycle tours for groups.
Mid-Atlantic Center for the Arts
1048 Washington Street, Cape May, NJ 08204.
Tel: 609-884-5404.
Walking and trolley-bus tours of Cape May's historic district and surrounding area *(see page 230)*.

Security and Crime

As with other big cities, crime is a concern in Philadelphia, but with a few precautions you shouldn't run into any trouble. Don't carry large sums of cash or wear flashy or expensive jewelry. Hang on to your purse and keep your wallet in your front pocket. Women should not travel alone at night, and no one should go into a strange or deserted area alone at night. Your best asset is knowing where you are and where you're going. With forward planning, you should be able to avoid dangerous areas.

If you need to take the subway at night, stand near other people, or, if possible, a SEPTA police officer (see page 266). Avoid riding in a car with just a few people in it. If you get on an empty bus, sit near the driver.

If you are mugged, or run into some other trouble, call or go to the nearest police station and report the crime. The police may not be much help finding your assailant, but they can do the proper paperwork for insurance claims. There is no good response to a mugging. Your safest bet is to give the mugger your money and then run away as quickly as possible, making as much noise as possible. Report the crime immediately to the police.

Loss of Belongings

If any of your possessions are lost or stolen in Philadelphia, report it to the police at once. It is unlikely that your property will be returned, but they will file reports necessary to make an insurance claim. Car theft and break ins are a real problem in Philadelphia. Keep your car doors locked even when you're in the car and lock all belongings in the trunk. If you have anything particularly valuable, you can ask your concierge to lock it in the hotel safe.

If you lose or have your credit cards or travelers' checks stolen, contact the following numbers:
American Express
Tel: 1-800-528-4800.
Visa
Tel: 1-800-336-8472.

Emergency Numbers

For police, medical or fire emergencies, dial **911** from anywhere in the city.

Carte Blanche/Diners Club
Tel: 1-800-234-6377.
MasterCard
Tel: 1-800-826-2181.

Medical Services

For a medical emergency, call 911 or go to the nearest hospital emergency room. There are over 50 hospitals in the Philadelphia area. The following are among the largest:

Children's Hospital of Philadelphia
34th Street and Civic Center Boulevard.
Tel: 215-590-1000.
Albert Einstein Medical Center
5501 Old York Road.
Tel: 215-456-7890.
Presbyterian Medical Center
39th and Market streets.
Tel: 215-662-8000.
Hahnemann University Hospital
Broad and Vine streets.
Tel: 215-762-7000.
Hospital of the University of Pennsylvania
3400 Spruce Street.
Tel: 215-662-4000.
Thomas Jefferson University Hospital
11th and Walnut streets.
Tel: 215-955-6000.
Temple University Hospital
Broad and Ontario streets.
Tel: 215-707-2000.
Pennsylvania Hospital
8th and Spruce streets.
Tel: 215-829-3000.
Friends Hospital
4641 Roosevelt Boulevard.
Tel: 215-831-1560.
Northeastern Hospital
2301 East Allegheny Avenue.
Tel: 215-291-3000.
Methodist Hospital
2301 South Broad Street.
Tel: 215-952-9000.
Medical College of Pennsylvania Hospital
3300 Henry Avenue.
Tel: 215-842-6000.
Graduate Hospital
1800 Lombard Street.
Tel: 215-893-2000.
Mercy Hospital
501 South 54th Street.
Tel: 215-748-9000.

Pharmacies
Pharmacies sell over-the-counter drugs without a doctor's prescription. For controlled drugs, including narcotics and antibiotics, you must obtain a written doctor's prescription or, in some cases, you can ask the doctor to call the pharmacy directly. There are 24-hour CVS and Rite Aid pharmacies at a number of locations, including a CVS at 1826–30 Chestnut Street (tel: 215-972-1401) and a Rite Aid at 2017–23 Broad Street in Center City.

Religious Services

The following places of worship are part of the Old Philadelphia Congregations (see page 118). You can get more information from the Old Congregations website at: www.holyexperiment.com

Gloria Dei (Old Swedes') Church
916 Swanson Street.
Tel: 215-389-1513.
Open Monday–Saturday 9am–5pm.
Cathedral Church of the Savior
3723 Chestnut Street.
Philadelphia.
This is the Episcopal Cathedral of this diocese. It's in University City, and has many activities, including jazz concerts, etc.
Christ Church
20 North American Street.
Tel: 215-922-1695.
Open Wednesday–Saturday 9am–5pm, Sunday services.
Old First Reformed Church
151 North 4th Street.
Tel: 215-922-4566.
Open by appointment.
Old St Joseph's Catholic Church
321 Willings Alley.
Tel: 215-923-1733.
Open daily 1–4pm.
Congregation Mikveh Israel
44 North 4th Street.
Tel: 215-922-5446.
Open Monday–Thursday 10am–3pm, Friday noon–5pm.
St Peter's Church
3rd and Pine streets.
Tel: 215-925-5968.
Open Monday–Friday 8am–4pm, Saturday–Sunday 1–3pm.

St Mary's Catholic Church
252 South 4th Street.
Tel: 215-923-7930.
Open Monday–Saturday
9am–4:30pm, Sunday.

Old Pine Street Presbyterian Church
412 Pine Street.
Open Monday–Friday 10am–4pm.

Old St George's Methodist Church
235 North 4th Street.
Tel: 215-925-7788.
Open Monday–Friday 10am–3pm,
Saturday–Sunday by appointment.

Holy Trinity Catholic Church
6th and Spruce streets.
Tel: 215-923-7930.
Open May–October daily 1:30–4pm.

Mother Bethel (African Methodist) Church
419 South 6th Street.
Tel: 215-925-0616.
Open Tuesday–Saturday 10am–3pm.

St Augustine's Church
4th Street, between Race
and Vine streets.
Tel: 215-627-1838.
Open Monday–Friday 11:30am–
1:30pm, Sunday 8am–1:30pm.

Arch Street Friends Meeting-house
320 Arch Street.
Tel: 215-627-2667.
Open Monday–Saturday
10am–4pm.

Society Hill Synagogue
418 Spruce Street.
Tel: 215-922-6590.
Open Monday–Friday 10am–3pm.

Seamen's Church Institute
249 Arch Street.
Tel: 215-922-2562.
Open Monday–Friday 9am–4:30pm.

Tipping

As elsewhere, service personnel in Philadelphia depend on tips for a large part of their income. With few exceptions, tipping is left up to your discretion; gratuities are not automatically added to the bill.

In most cases 15–20 percent is the going rate for tipping waiters, taxi drivers, bartenders, barbers and hairdressers. Porters and bellmen usually get about 75¢–$1 per bag, but never less than $1 total.

Getting Around

Thanks to William Penn, getting around Center City is fairly easy. The streets are laid out in an orderly grid. Traffic isn't too bad, although rush hours tend to be congested. If you're driving, it's helpful to learn in which direction the one-way streets run. There is plenty of public transportation too, but the best way to get around is on foot. From City Hall, you can walk just about anywhere in Center City within about 45 minutes.

Outside of Center City, Philadelphia seems to sprawl interminably. Public transportation is necessary to visit surrounding areas. Driving is convenient too, although finding a parking spot may be difficult.

SEPTA (Southeastern Pennsylvania Transportation Authority) operates an extensive public transit system with buses, trolleys, subways, and surface-subway cars able to take you anywhere in the city center, as well as commuter rail lines (like the famous Main Line) linking the city with the suburbs.

SEPTA
Tel: 215-580-7800.

On Arrival

The least expensive way to travel between the airport and Center City is SEPTA's Airport Rail Line (R1), which operates daily 6am–midnight, every half hour. The train departs from Market East, Suburban Station and 30th Street Station and services terminals A, B, C, D and E. The trip takes under 30 minutes. Purchase tickets before boarding.

Taxis and shuttle vans are also available, although a shuttle van costs much less. Some hotels offer complimentary shuttle service. Ask the hotel when making your reservations.

Public Transportation

BUS

SEPTA offers bus services throughout the city. The most useful bus route for visitors is the Route 76 Ben Franklin, which makes a round-trip from the Independence National Historical Park Visitor Center at 3rd and Chestnut, runs along Market Street to City Hall and then up the Benjamin Franklin Parkway to the Museum of Art and up to the zoo. Route 42 is also convenient. It runs crosstown along the Chestnut Street Transitway between 2nd and 17th streets and then crosses into West Philadelphia on Walnut Street.

Maps, timetables and tokens are available at the SEPTA customer service center at 841 Chestnut Street (open Monday–Friday 8am–4:30pm). Exact change is necessary on all routes. If you plan on using public transit often, a weekly or monthly Transpass, or daily DayPass may be worthwhile. Passes can be purchased at Market East Station, Suburban Station, 30th Street Station and 16th and JFK Boulevard.

The new Philly Phlash is also convenient. The purple shuttle bus makes a loop from Logan Circle through Center City to South Street and the waterfront 10am–6pm. An all-day pass costs $4.00.

New Jersey Transit offers a bus service from the Greyhound terminal at 10th and Filbert streets to Atlantic City, New York City and other destinations.

New Jersey Transit
Tel: 215-569-3752.

SUBWAY, TRAIN AND TROLLEY

Four subway lines run through the heart of Philadelphia:

The Market-Frankford Line runs along Market Street from 69th Street to 2nd Street and then north to the Frankford Terminal. The Subway-Surface Line runs along Market Street from 13th Street to 33rd Street and then branches off into West Philadelphia. The Broad Street Line runs along Broad Street from Fern Rock (in North Philadelphia) to Pattison Avenue (at the South Philadelphia Sports Complex), with a spur from Girard Street to 8th and Market.

Patco operates a rail link across the Delaware River between Philadelphia and Camden terminating at Lindenwold, New Jersey. Patco has four underground stations in Center City: Locust Street at 16th, 13th and 10th streets, and 8th and Market streets. Trains depart every 12 minutes weekdays 9am–midnight, every 40 minutes at other times. For further information, tel: 215-922-4600.

A network of regional rail lines link the city with suburbs in Bucks, Montgomery, Delaware and Chester counties. Board the regional lines at 30th Street Station, Suburban Station or Market East Station.

Philadelphia once had one of the country's most extensive trolley systems. Today, a few trolley tour companies run continuous loops around the city (see page 264).

Taxis

Taxis are usually available at Center City tourist spots. Rates are fairly reasonable. A 15 percent tip is customary. Call at least 30 minutes ahead for a door-to-door service to take you anywhere in the city.

These are a few of the largest taxi companies:

Yellow Cab
Tel: 215-922-4222.
Quaker City Cab
Tel: 215-726-6000.
Academy Cab
Tel: 215-333-3333.
Olde City Taxi
Tel: 215-338-0838.

Carriages

Horse-drawn carriages are a romantic (although expensive) way to see the historic district of Philadelphia. Drivers, many in 18th-century costume, act as guides. You can almost always catch a carriage at Head House Square or Independence Hall. For more information or to make reservations, contact:
Philadelphia Carriage
Tel: 215-922-6840.
76 Carriage
Tel: 215-923-8516.

Ferries

The **RiverLink Ferry** crosses the Delaware River between Penn's Landing (Delaware and Walnut streets) and the New Jersey Aquarium in Camden every 30 minutes from Camden, April–December 10am–5pm.
RiverLink Ferry
Tel: 925-LINK.

By Car

CAR RENTAL

Cars may be rented at the airport, and in many hotels and rental agencies throughout the city and suburbs. You must be at least 21 years old, have a valid driver's license and at least one major credit card to rent a car. Be sure that you are properly insured for both collision and liability. Insurance is usually not included in the base rental fee. You may already be insured by your own insurance or credit card company. It is also a good idea to inquire about an unlimited mileage package. If not, you may be charged extra per mile over a given limit.

Rental fees vary depending on the time of year, how far in advance you book your rental, and whether you are traveling on weekdays or weekends. Inquire about any discounts or benefits you may be eligible for, including corporate, credit card or frequent flyer programs. The smaller companies offer the best deals.

Below is a list of the best known rental companies:
Alamo
Tel: US 1-800-327-9633.
Tel: International +1-305-522 0000.

Center City Streets

Market Street, running east-west, and Broad Street, running north-south, are two main avenues which intersect at City Hall. Streets named by number run north and south (14th Street is Broad Street, also known as Avenue of the Arts.) South of Market, many of the streets running east-west are named after trees.

Avis
Tel: US 1-800-331 1212.
Tel: International +1-918-664 4600.
Budget
Tel: US 1-800-527-0700.
Tel: International +1-214-404 7600.
Dollar
Tel: US 1-800 800 4000.
Tel: International +1-813-877 5507.
Enterprise
Tel: US 1-800-325-8007.
Tel: International +1-314-781 8232.
Hertz
Tel: US 1-800-654-3131.
Tel: International +1-405-749 4424.
National
Tel: US 1-800-227-7368.
Tel: International +1-612-830 2345.
Thrifty
Tel: US 1-800-331-4200.
Tel: International +1-918 669 2499.

DRIVING IN PHILADELPHIA

Three major arteries cross Philadelphia. Although often slowed by rush-hour traffic, they make it easy to get from one end of the city to the other during off-peak hours.

I-76, or the Schuylkill Expressway, runs along the Schuylkill River from northwest Philadelphia to the Walt Whitman Bridge in South Philadelphia. I-95 runs north-south through the city along the Delaware River; 676, or the Vine Street Expressway, runs east-west across Center City.

If you plan to do a lot of driving during your visit, it's worth buying a membership to the **Automobile Association of America** (AAA), which, in addition to free maps and guidebooks, provides emergency road service, insurance and bail bond protection.

Automobile Association of America
2040 Market Street.
Tel: 215-864-5000.
Emergency Road Service
Tel: 215-569-4411.

PARKING

Two words strike fear in the heart of every Philadelphia motorist: meter maid! The Parking Violations Bureau is extremely efficient. If you park illegally, you will get a ticket. And if you don't pay the fine within the allotted time, you will get slapped with a hefty penalty.

Street parking in Center City can be frustrating. Spaces are often scarce, and most parking meters accept quarters only. If you can't find a space, it is almost always cheaper to leave the car in a parking lot or garage than to pay a parking ticket. There are garages and parking lots throughout Center City; rates tend to be lower in Chinatown. For information on locations and rates, check the telephone directory.

Limousines

Luxurious but expensive, most limousine companies charge a minimum fee plus an hourly and/or mileage rate. Here are just a few of the many companies (check out the *Yellow Pages* for a complete listing.)

Boston Coach
Tel: 1-800-672-7676.
Limelight Limousine
Tel: 215-533-6169.
Dave's Best Limousine
Tel: 215-288-1000.
Liberty Limousine
Tel: 1-800-654-6614.
Carey Limousine
Tel: 610-595-2800
or 1-800-336-4646.
RV Limousine
Tel: 215-743-2700.

Where to Stay

Choosing a Hotel

The opening of numerous high-quality hotels in recent years has encouraged competitive prices, making Philadelphia hotels especially good value, with a wide range of options. At most hotels, rates fluctuate widely based on day of the week, season, availability, and applicable discounts. Reservations are essential at nearly all Center City hotels, especially during the May to September season. If you reserve by telephone, you will need a credit card to guarantee the room. If you do not have a credit card, you may be asked to send a deposit by mail. Be sure to ask about weekend and other specials. Many hotels rely on the business trade and are willing to offer discounts in order to boost occupancy rates over the weekend.

There are many chain motels outside the city most of which are clean, simple and reasonably priced.

Hotels are listed by region in the same order as the Places section of this guide, and then alphabetically by town. Philadelphia hotels are listed by area and price category.

Hotel Listings

CENTER CITY

Deluxe
Four Seasons Hotel
18th Street and B. Franklin Parkway.
Tel: 215-63-1500; fax; 215-963-9506; toll free 1-800-332-3442.
www.fourseasons.com
Elegant hotel on Logan Square near Franklin Institute and Museum of Art. Amenities include first-class Fountain Restaurant and Swann Café, concierge, indoor pool, spa,

massage, air-conditioning, minibar, TV and valet parking.
Rittenhouse Hotel
210 West Rittenhouse Square.
Tel: 215-546-9000; fax: 215-732-3364; toll free: 1-800-635-1042.
www.ritzcarlton.com
Luxury and convenience in a modern concrete-and-glass tower on Rittenhouse Square. Amenities: fine dining at Treetops overlooking the park, Boathouse Row Bar, and afternoon tea at the cozy Cassatt Tea Room (the hotel is on the site of the former Cassatt mansion), fitness club, indoor pool, business center, bank, minibar, air-conditioning, TV.
Ritz-Carlton
10 Avenue of the Arts.
Tel: 215-735-7700; fax: 215-735-7710; toll free: 1-800-241-3333.
Beautiful renovation of historic Girard/Mellon Bank building near City Hall. This elegant 330-room hotel offers fine dining at the Pantheon, Paris Bar & Grill and Vault restaurants and afternoon tea or drinks at the rotunda lobby lounge.

Expensive
Crown Plaza
18th and Market streets.
Tel: 215-561-7500; fax: 215-561-4484; toll free: 1-800-227-6963.
email: skirby@bristolhotels.com
A comfortable chain hotel with 445 rooms within walking distance of Rittenhouse Square, City Hall, Liberty Place and Logan Square. Amenities: restaurant, lounge, pool, gift shop, small fitness room, air-conditioning, TV, parking.
Doubletree Hotel
Broad and Locust streets.
Tel: 215-893-1600;
toll free: 1-800-222-TREE.
On the Avenue of the Arts, across from the Academy of Music and Merriam Theatre, adjacent to the Wilma Theatre, this 427-room high rise hotel includes a restaurant, lounge, health club, and pool.
Embassy Suites Center City
1776 Benjamin Franklin Parkway.
Tel: 215-561-1776; fax 215-963-0122; toll free: 1-800-EMBASSY.
Reliable good value chain in the Parkway Museum District. Two-room suites with bars, complementary

cooked-to-order breakfast, bar, reception, and exercise facility.

Holiday Inn Independence Mall
4th and Arch streets.
Tel: 215-923-8660;
toll free 1-800-465-4329.
Old City hotel with Early American-style decor; walking distance from Independence Hall and Liberty Bell. Amenities: restaurant, lounge, café, outdoor pool, air-conditioning, TV, parking.

Hotel Sofite Philadelphia
17th and Sansom streets.
Tel: 215-569-8300; fax: 215-569-1492. www.sofitelphiladelphia.com
New French hotel in renovated former Philadelphia stock exchange building features dining in French bistro, and live music nightly in the lobby bar. Amenities include internet service, concierge, fitness center, valet parking, gift shop.

The Inn on Locust
1234 Locust Street.
Tel: 215-985-1905.
Boutique hotel with state of the art technology in a Georgian revival building; geared to business travelers, with internet access, room-to-room computer terminal connections, kitchenettes, 2-line telephones, and rooms which convert to conference rooms. Dining at Globar, on the ground floor.

The Latham Hotel
17th and Walnut streets.
Tel: 215-563-7474,
toll free 1-877-528-4261.
Renovated old-world style hotel near Rittenhouse Square. Amenities: restaurant, lounge, concierge, laundry service, exercise facility, air-conditioning, minibar, TV.

Loews Philadelphia Hotel
1200 Market Street.
Tel: 215-627-1200;
fax: 215-564-1985.
New Art Deco decor in architectural landmark, the PSFS tower, with 583 guest rooms, exercise facility and restaurants across from the Convention Center. Amenities: minibar, cordless phone, and printer/fax/copier.

Omni Hotel at Independence Park
401 Chestnut Street.
Tel: 215-925-0000;
toll free 1-800-THE-OMNI.

Plush, sleek, hotel located in Old City adjacent to Independence National Park. Amenities: Azalea, a gourmet restaurant, lounge; indoor pool, health club, sauna, concierge, air-conditioning, TV.

Park Hyatt at the Bellevue
Broad and Walnut streets.
Tel: 215-893-1776;
toll free 1-800-233-1234.
Elegant but unpretentious, the revamped Bellevue is comfortable with an airy central atrium and lovely city views; near City Hall and the Academy of Music. Amenities: Founders, a gourmet restaurant with breathtaking views, health club with indoor pool, smart shops on lower level, valet parking, concierge, air-conditioning, TV, VCR, minibar.

Philadelphia Downtown Marriott
1201 Market Street.
Tel: 215-625-2900; fax: 215-625-6000; toll free 1-800-228-9290.
This comfortable new chain hotel designed for business travelers is connected by skywalk to Convention Center. Amenities: TV, three restaurants, coffee house, health club, indoor pool, air conditioning, airport shuttle.

St Regis Hotel
17th and Chestnut streets at Liberty Place.
Tel: 215-563-1600;
toll free 1-800-325-3589.
Part of the Liberty Place complex in business/financial district; tasteful decor evokes Federal Philadelphia. Amenities: two restaurants and bar, several restaurants elsewhere in Liberty Place complex, fitness center, currency exchange, gift shop, concierge, air-conditioning, minibar, TV, valet parking.

Sheraton Rittenhouse Square Hotel
18th and Locust streets.
Tel: 215-546-9400;
toll free: 1-800-325-3535.
www.sheratonphiladelphia.com
Environmentally conscious non-smoking hotel with 193 rooms with freshly filtered air and unbleached cotton bedding. Internet access.

Sheraton Society Hill
1 Dock Street.
Tel: 215-238-6000;
toll free 1-800-325-3535.

Price Guide

The price guide below indicates approximate rates for a standard double room.
$$$$ Deluxe: over $300
$$$ Expensive: $175–$300
$$ Moderate: $125–$175
$ Budget: under $125

Understated Society Hill hotel with Colonial style furnishings, convenient to Independence Park historic district, South Street and river front. Amenities: restaurant, lounge, indoor pool, health club, concierge, laundry service, valet parking, air-conditioning, minibar, TV.

Moderate

Alexander Inn
12th and Spruce streets.
Tel: 215-923-3535;
fax. 215-923-1004.
www.alexanderinn.com
Boutique 48-room hotel near Antique Row in Washington Square district features Continental breakfast buffet and fitness center.

Best Western Independence Park Inn
235 Chestnut Street.
Tel: 215-922-4443; fax: 215-922-4487; toll free 1-800-624-2988.
www.bestwestern.com
Smaller five-story Victorian hotel, newly renovated, with homey Colonial-style decor. Amenities: morning paper, afternoon tea, concierge, air-conditioning, TV, free Continental breakfast.

Clarion Suites
1010 Race Street.
Tel: 215-922-1730;
toll free 1-800-228-5151.
Located in the heart of Chinatown, with 96 suites decked out in interesting Chinese-style decor. Amenities: conference facilities, free Continental breakfast, air-conditioning, TV, free parking (on first-come-first-served basis.)

Hawthorn Suites
1100 Vine Street.
Tel: 215-829-8300; fax: 215-829-8104; toll free 1-800-527-1133.
Hotel near the Convention Center with one- and two-room suites.

Complimentary breakfast, exercise facilities, store, air-conditioning, TV, parking.

Hilton Garden Inn
1100 Arch Street.
Tel: 215-923-0100.
Adjacent to the Convention Center and The Gallery shopping mall in Center City, within walking distance of Reading Terminal Market, historic district, Chinatown, theaters and shopping. The 279 rooms and suites are equipped with desk, 2-line telephones with speaker phone, voice mail and dataport, microwave, refrigerator and coffee-makers. Amenities include business center, restaurant, lounge, indoor pool, fitness center, and whirlpool spa.

Korman Suites Hotel
20th and Hamilton streets.
Tel: 215-569-7200.
Luxury hotel and conference center especially designed for business travelers and long-term visitors, located near Benjamin Franklin Parkway. Amenities: restaurant, health club, outdoor pool, kitchenettes and washer-dryers, meeting facilities, shuttle service to Center City, air-conditioning, TV, parking.

Penns View Inn
14 North Front Street.
Tel: 215-922-7600;
toll free 1-800-331-7634.
Converted 19th-century warehouse in Old City, on the National Register of Historic Places, with 28 tastefully furnished rooms overlooking the Delaware River. Amenities: fine dining at Ristorante Panorama, some rooms with Jacuzzi and fireplace, complimentary breakfast, air-conditioning, TV, parking.

Thomas Bond House
129 South 2nd Street.
Tel: 215-923-8523;
toll free 1-800-845-2663.
A charming Federal-style bed-and-breakfast maintained by the National Park Service with 10 rooms and two suites in the heart of historic district. Amenities: some rooms with fireplace, whirlpool, sofa bed, free Continental breakfast.

The Warwick
17th and Locust streets.
Tel: 215-735-6000;
toll free 1-800-523-4210.

Luxurious, European-style former apartment building located near Rittenhouse Square and Liberty Place, lavishly decorated with painstaking attention to detail. Amenities: fine dining at The Prime Rib, Capriccio Café, bar and grill, concierge, free use of nearby health club, air-conditioning, TV.

Wyndham Franklin Plaza
17th and Race streets.
Tel: 215-448-2000; fax: 215-448-2864; toll free 1-800-822-4200.
Modern hotel with thoughtful contemporary details located near Logan Square. Amenities: two restaurants, indoor pool, fitness center, tennis courts, concierge, air-conditioning, TV, valet parking.

Budget
Comfort Inn at Penn's Landing
100 North Columbus Boulevard.
Tel: 1-800-228-5150.
Comfortable lodging near Penn's Landing between busy river front street and I-95. Amenities: lounge, shuttle to historic district, air-conditioning, TV, free parking, free Continental breakfast.

Holiday Inn Express
1305 Walnut Street.
Tel: 215-735-9300;
toll free 1-800-465-4329.
Mid-range accommodation near City Hall. Amenities: restaurant, lounge, pool, air-conditioning, TV, parking.

Rodeway Inn
1208 Walnut Street.
Tel: 215-546-7000;
toll free: 1-800-887-1776.
Near Avenue of the Arts. Amenities: air-conditioning, free Continental breakfast, TV, concierge.

UNIVERSITY CITY

Expensive
The Inn at Penn
3600 Samson Street.
Tel: 215-222-0200/4600;
toll free 1-800-222-8733.
A classy new Doubletree addition to University City. Each of the 238 rooms has two dual-line phones, voice mail, dataports and Internet access. Concierge, fitness center, valet parking, restaurants including

Ivy Grill Bar, the Ivy Grill, and the cozy Living Room lounge.

Penn Tower Hotel
Civic Center Boulevard and 34th Street.
Tel: 215-387-8333;
toll free 1-800-356-7366.
A pleasant modern hotel owned by the University of Pennsylvania. Close to the Civic Center, University Museum, Franklin Fields and other campus sites. Amenities: breakfast, fresh flowers, restaurant, lounge, concierge, meeting facilities, gift shop, air-conditioning, TV, parking.

Moderate
Sheraton University City
36th and Chestnut streets.
Tel: 215-387-8000;
toll free 1-800-325-3535.
www.sheraton.com/universitycity
Comfortably appointed with surprisingly pleasant decorative touches, popular with business people and tourists, and within walking distance to University of Pennsylvania campus and Civic Center. Amenities: restaurant, gift shop, outdoor pool, shuttle to airport and 30th Street Station, air-conditioning, TV, parking.

Budget
The International House
3701 Chestnut Street.
Tel: 215-387-5125.
Clean but minimal dormitory-style lodging near University of Pennsylvania campus; popular with students. Amenities: shared bath, bring your own soap and toiletries.

NORTH AND WEST PHILADELPHIA

Expensive
Philadelphia Marriott West
111 Crawford Avenue (Matson Ford at Front Street), Conshohoken.
Tel: 610-941-5600; fax 620-941-4425; toll free: 1-800-237-3639.
Located just off I-76 and I-476 between Philadelphia and Valley Forge, this high-rise luxury hotel has easy access to attractions in both areas. Amenities: parking, fitness center, indoor pool, restaurants.

Moderate
Adams Mark Philadelphia
City Line Avenue and Monument
Road, PA 19131.
Tel: 215-581-5000; fax: 215-581-
5000; toll free 1-800-444-2326.
www.adamsmark.com
Contemporary hotel in western
flank of city, 15-minute drive from
Center City. Amenities:
restaurants, nightclub, bar,
meeting facilities, indoor and outdoor pools, health club, air-
conditioning, TV, parking.
Doubletree Club Hotel
9461 Roosevelt Boulevard,
PA 19114.
Tel: 215-671-9600;
toll free 1-800-325-3535.
Chain hotel in northeast Philadelphia about 30 minutes from Center
City. Amenities: restaurant, lounge,
gift shop, fitness facilities, pool, air-
conditioning, TV, parking.
Holiday Inn-City Line
4100 Presidential Boulevard,
PA 19131.
Tel: 215-477-0200;
toll free: 800-HOLIDAY.
Modern hotel on the western edge of
the city 15 minutes from downtown.
Amenities: restaurant, meeting
rooms, gift shop, swimming pool, air-
conditioning, TV, free parking.

Budget
Best Western
11580 Roosevelt Boulevard,
PA 19116.
Tel: 215-464-9500;
toll free 1-800-528-1234.
Good, clean motel about 25–30
minutes north of Center City.
Amenities: restaurant, lounge,
fitness center, outdoor pool, games
room, air-conditioning, TV, parking.

AIRPORT AREA

Expensive
Embassy Suites Hotel
9000 Bartram Avenue, PA 19153.
Tel: 215-365-4500;
toll free 1-800-362-2779.
Well-appointed business hotel with
two-room suites, close to the airport and 15–20 minutes' drive from
Center City. Amenities: restaurant,

indoor pool, health club, airport
shuttle, complimentary breakfast,
air-conditioning, TV, free parking.

Moderate
Hilton Philadelphia Airport
4509 Island Avenue, PA 19153.
Tel: 215-365-4150;
toll free 1-800-445-8667.
Business hotel near airport.
Amenities: exercise room, gift shop,
restaurant, free airport shuttle, air-
conditioning, TV, free parking.
Marriott Philadelphia Airport
8950 Essington Avenue, PA 19153.
Tel: 215-492-9000;
toll free 1-800-228-9290.
Hotel for business travelers,
connected to the airport by a
skywalk. Amenities: exercise room,
indoor pool, gift shop, lounge, two
restaurants, air-conditioning, TV,
free parking.

Price Guide

The price guide below indicates
approximate rates for a standard
double room.
$$$$ Deluxe: over $300
$$$ Expensive: $175–$300
$$ Moderate: $125–$175
$ Budget: under $125

**Westin Suites Philadelphia
Airport**
4101 Island Avenue, PA 19153.
Tel: 215-563-1600;
toll free 1-800-937-8461.
Plush accommodation popular with
business travelers, 15–20 minutes
south of Center City. Amenities:
restaurant, health club, indoor pool,
breakfast, air-conditioning, TV, free
parking, airport shuttle.

BRANDYWINE RIVER
VALLEY

Wilmington
Hotel du Pont
11th and Market streets, Delaware
PA 19801.
Tel: 302-594-3100; fax: 302-594-
3108; toll free 1-800-441-9019.
Early 20th-century grandeur in the
historic heart of Wilmington. **$$**

PENNSYLVANIA DUTCH
COUNTRY

Gettysburg
Historic Farnsworth House Inn
401 Baltimore Street, PA 17033.
Tel: 717-334-8838.
Authentically restored inn *circa*
1810, with some guest rooms that
are reportedly haunted. **$$**

Hershey
Hotel Hershey
Hotel Road, PA 17033.
Tel: 717-533-2171.
A grand hotel in the finest European
tradition, the newly restored Hotel
Hershey offers 235 deluxe guest
rooms, four suites and The Milton
Hershey Presidential Suite, indoor
and outdoor pools, tobogganing and
cross-country skiing. **$$$$**

Narvon
Inn at Twin Lindens
2092 Main Street, PA 17555.
Tel: 717-445-7619;
fax: 717-445-4656.
Historic inn with eight elegant
rooms and suites. Gourmet breakfast and afternoon tea by nationally
renowned chef; Saturday night
dinner by reservation only. Outdoor
Jacuzzi overlooks Amish farms. **$$$**

BUCKS COUNTY

Doylestown
Pine Tree Farm Bed & Breakfast
2155 Lower State Road, PA 18901.
Tel: 215-348-0632.
Stone farmhouse dating to 1730 on
16 acres just outside town, with
four guest rooms. Amenities: pool,
lounge, library, air-conditioning,
parking, breakfast. **$$$$**

Erwinna
Evermay on the Delaware
River Road, P.O. Box 60, PA 18920.
Tel: 610-294-9100, 877-864-2365;
fax: 610-294-8249.
e-mail: moffly@evermay.com
Eighteen rooms on 25-acre garden
spot on Delaware River. Amenities:
private bath, meeting facilities,
dinner served Friday–Sunday, free
breakfast. **$$$$**

Holicong
Barley Sheaf Farm
Route 202, PA 18928.
Tel: 215-794-5104.
Ivy-covered stone house dating from 1740 on 30 acres, 5 miles (8 km) west of New Hope. Amenities: private bath, antiques, garden, some rooms with fireplaces, complimentary breakfast. **$$$–$$$$**

Lahaska
Golden Plough Inn
Route 202 and Street Road, PA 19831.
Tel: 215-794-4004; fax: 215-794-4008. www.goldenploughinn.com
Country inn in the Peddlar's Village shopping complex. Amenities: many four-poster and canopy beds, TV, bath, refrigerator, air-conditioning, some rooms with fireplace and/or whirlpool, VCR and balcony, parking, free Continental breakfast. **$$–$$$**

Lumberville
Black Bass Hotel
River Road, PA 18933.
Tel: 215-297-5770/862-9139; fax: 215-862-3244.
Delightful historic inn on the Delaware River with seven rooms and three suites. Amenities: shared bath, river views, restaurant open for lunch and dinner, bar, small corporate meeting room facilities, parking. **$$$$**

New Hope
Aaron Burr House
80 West Bridge Street, PA 18938.
Tel: 215-862-2520; fax: 215-862-2570. e-mail: stay@newhope.com
A lovely Victorian bed-and-breakfast in town with 10 rooms. Amenities: some rooms with canopy beds and/or fireplaces, air-conditioning, parking. **$$$**
Center Bridge Inn
2998 North River Road, Route 32, PA 18938.
Tel: 215-862-2048/9139; fax: 215-862-3244.
e-mail: inn@centerbridgeinn.com
Modern inn less than 4 miles (7 km) from town with views of river. Amenities: complimentary breakfast, dining room, canopy, brass or four-poster beds, deck, private bath,

Price Guide

The price guide below indicates approximate rates for a standard double room.
$$$$ Deluxe: over $300
$$$ Expensive: $175–$300
$$ Moderate: $125–$175
$ Budget: under $125

some rooms with TV and air-conditioning, parking. **$$$$**
Logan Inn
10 West Ferry Street, PA 18938.
Tel: 215-862-2300; fax: 215-862-3931.
Renovated inn dating from 1727 with 16 rooms decorated in Colonial style. Amenities: four-poster beds, antiques, private bath, restaurant, tavern, air-conditioning, TV, parking, free full breakfast. **$$**
New Hope Inn
36 West Mechanic Street, PA 18938.
Tel: 215-862-2078, 888-272-2078; fax: 215-862-9119.
Modern lodging in center of town with 33 guest rooms, studios and suites. Amenities: some rooms with fireplaces, outdoor pool, TV. **$$$**
New Hope Motel in the Woods
400 West Bridge Street, Route 179, PA 18938.
Tel: 215-862-2800.
Comfortable but modest lodging on five wooded acres less than 1 mile (2 km) from town center. Amenities: heated pool, color cable TV, parking, refrigerator, bath. AAA approved. **$**
The Wedgewood Inn of New Hope
111 West Bridge Street, PA 18938.
Tel: 215-862-2570; fax: 215-862-2570.
Lovely bed-and-breakfast on 2-acre landscaped grounds with 12 rooms and suites near town center. Amenities: air-conditioning, private baths, some rooms with fireplaces, pool and tennis club privileges, free breakfast. 3-diamond, AAA approved. **$$$**

Point Pleasant
Tattersall Inn
River and Cafferty roads, PA 18950.

Tel: 215-297-8233; fax: 215-297-5093; toll free 1-800-297-4988.
e-mail: tattersallinn@aol.com
Bed-and-breakfast in historic Stover Mansion on the Delaware. Amenities: breakfast in room, dining room or on veranda, bath, lounge with fireplace, air-conditioning, parking. **$$$**

Bed-and-Breakfasts

Scores of people in the city, suburbs and countryside open their homes to guests. Situations and rates vary widely, from inexpensive and modest to the truly elegant and unique. For further information contact:
Bed and Breakfast Connection of Philadelphia
PO Box 21, Devon, PA 19333.
Tel: 610-687-3565; toll free 1-800-448-3619.
e-mail: bnb@bnbphiladel phia.com
www.bnbphiladelphia.com
La Reserve
1804 Pine Street.
Tel: 215-735-1137.
www.centercitybed.com
1853 townhouse in the heart of Rittenhouse Square. Eight guest rooms, private and shared baths. Drawing room, living room with 1903 Steinway piano on which guests are welcome to play, library, private garden and breakfast in the chandeliered dining room. **$–$$**

Youth Hostels

Chaminoux Mansion
West Fairmount Park.
Tel: 215-878-3676.
Early 19th-century country estate serves as Philadelphia's youth hostel. Accommodations (dormitory-style) and fees are minimal. Closed: 15 December–15 January.

Campsites

Campsites are available at state parks throughout the Philadelphia area. For information, contact:
Department of Environmental Resources
Bureau of State Parks, P.O. Box 8551, Harrisburg, PA 17105.
Tel: 717-772-0239; toll free 1-800-637-2757.

Where to Eat

What to Eat

Visitors are often surprised at the variety and quality of Philadelphia dining. The fact is, Philly is a great restaurant town, with a wide range of ethnic eateries, truly fine cuisine, casual spots and hotel dining.

Dining here is good value too, especially at the high end. With the exception of the fancier places, casual but neat dress is suitable for just about any occasion. Reservations may be required at the fancier restaurants and are strongly recommended elsewhere.

For those who have never experienced Philly food there are a few local specialties that you may not be familiar with, many of which come from the city's rich Pennsylvania Dutch heritage. Often served with breakfast, scrapple is a spicy mixture of ground meat and cornmeal fried up and served hot as a side dish. Philadelphia's favorite snack, soft pretzels with mustard, is another Pennsylvania Dutch treat and is sold by street vendors throughout Center City (see page 89). If a waiter asks you whether you like your bottom wet or dry, don't be offended. He's probably talking about shoofly pie, a rich molasses pie which may be served with a sticky wet base or a dry crumbly base.

Philadelphia is also home to the cheesesteak, a hot sandwich made with paper-thin strips of grilled beef smothered in gooey orange cheese, garnished with fried onions, hot peppers and mushrooms (optional), and served on a hoagie roll. What's a hoagie? In other towns, they're called submarine sandwiches or grinders. In Philly, these long overstuffed sandwiches are called hoagies, a name which some Philadelphians

believe is a reference to the preferred repast at the old Hog Island Shipyard, the largest of its day. If you're prowling South Philly for good eats, you may also see signs for water ice, a refreshing combination of crushed ice and pulpy juice known elsewhere as Italian ice.

Liquor Laws

Thanks to the city's Quaker heritage, Philadelphia's liquor laws are arcane and restrictive. Hard liquor and wines (but not chilled wine) are sold at state liquor stores. Cold beer can be purchased at licensed convenience stores, delicatessens, taverns or restaurants but tends to be expensive. For large quantities of beer at a decent price, you have to go to a beer distributor. Wine, beer and mixed drinks are available by the bottle or by the glass at restaurants with a liquor license. Restaurants that do not serve alcohol often permit customers to bring their own (and are typically identified by the designation BYOB.)

The legal drinking age is 21. You may be asked to show picture identification proving your age at bars, restaurants or liquor stores. Alcohol may not be served at bars or restaurants after 2am, or 3am at private clubs.

Restaurant Listings

Restaurants are arranged in alphabetical order first by cuisine and style of dining (cafés, steak-houses, etc.) in and near Center City and by location out of Center City. As restaurants establish unique identities, the categories below may overlap, as in American and steak or seafood houses, or international with the particular international cuisines.

American

American food, like America itself, can be plain or fancy, bland or spicy. It can mean old standbys like roast chicken or hamburgers, or finely tuned regional cuisine like Southern Cajun or Creole.

Astral Plane
1708 Lombard Street.
Tel: 215-546-6230.
A romantic, artsy hideaway with an inventive American menu. Lunch weekdays, dinner daily, Sunday brunch. $$$

Bridget Foy's
2nd and South streets.
Tel: 215-922-1813.
A South Street institution specializing in seasonal American cuisine. Lunch, dinner, Sunday brunch, late night. $$

Café Nola
117 South Street.
Tel: 215-351-6652 (NOLA).
A South Street favorite. A casual café includes a French Quarter raw seafood bar, and the main dining room offers tantalizing Cajun and creole dishes. Lunch Saturday–Sunday, dinner daily. $$$

Circa
1518 Walnut Street.
Tel: 215-545-6800.
Contemporary American, seafood and pasta dishes served in an ornate former bank in a lively atmosphere. Lunch, dinner, late night. $$

City Tavern
2nd and Walnut streets.
Tel: 215-413-1443.
This reconstructed 18th-century tavern serving Colonial-style cuisine makes a great stop for history buffs trying to round out the Old City experience. Lunch and dinner daily. $$$$

Copa, Too
263 South 15th Street.
Tel: 215-355-0848.
Boisterous bar-and-burger place with Tex-Mex dishes. The Spanish fries are a greasy treat. South Street and Rittenhouse locations. Lunch and dinner served daily. $

Price Guide

The price guide indicates approximate cost of dinner excluding beverages, tax and tip.
$ = under $15
$$ = $15–$25
$$$ = $25–$40
$$$$ = over $40

Cutters Grand Café
2005 Market Street.
Tel: 215-851-6262.
Smart and swanky establishment which has won kudos for wide-ranging menu, terrific two-story bar and high-profile atmosphere. Lunch Monday–Friday, dinner daily. **$$$**

Dock Street Brewing Company Brewery and Restaurant
18th and Cherry streets.
Tel: 215-496-0413.
A contemporary tavern/restaurant/brewery serving hearty eclectic fare and a variety of ales and lagers brewed on the premises. Located off the Parkway near the museum district. Lunch and dinner daily, Sunday brunch. **$$**

Hard Rock Café
12th and Market streets.
Tel: 215-238-1000.
Music and rock memorabilia surround you in this popular theme chain. Lunch, dinner, late night. **$$**

Jack's Firehouse
2130 Fairmount Avenue.
Tel: 215-232-9000.
Innovative (occasionally unusual) American regional country cooking presented in a converted firehouse near the Museum of Art. Lunch, dinner daily, Sunday brunch. **$$$**

Johnny Rockets
443 South Street.
Tel: 215-829-9222.
A 1940s-era malt/burger shop with jukeboxes on the tables and counter seating, and a kid-friendly menu. Breakfast, lunch, dinner, late night. **$**

Judy's Café
3rd and Bainbridge streets.
Tel: 215-928-1968.
A friendly longstanding Queen Village spot known for hearty American specialties and warm, neighborhood atmosphere. Dinner, Sunday brunch. **$$**

Melrose Diner
1501 Snyder Avenue.
Tel: 215-467-6644.
South Philadelphia's monument to the gum-chewing waitress. Solid diner fare. Usually fun for a late-night stop, although the service is occasionally too gruff for some people's liking. 24 hours. No credit cards accepted. **$**

Novelty
15 South Third Street.
Tel: 215-627-7885.
Renovated early 20th-century warehouse, former home of the General Novelty Store, provides a dramatic setting of exposed bricks and pipes for a creative mix of American cuisine with ethnic influences by chef-owner Bruce Cooper, the creator of Manayunk's popular Jakes (see page 280). Lunch Monday–Friday, dinner daily, Sunday brunch. **$$$**

Ortliebs Jazz Haus
847 North 3rd Street.
Tel: 215-922-1035.
Brewery tavern serving Cajun and Continental cuisine. Known for its nightly jazz. Dinner only. **$$**

Ron's Ribs
1627 South Street.
Tel: 215-545-9160.
Stripped-down rib joint that does one thing and does it right. Takeout, too. Lunch and dinner Monday–Saturday, Sunday brunch. **$**

Rouge
205 South 18th Street.
Tel: 215-732-6622.
Well-prepared seafood and meats served with cocktail classics in a sociable setting overlooking Rittenhouse Square. **$$$**

White Dog Café
3420 Sansom Street.
Tel: 215-386-9224.
A perfect fit in University City's politically correct, artsy atmosphere, with imaginative cuisine, great desserts and a lively bar. Lunch Monday–Friday, dinner daily, brunch Saturday–Sunday. **$$–$$$**

Warmdaddy's
Front and Market streets.
Tel: 215-627-2500/8400.
Live blues and Southern soul food. Dinner only Tuesday–Sunday. **$$$**

Zanzibar Blue
200 South Broad Street.
Tel: 215-732-5200.
Great jazz and cuisine featuring grilled fish and fiery gumbos. Dinner daily, Sunday brunch. **$$**

Asian
This is a broad category these days, encompassing everything from basic Chinatown establishments with authentic food and minimal decor, to up-scale, often mixed cuisine.

Buddakan
325 Chestnut Street.
Tel: 215-574-9440.
Contemporary Asian dishes and more presented in a spacious, bustling atmosphere overseen by a gilded Buddha. One of local restaurateur Stephen Starr's productions. **$$$**

Imperial Inn
1426 North 10th Street.
Tel: 215-627-2299.
Well known longstanding Chinatown restaurant with reasonably priced and consistently good, if not dazzling, food and service. Lunch, dinner, late night daily. **$$**

Joe's Peking Duck House
925 Race Street.
Tel: 215-922-3277.
The decor is non-existent, the ambience loud and crowded, but many think this is the best Chinese food in town. Lunch Monday–Friday, dinner daily. **$$**

Joseph Poon Asian Fusion Restaurant
1002 Arch Street.
Tel: 215-928-9333.
Asian fusion cuisine – Peking duck, and fresh seafood in a modern decor. Free parking after 4pm. Lunch, dinner, late night. **$$**

Meiji-En
Pier 19, Delaware Avenue and Callowhill Street.
Tel: 215-592-7100.
A large Japanese restaurant on the Delaware River with great views and a wide-ranging menu. Dinner daily, Sunday brunch. **$$$$$**

Oasis
1709 Walnut Street.
Tel: 215-751-0888.
Waterfalls and skylights provide dramatic decor for this Rittenhouse

Row restaurant. Eclectic fare includes Korean barbecue and sushi, salads and pasta, and an upstairs *sake* bar. Lunch, dinner daily. **$$**

Penang Malaysian Cuisine
117 North 10th Street.
Tel: 215-413-2531.
Open kitchen and extensive menu representing cuisines of India, Thailand and China. No credit cards. Lunch, dinner daily. **$$**

Pod
3636 Sansom Street.
Tel: 215-387-1803.
High concept, futuristic Asian decor, a Stephen Starr production, white surroundings with accents of glowing color, Asian video imagery and a conveyor belt sushi bar. Lunch, dinner daily. **$$–$$$**

Ray's Café
141 North 9th Street.
Tel: 215-922-5122.
A favorite Chinatown meeting place serving well-prepared food and gourmet coffee. Breakfast, lunch and dinner daily. **$$$**

Siam Cuisine Thai Restaurant
925 Arch Street.
Tel: 215-922-7135.
Exceptional Thai cuisine in Chinatown, rated by Zagat and praised by *Philadelphia* magazine. Lunch, dinner daily. **$$**

Susanna Foo
1512 Walnut Street.
Tel: 215-545-2666.
Elegant, up-scale Chinese cuisine, regarded by some critics as one of the finest Chinese restaurants in the country. Rather expensive compared to other Chinese restaurants, but truly in a class by itself. To be experienced. Lunch Monday–Friday, dinner daily. **$$$–$$$$**

Thai Garden
349 South 47th Street.
Tel: 215-471-3663.

Thai Garden East
101 North 11th Street.
Tel: 215-629-9939.
Both locations offer a relaxing setting for excellent Thai cuisine served by an attentive staff. Lunch and dinner daily. **$$**

Vietnam
221 North 11th Street.
Tel: 215-592-1163.
Fragrant and fresh authentic

Vietnamese cuisine in recently renovated house with wood tones and soft lights. Lunch and dinner daily. **$–$$**

Cafés and delis

Essene Café
719 South 4th Street.
Tel: 215-928-3722.
Organic vegetarian and seafood dishes are featured at this informal Queen Village café. Breakfast, lunch (except Tuesday) and dinner daily, Sunday brunch. **$$**

Famous 4th Street Delicatessen
700 South 4th Street.
Tel: 215-922-3274.
A busy Jewish deli one block from South Street, famous for its over-stuffed sandwiches and chocolate-chip cookies. Monday–Saturday 7am–6pm, Sunday 7am–4pm. **$**

Geno's Steaks
1219 South 9th Street.
Tel: 215-89-0659
The challenger in the great South Philly cheesesteak war has won its place at the highest tier of the cheesesteak hierarchy; located at the southern end of the Italian Market *(see page 199)*. Outdoor tables only. Open 24 hours. No credit cards accepted. **$**

Jim's Steaks
400 South Street.
Tel: 215-928-1911.
Many cheesesteak connoisseurs consider this funky little place the tastiest in town. Open daily. No credit cards accepted. **$**

More Than Just Ice Cream
1119 Locust Street.
Tel: 215-574-0586.
Famous for its gargantuan helpings of ice cream and mountainous slices of apple pie, this fun, often crowded, little place also offers burgers, sandwiches and other light fare. Lunch, dinner, late night. **$**

Old City Coffee
221 Church Street.
Tel: 215-629-9292.
A comfy café located on a narrow alley near Christ Church with freshly baked goods, wonderful coffees and a lively clientele. Open daily. **$**

Pat's King of Steaks
1237 East Passyunk Avenue.
Tel: 215-468-1546.

The original cheesesteak king is still holding its own at the southern end of the Italian Market *(see page 201)*. Open 24 hours. No credit cards accepted. **$**

Pink Rose Pastry Shop
630 South 4th Street.
Tel: 215-592-0565.
A pretty little pastry shop/café in Queen Village; a great place to decompress after cruising South Street. Open Tuesday–Sunday, breakfast– late. No credit cards accepted. **$**

Reading Terminal Market
12th and Arch streets.
Tel: 215-922-2317.
A carnival of good food with everything from sushi to soul food in a cavernous train shed engulfed by the Convention Center; an essential Philadelphia experience *(see page 159)*. Open 8am–6pm Monday–Saturday, but hours at some places vary. **$–$$**

French

Beau Monde
624 South 6th Street.
Tel: 215-592-0656.
Unassuming creperie with a fire-place in winter and outdoor seating in the summer, has gathered national accolades in *Travel and Leisure* and *Bon Appetit* magazines. Lunch, dinner, Sunday brunch. **$**

The Blue Angel
706 Chestnut Street.
Tel: 215-925-6889.
A Stephen Starr bistro which has garnered rave reviews for its ambience as well as for its twist on classic French bistro fare. Lunch, dinner, late night, Sunday brunch. **$$**

Bistro St Tropez
2400 Market Street, 4th Floor.
Tel: 215-569-9269.
Romantic French provincial cuisine won a Best of Philly award from *Philadelphia Magazine* in 1996. Lunch, dinner daily. **$$**

Brasserie Perrier
1619 Walnut Street.
Tel: 215-568-3000.
Well-known chef Georges Perrier's up-scale restaurant serving French-Asian dishes and memorable desserts. Lunch, dinner. **$$$**

Ciboulette
200 South Broad Street at the Bellevue.
Tel: 215-790-1210.
Fine provençale French cuisine, convenient to the Academy of Music. Dinner only. **$$$–$$$$**

Deux Cheminées
1221 Locust Street.
Tel: 215-790-0200.
Highly praised French cuisine by chef Fritz Blank in an elegant building designed by Frank Furness. Dinner Tuesday–Saturday. Reservations recommended. **$$$$**

La Terrasse
3432 Sansom Street.
Tel: 215-386-5000.
Popular French restaurant in University City. Lunch, dinner, Sunday brunch, late night. **$$**

Le Bec Fin
1523 Walnut Street.
Tel: 215-567-1000.
Regarded as one of the finest restaurants in the country, this very expensive French favorite by renowned chef Georges Perrier near Rittenhouse Square garners rave reviews from critics and clients alike. Reservations required. In the downstairs bistro an *à la carte* menu is served; no reservations required. Lunch Monday–Friday, seatings at 11:30am and 1:30pm; dinner Monday–Saturday, seatings at 6pm and 9pm. **$$$$**

Philippe on Locust and ChinChin Bar & Lounge
1614 Locust Street.
Tel: 215-735-7551.
Elegant French-Asian cuisine by award-winning master chef Philippe Chin served in a grand old building. Lunch, dinner, late night. Live music at Chinchin Bar and Lounge on Wednesday and Saturday. **$$$**

Hotel Dining
The proliferation of new up-scale hotels has increased Philadelphia's dining options, as nearly every new hotel has brought with it one or more fine restaurants.

Azalea
Omni Hotel, 401 Chestnut Street.
Tel: 215-925-0000.
Four-diamond, four-star, elegant, comfortable hotel dining room featuring regional American cuisine in the heart of the historic district. Breakfast, lunch and dinner daily, Sunday brunch. **$$$**

Boathouse Row Bar
The Rittenhouse Hotel, 210 West Rittenhouse Square.
Tel: 215-790-2533.
Casual pub fare with big screen TV. Lunch, dinner, late night. **$**

Capriccio
Warwick Hotel, 1701 Locust Street.
Tel: 215-735-9797.
Classy café near Rittenhouse Square with tasty baked goods, sandwiches, ice cream, *cappuccino* and other light fare. Breakfast, lunch and dinner daily. **$$$**

Chez Colette
Hotel Sofitel, 120 South 17th Street.
Tel: 215-569-8300.
Parisian-style brasserie serving entrées such as *salmon papilote*, *soupe au pistour*, and *escargots*. Desserts include *Ile flottant* and *Café Liegeois*. Breakfast, lunch, dinner and Sunday brunch, late night. **$$**

Circle Off the Square
Warwick Hotel, 1701 Locust Street.
Tel: 215-545-4655.
Mediterranean cuisine served in the high-class lobby of this handsome old hotel. Breakfast, lunch and dinner daily. **$$$**

Founders Restaurant
Park Hyatt at the Bellevue, 19th Floor, 200 South Broad Street.
Tel: 215-893-1776.
Breathtaking views from this formal, sky-high dining room as well as live music compliment fine French and Continental cuisine. Breakfast, lunch and dinner daily, Sunday brunch. **$$$$**

The Fountain
Four Seasons Hotel, Logan Square, 18th Street and Benjamin Franklin Parkway.
Tel: 215-963-1500.
Highly praised international cuisine offered in a sumptuous hotel dining room overlooking the Swann Fountain. Breakfast, lunch, dinner daily, Sunday brunch. **$$$$**

Paris Bar and Grill
Ritz-Carlton Hotel, 10 Avenue of the Arts.
Tel: 215-735-7700.
Open kitchen and comfortable elegance accompany classic cuisine without heavy sauces in the new Ritz-Carlton Hotel. Lunch Monday–Friday, dinner daily. **$$$–$$$$**

Prime Rib
Warwick Hotel, 1701 Locust Street.
Tel: 215-772-1701.
Prime beef, chops and seafood served in elegant surroundings. Jackets required for men. Lunch, dinner daily. **$$$$**

Square Bar
Sheraton Rittenhouse Square Hotel, 18th and Locust streets.
Tel: 215-546-9400.
International cuisine on Rittenhouse Square. Breakfast, lunch, dinner, late night. **$$**

Swann Café
Four Seasons Hotel, 18th Street and Benjamin Franklin Parkway.
Tel: 215-963-1500.
An elegant setting in the Museum District for inventive American cuisine, especially good for lighter fare. Lunch and dinner daily, late night, Sunday brunch. **$$$.**

TreeTops
The Rittenhouse Hotel, 210 West Rittenhouse Square.
Tel: 215-790-2533.
Plush dining room specializing in imaginative American dishes. Breakfast, lunch and dinner daily. **$$$**

International

Audrey Claire
276 South 20th Street.
Tel: 215-731-1222.
Mediterranean menu in intimate bistro near Rittenhouse Square. BYOB. No credit cards. Dinner, Tuesday–Sunday. **$$$**

The Bards
2013 Walnut Street.
Tel: 215-569-9585.
Irish pub with outstanding, authentic Irish food, drinks and decor. **$$**

Bleu
227 18th Street.
Tel: 215-545-0342.
Trendy bistro by Neil Stein on Rittenhouse Square with menu with a French-Asian flavor. Lunch, dinner, late night daily. **$$$–$$$$**

Continental Restaurant and Martini Bar

138 Market Street.
Tel: 215-923-6069.
Diner turned chic Martini bar with *tapas* menu of tasty snacks such as seared tuna over mushroom risotto. Dinner, late night, and Sunday brunch. **$$**

Dickens Inn

421 South 2nd Street.
Tel: 215-928-9307.
A cheerful English pub featuring authentic English dishes and a great selection of draft beer. Lunch and dinner daily. **$$**

Fork

306 Market Street.
Tel: 215-625-9425.
Well prepared dishes, seasonal vegetables a specialty, in an artsy, bistro atmosphere. Lunch, dinner, Sunday brunch, late night. **$$$**

Friday Saturday Sunday

261 South 21st Street.
Tel: 215-546-4232.
A friendly standby near Rittenhouse Square with creative international fare and a lovely romantic atmosphere. Lunch Monday–Friday, dinner daily. **$$–$$$**

Price Guide

The price guide indicates approximate cost of dinner excluding beverages, tax and tip.
$ = under $15
$$ = $15–$25
$$$ = $25–$40
$$$$ = over $40

The Garden

1617 Spruce Street.
Tel: 215-546-4455.
An elegant townhouse with outdoor dining in warm weather, known for superior Continental cuisine. Lunch Tuesday–Friday, dinner Monday–Saturday. **$$$$**

Knave of Hearts

230 South Street.
Tel: 215-922-3956.
A romantic, funky South Street pioneer that still pleases with creative Continental fare and a cozy setting. Lunch and dinner daily, Sunday brunch. **$$–$$$**

Le Champignon

122 Lombard Street.
Tel: 215-922-2515.
French, Japanese and Thai cuisines. Dinner, late night. **$$**

Ludwig's Garden

1315 Sansom Street.
Tel: 215-985-1525.
German tavern with German menu and wide selection of beers.

Monks Café

264 South 16th Street.
Tel: 215-545-7005.
A Belgian tavern serving a wide variety of beers and excellent traditional dishes. Lunch, dinner. **$**

Moshulu

735 Columbus Boulevard.
Tel: 215-923-2500.
Restored turn-of-the-century sailing ship whose menu reflects its ports-of-call *(see page 129).* Lunch, dinner, Sunday brunch. Music and dancing on weekends. **$$$**

Opus 251 at the Philadelphia Art Alliance

251 South 18th Street.
Tel: 215-735-6787.
Gourmet food prepared by master chef Alfonso Contrisciani and served in a museum setting. Lunch, dinner, late night, Saturday and Sunday brunch. **$$$**

Pasion!

210 South 15th Street.
Tel: 215-875-9895.
Nuevo Latino menu, accompanied by music art, and *serviche* bar for those who want to watch award-winning chef Guillermo Pernot. Lunch, dinner daily. **$$**

The Plough and the Stars

2nd and Chestnut streets.
Tel: 215-733-0300.
Western European food served in the beautifully restored Corn Exchange building. Lunch, dinner, late night, Sunday brunch. **$$**

Rembrandt's

23rd and Aspen streets.
Tel: 215-763-2228.
Reasonably priced international dishes in a romantic atmosphere surrounded by prints of the famous artist, in the Museum of Art area. Lunch, dinner, Sunday brunch. **$$**

Rococo

123 Chestnut Street.
Tel: 215-629-1100.
Opulent, architecturally detailed space provides the backdrop for contemporary American dishes with Asian influences. **$$**

Serrano

20 South 2nd Street.
Tel: 215-923-0770.
International home-cooking in the South Street neighborhood, with entrées ranging from Nori Wrapped Ahi Tuna to Malaysian pork chops. Dinner only. **$$–$$$**

Tangerine

232 Market Street.
Tel: 215-627-5116.
Eclectic nouvelle Mediterranean cuisine with a Moroccan flair. This hot new Stephen Starr eatery is adorned with opulently draped walls, pillow strewn banquets, and votive lights. **$$–$$$**

Waldorf Café

2000 Lombard Street.
Tel: 215-985-1836.
Homey bistro with eclectic international cuisine. Dinner only. **$$$**

Italian

Avenue B

260 Avenue of the Arts.
Tel: 215-790-0705.
Tuscan-inspired Italian cuisine in a high-style setting is the new production by Neil Stein of Striped Bass, Rouge, Bleu, and Fishmarket fame. Choose from an elegant dining room, casual bar and lounge, and outdoor garden café. Lunch, dinner, late night night, daily in café. Lunch, Monday–Friday, dinner daily in Dining Room. **$$–$$$$**

Bistro Romano

120 Lombard Street.
Tel: 215-925-8880.
A former granary now a historic landmark is the setting for Italian classics. Upstairs is the site of Philadelphia's original Mystery Theater. Dinner, late night. **$$$**

Coco Pazzo

1650 Market Street, Liberty Place.
Tel: 215-851-8888.
Snazzy contemporary restaurant and bar with a tantalizing Italian menu. Lunch and dinner daily. **$$$**

Dante's and Luigi's

762 South 10th Street.
Tel: 215-922-9501.
One of the country's oldest Italian

restaurants, serving traditional Italian entrées, with a 20-ounce grilled veal chop a specialty. Mafia hit some years back adds mystique. Lunch and dinner daily. **$$**

La Famiglia
8 South Front Street.
Tel: 215-922-2803.
An Old City favorite for high-class Italian food in a lovely formal setting. Lunch Tuesday–Friday, dinner Tuesday–Sunday. **$$$$**

Girasole
1305 Locust Street.
Tel: 215-985-4659.
A lovely authentic ristorante a few steps from the Avenue of the Arts serving light but tasty dishes in a contemporary setting. Lunch Monday–Friday, dinner daily. **$$**

Price Guide

The price guide indicates approximate cost of dinner excluding beverages, tax and tip.
$ = under $15
$$ = $15–$25
$$$ = $25–$40
$$$$ = over $40

Marras
1700 East Passyunk Avenue.
Tel: 215-463-9249.
Home-style eatery with tasty pizza, pastas and specialties (try the mussels) in South Philly shopping district. Lunch Tuesday–Saturday, dinner Tuesday–Sunday. **$$**

Michael's Ristorante
824 South 8th Street.
Tel: 215-922-3986.
Classic and contemporary Italian food. Located in South Philly. **$$**

Monte Carlo Living Room
2nd and South streets.
Tel: 215-925-2220.
Sophisticated restaurant offering fresh pasta, seafood, veal and beef and excellent service. Dinner, late night. **$$$–$$$$**

Ralph's Italian Restaurant
760 South 9th Street.
Tel: 215-627-6011.
Landmark neighborhood institution at the top of the Italian Market in South Philadelphia. No credit cards accepted. **$**

Saloon
750 South 7th Street.
Tel: 215-627-1811.
Highly regarded gathering spot of local movers and shakers, known for excellent steaks and Italian dishes. Reservations required. Lunch Tuesday–Friday, dinner Monday–Saturday. **$$$–$$$$**

Toto
1407 Locust Street.
Tel: 215-546-2000.
A sumptuous, romantic dining room, featuring fine Northern Italian cuisine. Located near the Academy of Music and convenient to Ritten-house Square and City Hall. Lunch Monday–Friday, dinner Monday–Saturday. **$$$$**

Vetri
1312 Spruce Street.
Tel: 215-732-3478.
Intimate setting for traditional and contemporary Italian dishes. distinctively prepared by owner-chef Marc Vetri. Dinner only. **$–$$$**

Victor Café
1303 Dickinson Street.
Tel: 215-468-3040.
Opera is the big attraction at this South Philly Italian restaurant where the waiters are as likely to serve up arias as antipasto. An interesting experience. Dinner daily. **$$$**

Mexican

Mexican Post
104 Chestnut Street.
Tel: 215-923-5233.
Informal, friendly service, with basic Mexican fare and eight flavors of margaritas, popular with the after-movie crowd coming from the Ritz. Lunch, dinner, late night. **$**

Tequilas
1511 Locust Street.
Tel: 215-546-0181.
A high-class Mexican restaurant, more expensive than most but a cut above the average cantina. Lunch Monday–Friday, dinner Monday–Saturday. **$$–$$$**

Zocalo
3600 Lancaster Avenue.
Tel: 215-895-0199.
A colorful Mexican restaurant in University City with spicy food, and a bar. Lunch Monday–Friday, dinner daily. **$$–$$$**

Seafood

Bookbinders Seafood House
215 South 15th Street.
Tel: 215-545-1137.
An old-time Philadelphia eatery near the Academy of Music specializing in seafood and steaks, popular with businessmen. Lunch Monday–Friday, dinner daily. **$$$**

Chart House
555 South Columbus Avenue.
Tel: 215-625-8383.
Large, modern establishment overlooking the Delaware River at the south end of Penns Landing, a favorite for those who love fresh seafood, juicy steaks and bountiful salads and desserts. Dinner daily, Sunday brunch. **$$$–$$$$**

Devon Seafood Grill
225 South 18th Street.
Tel: 215-546-5940.
Popular seafood house on Rittenhouse Square. Menu changes to reflect the particular fresh seafood arrived from both coasts. Lunch and dinner daily. **$$$**

DiNardo's Famous Crabs
312 Race Street.
Tel: 215-925-5115.
A well-known Old City seafood favorite that lures hordes of crab-lovers with its spicy hard-shell crabs and casual atmosphere. Lunch Monday–Saturday, dinner daily. **$$**

Hardshell Café
9th and Market streets.
Tel: 215-592-9110.
Casual Center City spot specializing in crabs and other seafood. Lunch, dinner, late night. **$$**

Olde City Seafood
319 Market Street.
Tel: 215-928-1115.
Praised for its fresh seafood at reasonable prices. BYOB. Lunch and dinner daily. **$$–$$$**

Old Original Bookbinders
125 Walnut Street.
Tel: 215-925-7027.
This seafood spot is a favorite with out-of-towners, and locals are showing renewed interest since the addition of a raw bar. Lunch Monday–Friday, dinner daily. **$$$**

Philadelphia Fish & Co.
207 Chestnut Street.
Tel: 215-625-8605.
Popular Old City seafood restaurant

known for fresh, consistently pleasing fare; outdoor dining in warm weather. Lunch Monday–Saturday summer, Monday–Friday winter, dinner daily. **$$–$$$**

Sansom Street Oyster House
1516 Sansom Street.
Tel: 215-567-7683.
A fun, informal seafood place with solid food and no pretensions. The Samuel Adams Brew House (tel: 215-563-2326), serving bar food and beer brewed on the premises, is upstairs. Lunch and dinner Monday–Saturday. **$$**

Sotto
231 South Broad Street.
Tel: 215-546-6800.
Contemporary styling and global seafood, including a raw bar, on Avenue of the Arts. Lunch, dinner, late night. **$$**

Striped Bass
1500 Walnut Street.
Tel: 215-732-4444.
Fish and shellfish prepared in full view of customers in expansive dining room which was the site of the anniversary dinner in the movie, The Sixth Sense. Lunch Monday–Friday, dinner daily, Saturday brunch. **$$$$**

Steakhouses

JW's Steakhouse
1201 Market Street.
Tel: 215 625-6024.
Succulent steaks in a three-story setting at the Philadelphia Marriott. Dinner only. **$$$**

Mortons of Chicago
1411 Walnut Street.
Tel: 215-557-0724.
A favorite among carnivores, this classy, convivial steakhouse features beef, lobster, veal and attentive service. Lunch Monday–Friday, dinner daily. **$$$–$$$$**

The Palm
200 South Broad Street.
Tel: 215-546-7256.
A clubby steakhouse located at the Bellevue known for its giant slabs of beef and high-powered clientele. Lunch Monday–Friday, dinner daily. Reservations necessary. **$$$–$$$$**

Ruth's Chris Steakhouse
260 South Broad Street.
Tel: 215-790-1515.
Humungous slabs of beef are the

specialty here; a favorite among businessmen and other power-munchers; convenient to the Academy of Music and City Hall. Lunch Monday–Friday, dinner daily. **$$$$**

Shula's Steak 2
3600 Chestnut Street.
Tel: 215-386-5556.
Casual steakhouse and sports bar with 80 TV screens and sports memorabilia in the Sheraton University City. Breakfast, lunch, dinner, late night. **$$**

Smith & Wollensky
The Rittenhouse Hotel, 210 Rittenhouse Square.
Tel: 215-546-9000.
Award-winning New York steakhouse and wine list has opened on Rittenhouse Square, serving steak and seafood and its famous pea soup. Lunch, dinner, late night, Sunday brunch. **$$$**

URBAN VILLAGES

Chestnut Hill

Cincin
7838 Germantown Avenue.
Tel: 215-242-8800.
Chinese cuisine with French flair. Lunch, dinner. **$$**

Melting Pot
8229 Germantown Avenue.
Tel: 215-42-3003.
Popular fondue restaurant only 20 minutes from Center City with a wide range of appetizers, meals and desserts. **$$**

Manayunk

Arroyo Grille
Main and Leverington streets, Venice Island.
Tel: 215-487-1400.
Well prepared Tex-Mex classics complimented with a variety of tequilas. Lunch, dinner, Sunday brunch. **$$**

Grasshopper
4427 Main Street.
Tel: 215-483-1888.
Imaginatively prepared French cuisine with additional Asian fusion accents for variation. Dinner only, Tuesday–Saturday. **$$**

Hikaru
4348 Main Street.
Tel: 215-487-3500.
Large sushi selection or grilled dishes; *tatami* room available. Other locations in the city. Lunch, dinner. **$$$**

Jake's Restaurant
4365 Main Street.
Tel: 215-483-0444.
A Manayunk favorite run by chef-owner Bruce Cooper featuring distinctive American cooking, an outstanding wine list and a lively social scene. Lunch, dinner, Sunday brunch. **$$$**

Kansas City Prime
4417 Main Street.
Tel: 215-482-3700.
A lively Manayunk eatery featuring hefty servings of char-grilled steaks. Fish and chicken dishes are also choices on the menu. Lunch Monday–Friday, dinner daily. **$$$$**

LeBus Main Street
4266 Main Street.
Tel: 215-487-2663.
Exposed brick and pipes, a friendly atmosphere and a varied selection of entrées, and homemade breads. Lunch, dinner, Sunday brunch. **$$**

Manayunk Brewery & Restaurant
4120 Main Street.
Tel: 215-482-8220.
Regional American fare with a selection of homemade ales, lagers and cocktails overlooking the Schuylkill. Live jazz and blues. Lunch, dinner, Sunday brunch. **$$**

Sonoma
4411 Main Street.
Tel: 215-83-9400.
A lovely Manayunk location serving a light combination of Italian and Californian cuisine. Lunch and dinner daily. **$$$**

US Hotel Bar & Grill
4439 Main Street.
Tel: 215-483-9222.
A welcoming neighborhood bar dating to the early 1900s, once part of Manayunk's best hotel during this mill town's boom years.

Vega Grill
4141 Main Street.
Tel: 215-487-9600.
Latino cuisine with patio dining. Lunch, dinner, late night. **$$$**

BRANDYWINE RIVER VALLEY

Chadds Ford
Chadds Ford Inn
Routes 1 and 100, PA 19317.
Tel: 610-388-7361.
Across the street from the Brandy-wine River Museum, this Colonial inn's wide-ranging menu for lunch, dinner and Sunday brunch has been pleasing guests since its opening in 1736. **$$$**
Chadds Ford Tavern
Route 1, PA 19317.
Tel: 610-459-8453.
This historic roadside tavern once served the generals of the Battle of Brandywine, but today caters to local artists. The inexpensive menu offers tasty American cuisine. **$**

Price Guide

The price guide indicates approximate cost of dinner excluding beverages, tax and tip.
$ = under $15
$$ = $15–$25
$$$ = $25–$40
$$$$ = over $40

Wilmington
Brandywine Room/Green Room
Hotel du Pont, 11th and Market streets, DE 19801.
Tel: 302-594-3251.
Two award-winning restaurants in one hotel; the Brandywine Room, with walnut-paneled walls and original Wyeth paintings, offers American cuisine and flawless service. The elegant Green Room offers French dining to the accompaniment of harp music. Reservations recommended. **$$$$**

PENNSYLVANIA DUTCH COUNTRY

Gettysburg
Historic Farnsworth House Restaurant
401 Baltimore Street, PA 17033.
Tel: 717-334-8838.
Authentically restored dining room with photos by Civil War photo-grapher Matthew Brady, specializes in period fare. Reservations suggested. **$$**

Hershey
Hotel Hershey Circular Dining Room
Hotel Hershey, Hotel Road, PA 17033.
Tel: 717-534-8800.
Famous for its elegant dining and unique setting, with the finest classical cuisine and exquisite chocolate desserts. With breathtaking views of the gardens and tranquil reflecting pools, this most formal of Hershey Resorts restaurants serves breakfast, lunch, dinner, a renowned Sunday brunch, and a formal tea (on select days). Reservations, jacket required. **$$$$**

Lancaster
Gibraltar
College Square, 931 Harrisburg Pike, PA 17603.
Tel: 717-397-2790.
This little Mediterranean restaurant bordering the campus of F&M College offers a wide range of simple, fresh and well-prepared meals accompanied by an outstanding wine list. Patio dining in summer. Reservations. **$$$**

Reading
Green Hills Inn
2444 Morgantown Road (Route 10), PA 19607.
Tel: 610-777-9611.
A lovingly restored country farmhouse featuring an elegant garden room and award-winning dining. Reservations advisable. **$$$$**

York
Accomac Inn
6330 South River Drive, PA 17406.
Tel: 717-252-1521.
This historic stone former inn on the banks of the Susquehanna River offers superb Continental cuisine and a renowned wine list in a romantic setting. Dining available on the porch in summer or by the fireplace on the first floor. Reservations advisable. **$$$$**

BUCKS COUNTY

Carversville
Carversville Inn
Aquetong and Carversville roads.
Tel: 215-297-0900.
A charming country inn located in a quiet village, serving solid American dishes. Lunch Wednesday–Sunday, dinner Tuesday–Sunday. **$$$**

Doylestown
Sign of the Sorrel Horse
4424 Old Easton Road.
Tel: 215-230-9999.
French cuisine lovingly prepared and served in a romantic dining room. Dinner Wednesday–Saturday. Reservations required. **$$$**

Erwinna
Evermay on the Delaware
River Road.
Tel: 215-294-9100.
This gorgeous Victorian mansion set on lovely grounds offers a menu of consistently pleasing French-influenced cuisine. One seating at 7:30pm Friday–Sunday only. **$$$$**

Lumberville
Black Bass Inn
River Road.
Tel: 215-297-5770.
Fine country fare with European touches presented at a lovely inn dating to 1745 perched on the banks of the Delaware River. Lunch Monday–Saturday, dinner daily, Sunday brunch. **$$$**
Cuttalossa Inn
River and Cuttalossa roads.
Tel: 215-297-5082.
Imaginative international cuisine in a peaceful, creatively furnished 18th-century building. Lunch, dinner Monday–Saturday. **$$$–$$$$**

New Hope
Havana
105 South Main Street.
Tel: 215-862-9897.
Eclectic menu at a fun-loving bar/restaurant, great for watching the carnival on Main Street. Live music, karaoke, comedy. Open daily (closed Tuesday–Wednesday January–March.) **$$**

Odettes
River Road near Route 232.
Tel: 215-862-2432.
Imaginative Continental dishes at a historic and cheerful riverside place, with nightly piano bar, seasonal weekend cabaret shows. Lunch Monday–Saturday, dinner daily, Sunday brunch. **$$–$$$**

Cafés and Bars

Dock Street Brewery and Restaurant
2 Logan Square.
Tel: 215-495-0413.
Six varieties of home brewed ale. Live music Friday–Saturday.

Bar Noir
112 South 18th Street.
Tel: 215-569-9333.
Cocktails and bottled beer in a trendy New Wave underground bar off Rittenhouse Square.

Boathouse Row Bar
The Rittenhouse Hotel, 220 West Rittenhouse Square.
Tel: 215-546-9000.
A classy spot filled with rowing memorabilia.

Cassatt Tea Room
The Rittenhouse Hotel, 210 West Rittenhouse Square.
Tel: 215-546-9000.
Afternoon tea is a tradition at this lovely, up-scale room in a modern hotel with a garden view. Daily tea 2–5pm, cocktails 5–11pm. **$$**

The Continental
2nd and Market streets.
Tel: 215-923-6069.
Creative Martinis and classic cocktails along with tantalizing dishes in a very hip atmosphere.

Crimson Moon
2005 Sansom Street.
Tel: 215-564-2228.
Popular coffee bar.

Fergie's Pub
1214 Sansom Street.
Tel: 215-928-8118.
Lively Irish pub in the heart of Center City.

Happy Rooster
118 South 16th Street.
Tel: 215-563-1481.
Music ranging from salsa to European and a wide assortment of after dinner drinks.

Il Bar
14 North Front Street.
Tel: 215-922-7800.
In the Penns View Inn, romantic with a large selection of wines.

The Library Lounge
Park Hyatt at the Bellevue, Broad and Walnut streets.
Tel: 215-893-1776.
A plush bar perfect for having a relaxing drink and conversation.

New Wave Café
784 South 3rd Street.
Tel: 215-922-8484.
Friendly neighborhood bar which hosts Quizzo on Monday nights.

The Rotunda Lounge
Ritz-Carlton, 10 Avenue of the Arts.
Tel: 215-735-7700.
Afternoon tea and evening cocktails in magnificent rotunda lobby of historic former bank building.

Samuel Adams Brew House
1516 Sansom Street.
Tel: 215-563-2326.
Home-brewed ales, and an oyster house on the first floor.

Swanky Bubbles
10 South Front Street.
Tel: 215-928-1200.
Distinctive for its champagne lounge and sushi bar.

Tellers Lounge at PSFS
1234 Market Street.
Tel: 215-629-1200.
Sleek, Art Deco cocktail lounge.

The Vault
Ritz-Carlton, 10 Avenue of the Arts.
Tel: 215-735-5200.
Intimate lounge for those who like cigars and after-dinner drinks.

Dinner Cruises

Spirit of Philadelphia
Penn's Landing between Market and Chestnut streets.
Tel: 215-923-1419.
Dining cruises on the Delaware River with live entertainment. Lunch Monday–Saturday, dinner daily, Sunday brunch.

Liberty Belle Charters
337A North Front Street.
Tel: 215-629-1131.
Daily lunch, dinner and sightseeing cruises on the Delaware River.

Nightlife

Nightclubs, Comedy Clubs, Music Venues

Artful Dodger
400 South 2nd Street.
Tel: 215-922-1790.
A traditional English pub on Head House Square with full menu and live entertainment Thursday–Saturday nights.

The Balcony Bar
10th and Arch streets, above the Trocadero.
Tel: 215-922-5483.
Local and national indie rock bands nightly. Credit cards not accepted.

Brasils
112 Chestnut Street.
Tel: 215-13-1700.
Philadelphia's premier Latin nightspot. Food, music and dancing.

Catch a Rising Star
211 South Street.
Tel: 215-440-3131.
Comedy shows at 8:30pm Tuesday–Sunday, also 11pm shows Friday–Saturday.

Chestnut Cabaret
38th and Chestnut streets.
Tel: 215-382-1201.
Local and national acts in rock, pop, R&B, reggae. Tuesday–Saturday.

Circa
1518 Walnut Street.
Tel: 215-545-6800.
A variety of music from disco to techno. From 9pm Friday–Saturday.

Comedy Cabaret
1010 Race Street.
Tel: 215-625-JOKE.
Comedy club and comedy classes.

Dave & Busters
Pier 19, 325 North Columbus Boulevard.
Tel: 215-413-1951.
Food, drink, billiards, over 300 electronic virtual-reality games, and a bar with over 20 TVs tuned to

sports. Saturday night murder mystery theater.

David Brenner's Laugh House
221 South Street.
Tel: 215-440-4242.
Comedy club seats 250, attracting large and local talent alike.

Edge
Main Street and Shurs Lane.
Tel: 215-483-4100.
A large and usually crowded disco and restaurant with a raw bar, games room and outdoor deck.

Egypt
Christopher Columbus Boulevard at Spring Garden Street.
Tel: 215-922-6500.
Concert-quality sound and light system on a two-level dance floor. One of several popular night spots on the Delaware River.

The Five Spot
5 South Bank Street.
Tel: 215-574-0070.
Retro, two-floor lounge for dining, dancing and cocktails, featuring swing and other favorites. Local and national bands most evenings.

Fluid
613 South 4th Street.
Tel: 215-629-3686.
Intimate yet pulsating dance club just off of South Street.

Grape Street Pub
Grape Street, near Main Street, Manayunk.
Tel: 215-483-7084.
Manayunk favorite for drink and local rock bands. No credit cards.

Irish Pub
1123 Walnut Street.
Tel: 215-925-3311.
Lively Irish tunes and beer in the Washington Square District.

Jake and Olivers
22 South 3rd Street.
Tel: 215-627-4825.
Former church now pulses with techno and house music Monday–Saturday.

Kathmandu
Pier 25, Delaware Avenue and Willow Street.
Tel: 215-629-1101.
Popular outdoor bar on the riverfront in the shadow of the Ben Franklin Bridge with live world music, reggae, rock, dance and outdoor dining. May–October only.

The Khyber
56 South 2nd Street.
Tel: 215-238-5888.
Rock club in Old City with live local alternative and hard rock bands nightly; a little rough around the edges but much beloved by regulars and visitors alike. No credit cards.

Pontiac
304 South Street.
Tel: 215-925-4053.
This down and dirty rock club with live local talent has been a South Street institution for years.

Polly Esthers
1201 Race Street.
Tel: 215-851-0776.
Large club with three dance floors, and featuring DJs and music from the 1970–80s. Located near the Convention Center. No credit cards.

Rock Lobster
Columbus Boulevard at Vine Street.
Tel: 215-627-7625.
Riverfront bar and restaurant with outdoor dining and live music. Open seasonally.

Shampoo
417 North 8th Street.
Tel: 215-922-7500.
Large, energetic dance club with numerous special nights. Gay party on Friday night.

Silk City Lounge
5th and Spring Garden streets.
Tel: 215-592-8838.
Small club attached to American Diner. Caters to a young crowd with hip new music, live acts weekly.

Tin Angel
20 2nd Street.
Tel: 215-928-0978.
Cozy café with coffees, liqueurs, beer and wine and acoustic music.

Trocadero
1003 Arch Street.
Tel: 215-922-LIVE.
A wide variety of everything from rock to hip hop.

Upstairs at Nick's
16 South 2nd Street.
Tel: 928-0665.
Rock club featuring local and national bands. No credit cards.

Xero
613 South 4th Street.
Tel: 215-629-0565.
Food, drink, dance and DJs on the weekends.

Jazz and Blues

Blue Moon Jazz Club
The Bourse, 21 South 5th Street.
Tel: 215-413-2272.
Jazz from house performers Wednesday–Saturday.

Liberties
705 North 2nd Street.
Tel: 215-238-0660.
A classy, convivial spot north of Old City with interesting antique decor and live jazz on weekends.

Maui
Pier 53, 1143 North Delaware Avenue.
Tel: 215-423-8116.
Outdoor tropical setting includes palm trees, beach grill and volleyball court.

Ortlieb's Jazzhaus
847 North 3rd Street.
Tel: 215-922-1035.
The city's jazz favorite for years, a casual old-time nightclub and restaurant in the Northern Liberties with local and national jazz talent and jam sessions.

Warmdaddy's
Front and Market streets.
Tel: 215-627-8400.
Blues club featuring live music and Southern cooking.

Zanzibar Blue
Broad and Walnut streets at the Bellevue.
Tel: 215-732-5200.
Up-scale nightclub and restaurant with live jazz nightly, Sunday jazz brunch and food as electrifying as the music.

Gay and Lesbian Venues

These are the biggest clubs for women and men, respectively. Aside from gay bars, a number of restaurants and clubs consider themselves gay-friendly. For more information, take a look at *Philadelphia Gay News*, available at newsstands *(see page 262)*.

Sisters
1320 Chancellor Street.
Tel: 215-735-0735.

Woodys
202 South 13th Street.
Tel: 215-545-1893.

Culture

Art Galleries

Many art galleries in the Old City area coordinate their openings for "First Fridays," the first Friday of every month except July and August. For further information, visit the website www.gallery-guide.com.

The following list contains details of the most popular galleries in the city:

I. Brewster & Co
1628 Walnut Street.
Tel: 215-731-9200.
Monday–Saturday 11am–6pm.
Displaying a wide range of styles and media.

Calderwood Gallery
1427 Walnut Street.
Tel: 215-568-7475
www.calderwoodgallery.com
Tuesday–Friday 11am–5:30pm,
Saturday noon–5:30pm.
Art Deco and 20th-century decorative arts.

The Clay Studio
139 North 2nd Street.
Tel: 215-925-3453.
www.theclaystudio.org
Tuesday–Sunday noon–6pm.
Work in clay.

deVecchis
404 South Street.
Tel: 215-922-5708.
Tuesday–Thursday, Saturday
10:30am–6pm, Friday
10:30am–8pm, Sunday noon–5pm.
Contemporary graphics,
photography and posters.

Eyes Gallery
402 South Street.
Tel: 215-925-0193.
www.eyesgallery.com
Monday–Thursday 11am–7pm,
Friday–Saturday 11am–8pm,
Sunday noon–6pm.
Latin American folk art, ethnic jewelry and exotic clothing.

Helen Drutt: Philadelphia
1721 Walnut Street.
Tel: 215-735-1625.
www.helendrutt.com
Wednesday–Friday noon–5pm,
Saturday 11am–2pm, and by appointment.
Represents international artists who work in ceramics and metal.

F.A.N. Gallery
221 Arch Street.
Tel: 215-922-5155.
Wednesday–Sunday noon–6pm.
Contemporary American realist art, sculpture and works on paper.

Fleisher Art Memorial
719 Catharine Street.
Tel: 215-922-3456.
www.fleisher.org
Monday–Friday 11am–5pm and,
while school is in session,
Monday–Thursday 6:30–9:30pm,
Saturday 10am–3pm, closed August.
This free art school, over 100 years old, shows work by faculty students.
The Challenge Series, a juried regional exhibition, showcases 12 individual artists each year.

Fleisher Ollman Gallery
211 South 17th Street.
Tel: 215-545-7562.
Monday–Friday 10:30am–5:30pm,
Saturday 11am–5:30pm.
Contemporary American art.

Jeffrey Fuller Fine Art Ltd
730-32 Carpenter Lane.
Tel: 215-991-1900.
Monday–Friday 9:30am–5:30pm.
19th- and 20th-century American and European masters.

Hahn Gallery
8439 Germantown Avenue.
Tel: 215-247-8439.
www.hahngallery.com
Tuesday–Saturday 10am–5:30pm.
A wide range of styles and media.

Highwire Gallery
137 North 2nd Street.
Tel: 215-829-1255.
Thursday–Friday noon–6pm,
Saturday–Sunday noon–5pm.
Cooperative gallery with group and individual shows.

Hot Soup Hot Glass Studio and Gallery 2
6 South Strawberry Street.
Tel: 215-922-2332.
www.hotsoupstudio.com
Daily 10am–10pm.

Public access glass-blowing studio and gallery.

Indigo
151 North 3rd Street.
Tel: 215-922-4041.
www.indigoarts.com
Monday–Saturday 11am–7pm,
Sunday noon–6pm.
Art and artifacts from Asia, Africa and the Americas.

Esther M. Klein Art Gallery
University City Science Center lobby,
3600 Market Street.
Tel: 215-387-2255.
Monday–Friday 9am–5pm.
Wide range of styles and media.

Gilbert Luber Collection
Tel: 215-545-4975.
www.lubergallery.com
Antique and contemporary
Japanese graphics sold on website or by appointment.

Lucien Crump Art Gallery
6380 Germantown Avenue.
Tel: 215-843-8788.
www.luciencrump.com
Monday–Saturday noon–6pm,
Sunday 1–5pm.
Modern and African-American art.

Newman Galleries
1625 Walnut Street.
Tel: 215-563-1779.
www.newmangalleries1865.com
Monday–Friday 9am–5:30pm,
Saturday 10am–4:30pm, closed
Saturday during summer.
19th- and 20th-century art.

Nexus Foundation for Today's Art
137 North 2nd Street.
Tel: 215-629-1103.
Tuesday–Friday noon–6pm,
Saturday–Sunday noon–5pm.
Contemporary work.

October Gallery
68 North 2nd Street.
Tel: 215-629-3939.
Monday–Friday 11am–6pm,
Saturday noon–5pm.
African-American art.

Old City Arts Association
139 North 2nd Street.
Tel: 215-625-9200.

Painted Bride Art Center
230 Vine Street.
Tel: 215-255-9914.
www.paintedbride.org
Monday–Friday 10am–6pm,
Saturday noon–6pm.

Contemporary work and performance art.

Pentimenti Gallery
133 North 3rd Street.
Tel: 215-625-9990.
www.pentimenti.com
Monday–Tuesday by appointment,
Wednesday–Friday noon–5:30pm,
Saturday noon–5pm.
Contemporary art ranging from representational to experimental abstract. Paintings, photography, sculpture.

Philadelphia Art Alliance
251 South 18th Street.
Tel: 215-545-4302.
www.libertynet.org/paa
Tuesday–Sunday 11am–5pm,
closed August.
Mixed-media gallery featuring visual, performance and literary art.

The Print Center
1614 Latimer Street.
Tel: 215-735-6090.
www.libertynet.org/print
Tuesday–Saturday 11am–5:30pm,
call ahead to confirm hours.
Contemporary prints and photographs.

Rosenfeld Gallery
113 Arch Street.
Tel: 215-922-1376.
Wednesday–Saturday 10am–5pm,
Sunday noon–5pm.
American artists in all media.

Arthur Ross Gallery
University of Pennsylvania, 220 South 34th Street.
Tel: 215- 898-4401.
www.upenn.edu/ARG
Tuesday–Friday 10am–5pm,
Saturday–Sunday noon–5pm.
Eclectic work, all media.

Sande Webster Gallery
2018 Locust Street.
Tel: 215-732-8850.
www.sandewebstergallery.com
Monday–Friday 10am–6pm,
Saturday 11am–4pm.
Contemporary work in a variety of media and styles.

Snyderman Gallery
303 Cherry Street.
Tel: 215-238-9576.
www.snyderman-works.com
Tuesday–Saturday 10am–6pm.
One-of-a-kind furniture, glass works and sculpture.

Space 1026
1026 Arch Street, 2nd Floor.
Tel: 215-574-7630.
www.space1026.com
Wednesday–Saturday 2–8pm.
Contemporary work in a variety of media.

Taller Puertorriqueño
2721 North 5th Street.
Tel: 215-426-3311.
Tuesday 2–6pm, Wednesday–
Saturday 10am–1pm, 2–6pm.
Emphasis on Puerto Rican and Latin American artists and culture.

University of the Arts
Haviland Hall Gallery, Mednick Gallery, Rosenwald-Wolf Gallery, Broad and Pine streets.
Tel: 215-717-6480.
www.uarts.edu
Monday–Friday 10am–5pm,
Wednesday 10am–9pm,
Saturday–Sunday noon–5pm.
Contemporary work.

Vox Populi
141 North 2nd Street.
Tel: 215-255-1841.
Thursday, Saturday, Sunday noon–6pm, Friday noon–9pm.
Contemporary work by local artists.

The Works Gallery
303 Cherry Street.
Tel: 215-922-7775.
www.snyderman-works.com
Tuesday–Saturday 10am–6pm.
Contemporary crafts in clay, fiberglass and jewelry.

Ruth Zafrir Gallery
13 South 2nd Street.
Tel: 215-627-7098.
Monday–Friday noon–6pm; call ahead to confirm hours.
Sculpture by local artists.

Cinema

For information on films currently playing in Philadelphia and theater locations, call MovieFone at 215-222-3456 or visit the website www.moviefone.com.
    The following are a few of the film venues in the city:

Annenberg Center
3680 Walnut Street.
Tel: 215-898-6791.
www.upenn.edu/annenberg-center
Documentary films.

Cinemagic 3 at Penn
3925 Walnut Street.
Tel: 215-222-5555.
First-run and other films.

GCC Franklin Mills 14
903 Franklin Mills Circle.
Tel: 215-281-2750.
www.generalcinema.com
First-run films shown on multiple screens.

International House
3701 Chestnut Street.
Tel: 215-895-6542.
www.libertynet.org/ihouse
Independent and foreign films.

Ritz 5
214 Walnut Street.
Tel: 215-925-7900.
www.ritzfilmbill.com
Independent, limited-run, foreign films, some first run.

Ritz at the Bourse
4th and Chestnut streets.
Tel: 215-925-7900.
www.ritzfilmbill.com
Independent, limited-run and foreign films.

Ritz East
2nd Street between Chestnut and Walnut streets.
Tel: 215-255-7900.
www.ritzfilmbill.com
Independent, limited-run, foreign films, some first run.

The Roxy
2023 Sansom Street.
Tel: 215-233-6699.
Independent, limited-run, foreign films.

Sundance Cinema
40th and Walnut streets.
Variety of films on seven screens with restaurant, *tapas* bar, media research library and *espresso* bar. Reservations necessary.

Tuttleman IMAX Theater
Franklin Institute, 20th and Benjamin Franklin Parkway.
Tel: 215-448-1111.
www.fi.edu
IMAX (large screen) films.

United Artists
3729 Main Street, Manayunk.
Tel: 215-482-6230.
www.uatc.com
First-run films on multiple screens.

United Artists King of Prussia Stadium 15 and IMAX
232 Mall Boulevard, King of Prussia.

First-run films on multiple screens and IMAX films.

United Artists Riverview Plaza 17
Delaware Avenue and Reed Street.
Tel: 215-755-2219.
First-run and other films shown on multiple screens.

United Artists Sameric
1908 Chestnut Street.
Tel: 215-677-0604.
www.uatc.com
First run films shown on multiple screens.

Music

Academy of Music
Broad and Locust streets.
Tel: 215-893-1999.
www.philorch.org
Home of the Philadelphia Orchestra until December 2001, when the orchestra moves to the Kimmel Center. *(see under theater page 287)* Thereafter home to the Philadelphia Ballet, the Philadelphia Opera, touring Broadway shows, and other music events.

Blockbuster-Sony Music Centre
1 Harbor Boulevard, Camden, NJ.
Tel: 609-365-1300.
www.electricfactory.com
7,000-seat outdoor spring/summer, indoor fall/winter, venue for a variety of concerts and events.

Choral Arts Society
1420 Locust Street.
Tel: 215-545-8634.
www.choralarts.com
150-member symphonic chorus; performances at the Academy of Music and other sites in the city.

Concerto Soloists of Philadelphia
Tel: 215-545-5451.
Chamber music group featuring many members of the Philadelphia Orchestra.

First Union Center
Broad Street. and Pattison Avenue.
Tel: 215-336-3600.
www.comcastspectacor.com
20,000-seat arena, home of sports teams *(see page 296)* and host to major concerts and other events.

City of Philadelphia Recreation Department
1515 Arch Street, 10th Floor.
Tel: 215-683-3600.
www.phila.gov/departments/recreation
The City of Philadelphia sponsors outdoor jazz, classical and pop concerts at various sites, including JFK Plaza next to City Hall, Penn's Landing, Rittenhouse Square, Robin Hood Dell East in Fairmount Park and Independence Mall.

Curtis Institute of Music
1726 Locust Street.
Tel: 215-893-5252.
www.curtis.edu
Over 80 free concerts, opera and recitals are held at the Institute's small concert hall.

Delaware Valley Opera Company
1731 Chandler Street.
Tel: 215-725-4171.
www.libertynet.org/dvoc
Summer performances in an outdoor amphitheater at the Hermitage Mansion in Fairmount Park.

The Electric Factory
421 North 7th Street.
Tel: 215-627-1332.
www.electricfactory.com
Large, general admission rock music venue with both seating and standing areas.

Electric Factory Concerts
Tel: 215-568-3222.
www.electricfactory.com
Sponsors most concerts at major Philadelphia venues.

Hersheypark Arena & Stadium
P.O. Box 866, Hershey, PA.
Tel: 717-534-3911.
The 7,225-seat Hersheypark Arena is a sports venue *(see page 296)* also renowned for its variety of concerts and annual family shows including Disney On Ice and Barnum & Bailey circus. The 30,000-seat stadium also features a summer concert series. Smaller concerts are held at the Star Pavilion.

Buying Tickets

For information on major concerts, contact **Ticketmaster** tel: 215-336-2000 or www.ticketmaster.com

International House
3701 Chestnut Street.
Tel: 215-387-5125.
www.libertynet.org/ihouse
International music, dance and film.

Keswick Theatre
291 Keswick Avenue, Glenside.
Tel: 215-572-7650.
www.keswicktheater.com
Historic 1,200-seat theater for a variety of concerts and events.

Mann Center for the Performing Arts
52nd Street and Parkside Avenue, West Fairmount Park.
Tel: 215-677-0707.
www.manncenter.org
Large indoor/outdoor venue for a variety of concerts and summer home of the Philadelphia Orchestra.

Mendelssohn Club of Philadelphia
Tel: 215-735-9922.
www.libertynet.org/mcchorus
Men's and women's choir performing choral works at the Academy of Music and other venues.

Merriam Theater
250 South Broad Street.
Tel: 215-732-5446.
www.merriamtheater.com
A restored historic landmark featuring dance, theater, music and other performing arts.

Opera Company of Philadelphia
510 Walnut Street, Suite 1500.
Tel. 215-928-2100.
www.operaphilly.com
The city's premier opera company presents four operas a year at the Academy of Music.

Painted Bride Art Center
230 Vine Street.
Tel: 215-925-9914.
www.paintedbride.org
Contemporary performing and visual arts and workshops.

Penn's Landing
Columbus Boulevard (between Market and Walnut streets).
Tel: 215-928-8801.
www.pennslandingcorp.com
Summer series of outdoor jazz and pop concerts, many free.

Philadelphia Boy's Choir
Tel: 215-222-3500.
www.phillyboyschoir.com
Acclaimed ensemble of 90 boys and 30 men; performs at venues throughout the city and the world.

Dance Companies

For information about local dance companies and performances, contact:
Philadelphia Dance Alliance
1429 Walnut Street.
Tel: 215-564-5270.
www.libertynet.org/dance
Pennsylvania Ballet
1101 South Broad Street.
Tel: 1-800-551-7000.
www.paballet.org
Philadelphia's premier ballet

Philadelphia Clef Club of Jazz and Performing Arts
736 South Broad Street.
Tel: 215-893-9912.
www.metrotron.com/norton/pcc
Organization dedicated to jazz performances and education.
Philadelphia Folksong Society
7113 Emlen Street.
Tel: 215-247-1300.
www.pfs.org
American and international folk music presented at the Commodore Barry Club; the society also sponsors the annual Philadelphia Folk Festival at the Old Poole Farm in Schwenksville, PA.
Philadelphia Orchestra
Academy of Music, 1420 Locust Street.
Tel: 215-893-1999.
www.philorch.org
World-famous ensemble formerly conducted by Leopold Stokowski, Eugene Ormandy and Riccardo Muti, now under the baton of Wolfgang Sawallisch. Performs at the Academy of Music (see page 285), with summer concerts at the outdoor Mann Center for the Performing Arts (see page 186).
Philly Pops
Tel: 215-735-7506.
Performances at the Academy of Music, October to May.
Prince Music Theater
100 South Broad Street.
Tel: 215-569-9700.
www.princemusictheater.org
New and innovative musical theater ranging from musical comedy to opera to experimental works.

company performs at the Academy of Music and Merriam Theater; the annual *Nutcracker* is a tradition.
Philadanco
9 North Preston Street.
Tel: 215-387-8200.
A contemporary company which performs at the Zellerbach Theater, the Annenberg Center, the Walnut Street Theatre and the Mandell Theater.

Relache
Tel: 215-574-8246.
Contemporary experimental music presented at Drexel University's Mandell Theater, the Philadelphia Ethical Society on Rittenhouse Square, and other venues throughout the city.
Savoy Company
Tel: 215-735-7161.
www.savoy.org
Gilbert and Sullivan troupe performing at the Academy of Music and Longwood Gardens (see page 225).
Theater of the Living Arts
334 South Street.
Tel: 215-922-1011.
www.electricfactory.com
Pop, jazz, rock and folk at this South Street institution; general admission for 800 people.
Tower Theater
69th and Ludlow streets, Upper Darby, PA.
Tel: 610-352-0313.
www.electricfactory.com
3,000-seat rock music venue.
Trocadero Theater
10th and Arch streets.
Tel: 215-922-6888.
www.trocaderotheater.com
Historic rock music venue with seating and standing areas.

Theater

There is a lively theater scene in Philadelphia. Many of the larger theaters have their own companies and/or host touring companies. Other theaters are home to several companies, and a number of smaller companies perform in

various spaces around the city. The **Theater Alliance of Greater Philadelphia**, a service organization with over 60 non-profit theater companies, has a website with member listings and information about current performances: www.theatrealliance.org. You can also check local listings in the newspaper (see page 262) and/or call theaters direct. Here are some of the venues and companies:
The Adrienne Theatre
2030 Sansom Street.
Home to Second Stage (tel: 215-563-4330), InterAct Theatre Company (tel: 215-568-8077), and other companies.
Arden Theatre Company
40 North 2nd Street, north of Market.
Tel: 215-922-8900.
www.libertynet.org/arden
A number of productions each year including original literary adaptations, musicals, modern dramas and classics.
Arts Bank
601 South Broad Street.
Tel: 215-875-2232.
www.uarts.edu
A rehearsal and performance venue operated by the University of the Arts used by students and a variety of theater and music organizations.
Brick Playhouse
623 South Street.
Tel: 215-592-1183.
www.libertynet.org/thebrick
Intimate theater featuring comedy shows, plays, and various stage performances.
Bucks County Playhouse
70 South Main Street, New Hope.
Tel: 215-862-2041.
www.buckscountyplayhouse.com
Musicals, comedies and dramas by a professional theater company.
Forrest Theatre
1114 Walnut Street.
Tel: 215-923-1515.
www.forresttheatre.com
Several big-time Broadway road shows each year.
Freedom Theatre
1346 North Broad Street.
Tel: 215-765-2793.
A top notch African-American theater company in historic Edwin

Forrest Mansion stages six or seven productions each year.

Fulton Opera House
12 North Prince Street, Lancaster.
Tel: 717-394-7133.
The oldest continuously operating theater in the US, one of only three National Historic Landmark theaters. Renovated in 1995, it includes a lobby with sweeping staircase and crystal chandelier, and a seating plan that makes every seat in the house a good one.

Hedgerow Theatre
64 Rose Valley Road, Media.
Tel: 610-565-4211.
www.hedgerowtheater.com
Longest-running residential repertory theater in the country, performing in a 19th-century mill.

Hershey Theater
15 East Caracas Avenue, Hershey.
Tel: 717-534-3405 (box office);
717-534-3411 (general office);
fax: 717-533-2882.
This magnificent theater has established itself as the area's premier performing arts center, presenting the finest in touring Broadway shows, classical music and dance attractions, and world-renowned entertainers.

Kimmel Center for the Performing Arts
Broad and Spruce streets.
Tel: 215-790-5800.
www.rpac.org
Scheduled to open in December 2001, this will be one of the largest performing arts centers in the country, with a 2,500-seat concert hall, 650-seat recital theater, 150-seat black box theater, a rooftop garden terrace, an arts education center, and a restaurant.

Mask & Wig Theatre
310 South Quince Street.
Tel: 215-898-9999.
This charming theater tucked away in an alley in Washington Square West is home to the University of Pennsylvania's theater troupe and the Philadelphia Area Repertory Theater.

McCarter Theater
91 University Place, Princeton, NJ.
Tel: 609-258-2787.
www.mccarter.org
A wide range of performances,

including musicals, classical dramas, comedies and new works.

Media Theatre for the Performing Arts
State and Monroe streets, Media.
Tel: 610-566-4020/800-568-7771.
www.mediatheatre.com
Elegantly restored 1927 movie palace 20 minutes from the city of Philadelphia. Venue for Broadway-style musical productions as well as new work. Hosts the region's premier music theater company as well as the Society for the Performing Arts.

Mount Hope Estate & Winery
Manheim, PA 17016.
Tel: 717-665-7021.
Pennsylvania Renaissance Faire's Professional Acting Company bring interactive theater to life in the beautiful 200-year-old Victorian Mount Hope Mansion. Shows include the annual Charles Dickens Victorian Christmas, Poe Evermore (Hallowe'en), and the ever popular summer Renaissance Faire (see page 242).

Mum Puppet Theater
115 Arch Street.
Tel: 215-925-8686.
www.libertynet.mum
Puppet troupe performs original and other works in its theater in Philadelphia and around the world.

Painted Bride Art Center
230 Vine Street.
Tel: 215-925-9914.
Cutting-edge dance, performance music, mime, puppetry and more.

PENN Presents
Annenberg Center, 3680 Walnut Street and the Irvine Auditorium, 3401 Spruce Street.
Tel: 215-898-3900.
www.pennpresents.org
A complex of theaters at the University of Pennsylvania run by PENN Presents, a professional arm of the university, presenting world-class dance, theater, music and jazz, including the Philadelphia International Children's Theater Festival.

People's Light and Theatre Company
39 Conestoga Road, Malvern.
Tel: 610-644-3500.
www.peopleslight.com

Exciting adaptations of contemporary and classical dramas presented in a 200-year-old converted barn, 45 minutes outside Center City.

Philadelphia Shakespeare Festival
2111 Sansom Street.
Tel: 215-496-8001.
Three Shakespearean works presented each year.

Plays and Players Theater
1714 Delancey Street.
Tel: 215-735-0630.
www.libertynet.org/ppt
The oldest community theater in the country presents its own productions and is home to the innovative Philadelphia Theatre Company (tel: 215-985-1400) and others. The Philadelphia is one of the city's leading theater companies, combining local talent with the skills of Tony Award winning actors and directors. The 324-seat auditorium offers great views and acoustics.

Society Hill Playhouse
507 South 8th Street.
Tel: 215-923-0210.
www.societyhillplayhouse.com
Historic venue with two theaters (cabaret and main stage), presenting contemporary musicals, comedies and dramas.

Sight and Sound Millennium Theater and Living Waters Theater
Route 896, Strasburg.
Tel: 717-687-7800.
www.bibleonstage.com
In Lancaster county. Dramatic representation of the scriptures.

Walnut Street Theatre
Broad and Spruce streets.
Tel: 215-574-3550.
www.wstonline.org
The oldest continuously operated theater in the country presents musicals, dramas, classics and Broadway road shows as well as four new plays each year at adjacent smaller theaters.

Wilma Theater
265 South Broad Street.
Tel: 215-546-7824.
www.wilmatheater.org
A state-of-the-art 296-seat theater on the Avenue of the Arts featuring cutting-edge drama and comedy, both grandiose and intimate.

Festivals

Listings and advertisements for upcoming special events can be found in *The Daily News*, *Philadelphia Inquirer*, *Philadelphia Magazine*, *The Philadelphia Tribune* (the city's African-American newspaper) and *Philadelphia Gay News*, as well as in weekly newspapers like *The City Paper* and *Philadelphia Weekly*.

The following is a list of some of the annual traditions you'll find in Philadelphia. A number of events are held at Penn's Landing, and with the construction of the new Entertainment Center, some events may be subject to change.

All Year

First Friday. An ongoing art fest held at Old City galleries on the first Friday of every month between December and June.

January

Mummers' Parade. 30,000 high-struttin' Mummers march all the way up Broad Street (or some years, west on Market Street) to City Hall on New Year's Day *(see page 81)*. Tel: 215-336-3050 for details.
Philadelphia International Auto Show. Scores of new car models and spiffy foreign imports exhibited at the Pennsylvania Convention Center.
Benjamin Franklin's Birthday. The Franklin Institute celebrates the birth of its namesake and inspiration. Look for the kite-flying festival at Independence Mall in honor of Franklin's famous experiments with electricity. Tel: 215-448-1200 for details.

Edgar Allan Poe Birthday. Special tours, programs and exhibits are presented at the Poe National Historic Site *(see page 216)*.
Martin Luther King, Jr. Birthday. Ceremonies, special performances and lectures in honor of Dr King.
Philadelphia Boat Show. The latest in yachts, sailboats and motorboats, with more than 500 vessels on display at the Convention Center.

February

Black History Month. A series of special exhibits, performances and presentations at venues throughout the city. Call the Afro-American Historical and Cultural Museum for information tel: 215-574-0380.
Mummers String Band Show of Shows. Outlandishly costumed Mummers bring their fun-loving brand of music to the Convention Center.
Philadelphia Home Show. Products and plans for remodeling, renovating, furnishing and decorating your home exhibited at the Convention Center.
Presidents' Day. Look for special tours and events at Independence Park and Valley Forge National Historical Park, and other historic sites throughout the area in celebration of Washington's and Lincoln's birthdays.
Chinese New Year. Chinatown celebrates the new year with traditional processions and festivities, and banquets at the Chinese Cultural Center.
Presidential Jazz Weekend. Four days of jazz at venues throughout the city featuring local talent and international jazz legends. Tel: 215-636-1666.
US Pro Indoor Tennis Championship. The world's top tennis players compete for a $1 million crown at the Spectrum. Tel: 215-947-2530.

March

Philadelphia Flower Show. The Convention Center is transformed into a many-colored sea of petals and pollen at the largest flower

show in the country. The show is sponsored by the Pennsylvania Horticultural Society. Tel: 800-611-5960 for details.
St Patrick's Day Parade. A celebration of Philadelphia's Irish heritage along Benjamin Franklin Parkway and Chestnut Street to Independence Hall.
The Book and the Cook. The city's finest and most innovative chefs hitch up with well-known cookbook authors and food critics for a celebration of food and drink. Tel: 215-686-3662.
Women's History Month. Look for the Women's Festival at the Bourse plus other events in the city.
Poetry Week. The American Poetry Center honors the muse with readings, lectures, exhibits and other events for local literati.

April

Easter Parade. An age-old tradition on Rittenhouse Square, showcasing imaginative fashions and music.
Manayunk in Bloom. Easter Sunday festival along Main Street, with Easter Bunny, floral window displays, and special holiday menus in restaurants.
Penn Relays. The country's oldest and largest amateur track meet is held at Franklin Fields on the University of Pennsylvania campus. Tel: 215-898-6148.
Valborgsmassoafton. A traditional Swedish rite of spring with folk music, dance and food at the American Swedish Historical Museum in South Philadelphia's Franklin Park. April 30th. Tel: 215-389-1776.
Philadelphia Open House. Bus and walking tours through the homes, churches, gardens and other notable sites in the city's many historic neighborhoods. Tel: 215-928-1188.
Philadelphia Antiques Show and Sale. A tradition among the metropolitan area's dealers and collectors and one of the finest shows in the country; 103rd Engineers Armory, 33rd and Market streets. Tel: 215-387-3500. www.philaantiques.com.

Philadelphia Folk Fair. Held at the Convention Center every even-numbered year, the fair features arts, crafts, song, dance and food from the city's many ethnic communities and visitors from around the world.

Spring Tours of Fairmount Park. Trolley-buses run a special route along Wissahickon Creek. Tel: 215-636-1666.

May

Africamericas Festival. A 12-day celebration of African American culture with music, parades, films, theater and dance at sites throughout the city.

Philadelphia Festival of World Cinema. A two-week festival featuring the finest new films from around the world screened at various theaters throughout the city. Tel: 1-800-WOW-PFWC.

Strawberry, Flower & Garden Festival. Weekend devoted to gardening enthusiasts. Tel: 215-794-4000. www.peddlersvillage.com.

Brandywine River Blues Festival. A celebration of wine, music and soul. Tel: 610-388-6221. www.chaddsford.com.

Rittenhouse Row Spring Festival. Street cafés, music, art, fashion and culture along Walnut Street from Avenue of the Arts to Rittenhouse Square. Tel: 215-735-4899.

Dad Vail Regatta. With more than 3,000 rowers, the largest collegiate regatta in the country floats down the Schuylkill River near Strawberry Mansion and Boathouse Row. www.dadvail.org.

Armed Forces Weekend. Philadelphia honors the men and women of America's military at Penn's Landing with entertainment, exhibits and tours of a naval vessel.

Israel's Independence Day. A celebration with a parade down Chestnut Street, culminating with entertainment and an Israeli bazaar at Independence Mall. Second or third Sunday of the month. Tel: 215-922-7222.

Israel Independence Celebration at Penn's Landing. Part of PECO Energy Multicultural Series.

Italian Market Festival. A day of music and outdoor food stands at the 9th Street Market.

International Theater Festival for Children. Five days of theater, folktales, puppet shows and dance at the Annenberg Center, Walnut Street Theater and other venues. Tel: 215-898-6791.

Devon Horse Show and Country Fair. One of the country's largest horse shows, and a Main Line tradition since 1896, at the Devon Fairground about 45 minutes from Center City. Tel: 610-964-0550.

Jam on the River. A three day blast at Penn's Landing with music, Southern cuisine and cultural celebrations. Originally a homage to New Orleans, now includes blues as well as jazz. Tel: 215-922-2FUN www.pennslandingcorp.com.

Memorial Day Observance. A formal observance is held aboard the 19th-century USS *Olympia* at Penn's Landing.

Rittenhouse Square Flower Market. An annual tradition for more than 75 years, featuring thousands of flowering plants and food stands. Tel: 215-525-7182.

Manayunk Canal Day. A parade and day-long festival showcasing the colorful shops and restaurants along this old mill town's gentrified Main Street.

Mozart on the Square. Two weeks of performances at venues around Rittenhouse Square honor the genius of Wolfgang Amadeus Mozart. Tel: 215-668-1799.

Penn's Landing Summer Season. Dozens of free concerts and ethnic festivals are offered at this waterfront venue. One of the best entertainment values in the city; weekends through to September.

Head House Square Crafts Fair. Local crafts people and artists exhibit their work, weekends from Memorial Day weekend through to mid-September. Tel: 215-790-0782.

June

WPEN Big Band Series Kick Off at Penn's Landing. Music from the big bands. Swing dance instruction every Thursday.

Marine Day. Celebration of the Delaware Valley's maritime industry at Penn's Landing.

Safe Boating Weekend. Live air/sea rescue demonstrations, and marine vessels open for tours. Penn's Landing.

Elfreths Alley Day. The residents of the oldest residential street in the country, many in colonial dress, open their charming homes to visitors. Colonial crafts and baked goods are sold at the Museum House. First weekend of the month. Tel: 215-574-0560.

Italian National Day. A tribute to the people, history and culture of Italy at Penn's Landing on the occasion of Italy's national holiday.

Islamic Festival. Celebration of the arts, crafts, culture and cuisine of Islam. Penn's Landing (PECO Multicultural Series).

Portuguese Heritage Day. Live bands, art performances and displays, Portuguese cuisine. Penn's Landing (PECO Multicultural Series).

Irish Festival. Celebration of the music, customs, food and artwork of Ireland, complete with string bands, bagpipers, and other musical entertainment. Penn's Landing (PECO Multicultural Series).

Midsommerfest. A traditional celebration of summer with folk dancing, music and food at the American Swedish Historical Museum situated in South Philadelphia. Tel: 215-389-1776

Rittenhouse Square Fine Arts Annual. Many of the area's most talented artists exhibit thousands of works at this five-day open-air clothesline exhibit.

Flag Day. Old Glory is celebrated with a parade and ceremonies at the Betsy Ross House.

Phillyfest. A series of free lunchtime performances featuring jazz, pop and ethnic musicians as well as sports competitions and other entertainment at JFK Plaza adjacent to City Hall; weekdays through to August.

Mellon Jazz Festival. Some of the biggest names in jazz converge on Philly for concerts, master classes and jam sessions at venues in Center City.

Mann Music Center Summer Concerts. A set of open-air performances by the world-renowned Philadelphia Orchestra in beautiful Fairmount Park. Free tickets are available on the day of the concert at the JFK Visitors Center.

Manayunk Cycling Celebration. A two-day festival before the Pro-Cycling Championship with sidewalk sales, entertainment, food and family fun.

First Union Pro Cycling Championship. A grueling 156-mile (250-km) international bicycle race including the punishing climb up the Manayunk Wall. The race begins and ends in front of the Museum of Art on the Benjamin Franklin Parkway. Tel: 215-482-9565. www.firstunioncycling

Kutztown Folk Festival. Perhaps the area's best opportunity to experience Pennsylvania Dutch and Amish culture, crafts, food and people at this nine-day festival at the Kutztown Fairgrounds, approximately 15 miles (25 km) northeast of Reading *(see page 242)*.

Manayunk Arts Festival. Outdoor juried arts and crafts show with 250 professional artists from across the nation. Tel: 215-482-9565. www.manayunk.com.

July

WPEN Big Band Series. Swing dance every Thursday in July and August at Penn's Landing.

Welcome America! Festival. Independence Day is a big event in Philadelphia. In addition to the traditional parade and fireworks, there are Mummers' bands, a hot-air balloon race, a restaurant festival, sporting events and more. Most of the week's action is centered around Independence Hall, but events are held at Rittenhouse Square, the Museum of Art, JFK Plaza, Penn's Landing and other venues. Check the papers for a detailed list of events.

Concerts in Fairmount Park. Philadelphia Orchestra Summer Concerts at the Mann Music Center, Pop Concerts at the Mann and at Robin Hood Dell East.

Fitness Fun Fest. An afternoon of fun and fitness with family activities at Penn's Landing.

Hispanic Fiesta. Music, dance, food and crafts from Puerto Rico and Latin America. Penn's Landing. (PECO Multicultural Series)

Children's Special Sundays. Sunday afternoons in July and August at Penn's Landing mean jugglers, musicians, shows, and other activities for children.

Singer-Songwriter Festival. A three-day series of performances by contemporary singer-songwriters at Penn's Landing.

RiverBlues Festival. A fantastic opportunity to hear some of the country's best blues musicians at a three-day celebration of American music, food and fun around Penn's Landing's outdoor stage.

International Folk Dancing. Folk dancing exhibitions are offered Tuesday evenings at the Philadelphia Museum of Art terrace.

Pennsylvania Renaissance Faire. A recreation of 16th-century life at a 38-acre (15-ha) English village complete with costumed performers, jousting knights, ladies, lords, minstrels, dramas, jugglers, craftspeople and food merchants; weekends through early October; Mount Hope Estate and Winery *(see page 242)*.

August

WJJZ Jazz Series. Every Friday evening (6:30–9pm) in August, jazz concerts at Penn's Landing.

German Festival. Three-day festival showcasing German music, dance, food and crafts. Penn's Landing. (PECO Energy Multicultural Series.)

Festival of India. Indian dancing, cuisine and crafts. Penn's Landing. (PECO Energy Multicultural Series.)

Caribbean Festival. Celebrates the cultures of Antigua, Bahamas, Barbados, Haiti, Grenada, Guyana and St Thomas, with music and food. (PECO Energy Multicultural Series.)

African-American Cultural Extravaganza. Dance, music, food, and crafts celebrating African-American culture. (PECO Energy Multicultural Series.)

Philadelphia Folk Festival. A weekend of international folk music performed outside Philadelphia at Old Poole Farm in Schwenksville. www.folkfest.org.

Pennsylvania Dutch Festival. Demonstrations of arts, crafts and food from Pennsylvania Dutch country; Reading Terminal Market.

Polish Festival. A two-day celebration of Polish dance, music, food and culture at Penn's Landing. (PECO Energy Multicultural Series)

Pennsylvania Dutch Days. A festival of food, crafts and culture in Hershey, America's chocolate capital *(see page 242)*.

Goschenhoppen Folk Festival. Another Pennsylvania Dutch festival, this one in East Greenville.

September

Labor Day Weekend at Penn's Landing. Music, food and other entertainment.

Philadelphia Fringe Festival. Ten-day festival with art performances and exhibitions by local, national and international artists in galleries, on sidewalks, in cafés and vacant lots throughout Old City. Tel: 215-413-9006.

Mexican Independence Day. Mexican entertainment, food and crafts at Penn's Landing. (PECO Multicultural Series.)

Sippin' by the River. Wine- and beer-tasting festival with gourmet food and silent auction. Admission fee. Penn's Landing.

Dressage at Devon. A world-class equestrian competition featuring the country's finest horses and riders. Devon Fairground. Tel: 610-449-2452.

Von Steuben Day Parade. A tribute to the German general who whipped the Continental Army into fighting shape at Valley Forge and a salute to the city's rich German heritage. The procession runs down the Benjamin Franklin Parkway and then heads to Independence Mall.

Puerto Rican Day Parade. A celebration of Philly's Puerto Rican community. This parade starts on the Parkway, too.

Philadelphia Distance Run. A half-marathon through Center City and Fairmount Park drawing a field of some 7,500 runners. The finish line is next to City Hall at JFK Plaza.
Harvest Show. A flower and garden show at the Horticultural Center in Fairmount Park, with entertainment, food and children's activities.
Fairmount Park Festival. A series of events including sports competitions, special tours, exhibitions and other recreational activities; through to November.
Pennsbury Manor Fair. A recreated 17th century country fair on the grounds of William Penn's Bucks County estate with costumed players, crafts demonstrations, puppeteers, musicians, food and dancers.
Battle of Brandywine. Re-enactment of the historic clash between rebels and redcoats south of Philadelphia at Brandywine Battlefield State Park.
Manayunk Indian Summer Festival. Food and family fun along Main Street. Pumpkin painting, scarecrow making and other activities.

October

Columbus Day. The city celebrates Columbus' voyage of discovery with a parade followed by a festival at Penn's Landing.
Pulaski Day Parade. A parade honoring the Polish patriot who rallied with American rebels during the Revolutionary War and the city's substantial Polish-American community.
Super Sunday. Sponsored by the cultural institutions along the Benjamin Franklin Parkway, this is a day-long party featuring games, rides, food stalls, entertainment, exhibits, a flea market and more on the Parkway between Logan Circle and the Museum of Art.
Thomas Eakins Regatta. Collegiate crews across the country come out for a row down the Schuylkill River in honor of the city's famed artist, who immortalized rowers and the river in many of his finest works.
William Penn's Birthday. The founder's birth is celebrated in period costume with a special party

at Pennsbury Manor (Penn's country estate in Bucks County) as well as at various events in the city.
Battle of Germantown. Washington's heroic but failed attempt to dislodge the British from Germantown in 1777 is commemorated with a historic re-enactment and country fair at Cliveden.
Hallowe'en. Celebrations, including the Philadelphia Orchestra's Hallowe'en concert, at which everyone (orchestra included) is encouraged to come in costume, and the annual Trick or Treat Parade in Manayunk when children parade, trick or treating at stores along Main Street the Sunday nearest Hallowe'en.

November

Thanksgiving Day Parade. The oldest of its kind, the parade files down Market Street and west on the Parkway with giant balloons, colorful floats, brass bands, clowns and a cast of thousands.
Books, Toys and Tinkertoys. Both children and adults will get a kick out of the Giant Tinkertoy Extravaganza at the Franklin Institute.
Old Fort Mifflin. The siege of this historic fort in 1777 is re-enacted by soldiers in period costume. Scores of Americans died during the battle in order to protect Washington's army from a British attack on Valley Forge (see page 229).
Philadelphia Crafts Show. A four-day juried crafts fair at the Convention Center featuring the work of 100 artists from around the US
Philadelphia Marathon. Marathon starts at the Museum of Art, runs through Fairmount Park, Center City and Independence Hall area, and back to the museum.
Virginia Slims Tennis Classic. The finest women tennis players compete at the Spectrum in South Philadelphia.

December

Army-Navy Football Classic. West Point and the Naval Academy face off in Philly for their annual gridiron grudge match.

One City, One Song. Community caroling at the Museum of Art precedes the lighting of the city's Christmas tree at City Hall.
Christmas Tours of Historic Houses. The mansions of Fairmount Park are decked with Christmas cheer for special tours. Holiday tours of Germantown's historic houses, and a Christmas party at the Ebenezer Maxwell Mansion, are offered, too. Contact the staff at Cliveden or at the Maxwell Mansion for details (see page 209–210).
Lucia Fest. A traditional Swedish winter festival with folk music, crafts, food, a candlelight procession and a Christmas fair at the American Swedish Historical Museum in South Philadelphia and Gloria Dei (Old Swedes') Church in Queen Village.
Kwanzaa. The African-American winter holiday is celebrated with a parade, special exhibits and other events. Contact the Afro-American Historical and Cultural Museum (see page 160).
Charles Dickens Christmas Past. Dickens and the characters from A Christmas Carol and other works are brought to life at the Mount Hope Estate and Winery.
Washington's Crossing of the Delaware. Washington's bold river crossing in 1776 is re-enacted on Christmas Day at Washington Crossing State Park in Bucks County.
The Nutcracker. The Pennsylvania Ballet performs Tchaikovsky's Nutcracker at the Academy of Music throughout the month. Tel: 215-551-7014.
New Year's Eve Celebration. Ring in the New Year with fireworks, music and hundreds of fellow revelers at Penn's Landing. Dress warmly.

Shopping

CENTER CITY

The largest shopping district in the city is on Market Street east of Broad Street. Here you'll find **Lord & Taylor**, formerly John Wanamaker, (13th and Market streets; tel: 215-241-9000; open Monday–Tuesday, Thursday–Saturday 10am–7pm, Wednesday 10am–8pm, Sunday noon–5pm), the granddaddy of Philadelphia department stores housed in a landmark building across from City Hall. Lord & Taylor has five floors of retail space with a grand central court where shoppers can grab a bite at the gourmet counter, take in the daily organ concerts (performed on the world's largest organ) during the Christmas season at 11:15am and 5:15pm or enjoy the Christmas light show.

Further east on Market Street, past discount shops, sporting goods, electronics, shoes and clothing stores, is **The Gallery**, a modern shopping mall that occupies three square blocks and four levels between 11th and 8th streets. There are over 200 shops and restaurants around the airy, skylit atrium including three department stores (Kmart, J.C. Penney and Strawbridges) and a surprisingly interesting food court that's convenient for quick and inexpensive meals or snacks. The Gallery (tel: 215- 625-4962) has the same opening times as Lord & Taylor.

Market Place East (tel: 215-592-8905) is next to The Gallery. Housed in a magnificent cast-iron structure once occupied by Little Bros Department Store, this block-long complex is divided between offices, stores and restaurants.

Also in the area, facing the Liberty Bell near Independence Mall, is the **Bourse** (tel: 215-625-0300), a 19th-century commercial exchange with a glorious six-story central hall now occupied by stores, restaurants and offices. The location is perfect for a shopping or dining break.

A short walk away, **Jewelers Row Sansom Street** between 7th and 8th streets is devoted exclusively to precious gems and metals. If you're looking for a gift, or thinking about getting hitched, the selection and prices can't be beaten in Philadelphia.

Running parallel to Market Street is Chestnut Street. Most of the retailers on this strip are discount stores or specialty shops. The snazzy **The Shops at Liberty Place** (tel: 215-851-9055) complex is between 16th and 17th streets. The 70 shops and restaurants including Warner Bros, J. Crew, Godiva Chocolates, Coach, and Rand McNally Travel Bookstore are set around a two-story glass rotunda. The shops are open Monday–Saturday 9:30am–7pm, Wednesday until 8pm, Sunday noon–6pm.

For even fancier pickings, try the **Shops at the Bellevue** (tel: 215-875-8350), a posh marketplace beneath the The Park Hyatt at the Bellevue at Broad and Walnut streets, where retailers like Ralph Lauren's Polo, Nicole Miller, Rizzoli and Tiffany & Co. do business in beautifully appointed shops. Most shops are open Monday–Saturday 10am–6pm, and until 8pm on Wednesday. There's also a huge, good-value food court downstairs.

Walnut Street near Rittenhouse Square also has its share of fancy retailers, including Rodier of Paris, Burberrys, and fashion stops, Jones NewYork and Toby Lerner.

For more adventurous tastes, **South Street** is the place to go. The shops and eateries on or near South Street from 9th to Front streets include everything from punk shops and art galleries to rock bars and fine restaurants. This is the hip, edgy part of town, popular

with, but certainly not limited to, young people. It tends to be a bit of a carnival on Friday and Saturday nights, but it's almost always interesting. At one time, South Street ran through a large Jewish neighborhood. A remnant of those days can still be found on Fabric Row, which runs along 4th Street south of South Street.

BEYOND CENTER CITY

Manayunk's Main Street is lined with unique boutiques and galleries, not to mention numerous eateries. **Chestnut Hill** also has numerous specialty shops in which to browse.

In the far northeastern corner of the city, near the Bucks County border, **Franklin Mills** (tel: 215-632-1500, www.franklin-mills-mall.com) is a sprawling discount mall – the city's largest – with more than 200 outlet stores, 30 fast-food counters and restaurants, and a 10-screen cinema. The complex occupies more than 40 acres (16 ha) and is surrounded by a Carrefour Hypermarket and a complex of shops known as the Philadelphia Home and Design Center. From Center City, take I-95 north to the Woodhaven Road exit. Hours at Franklin Mills are Monday–Saturday 10am–9:30pm, Sunday 11am–6pm.

To the north of the city, **Plymouth Meeting Mall** (tel: 610-825-9351), off I-76, with department stores Boscovs and Strawbridges, is best-known for Ikea (tel: 610-834-1520), a Swedish furniture and house-wares company. The mall's hours of business are the same as Franklin Mills. Recent additions include a huge multiscreen movie theater.

Nearby, the **King of Prussia Mall**, off Route 202 about 30 minutes north of Center City, is a huge two-part complex (The Court, tel: 610-337-1210 and The Plaza, tel: 610-265-3353) with more than 300 stores and restaurants, including Bloomingdales, Nordstrom, Lord & Taylor, Macy's, Neiman Marcus, J.C. Penny, Sears and Strawbridges; open Monday–Saturday

10am–9:30pm, Sunday 11am–5pm. There's also a new multiscreen movie complex here, which includes an IMAX screen.

Across the Ben Franklin Bridge in Cherry Hill, New Jersey, the **Cherry Hill Mall** (Monday–Saturday 10am–9:30pm, Sunday 11am–6pm) is anchored by Macy's, Strawbridges and J.C. Penney (tel: 856-662-7440).

If it's outlet shopping you're interested in, check out the almost side-by-side outlets on Route 30 East in Lancaster in Pennsylvania Dutch Country: the **Tanger Outlet Mall** and **Rockvale Square Outlets**. Rockvale Square is an award-winning, 76-acre (31-ha) outlet shopping center housed in 14 brickfaced buildings showcasing 120 factory stores. Tanger adds another 63 stores to this shopping mecca.

In Bucks County, **Peddler's Village** (tel: 215 794 4000) on Route 202 between Doylestown and New Hope, offers 70 specialty shops featuring crafts, antiques and gifts as well as several restaurants in a pleasant country setting. **New Hope** (tel: 215-867-5880) on the Delaware River, is a center of art galleries, antiques shops, gift shops, crafts and fashion stores, as well as many fine restaurants.

What to Buy

ANTIQUES

Philadelphia is big on antiques. Once a major center of American craftsmanship, collectors and dealers still scour swap meets, flea markets and salvage operations in search of ancient treasures. The best place to start looking for antiques is **Pine Street** between 13th and 8th streets, otherwise known as Antique Row. There are about 20 or so antiques dealers along this strip as well as jewelers, craft shops and several interesting spots for a bite to eat. You might also want to try the nearby **Antiquarians Delight** (615 South 6th Street, tel: 215-592-0256), an indoor antiques market just off South Street with some 30 antiques dealers hawking their

wares under a single roof. There are dozens of other shops elsewhere in town, large and small, with a variety of specialties. Check the telephone directory's *Yellow Pages* for listings. If you're serious about antiques, you should also check the Weekend section of the *Philadelphia Inquirer* for listings of special antiques markets in and around the city *(see page 262)*, as well as the yearly Philadelphia Antiques Show, usually held in April at the 103rd Engineers Armory at 33rd and Market streets.

BOOKS AND MUSIC

There are lots of good bookstores in Philadelphia, many specializing in rare volumes or special themes. Check the *Yellow Pages* or the Internet for a large listing. For the widest selection, try one of the three largest stores, each with thousands of titles:

Barnes & Noble
1805 Walnut Street.
Tel: 215-665-0716.
Tower Books
425 South Street.
Tel: 215 925 0900.
Borders Books and Music
1727 Walnut Street.
Tel: 215-568-7400.

There are chain stores, including Waldenbooks and B. Dalton at The Gallery. Two independent shops with a good selection of art, photography, graphic arts and literature are **Hibberds** (1310 Walnut Street) and **Joseph Fox Bookstore** (1724 Sansom Street).

Among specialty bookstores are:

American Institute of Architecture Bookstore
17th and Sansom streets.
Academy of Fine Arts Museum Shop
Broad and Cherry streets.
Museum of Art Bookstore
Benjamin Franklin Parkway.
Art and architecture.
Garland of Letters
527 South Street.
New Age books.
Giovanni's Room
345 South 12th Street.
Gay and feminist subject matter.

Rand McNally
1 Liberty Place.
Travel guides and maps.
How-to-do-it Bookshop
1608 Sansom Street.
How-to books.
Whodunit
1931 Chestnut Street.
Mystery books and thrillers.
Cookbook Stall
Reading Terminal Market.
Book Trader
501 South Street.
Second-hand books.
W. Graham Arader
1308 Walnut Street.
Bauman Rare Books
1215 Locust Street.
Antique and rare volumes.

The annual Book and the Cook Fair brings together cookbook authors, food critics and the city's finest chefs for a two-day celebration of good eating and reading.

You'll find the city's best selection of compact discs and tapes at **Tower Records** (610 South Street) and **Tower Records Classical Annex** (539 South Street), open 9am–midnight seven days a week. Chain stores like **Borders Books and Music** and **Sam Goody** have several locations and a good selection of popular music. There are also a number of specialty shops, including **Nathan Muchnick** (1725 Chestnut Street) for classical and the **Book Trader Record Annex** (501 South Street) and **Philadelphia Record Exchange** (608 South 5th Street and 618 South 5th Street) for used and rare records.

FOOD

There are two spots in Philadelphia that gourmets and gourmands should not miss: Reading Terminal Market and the Italian – or 9th Street – Market. Housed in a historic train shed, **Reading Terminal Market** (12th and Arch streets, tel: 215-922-2317) has been enveloped by the new Philadelphia Convention Center. No matter, this is still one of the most entertaining spots in the city, with stall after stall of fresh fish, vegetables, meats and baked goods as well as counter service and restaurants offering everything from sushi to spaghetti shoofly pie. Reading Terminal Market is open Monday–Saturday 8am–6pm.

The **Italian Market** is a bit grungier but equally enticing. The offerings at this mostly outdoor market, stretching along 9th Street between Catharine and Wharton streets, are fresh and inexpensive. And at least a dozen good Italian restaurants are within easy walking distance, not to mention South Philly's cheesesteak royalty, Pat's and Geno's *(see page 199)*. Check Fantes for the latest cookware, cookbooks and culinary gadgets. Most outdoor stalls are open Tuesday–Saturday around 8:30am–5pm. Most shops, bakeries, delis and butchers are open Monday, too.

Among the city's many gourmet shops, **The Chef's Market** (231 South Street, tel: 215-925-8360, open Monday–Thursday 8:30am–9pm, Friday–Saturday 8:30am–11pm, Sunday 8am–9pm) is among the largest, with a huge choice of gourmet groceries, supplies and prepared foods.

Children

Philadelphia is a great place to bring the whole family. History comes alive in Independence Park, Fort Mifflin, and other sites around the city. Several museums are totally or partly devoted to kids, and apple orchards, pumpkin patches, theme parks and sandy beaches beckon not far from the city limits. Many hotels offer family packages. Check the daily newspapers or pick up a free copy of *Parents' Express* or *MetroKids* at newsstands throughout the city for more ideas.

Aquariums & Zoos

NJ State Aquarium & Camden Children's Garden
Delaware River between Federal Street & Mickle Boulevard, Camden.
Tel: 1-800-616-5297.
Open Monday–Saturday 10am–4pm. has one of the world's largest fish tanks with over 1,500 fish.

Insectarium
8046 Frankford Avenue.
Tel: 215-338-3000.
Open Monday–Saturday 10am–4pm. Entrance fee.
Two floors of the world's insects, including exotic roaches, scorpions, a beehive and a termite colony. Interactive games, including a crawl through bungee cord spider web.

Philadelphia Zoo
34th Street & Girard Avenue.
Tel: 215-243-1100.
www.philadelphiazoo.org
The oldest zoo in the country, home to nearly 2,000 animals. Children especially enjoy the Treehouse, a display of six different environments with a giant artificial ficus tree reaching up through the roof.

ZooAmerica
North American Wildlife Park, 100 W. Hersheypark Drive, Hershey.
Tel: 1-717-534-3860.
www.hersheypa.com
Open September–mid-June 10am–5pm, mid-June–August 10am–8pm. Entrance fee.
Eleven-acre (4-ha) wildlife sanctuary with animals from North America.

Farms & Orchards

Linvilla Orchards
137 West Knowlton Road, Media.
Tel: 610-876-7116.
Call for hours and times.
Depending upon the season, pumpkins, apples, hayrides, and a maze

Merrymead Farm
2222 Valley Forge Road.
Tel: 610-584-4410.
Call for hours and times.
Pumpkins, hayrides, cornfield maze and other activities in season.

Museums

Academy of Natural Sciences
19th Street and Parkway.
Tel: 215-299-1000. www.acnatsci.org
Open Monday–Friday 10am–4:30pm, Saturday–Sunday 10am–5pm. Entrance fee.
Butterflies, dinosaurs and other exhibits on natural history. Outside there is a children's activity area.

Franklin Institute
20th Street and Parkway.
Tel: 215-448-1200. www.fi.edu
Open Monday–Thursday 9:30am–5pm, Friday–Saturday 9:30am–9pm, Sunday 9:30am–6pm. Entrance fee.
Science museum for all ages, with planetarium, a SkyBike three stories off the ground, an IMAX theatre and interactive exhibits.

Garden State Discovery Museum
16 North Springdale Road, Cherry Hill, NJ.
Tel: 856-424-1233.
www.discoverymuseum.com
Open June–September Tuesday–Saturday 9:30am–5:30pm, October–May until 8:30pm Saturday. Up to age 10. Kids can enter a giant bubble, climb a wall, create artwork, music and more.

Independence Seaport Museum
Penn's Landing, Columbus
Boulevard & Walnut Street.
Tel: 215-413-8621.
www.libertynet.org/seaport
Open daily 10am–5pm. Entrance
fee, except children under 5.
Maritime museum with interactive
exhibits. Tour USS *Olympia*, Admiral
Dewey's flagship from the Spanish
American War and the USS *Becuna*,
a World War II submarine.
Please Touch Museum
210 North 21st Street.
Tel: 215-963-0667.
www.pleasetouchmuseum.org
Open daily 9am–4:30pm.
Entrance fee.
For kids aged seven and under, with
interactive exhibits and programs.

Theme Parks

**Dorney Park & Wildwater
Kingdom**
Dorney Park & Hamilton Boulevard,
Allentown.
Tel: 610-395-3724/1-800-386-8463.
www.dorneypark.com
Open seasonally and fall weekends.
Call for times. Entrance fee.
Amusement and water park.
Hershey Park
100 West Hersheypark Drive, Hershey.
Tel: 1-800437-7439.
www.hersheypa.com
Open seasonally and special week-
ends. Call for times. Entrance fee.
Sixty rides and attractions, including
8 rollercoasters, 6 water rides, and
20 rides for young children.
Sesame Place
100 Sesame Road, Langhorne.
Tel: 215-752-7070.
www.sesameplace.com
Open seasonally, and weekends in
October. Call for times. Entrance fee.
Theme park for children aged 2–13
based on *Sesame Street* TV
characters.
Six Flags Great Adventure
Route 537, Exit 16 off I-195,
Jackson, NJ.
Tel: 732-928-1821.
www.sixflags.com
Open seasonally and some
weekends. Call for times.
This large amusement park is part
of a chain, with rides and shows.

Sport

Philadelphia has professional teams
in all the major American sports:
football, baseball, basketball, hockey,
soccer and lacrosse *(see page 91)*.
Most play at First Union Veterans or
the First Union Center in South
Philadelphia, reached by SEPTA bus C
south on Broad Street or the Broad
Street subway south to Pattison
Avenue. Boxing spectators can visit
the famed Blue Horizon club in North
Philadelphia, which also hosts
wrestling matches and cabaret.

Spectator Sports

Baseball
Philadelphia Phillies
Veterans Stadium, Broad Street and
Pattison Avenue.
Tel: 215-463-5000.

Basketball
Philadelphia 76ers
First Union Center, Broad Street and
Pattison Avenue.
Tel: 215-339-7676.

Boxing and wrestling
**Blue Horizon Boxing and
Entertainment Club**
1314 North Broad Street.
Tel: 215-763-0500.

Football
Philadelphia Eagles
Veterans Stadium, Broad Street and
Pattison Avenue.
Tel: 215-463-5500.

Hockey
Hersheypark Arena
P.O. Box 866, Hershey,
PA 17033-0866.
Tel: 717-534-3911.
Hersheypark Arena has been the
home to the Hershey Bears Hockey
Club since 1938. In addition, the

arena offers concerts *(see page
285)* and other sporting events
including the Harlem Globetrotters.

Horse racing
Philadelphia Park
Street Road, Bensalem, PA.
Tel: 215-639-9000.
Garden State Park
Route 70, Cherry Hill, NJ.
Tel: 609-488-8400.
Off-Track Betting
7 Penn Center, 17th and Market
streets, lower level.
Tel: 215-246-1556.
One of a chain of off-track betting
parlors. Serves food and drink.

Soccer
Hersheypark Stadium
P.O. Box 866, Hershey,
PA 17033-0866.
Tel: 717 534 3911.
The 30,000-seat Hersheypark
Stadium is the most prominent
outdoor stadium facility between
Philadelphia and Pittsburgh. Home of
the Hershey Wildcats (professional
soccer) and is also the venue for
concerts.

Participant Sports

Balloon & helicopter rides
Wings of Gold Hot Air Ballooning
4201 Neshaminy Boulevard,
Bensalem.
Tel: 215-244-9323.
**Balloon Flights Daily by the US
Hot Air Balloon Team**
490 Hopewell Road, St Peters.
Tel: 1-800-763-5987.
Sterling Helicopter
Penn's Landing Heliport, Pier 36,
South Columbus Boulevard.
Tel: 215-271-2510.

Bicycling
For information on bike tours, call
the **Bicycle Club of Philadelphia**
(tel: 215-735-2453). Bikes may be
rented in Fairmount Park at **Lloyd
Hall**, 1 Boathouse Row, Kelly Drive.

Canoes and tubing
Bucks County River Country
2 Walters Lane, Point Pleasant.
Tel: 215-297-5000.
Tubing down the river.

**Bucks County River Country/
Point Pleasant Canoe**
Route 32, Upper Black Eddy,
Point Pleasant.
Tel: 215-297-8181.
**Northbrooke Canoe
Company**
1810 Beagle Road, West Chester.
Tel: 610-793-2279.

Golf courses
John F. Byrnes Golf Course
9500 Leon Street.
Tel: 215-632-8666.
18 holes.
Cobbs Creek Golf Course
72nd Street and Landsowne Avenue.
Tel: 215-877-8707.
Two 18-hole courses.

Juniata Golf Course
M and Cayuga streets.
Tel: 215-743-4060.
18 holes.
Walnut Lane Golf Course
Walnut Lane and Magdalena Street.
Tel: 215-482-3370.
18 holes.
Franklin D. Roosevelt Golf Course
20th Street and Pattison Avenue.
Tel: 215-462-8997.
18 holes.

Parks and Environment Centers

Fairmount Park Commission
Memorial Hall, North
Concourse Drive.
Tel: 215-685-0000.
The country's largest municipal
park stretches across more than
8,000 acres (3,237 ha) on both
sides of the Schuylkill River *(see
page 183)*.
The Fairmount Park Commission
also administrates:
Franklin D. Roosevelt Park
District #2, Broad Street and
Pattison Avenue.
Tel: 215-685-1837.
With 365 acres (148 ha),
American Swedish Museum,
Roosevelt Golf Course, Bellaire
Mansion, tennis courts, baseball
diamonds, Meadows Lake and
other recreational facilities.
Cobbs Creek Park
District #4, 63rd and
Market streets.
Tel: 610-352-8644.
800 acres (324 ha), baseball,
tennis courts, golf course, play-
grounds and other recreational
facilities.
Longwood Gardens
Route 1, Kennett Square.
Tel: 610-388-1000.
Botanical gardens *(see page 225)*.
Entrance fee.
Pennypack Park
District #5, Winchester Avenue
and Roosevelt Boulevard.
Tel: 215-685-0470.
With 1,300 acres (526 ha), hiking
trails, picnic areas, bird sanctuary
and other recreational facilities.
**Pennypack Environmental
Center**
Verree Road.
Tel: 215-671-0440.
Exhibit space and nature programs

in Pennypack Park. Open daily
9am–5pm.
Andorra Natural Area
Northwestern Avenue.
Tel: 215-685-9285.
Exhibits and nature programs in
the northern section of Fairmount
Park.
Penn Treaty Park
East Columbia Avenue and
Beach Street.
Six-acre (2-ha) site on the
Delaware River where William
Penn is said to have negotiated
his treaty with the Lenni-Lenape
Indians.
**Schuylkill Center for
Environmental Education**
8480 Hagys Mill Road.
Tel: 215-482-7300.
A 500-acre (202 ha) natural site:
guided walks and exhibits on local
ecology, plant and animal life. Open
Monday–Saturday 8:30am–5pm,
Sunday 1–5pm. Entrance fee.
**John Heinz National Wildlife
Refuge at Tinicum**
86th Street and Lindbergh
Boulevard.
Tel: 215-365-3118.
Has 1,200 preserved acres
(486 ha) in South Philadelphia's
wetlands; exhibits and guided
walks focus on local wildlife and
ecology. Open daily 9am–4pm.
Morris Arboretum
100 Northwestern Avenue.
Tel: 215-247-5777.
Formerly the summer estate of the
Morris clan, this 175-acre (71-ha)
site in Chestnut Hill is now
administered by the University of
Pennsylvania. Open daily
10am–4pm, with extended
summer hours (call for details).
Entrance fee.

Health clubs
Several hotels have fitness
facilities or links with nearby
clubs. If not, these clubs take
day visitors:
LifeSport
2112 Fairmount Avenue.
Tel: 215-236-0763.
Market West Athletic Club
1835 Market Street, 2nd floor.
Tel: 215-963-2700.
**Rittenhouse Square Fitness
Club**
2002 Rittenhouse Street.
Tel: 215-985-4095.
World Gym
2020 Sansom Street.
Tel: 215-972-0927.

Horseback riding
Gateway Stables
949 Merrybell Lane, Kennett Square.
Tel: 610-444-1255.

Ice skating
River Rink
Festival Pier at Penn's Landing.
Tel: 215-925-RINK.
Open late November–late February.
**University of Pennsylvania Class
of 1923 Ice Rink**
3130 Walnut Street.
Tel: 215-898-1923.
Public sessions September–March
Monday–Friday.

Skiing
Alpine Mountain
Route 447, Analomink, PA.
Tel: 570-595-2150.
Big Boulder
Route 903, Lake Harmony, PA.
Tel: 570-722-0100.
Jack Frost Mountain
Route 940, Blakeslee, PA.
Tel: 570-443-8425.

Shawnee Mountain
Shawnee-on-Delaware, PA.
Tel: 570-421-7231.
Tamiment Resort
Tamiment, PA.
Tel: 570-588-6652.
Tanglewood Ski Area
Off Route 390, Tafton, PA.
Tel: 570-226-7669.

Tennis
There are over 200 public tennis
courts in Philadelphia. For
information on locations,
reservations and special programs
contact **Fairmount Park** (tel: 215-
685-0051).

College Sports

Philadelphia is a great town for
college competition. The Big Five in
Philadelphia are: University of
Pennsylvania, and Temple,
Villanova, LaSalle and St Joseph's
universities.

Ice hockey
Philadelphia Flyers
First Union Center, Broad Street and
Pattison Avenue.
Tel: 215-755-9700.
Philadelphia Phantoms
AHL Hockey, First Union Spectrum,
Broad Street and Pattison Avenue.
Tel: 215 465 4522.

Lacrosse
Philadelphia Wings
First Union Center, Broad Street and
Pattison Avenue.
Tel: 215-398-9464.

Indoor soccer
Philadelphia Kixx
First Union Center, Broad Street and
Pattison Avenue.
Tel: 216-952-5499.

Tickets & Scores

Tickets for major sports events
may be purchased from **Ticketmaster** (tel: 215-336-2000). You
can hear the scores of major
games nationwide by calling the
**Philadelphia Inquirer Dial-A-
Score** (tel: 215-854-2500).

Further Reading

History and Culture

**An Architectural Guidebook to
Philadelphia** by Francis Morrone,
James Iska (Photographer), Gibbs
Smith (1999).
**Autobiography and Other Writings
by Benjamin Franklin**. New York:
Bantam (1982).
**Benjamin Franklin: His Life As He
Wrote It** by Esmond Wright, ed.
Cambridge, MA. Harvard University
Press (1990).
**Building Little Italy: Philadelphia's
Italians Before Mass Migration** by
Richard North Juliani. Penn State
University Press (1998).
**The Buried Past: An Archeological
History of Philadelphia** by John L.
Cotter, et al. University of
Pennsylvania Press (1993).
**Christ Church, Philadelphia: The
Nation's Church in a Changing City**
by Deborah Mathias Gough.
University of Pennsylvania Press
(1995).
**The Elite of Our People: Sketches
of Black Upper-Class Life in
Antebellum Philadelphia** by Joseph
Willson, Julie Winch, Editor. Penn
State University Press (2000).
Annotated edition of an 1841 text
written by an African-American who
had moved to Philadelphia from the
south provides insight into 19th-
century African-American life.
**Faces of Revolution: Personalities
and Themes in the Struggle for
American Independence** by Bernard
Bailyn. New York: Alfred A. Knopf,
(1990) Vintage Paperback (1992).
Franklin of Philadelphia by Esmond
Wright. Cambridge, MA. Harvard
University Press, (1986), paperback
(1988).
**Historic Houses of Philadelphia: A
Tour of the Region's Historic
Homes,** by Roger W. Moss, Tom
Crane (Photographer). University of
Pennsylvania Press (1998). A
beautiful look at historic homes in
and around Philadelphia.

**Jewish Quarter of Philadelphia: A
History & Guide 1881–1930** by
Harry D. Boonin. Jewish Walking
Tours of Philadelphia (1999).
**John Wanamaker, King of
Merchants: The Wanamaker Digest**
by William A. Zulker. Eaglecrest
Press (1993).
Larry Kane's Philadelphia by Larry
Kane, Dan Rather. Temple Univer-
sity Press (2000). Reflections on
Philadelphia by local anchorperson.
**Natural Lives, Modern Times:
People and Places of the Delaware
River** by Bruce Stutz. New York:
Crown Publishers (1992).
**Main Line Wasp: The Education of
Thatcher Longstreth** by W. Thatcher
Longstreth. W.W. Norton & Co.
(1990). Memoir of long-time City
Councilman Thatcher Longstreth.
**Making a Modern Classic: The
Architecture of the Philadelphia
Museum of Art** by David Bruce
Brownless, Graydon Wood
(Photographer). Philadelphia
Museum of Art (1997). A good gift
book with art, history, city politics
and stunning photographs.
**Mermaids, Monasteries,
Cherokees and Custer: The Stories
Behind Philadelphia Street Names**
by Robert I. Alotta. Bonus Books
(1990).
**Millennium Philadelphia: The Last
100 Years,** by the staff of the
Philadelphia Inquirer. Philadelphia:
Camino Books, Inc.1999. Essays
and pictorial history of Philadelphia
over the last century.
**Miracle at Philadelphia: The Story
of the Constitutional Convention,
May to September 1787** by
Catherine Drinker Bowen. Little
Brown (1986).
**Philadelphia Gentlemen: The
Making of a National Upper Class**
by Digby Baltzell. Transaction
Publishers (1989).
**Philadelphia Orchestra: A Century
of Music** by John Ardoin (ed).
Temple University Press (2000).
Essays that chart the history of the
Fabulous Philadelphians and the
musical artists who have shaped
their sound.
Philadelphia World Class, by
Marion Laffrey Fox. Community
Communications (1997).

Philadelphia: A 300-Year History
by Russell F. Weigley, ed. New
York: W.W. Norton & Company,
(1982).
**Philadelphia Stories: A
Photographic History, 1920–1960**
by Fredric Miller et al.
Philadelphia: Temple University
Press, (1988).
A Prayer for the City, by Buzz
Bissinger, New York: Random House
(1997). An engaging and intimate
look at the workings of Mayor Ed
Rendell's administration and its
efforts to combat the problems of
urban decline and revitalize
Philadelphia.
The Puzzles of Amish Life by
Donald B. Kraybill. Intercourse, PA:
Good Books, (1990).
The Riddle of Amish Culture by
Donald B. Kraybill. Intercourse, PA:
Good Books, (1990).
**W.East.B. Dubois, Race, and the
City: The Philadelphia Negro and
Its Legacy** by Michael B. Katz
(ed), Thomas J. Sugrue (ed).
University of Pennsylvania Press
(1998).

Food

**The City Tavern Cookbook: 200
Years of Classic Recipes from
America's First Gourmet
Restaurant** by Walter Staib, Beth
Daddono, John Mariani (1999). City
Tavern, opened in 1773, continues
to serve historically accurate fare.
Lancaster County Cookbook by
Louise Stoltzfus. Good Books
(1993).
**A Taste of Pennsylvania History: A
Guide to Historic Eateries and
Their Recipes** by Debbie Nunley and
Karen Jane Elliott. John F. Blair
(2000). Over 100 recipes culled
from restaurants all over the state.
**The Philadelphia Italian Market
Cookbook**, by Celeste A. Morello.
Philadelphia: Jefferies & Manz, Inc.
(1999). History and anecdotes are
interspersed with recipes for
neighborhood specialties, painting
an intimate portrait of South
Philadelphia's Italian Market.
**The Reading Terminal Market
Cookbook**, by Ann Hazan, Irina
Smith, Reading Terminal Market,

Camino Books (1997). Recipes
from a wide assortment of food
vendors from Philadelphia's historic
Reading Terminal Market include
both prepared foods and recipes
using fresh ingredients available at
the market.

Other Insight Guides

Three Insight Guides series cover
every continent and include 86
titles devoted to the United
States, from Alaska to Florida,
from Seattle to New Orleans.
Destinations in this particular
region include:
Insight Guide: New York City. A
comprehensive and beautifully
photographed guide to the city of
drama and dreams
Insight Guide: Boston. An expert
team of local writers and
photographers celebrates one of
America's most intriguing cities.
Insight Guide: Washington D.C.
Essential reading that conveys the
power and the story of America's
capital.

Feedback

We do our best to ensure the information in our books
is as accurate and up-to-date as possible. The books are
updated on a regular basis, using local contacts, who
painstakingly add, amend and correct as required.
However, some mistakes and omissions are inevitable
and we are ultimately reliant on our readers to put us in
the picture.

We would welcome your feedback on any details
related to your experiences using the book "on the
road". Maybe we recommended a hotel that you liked
(or another that you didn't), as well as interesting new
attractions, or facts and figures you have found out

about the country itself. The more details you can give
us (particularly with regard to addresses, e-mails and
telephone numbers), the better.

We will acknowledge all contributions, and we'll offer
an Insight Guide to the best letters received.

Please write to us at:
**Insight Guides
PO Box 7910
London SE1 1WE
United Kingdom**
Or send e-mail to:
insight@apaguide.demon.co.uk

ART & PHOTO CREDITS

Picture spreads

INSIGHT GUIDE
PHILADELPHIA

Cartographic Editor **Zoë Goodwin**
Production **Linton Donaldson**
Design Consultants
Carlotta Junger, Graham Mitchener
Picture Research
Hilary Genin, Natasha Babaian

Map Production: Stephen Ramsay
© 2001 Apa Publications GmbH & Co.
Verlag KG (Singapore branch)

Index

*Numbers in italics refer to
photographs*

a

Abele, Julian 149
academic prestige 58
Academy of Music 78, 155, *156*, 285
Academy of Natural Sciences 177
Adams, John 15, 30, 31, 125
Adamstown 237
The Adrienne Theatre 286
African-American Museum 77, *160*
African-Americans 60, 149
Albert Maranga Antiques 146
Algonquins 21
Allen, Richard 128
America map *16–17*
American Bandstand 47
American Civil War 38
American Indian Cultural Center of
the Delaware Valley 108
American Music Theater Festival 72
American Pie craft shop 135
American Swedish Historical
Museum 202
Amish *62*, 63–8, *236*
cottage industries *64*, *239*, *240*, 245
farming *66*, *238*
homesteads *240*
Old Order Brethren family *67*
transportation *241*, 245
Ammann, Jacob 63
Anabaptists 63
Andalusia 250
Anderson, Marion *see* Marion
Anderson Award
Annenberg Center 284
anthem 82
anti-slavery movement 37–8, 60, 224
Antique Row *145*, 146
bicycle store *141*
antique shops 146, 237
Aquarium 129
Arch Street Friends' Meeting
House 116
Arch Street Presbyterian Church 177
architecture 148–9, *169*, *178*
religious 177–8
Arden Theatre Company 72, 117, 286
art 18

art galleries 283–4
Delaware Art Museum 228
Independence Park Portrait
Gallery 112
Institute of Contemporary Art 77, 194
Locks Gallery 141
Museum of Art *14*, *75*, 76, 78, *178*
Philadelphia Museum of Art *148*, 149, *172–3*, 178
Woodmere Art Museum 210
art treasures 178–9
Arthur Ross Gallery 194, 284
Articles of Confederation 113
artists 250–2
Arts Bank 71, 286
Astor, John Jacob 214
Athenaeum Reading Room *140*
Atlantic City 230, 231
Atwater Kent Museum 143
Avalon 230
Azalea Garden 183

b

Balch Institute 143
Baldwin, Matthias 36
Barclay Hotel 167
Barnes Foundation 161
Barry, John *111*
Bartram's Gardens 195
Battle of Germantown *32*
Bell Atlantic Tower 178
Benjamin Franklin Bridge 115
Benjamin Franklin National
Memorial 177
Benjamin Franklin Parkway 149, 175
Betsy Ross House *116*
bicycle race *see* Corestates bicycle
race
Bingham Court 124
Bird-in-Hand 240
Bishop, John 137
Bishop White House 108
Black Thursday 42
Blockbuster-Sony Music Center 285
Blue Moon Jazz Club 283
blues 74–5, 283
Boathouse Row, Fairmount Park
98–9, *180–81*, 184
body piercing 136
Boelson Cottage *186*
Bohemian Arts 72
Bolt of Lightning 115
Book and Cook Festival and Fair 88

Book Trader 136
Boston Massacre *31*
Botanical Garden 195
Bourse 115
Bowman's Tower 254
Brandywine Battlefield Park 224
Brandywine River Museum 223
Brandywine River Valley 223–9
Tourist Information Center 225
Brandywine Workshop 156
Brewster, I. & Co. Gallery 283
Brick Playhouse 286
bridges 115, 255
Bridget Foy's eatery 135
Brigantine Island 230
Broad Street *56*, *151*, 155–7
Buckingham Valley Vineyards 255
Bucks County *218–19*, 249–55
Bucks County Playhouse 254, 287
Bull's Island State Park 255
Bushfire Theater 72
business district 151, 157

c

cakewalk 82
Calder, Alexander Milne 75, 151, 154, 175
Calderwood Gallery 283
Camac Street 145
Cape May 230, 231
carnival *133*
Carpenters' Hall 109, *112*
casinos 75
Cathedral of Saints Peter and Paul 176, *177*
Cedar Grove 186
Celluloid City 78–9
Centennial Exhibition 39
Center City 101
Central Market (Lancaster City) *65*, 239
Chadds Ford 223
Chadds Ford Museum *224*
Chadds Ford Winery 224, *226*, 255
Chain Gang 81
charitable trusts 60
Charlotte Cushman Club 145
Cheesesteaks 203
Chestnut Hill *70*, 210
Chestnut Hill Historical Society 210
Childhood see Wildwood
Chinatown 160
Chinese Cultural and Community
Center 160
Chinese Friendship Gate 160
chocolate 238, 242

Choral Arts Society 285
Chris's Jazz Café 74
Christ Church 53
Christ Church Burial Ground 116
Church of St. Luke and the
    Epiphany 146
churches 118–19
    Arch Street Presbyterian 177
    Cathedral of Saints Peter and
        Paul 176, 177
    Christ Church 53
    Gloria Dei 136, 137
    Holy Trinity Roman Catholic 145
    Mother Bethel African Methodist
        Episcopal 128
    Old Pine Street Presbyterian
        119, 126
    Old St. Joseph's 124
    Old Swedes' 136, 137
    St. Clement's Episcopal 177
    St. George's Greek Orthodox
        144
    St. John the Evangelist 158
    St. Luke and the Epiphany 146
    St. Mark's 165, 167
    St. Mary's 124
    St. Peter's Episcopal 127
Churchtown 235
cinema 77, 129, 194, 284, 285
    celluloid city 78–9
Cinemagic 3 at Penn 284
City Hall 52, 101, 148, 150, 151,
    157
City of Philadelphia Recreation
    Department 285
City Tavern 107
City Visitor Center 105
Civil Rights Movement 82
Civil War Library and Museum 169
Civil War Soldiers 178
Clark, Dick 47
classical music 73
Claudio's Italian Market Cheese
    200
Clay Studio 283
Clinton, President W. 45
Clinton Street 147
Cliveden 209
coal 35, 39
College Hall 194
colonial times 18, 53
Concerto Soloists Chamber
    Orchestra of Philadelphia 75, 285
Congregation Mikveh Israel 116
Congress Hall 114
Constitution 15, 33, 105, 113
Constitutional Convention 32
Convention Center 46, 101
Convention Center district 158–60

Corestates bicycle race 91
Corn Exchange Building 108
corruption 43
cottage industries 64, 239, 240,
    245
Cream Cheese 86
crime 41, 44, 45
culture 71–9
Curtis Centre 141
Curtis Institute of Music 167, 285

d

Dali, Salvador 161
dance companies 73, 287
Dante's and Luigi's eatery 201
Declaration House 143
Declaration of Independence 15,
    31, 113
    signing 26–7, 111
Delancey Place (Rittenhouse) 169
Delancey Street (Society Hill) 126
Delaware Art Museum 228
Delaware Canal 253
Delaware History Museum 228
Delaware Museum of Natural
    History 227
Delaware River 22, 23, 246–7, 249
    waterfront 22–3, 129
Delaware Toy and Miniature
    Museum 227
Delaware Valley Opera Company
    285
Deshler-Morris House 208
deVecchis Gallery 283
Devon Horse Show 59, 60
Devon Seafood Restaurant 167
Di Bruno Brothers' House of
    Cheese 200
Dilworth, Richardson 143
diner 84
Doneckers 237
Doylestown 250
Dragon Boat Racing 93
The Dream Garden 141
Drexel University 192
Du Pont Treasures 226–8
Dutch Wonderland amusement
    park 240

e

Eakins, Thomas 153
Eastern State Penitentiary 78, 213
Ebenezer Maxwell Mansion 210
Edgar Allan Poe National Historic
    Site 216
Electric Factory concert hall 74,
    285

Eleutherian Mills 227
Elfreth's Alley 117, 149
Elfreth's Alley Museum 117
English Village 170
Ephrata 237
epidemics 41, 186, 207
Erie Canal 36
Erwinna 255
Esther M. Klein Art Gallery 284
Ethical Society 166
ethnic diversity see
    multiculturalism
Fyes Gallery 283
Eyre, Wilson 168

f

Fabric Row 133–4
Fairmount 213
Fairmount Park 41, 183–6, 184,
    185
Fairmount Waterworks 183
fall 210–19, 222
Fallsington 249
Family Entertainment Center 128
F.A.N. Gallery 283
Fante's 200
fast food 85, 135
Ferry Dock 129
festivals 75, 117, 128, 245, 288
Fields, W. C. 79
Film Forum 77
films 78–9
Fine Arts Library 194
fire company 29
Firemen's Hall 117
First Bank of the United States
    107
First Fridays 77
First Union Center 74, 201, 285
First Union Sports Complex 201
Fleisher Art Memorial 283
Fleisher Ollman Gallery 283
folk culture 240–2, 255
Fonthill 250, 251
food 85–9, 86–8, 145, 155
    4th Street Deli 136, 159
    Delaware River waterfront 129
    ethnic influence 160
    haute cuisine 86, 167
    Italian 196–7, 200–1
    Jim's Steaks 203
    Johnny Rockets fast food 135
    Pat's King of Steaks 159, 201,
        203
    Reading Terminal Market 159
    Shady Maple Smorgasbord 236
    South Street 134–5
food trucks 85, 87

Forrest, Edwin 144
Forrest Theatre 72, 144, 287
Fort Christina 228
Fort Mifflin *202*
Founding Fathers 15
Franklin, Benjamin 25, 29, 31, 110, *188–9*
Franklin Court 111
Franklin Field 192
Franklin Institute 176
Free Library of Philadelphia 176
Free Quaker Meeting House 116
Freedom Theatre 72, 287
French Creek State Park 236
Fulton Opera House 240, 287
Furness, Frank 77, 148, 153, 168, 170, 192
Furness Library *195*

g

Gallery Ghetto 115–17
The Gallery shopping mall 159
gambling 231
gardens
  Azalea 183
  Botanical 195
  Longwood *224*, 225, *226*
  Morris Arboretum 210
  Nemours 227, *228*
  Philadelphia Zoological *186*
  Rockwood 228
  Rose 123
  Spring 213
  Winterthur 226, *227*
Garland of Letters 136
Gateway Regional Visitor Center 105
gay community 59, 146
gay and lesbian venues 77, 146, 283
Gazela 128
GCC Franklin Mills 14 cinema 285
Geno's cheesesteaks 201, 203
Germantown 207–9
Germantown Historical Society 208
Gettysburg 38, 242, 243
Gilbert Luber Collection 284
Giovanni's Room 146
Girard College *213*
Gloria Dei Church *136*, 137
Go West 3rd Thursdays 77
golden eagle (US symbol) *112*
Goode, W. Wilson 45
graduation day *191*
Graff House 143
Great Plaza 128
Green Dragon 237

Green, William J. 45
Grumblethorpe 208

h

Hagley Museum and Library 227
Hahn Gallery 283
Hamilton, Alexander 107
Hamilton Walk 194
Hands On House 238
Hans Herr House 241
haute cuisine 86
Haviland, John 213
Head House Square *124*, 128
  Saturday market *128*
Hedgerow Theatre 287
Heemet Fescht Home Festival 245
Helen Drutt Gallery 283
Henry George School 146
Henry, Patrick 30
Heritage Center of Lancaster County 240
Hershey 242
Hershey Theater 287
Hersheypark 242
Hersheypark Arena and Stadium 285
Hershey's Chocolate World 242
Hewitt, George 168
High Society 59, 79
high society 59
higher education 195
Highwire Gallery 283
historic houses 184–5
Historical Society of Pennsylvania 146
history 18–44
Holy Trinity Roman Catholic Church 145
Home Festival 245
Hopewell Furnace National Historic Site 236
Horn & Hodart's food automat 85
Horticultural Center 186
Hot Soup Hot Glass Studio and Gallery 2 283
Hudson, Henry 22
hunger marchers' protest *42*

i

IMAX theaters 177, 284
immigrants
  anti-slavery movement 37–8, 60, 224
  Italians 199
  living conditions 36–7
  post-Civil War years 39

sanctuary in Philadelphia 55, 57
Swedes 202
Independence 18, *26–7*, 29–32, 112–13
Independence Hall *13*, *37*, *100*, *105*, *111*, 113
Independence Mall 115
Independence National Historical Park Visitor Center 105
Independence Park Institute 105
Independence Park Portrait Gallery 112
Independence Seaport Museum 129
Independence Square 113
Indians 21, 22
Indigo antique shop 146, 284
industrialization 18, 35–39
Institute of Contemporary Art 77, 194
Intercourse 240
International Festival of Theater for Children 73
International Gay and Lesbian Film Festival 77
International House 72, 285
iron 35–6
Italian food *196–7*, *200*
Italian Market *48–9*, *57*, 199
Italians 199
Ivy League football 192

j

James A. Michener Museum 252
jazz 74–5, *144*, 160, 283
Jefferson, Thomas 15, 31
Jeffrey Fuller Fine Art Ltd. 283
Jewelers Row 143
Jewish community 116
Jim's Steaks 135, 203
John Chads House *223*
John F. Kennedy Plaza 175
John Heinz National Wildlife Refuge 202
Johnny Rockets fast food 135
Johnson House 209
Johnson, Russell 156
Jon's snacks 135
Joseph Fox Bookshop 167

k

Kalmar Nyckel Shipyard and Museum 228
Kelly Drive *183*
Kelly, Grace 59, 79, 93
Kennett Square 224, 225
Keswick Theatre 285

Kimmel Center for the Performing Arts 71, 73, 156
Knave of Hearts eatery 135
Kutztown folk festival 235
Kutztown Pennsylvania German Folk Festival 242, 244

l

Lake Nockamixon 255
Lancaster Central Market 65
Lancaster City 239–40
Lancaster County 89, 235, 236
Lancaster County Historical Society 239
Lancaster Walking Tours 240
Land Title Building 155
Landis Valley Museum 238
Laurel Hill 185
Le Bec Fin restaurant 167
Le Brun, Napoleon 148, 155, 176
Lee, Richard Henry 30
Lemon Hill 184
Lenni-Lenape 21
lesbian venues 77, 283
Levy, Nathan 145
Liberties 283
Liberty Bell 25, 104, 114
Liberty Medal 46
Liberty Place 40, 52, 157
Library Company of Philadelphia 146
Library Hall 113
Lights of Liberty show 114, 115
Lincoln, Abraham 38, 243
Lititz 238
Little Italy 199–201
  cheesestore 86
Lloyd Hall 184
Locks Gallery 141
Locktender's House 253
Locust Walk 193, 194
Logan Inn 253, 254
Logan, James 25, 175, 208
Logan Square 175–6
Long Beach Island 230
Longwood Gardens 224, 225, 226
Lord & Taylor department store 78, 158
Lucien Crump Art Gallery 284
Lumberville 255

m

M. Finkel and Daughter antique shop 146
McCarter Theater 73, 287
McManes, James 41

Madison, James 33
mafiosi 42, 45
Maide Franklin jewelry 146
A Man Full of Trouble Tavern 125
Manayunk 204–6, 211
Mann Center for the Performing Arts 73, 74, 186, 286
mansions 249–50
  Nemours 227, 228
  Parry 253
  Pennsbury Manor 249
  Stenton 288
  Strawberry 149, 185
  Van Rensselaer 166
manuscripts 169
Margaret R. Grundy Memorial Library and Museum 249
Margate 230
Mario Lanza Museum 136
Marion Anderson Award 46
Market East 157, 158, 159
Market Street 158
markets 85, 253
  Head House Square 128
  Italian 48–9, 57, 199
  Lancaster Central 65, 239
  Reading Terminal 89, 148, 159
Mask & Wig Theatre 287
Mask and Wig Club 145
Masonic Temple 152
Maui 283
Memorial Hall 186
Mendelssohn Club of Philadelphia 286
Mennonites 69, 235
  Information Center 209, 240
Mercer, Henry Chapman 250
Mercer Mile 250
Mercer Museum 248, 252
Merriam Theater 156, 285
Mikveh Israel Cemetery 145
minstrel shows 82
Moore College of Art 177
Moravian Pottery and Tile Works 251, 252
Morgantown 235
Morris Arboretum 210
Morris House 144
Moshulu sailing restaurant 129
Mother Bethel African Methodist Episcopal Church 128
Mount Airy 209
Mount Hope Estate and Winery 242, 287
Mount Pleasant 184
MOVE 44
multiculturalism 57, 143, 199
Mum Puppet Theater 287
Mummers 19, 80, 81–4

Mummers Museum 201
Mummers Parade 50–51, 81, 82, 83
Municipal Court 176
Mural Arts 76
muralist 57
Museum of Art 14, 75, 76, 78, 178
Museum District 176
museums
  African-American 77, 160
  American Swedish Historical 202
  Archeology and Anthropology (University of Pennsylvania) 192
  Atwater Kent 143
  Brandywine River 223
  Chadds Ford 224
  Civil War 169
  Delaware Art 228
  Delaware History 228
  Delaware Natural History 227
  Delaware Toy and Miniature 227
  Elfreth's Alley 117
  Hagley 227
  Independence Seaport 129
  James A. Michener 252
  Kalmar Nyckel 228
  Landis Valley 238
  Margaret R. Grundy 249
  Mario Lanza 136
  Mercer 248, 252
  Mummers 201
  Museum of Art 14, 75, 76, 78, 178
  Mutter 170
  National Liberty 112
  National Museum of American Jewish History 115
  New Hall Military 109
  Philadelphia Museum of Art 148, 149, 172–3, 178
  Phillips Mushroom 225
  Please Touch 177
  Railroad Museum of Pennsylvania 241
  Rockwood 228
  Rodin 77, 178
  Rosenbach 169
  Underground 112
  Wharton Esherick 77
  Wilbur Chocolates Candy Americana 238
  Woodmere Art 210
music 73–5, 164, 285
Musical Fund Hall 144
Mutter Museum 170

n

National Constitution Center 105
National Liberty Museum 112
National Museum of American
  Jewish History 115
National Park Visitor Center 105
neighborhoods 58, 167
Nemours Mansion and Gardens
  227, *228*
New Hall Military Museum 109
New Hope 253, 254
New Hope Canal Boat Company
  253
New Hope Tourist Information
  Center 253
New Hope Winery Inc. 255
New Jersey 230–31
New Jersey State Aquarium 129
Newman Galleries 284
Nexus Foundation for Today's Art
  284
North Philadelphia 213–16
Northern Liberties 213, 215
Not Just Ice Cream 146
Notman, John 148, 166, 176

o

Ocean City 230
October Gallery 284
Oh! Dem Golden Slippers 82
Ohio House 186
Old City 105–17
Old City Arts Association 77, 284
Old City Hall *14*, 113
Old Pine Street Presbyterian
  Church *119*, 126
Old St. Joseph's Church 124
Old Swedes' Church *136*, 137
One Liberty Place *40*, 148
Opera Company of Philadelphia 74,
  156, 286
Orchestra 2001 74
Ormiston 185
Ortlieb's Jazz House 74, 282

p

Painted Bride Art Center 117, 284,
  286, 287
Palestra arena 192
Paradise 240
Park Hyatt Atop the Bellevue 155
Parkway Museum District 175–9
Parry Mansion 253
Pastorius Park, Chestnut Hill *70*
pathology museum 170
Pat's King of Steaks 159, 201, *203*

Pearl S. Buck House 252
PECO Energy Liberty Center 114
Peddlar's Village 252
Penn Campus 188–9, 194
Penn Center 157
Penn Mutual Building 143
PENN Presents theater complex
  287
Penn Relays 192
Penn, William 15, 21–5, 107, 154,
  249
  statues *94–5*, *147*, *148*, 151
Penn's Landing *120–21*, *127*,
  128–9, 286
Pennsbury Manor 249
Pennsylvania 21
Pennsylvania Academy of Fine Arts
  14, *77*, *153*
Pennsylvania Ballet 71, 73, 156,
  287
Pennsylvania Convention Center
  74, 158
Pennsylvania Dutch Convention
  and Visitors Bureau 240
Pennsylvania Dutch Country
  235–43
Pennsylvania Dutch Folk Festivals
  85, 242, 244
Pennsylvania heartland *232–3*
Pennsylvania Hospital *138–9*, 147
Pennsylvania Opera Company 71
Pennsylvania Pro Musica 74
Pennsylvania Renaissance Faire
  242
Pennypack Park 216
Pentimenti Gallery 284
People's Light and Theater
  Company 72, 287
Philadanco 73, 286
Philadelphia Art Alliance 167, 284
Philadelphia Boys' Choir 286
Philadelphia Campaign 224
Philadelphia Chamber Music
  Society 71, 74
Philadelphia Clef Club for Jazz and
  the Performing Arts 71, 74,
  156, 286
Philadelphia Contributionship for
  the Insurance of Houses 123
Philadelphia Dance Alliance 287
Philadelphia Festival of World
  Cinema 77
Philadelphia Folk Song Society 74,
  286
Philadelphia Gay News 146
Philadelphia International Airport
  202
Philadelphia (Merchant's)
  Exchange 107, *108*

Philadelphia Museum of Art *148*,
  149, *172–3*, 178
Philadelphia Orchestra *73*, 155,
  286
Philadelphia Pretzel Museum 89
Philadelphia Shakespeare Festival
  72, 287
Philadelphia Sketch Club 145
Philadelphia Stock Exchange 157
The Philadelphia Story 59
Philadelphia Theatre Company 72
Philadelphia Vietnam Veterans
  Memorial 129
Philadelphia Visitors Center 175
Philadelphia Zoological Gardens
  186
Phillips Mushroom Museum 225
Philly Pops 286
Physick House 126
Pilbrow, Richard 156
Pine Street *145*, 146
Pitt, Brad 78
Plastic Club 146
Plays and Players Theater 72, 169,
  287
Please Touch Museum 177
Poe, Edgar Allan 55, 216, 217
Point Pleasant *255*
port *24*
Portico Row 145
post-war years 43
Powel House 125
Powelton Village 195
power 59
Presbyterian Historical Society
  127
Presbyterian Ministers' Fund 166
prestige 59
pretzels *89*, 238
Prince Music Theater 71, 72, 155,
  286
Print Club 168
printing centers 141, 284
Prohibition 41–2
PSFS Building 158

q

Quakers *18*, *20*, 21–5, 213
  pacifists 43
  wedding *39*
Queen Village *131–2*, 136–7
Quince Street 145

r

racial conflict 37
Railroad Museum of Pennsylvania
  241

railroads 36
Ralph Stover State Park 255
Ralph's restaurant 201
rare books 169
Reading Terminal Market 89, *149*, *159*
Reese's antiques 146
Relache experimental music 286
religious liberty 118–19
renaissance 19
Rendell, Ed *45*, 55, 71
Republican National Convention 53
restaurants *see* food
revolution 18, *28*, 30
Ringing Rocks County Park 255
riots *36*
Rittenhouse 101, 165–70
Rittenhouse Hotel 166
Rittenhouse Row 168
Rittenhouse Square *58*, *162–3*, 165, *167*, *168*
Rittenhouse Town 210
Ritz 5 77, 285
Ritz at the Bourse 77, 285
Ritz Carlton Hotel *155*
Ritz East Cinema 285
Rizzo, Frank 44, 45
rock music 74–5
rock n' roll 47
Rockland 185
Rockwell, Norman 143
Rockwood Museum and Gardens 228
Rocky 79, *179*, 200
Rodin Museum 77, *178*
Rose Garden 123
Rosenbach Museum 169
Rosenfeld Gallery 284
The Roxy 285
Rumspringa 66
Runge, Gustave 155
Ruth Zafrir Gallery 284

s

Sailors Memorial 178
St. Clement's Episcopal Church 177
St. George's Greek Orthodox Church 144
St. John the Evangelist Church 158
St. Mark's Church *165*, 167
St. Mary's Church 124
St. Peter's Episcopal Church 127
The Saloon restaurant 201
Samuel Memorial 185
Samuel S. Fleisher Art Memorial 136
Sand Castle Winery 255

Sande Webster Gallery 284
Sansom Row 193
Sansom Street 167
Sarcone's Bakery 200
Savoy Company 286
Schaffer Antiques 146
Schoolhouse 209
Schuylkill River 175, *182*, 183, 192
Schuylkill River Park 170
Schuylkill River Trail 184
science 177, *195*, *215*
sculptures *143*, 153, 155
Sea Isle City 230
Seamen's Church Institute 117
Second Bank of the United States 112
Sesame Place 250
Shady Maple Smorgasbord 236
shopping 126–8
Sight and Sound Millenium Theater 241
The Signer 112
Sisters 283
skyscrapers *40*, 148
slavery *see* anti slavery movement
Smith Civil War Memorial 186
Smith, Robert 109
Smucker's Harness Shop 238
Snyderman Gallery 284
Society Hill *13*, *96–7*, 123–8
Society Hill Playhouse 287
Society Hill Synagogue 126
Sony's E-Center 74
South Philly 199–202
South Street *130–2*, 133–6, *137*
Sparks Shot Tower *137*
Spice Corner 200
Spirit of Philadelphia 129
sports 91–3, *191*, 192, 201
Spring Garden 213
Spruce Street 125–6, 145–6, 168
squares
    Head House *124*, 128
    Independence 113
    Kennett 224, 225
    Logan 175–6
    Rittenhouse *58*, *162–3*, 165, *167*, *168*
    Washington 78, 101, 141–9
Stallone, Sylvester 78, 79, 179, 200
Stamp Act 29, *30*
Starman in the Ancient Garden sculpture *143*
Statue of Religious Liberty *119*
steam locomotives *34*
Stenton Mansion *208*
Stetson, John B. *35*

stock exchange 107, 157
Stone Harbor 230
Strasburg 241
Strawberry Mansion 149, 185
Street, John *46*, 60
Strickland, William 107, 112, 113, 144, 148
Sturgis Pretzel House 238
Sundance Cinema 285
Sundance Cinema Center 194
Superior Ravioli 200
Susanna Foo restaurant 167
Swann Memorial Fountain 75, 149, 175
Swedes 22, 202
Sweetbriar 186
symbol, US *112*

t

Tall Ships 128, 137, *228*
Taller Puertorriqueño 210, 284
Talluto's eatery 200
taxes 29
Temple Beth Zion-Beth Israel 168
Temple University 215
Temple University Cinematheque 77
Termini Bros. 201
Thaddeus Kosciuszko National Memorial 127
Theater Alliance of Greater Philadelphia 72, 286
Theater of the Living Arts 135, 286
theater/s 71–3, 241, 286–7
The Thinker, Rodin *175*
Thirtieth Street Station 191
Thompson-Neely House 254
tickets 285
Tinicum Park *249*, 255
Todd House 108
Tomb of the Unknown Soldier 141, *144*
tourist information centers
    Brandywine River Valley 225
    City Visitor Center 105
    Gateway Regional Visitor Center 105
    National Park Visitor Center 105
    New Hope 253
    Philadelphia Visitors Center 175
Tower Books 136
Tower Records 136
Tower Theater 286
Townshend Acts 29
train sheds *149*
Travolta, John 78
Trocadero Theater 286

Tuttleman IMAX Theater 177, 285
Twain, Mark 54

u

Uhlerstown 255
Underground Museum 112
United Artists Cinema 285
United Artists King of Prussia
    Stadium 15 and IMAX 285
United Artists Riverview Plaza
    285
United Artists Sameric 285
University of the Arts 156, 284
University City 191–98
University Gate mural *56*
University of Pennsylvania Museum
    of Archeology and Anthropology
    192
University of the Sciences in
    Philadelphia 195
urban villages 207–12
US Customs Building 108, *123*
US Mint 116
USS *Becuna* *127*, 129
USS *Olympia* *127*, 129

v

V–J Day *43*
Valley Forge 224, 229
Van Rensselaer Mansion 166
Vansant House 253
Vare Brothers 41
Ventnor 230
Venturi, Robert 108
Veterans Stadium 91, *198*, 201

Vine Street 213
Viñoly, Rafael 156
visual arts 75–6
Vox Populi Gallery 284

w

Wagner Free Institute of Science
    215
Walnut Street 167
Walnut Street Theatre 72, 143,
    287
Walter, Thomas U. 213
Wanamaker, John 158
Warmdaddy's blues club 74, 283
Warwick Hotel 167
Washington Crossing Memorial
    Building 254
Washington Crossing State Park
    254
Washington, Denzel 78, 79
Washington, George *33*, *125*,
    144
    Constitutional Convention 32
    Declaration of Independence 30,
        31
    Valley Forge 229
Washington Square 78, 101,
    141–9
Welcome America Festival 46
Welcome sailing ship *18*
West, Benjamin 77
Wharton Escherick Museum 77
Wheatland 239
White Dog Café 193
White, Stanford 168
Whitman, Walt 55, 151

Wilbur Chocolates Candy
    Americana Museum 238
Wildwood 230, 231
Willis, Bruce 78
Wilma Theater 71, 72, 156, 287
Wilmington 228
wine
    Chadds Ford Winery 224, *226*,
        255
    Mount Hope Estate and Winery
        242, 287
    New Hope Winery Inc. 255
    Sand Castle Winery 255
Winfrey, Oprah 78
Winterthur *226*, *227*
Winterthur Museum and Gardens
    226, *227*
Wissahickon River 175
Witness 68
Woodford manor house 185
Woodlands Cemetery 195
Woodmere Art Museum 210
Woodys 282
The Works Gallery 135, 284
World War I *41*
World War II 42–3
writers 250–2
Wyeth, N. C. 223

x

Xog boutique 135

z

Zanzibar Blue Club 74, 155, 283
Zipperhead Boutique 136

A
C
D
E
F
G
H
I
J
a
b

d
e
f
g
h
i
j
k
l

"I was first drawn to the Insight Guides by the excellent "Nepal" volume. I can think of no book which so effectively captures the essence of a country. Out of these pages leaped the Nepal I know – the captivating charm of a people and their culture. I've since discovered and enjoyed the entire Insight Guide series. Each volume deals with a country in the same sensitive depth, which is nowhere more evident than in the superb photography."

Sir Edmund Hillary

Insight Guides portray destinations in depth, providing the complete picture and the top photography

Insight Pocket Guides focus on the best choices for places to see and things to do and include large fold-out maps

Insight Compact Guides' portability makes them the perfect books to carry with you for on-the-spot reference

Three types of guide for all types of travel

INSIGHT GUIDES Different people need different kinds of information. Some want *background information* to help them prepare for the trip. Others seek *personal recommendations* from someone who knows the destination well. And others look for *compactly presented data* for on-the-spot reference. With three carefully designed series, Insight Guides offer readers the perfect choice. Insight Guides will turn your visit into an experience.

The world's largest collection of visual travel guides

✖ INSIGHT GUIDES

The world's largest collection of visual travel guides

Insight Guides – the Classic Series
that puts you in the picture

Alaska	China	Hungary	Munich	South Africa
Alsace	Cologne			South America
Amazon Wildlife	Continental Europe	Iceland	Namibia	South Tyrol
American Southwest	Corsica	India	Native America	Southeast Asia
Amsterdam	Costa Rica	India's Western	Nepal	Wildlife
Argentina	Crete	Himalaya	Netherlands	Spain
Asia, East	Cuba	India, South	New England	Spain, Northern
Asia, South	Cyprus	Indian Wildlife	New Orleans	Spain, Southern
Asia, Southeast	Czech & Slovak	Indonesia	New York City	Sri Lanka
Athens	Republics	Ireland	New York State	Sweden
Atlanta		Israel	New Zealand	Switzerland
Australia	Delhi, Jaipur & Agra	Istanbul	Nile	Sydney
Austria	Denmark	Italy	Normandy	Syria & Lebanon
	Dominican Republic	Italy, Northern	Norway	
Bahamas	Dresden	Italy, Southern		Taiwan
Bali	Dublin		Old South	Tenerife
Baltic States	Düsseldorf	Jamaica	Oman & The UAE	Texas
Bangkok		Japan	Oxford	Thailand
Barbados	East African Wildlife	Java		Tokyo
Barcelona	Eastern Europe	Jerusalem	Pacific Northwest	Trinidad & Tobago
Bay of Naples	Ecuador	Jordan	Pakistan	Tunisia
Beijing	Edinburgh		Paris	Turkey
Belgium	Egypt	Kathmandu	Peru	Turkish Coast
Belize	England	Kenya	Philadelphia	Tuscany
Berlin		Korea	Philippines	
Bermuda	Finland		Poland	Umbria
Boston	Florence	Laos & Cambodia	Portugal	USA: On The Road
Brazil	Florida	Lisbon	Prague	USA: Western States
Brittany	France	Loire Valley	Provence	US National Parks: East
Brussels	France, Southwest	London	Puerto Rico	US National Parks: West
Budapest	Frankfurt	Los Angeles		
Buenos Aires	French Riviera		Rajasthan	Vancouver
Burgundy		Madeira	Rhine	Venezuela
Burma (Myanmar)	Gambia & Senegal	Madrid	Rio de Janeiro	Venice
	Germany	Malaysia	Rockies	Vienna
Cairo	Glasgow	Mallorca & Ibiza	Rome	Vietnam
Calcutta	Gran Canaria	Malta	Russia	
California	Great Britain	Mauritius, Réunion		Wales
California, Northern	Greece	& Seychelles	St Petersburg	Washington DC
California, Southern	Greek Islands	Melbourne	San Francisco	Waterways of Europe
Canada	Guatemala, Belize &	Mexico City	Sardinia	Wild West
Caribbean	Yucatán	Mexico	Scandinavia	
Catalonia		Miami	Scotland	Yemen
Channel Islands	Hamburg	Montreal	Seattle	
Chicago	Hawaii	Morocco	Sicily	
Chile	Hong Kong	Moscow	Singapore	

Complementing the above titles are 120 easy-to-carry Insight Compact Guides, 120 Insight Pocket
Guides with full-size pull-out maps and more than 100 laminated easy-fold Insight Maps